D1284340

OLD VIRGINIA

The Pursuit of a Pastoral Ideal

OLD VIRGINIA

The Pursuit of a Pastoral Ideal

William M. S. Rasmussen

Robert S. Tilton

HOWELL PRESS

Charlottesville, Virginia

Text © 2003 by the Virginia Historical Society

All rights reserved. This book, or any portions thereof, may not be reproduced or transmitted in any form or by any means, electronic or mechanical, including photocopying, recording, or by any information storage and retrieval system, without permission in writing from the publisher, except for brief quotations in critical reviews or articles.

Designed by Carolyn Weary Brandt

Library of Congress Cataloging-in-Publication Data

Rasmussen, William M. S. (William Meade Stith), 1946-
  Old Virginia : the pursuit of a pastoral ideal / William M. S.
Rasmussen, Robert S. Tilton
      p. cm.
Includes bibliographical references and index.
  ISBN 1-57427-139-3 (alk. paper) – ISBN 1-57427-140-7(pbk. : alk.
paper)
  1. Virginia–History–Colonial period, ca. 1600-1775–Pictorial works.
2. Virginia–History–1775-1865–Pictorial works. 3. Virginia–Social
conditions–Pictorial works. 4. Country
life–Virginia–History–Pictorial works. 5. Country
life–Virginia–History. 6. Plantation life–Virginia–Pictorial works.
7. Plantation life–Virginia. 8. Pastorial systems–Social
aspects–Virginia–History. 9. Landscape–Virginia–Pictorial works.
10. Landscape–Social aspects–Virginia–History. I. Tilton, Robert S.
II. Title.
  F229 .R36 2003
  975.5–dc21

                                              2002015805

Printed in Korea

12 11 10 09 08 07 06 05 04 03   10 9 8 7 6 5 4 3 2 1

Published by Howell Press, Inc.
1713-2D Allied Lane
Charlottesville, VA 22903
http://www.howellpress.com

Cover:
Edward Beyer, *Bellvue, The Lewis Homestead, Salem, Virginia in 1855*, detail,
oil on canvas, 38 x 50 in., private collection

Back cover:
Lefevre James Cranstone, *Slave Auction, Virginia*, ca. 1859,
oil on fabric, 13 x 21 in., Virginia Historical Society

Table of Contents

Foreword

As eighteenth-century Virginians searched for an identity that might redeem the reputation of their much maligned colony, they began to reimagine their rural, often backwater existence as embodying the precepts of what for centuries had been associated with the pastoral ideal. This country life, away from the chaos, commercialism, and temptations of the types of cities that were being developed in the North, has come to be associated with the term "Old Virginia." To some, Old Virginia conjures up images of gentility, wealth, abundance, and good and easy living on the land, the type of bucolic existence that would allow for the pursuit of humanistic learning and its attendant virtues. To others, however, Old Virginia will forever be synonymous with slavery, a dark period in America's history, during which exploitation and cruelty were at the heart of what appeared on the surface to be a civilized society. Despite the frequent use of this term over the past four centuries, no one has ever before studied how the idea of Old Virginia originated, why its use persisted, how its meaning changed over time, and what is to be found in its mythology that informs us about the actual history of the region. These are some of the many topics addressed in *Old Virginia: The Pursuit of a Pastoral Ideal*, which is the third collaborative project of Dr. William M. S. Rasmussen, Lora M. Robins Curator of Art at the Virginia Historical Society, and Dr. Robert S. Tilton, Associate Professor of English and Director of American Studies at the University of Connecticut. Our co-curators earlier produced two of the Society's most successful shows, *Pocahontas: Her Life and Legend* (1994) and *George Washington: The Man Behind the Myths* (1999). The latter won the prestigious Award of Merit from the American Association for State and Local History. We welcome their latest contribution to the study of Virginia's past.

The authors demonstrate early in their study that the notion of an idealized rural lifestyle dates back to the ancient world. The pastoral ideal was revived in the Renaissance, reconfigured in Augustan England, and ultimately exported to Virginia through colonials like William Byrd II of Westover and Landon Carter of Sabine Hall. What has appealed to its adherents throughout the centuries has been the belief that a life away from the vices of the city, in a rural, pastoral setting, can inspire virtue and provide the proper atmosphere for enlightened speculation about man's place in the political, theological, and social realms. There can be no doubt that the pastoral society of late colonial Virginia spawned many of the philosophers of the revolutionary era who crafted the government that we so highly value today. At the same time, however, this exhibition does not shy away from the problems attendant to slavery, an institution that routinely attracted the interest of foreign visitors to Virginia. While Jefferson, Madison, Mason, and many of their contemporaries denounced slavery, they could find no way to end what was clearly an immoral system, and their antebellum descendants, many of whom offered similar opinions, would not be compelled to free their slaves by the arguments of northern abolitionists. In this show visitors will find disturbing, often troubling images of blacks, as well as images and descriptions by contemporary painters and writers who were sympathetic to the victims of slavery. They admired blacks for enduring under adversity. And at a time when simple rural ways were valued, many travelers were charmed by what they saw as the picturesque lifestyles of slaves and black freedmen. They rightly credited African Americans for contributing markedly to the identity of early Virginia.

As the curators introduce the viewer to the extensive history of Old Virginia, they dispel much of the mythology that has long enveloped the heritage of our region. In the closing sections, which deal with the Colonial Revival and the New Ruralism of the late twentieth century, it becomes clear that while the term "Old Virginia" has gone out of vogue, some of the notions that provided its foundation are still with us. *Old Virginia: The Pursuit of a Pastoral Ideal* provides a new way to understand Virginia's past, as well as a mechanism for contemplating the state's present and future.

Charles F. Bryan, Jr.
President and Chief Executive Officer
Virginia Historical Society

Acknowledgments

Our previous exhibitions, *Pocahontas: Her Life and Legend* and *George Washington: The Man Behind the Myths*, examined the lives of the figurative "mother" and "father" of our country by comparing historical accounts to the works of writers and artists who had adapted their narratives to suit their own purposes. After the Washington show we began to think in broader terms about periods in our history about which our understanding was murky because any semblance of reality has been pushed into obscurity by the myths surrounding it. We thought first about the "Old South," but this vast subject is notoriously elusive. In fact, we came to fear that we would unwittingly contribute to a mythology that suggests that the lives being led in Richmond, Charleston, New Orleans, and the plantations of antebellum Alabama were somehow similar and comprehendible under a single rubric. We soon recognized that the Virginia portion of the "Old South" mythology was remarkably rich, and that a study that proceeded from the assumption that the idea of "Old Virginia" was brought into being and maintained for a purpose would allow us both to undertake the sort of myth versus reality study that we enjoy, and, we hoped, to come to some sort of conclusion about Americans' need to carve out easily digestible gobbets from our mytho-historic past. We decided that if we could unravel some of the legends that have given a mystique to Old Virginia, we would contribute to a better understanding of a particular American heritage.

We are indebted to a number of scholars who have taught us much about both the colonizing and coming-of-age of Virginia and about manifestations of the pastoral as they have related to American culture. Special mention must be made of such seminal works as Jack P. Greene's *Defining Virginia: Studies in the Formation of an Identity, 1584-1775*, Leo Marx's *The Machine in the Garden: Technology and the Pastoral Ideal in America*, Lewis P. Simpson's *The Dispossessed Garden: Pastoral and History in Southern Literature*, and *Virginia: The New Dominion* by Virginius Dabney. To these distinguished guides and all who have followed their trail we send our thanks. In this study we have endeavored to keep to the well-trodden path, but we ask your patience in advance for the occasional divergence.

As with every exhibition that emphasizes the visual record of Virginia's past, our greatest debt is to Lora Robins, whose vision and generosity have made possible the Society's collection of Virginia art that is named in her honor. Many of her paintings are featured in this exhibition. *Old Virginia: The Pursuit of a Pastoral Ideal* has been

underwritten by a number of generous grants. The E. Rhodes and Leona B. Carpenter Foundation funded the publication of this book, and the Windsor Foundation substantially funded the expense of mounting the exhibition. Additional support was provided by the Lettie Pate Whitehead Evans Exhibitions Fund and the Research Foundation of the University of Connecticut.

Dr. James C. Kelly of the Virginia Historical Society encouraged us to pursue the subject of Old Virginia and served as a valuable reader of our manuscript, ever ready to help us sharpen our focus as we plowed through four centuries of the region's history. Jim offered us many useful suggestions and always pointed us in the right direction when we were in danger of any overenthusiastic straying. We are, as ever, in his debt. Our sincere thanks also go to Dr. Nelson D. Lankford, who carefully edited the manuscript; while offering as well a number of thoughtful comments, he patiently pointed out that one can write about the seventeenth and eighteenth centuries without utilizing the grammatical and dictional consuetudes that were popular in those bygone days. And, as always, Dr. Charles F. Byran, Jr., the Society's President and C.E.O., was unswerving in his support for this project and in his confidence in us. We are extremely grateful to these colleagues.

Many others at the Virginia Historical Society also contributed to this often unwieldy undertaking. Stephanie Jacobe assembled the nearly three hundred images that illustrate this book, produced its index, and provided aid and comfort throughout the process. AnnMarie Price arranged the shipping for the exhibition. Robert F. Strohm, E. Lee Shepard, and Frances Pollard located significant books and manuscripts in the Society's collection. In the Bryan Reading Room, Toni Carter, Greg Stoner, Jon Bremer, and David Ward pulled and organized much material for us. Jeffrey Ruggles answered our questions about the art of photography. Missy Rogers, Graham Dozier, Lauranett Lee, Paulette Schwarting, and Bryan Clark Green assisted with specific queries. Ron Jennings took many of the photographs for this book. Canan Boomer translated German for us. Stacy Gibford-Rusch conserved works on paper. Dale Kostelny and Drew Gladwell installed the exhibition. We must also thank Pamela R. Seay, the Society's director of development, and Risha Stebbins, its grants officer, for securing the needed funding. Maribeth Cowan, our public relations director, and William B. Oborochta, the director of educational services, also contributed to this effort.

At the University of Connecticut Bob received sound

advice from Jack Manning, Tom Recchio, Michael Meyer, Jean Marsden, and Hans Turley of the English Department, and Richard D. Brown, Kenneth Gouwens, and W. Guthrie Sayen of the History Department. He would also like to thank Carolyn Graham for her occasional suggestions, as well as for allowing him to wander over to her apartment to look at her print of "The Plantation," John Christie for good conversations over pizza, and Thomas Moser the Younger and Catherine Ann Bledsoe for their support and wise counsel.

We also have been aided by the staffs at many museums, galleries, libraries, and institutions, as well as by private individuals who were willing to part with their items and their expertise. We are indebted to Ann J. Arcari, Richard Armstrong, Holly Bailey, Georgia Barnhill, Carrie Rebora Barratt, Judith Barter, Graham Beal, David Berreth, Dawn Bonner, Lonnie Burch, Sarah Cash, Joanna Catron, Trinkett Clark, Keith Claussen, Constance Clement, Minora Collins, Robert Conte, Malcolm Cormack, Deanna Cross, David Curry, John Cuthbert, Paula DeStefano, Heather Domencic, Claire Edwards, Marcia Erickson, Ken Garrett, Joan Gates, Eleanor Gillers, Timothy Goodhue, Lisa Kathleen Graddy, Grant Griswold, Catherine Grosfils, Peter Grover, Carrie Hedrick, Teresa Heinz, William Hennessey, Mr. and Mrs. William Maury Hill, Hsiu-ling Huang, Sylvia Inwood, Kenneth Jackson, Jennifer Jensen, Anne Johnson, Julie Katz, Peter Kenny, Robert H. Lamb, Tom Litzenburg, Calder Loth, William Martin, Diane Martz, Barbara McMillan, Christian Müller, Kelly O'Neil, Nancy Orth, Laura Pasch, Howell Perkins, Anne Richtarik, Philip Rhodes, Suzanne Savery, Jacquelyn Serwer, Rebekah Sobel, Kathryn Speckart, Mary Sullivan, Kimberly Terbush, James Tottis, Therasa Tremblay, Sarah Beth Walsh, Malcolm Warner, Catherine Jordan Wass, Lawrence Wheeler, and George Yetter. At Howell Press, our thanks go to Ross Howell and Dara Parker for producing this book, and to Carolyn Brandt for designing it.

William M. S. Rasmussen
Richmond, Virginia

Robert S. Tilton
Storrs, Connecticut

"Ould Virginia"
   —from the map by Robert Vaughan published in John Smith's *Generall Historie of Virginia* (1624)

"No, no, gentlemen! You may depend, Old Virginny's not going to let Congress carry on in her day!"
   — John Pendleton Kennedy, *Swallow Barn, Or A Sojourn in the Old Dominion* (1832)

"You are a good hand at questioning," said the youth, with a smile, "but, without asking a single question, I have found out all I wanted to know."
   "And what was that?" asked the other.
   "Whether you were friends to the Yorkers and Yankees, or to poor old Virginia."
   "And which *are* we for?" asked the laconic mountaineer.
   "For OLD VIRGINIA FOR EVER," replied the youth, in a tone in which exultation rung through a deeper emotion, that half stifled his voice.
   —Nathaniel Beverley Tucker, *The Partisan Leader, A Tale of the Future* (1836)

The floating scow of Old Virginny
   I work'd in from day to day,
A fishing 'mongst de oyster beds,
   To me it was but play.
But now I'm growing very old,
   I cannot work any more,
So carry me back to Old Virginny,
   To Old Virginny's shore.
         —E. P. Christy, "Carry Me Back to Old Virginia" (1847)

"Up, men, and to your posts! Don't forget today that you are from old Virginia."
   —General George Pickett, to his troops at Gettysburg (1863)

Carry me back to old Virginny,
   There's where the cotton and the corn and tatoes grow,
   There's where the birds warble sweet in the spring-time,
   There's where the old darke'ys heart am long'd to go,
   There's where I labored so hard for old massa,
   Day after day in the field of yellow corn,
   No place on earth do I love more sincerely
   Than old Virginny, the state where I was born.
         — James Bland, "Carry Me Back to Old Virginny" (1878)

"When I speak of Virginia it is not so much the present Virginia that I bear in mind as that 'Old Virginia,' whose eastern shores extended from her Floridian confines on the south to the forty-fifth degree of north latitude on the north, and whose border to the westward reached to 'the furthest sea'. . . . This spot [Jamestown] belongs to the continent. The heart of it is Old Virginia."
   — Thomas Nelson Page, *Address at the Three Hundredth Anniversary of the Settlement of Jamestown* (1907)

Introduction

Throughout the history of the colony and commonwealth there have been essential, sometimes visceral, disagreements about what is understood when a reference is made to Old Virginia. To some commentators in the nineteenth and twentieth centuries the term conjured up images of the region's proud past and traditions, of its great men and contributions to the cause of freedom, of a pastoral society governed by benevolent stewards of the land whose leisure time allowed them to develop enlightened political and social philosophies, and of an era in which society was ruled by a code of honor and decency that has largely fallen by the wayside under the pressures of the modern world. To others it signaled, and still signals today, an economic system based on oppression and racial segregation, and an apparently civilized way of life built upon a foundation of bondage and cruelty.

Our intention in *Old Virginia: The Pursuit of a Pastoral Ideal* is to have our visitors and readers think again about this multifaceted term. As we examine the various identities of Old Virginia we will note how the European ideal of the pastoral, and its associated ideas of simplicity and rural virtue, became linked to what is a largely imaginative entity. The pursuit of the pastoral would ultimately be perceived as a justification for the region's non-urban settlement, and its virtues seen to be the reward for a lifestyle led close to nature, even though that lifestyle was rooted in an immoral support system. Neither the multiple meanings of Old Virginia nor its complex mythology have ever been surveyed, despite the prominence of both in the state's long history.

It was perhaps inevitable that over the course of four centuries Old Virginia would assume multiple guises. The term first identified an emerging settlement; Captain John Smith coined "Ould Virginia" to distinguish the earliest colony from "New England," which was carved from the original territory of Virginia, and at the same time to hint at the importance of the region that he had helped to found. After the restoration of the English monarchy, however, the term "Old Virginia" was often displaced by Charles II's term "Old Dominion," which suggested both age and exclusivity.[1] During the eighteenth century, when the colonial gentry looked to fashion a society built on the model of the English aristocracy, Old Virginia was thought of as a world in transition, in which the wealth provided by the tobacco trade was financing an imaginative transformation of the colony from a loosely connected series of backwater settlements into a world of pastoral country estates.

In the early nineteenth century Old Virginia was again reinvented. Although the colonial period was not forgotten, by the 1830s the term more often was used to mean the region's antebellum society, a culture in decline yet proudly defensive, under simultaneous attack by northern mercantile and manufacturing interests, as well as by abolitionists who would see slavery ended at any cost, and further disrupted by the internal pressures of agricultural failure, urbanization, industrialization, and the ever-increasing prominence of the state's non-English populations. Through the teens and twenties, when no figures emerged on the political stage equal in stature to George Washington or Patrick Henry, Virginians of English ancestry became increasingly conscious of "old families," "old houses," and of the "true old Virginia breed" of gentry that also seemed in danger of vanishing.[2] In these trying circumstances, the idea of an Old Virginia to which the descendants of the great families could claim allegiance became an effective tool to combat challenges to the status quo, a function that it would retain through the Civil War years. During the postwar period, when the old plantation society—which Thomas Nelson Page defined as having been "the purest, sweetest life ever lived"—had passed out of actual existence, Old Virginia survived in the imaginations of those who had fought for the "Lost Cause" and wished that the "good old days" would come again.

Following the centenary of independence Old Virginia went through another transformation. During the Colonial Revival the term would again refer to the society that had spawned patriots, the genteel civilization that arose in the mid-eighteenth century, which had suffered such oppressions and economic setbacks that a number of its greatest men saw the need to rebel. At the same time, Old Virginia came to serve as a decorous reminder of the earliest voyages of discovery and of Jamestown, England's first permanent colony in America, which was celebrated at the tercentenary of 1907. As the colonial past, and only in this guise, would Old Virginia capture the American imagination, to the point where an entire city—what we now know as Colonial Williamsburg—would be restored to allow modern Americans to view it firsthand.

If by the early twentieth century the *idea* of Old Virginia had gained acceptance in reference to the glorious days of the eighteenth century, the *term* Old Virginia had become so imprecise that historians increasingly discarded it. More specific identifications, such as Colonial Virginia, Early National Virginia, and Antebellum Virginia, gained currency so that the much less precise Old Virginia, along with its negative connotations, was forced into the background. One could argue that this term has been saddled with much of the baggage, both offensive and nostalgic, of the commonwealth's past, thereby allowing its slightly younger variant, Old Dominion, to preserve a neutrality that accounts for its continued usage.

Rural settlement and gentility have long been components of what has been identified as the "pastoral ideal." At the opening of his seminal study, *The Machine in the Garden: Technology and the Pastoral Ideal in America*, Leo Marx points to its early application to the new-found lands in the West:

> The pastoral ideal has been used to define the meaning of America ever since the age of discovery, and it has not yet lost its hold upon the native imagination. The reason is clear enough. The ruling motive of the good shepherd, leading figure of the classic, Virgilian mode, was to withdraw from the great world and begin a new life in a fresh, green landscape. And now here was a virgin continent! Inevitably the European mind was dazzled by the prospect.[3]

From ancient Rome, to the Italian—and later, the English—Renaissance, to the British Augustan Age, and ultimately to colonial Virginia, a rural setting was considered a requirement for the development of such agreeable qualities as self-respect, dignity, courage, courtesy, and a love of ideas based on one's reading the classics of the day. For nearly two thousand years, men had believed that such contemplation could provide the foundation for a virtuous life. However, these attributes could not be properly inculcated without the right atmosphere, and enough leisure time to make the best use of it. In the South, as Lewis P. Simpson has remarked, it became possible to see "the plantation as a homeland of the life of the mind."[4] In his thoughtful monograph, *The Refinement of America*, Richard L. Bushman suggests that the houses built by those who aspired to a more genteel lifestyle "were in truth outward signs of what the inhabitants hoped would be an inward grace."[5] Pastoral bliss, however, came with a price. The pursuit of rural virtue engendered both the best and the worst in Virginia's history: the aspiration to lead a genteel lifestyle, and the use of a system of labor that divided the populace into an aristocracy and those who served it.

The development of the pastoral ideal during the colonial period, the drift away from its tenets in the nineteenth century, when Virginians looked more to defend their society than to improve it, and the reinvigoration of the earlier model in the twentieth when new ruralists revived the old ideas, form an arc of remembrance. In this continuum, the moments thought most to be praised or mourned in Virginia's past—those eras that have often come to be categorized as Old Virginia—emerge or disappear as the cultural concerns of the moment influenced

recollections of Virginia's history. From the colony's beginnings on through statehood, this adaptability allowed for competing representations of what Virginia was, is, or should be, to flourish simultaneously. These many, often conflicting associations have collectively given rise to what Raymond H. Pulley has called the "Old Virginia Mystique," a phenomenon that is at times rooted in these very contradictions.[6]

The confusion that we see as inherent in this mystique is attributable in some degree to the popularization of an image of antebellum Virginia as part of, and synonymous with, a mythic Old South, wherein the races live together happily on a bucolic plantation .That arcadia is described in a number of nineteenth-century songs and novels that look with nostalgia to an imagined setting that could be anywhere below the Mason-Dixon line.The intermingling of invocations of the South, antebellum Virginia, and antebellum Kentucky come together usefully in reference to a well-received painting by Eastman Johnson.

Negro Life in the South (1859) was among the first important paintings completed by Johnson in the years following his return from Europe (fig. 1). While there he had shared a studio with Emanuel Leutze and had worked for four years in the Netherlands, where he became to some the "American Rembrandt," an image that he would encourage by occasionally attending social events dressed as a seventeenth-century Dutch burgher.[7] Such was Johnson's popularity that he was offered, and would ultimately decline, the post of court painter at The Hague. After moving to Paris, he became interested in French genre painting and the picturesque, particularly as it was manifested in images of the peasantry. These influences are evident in *Negro Life in the South*, which Johnson exhibited at the National Academy of Design in 1859 to such acclaim that he was soon elected an Associate Member; he became a full academician in 1860.[8]

The figures here are at ease rather than at work. The ax and corn husks have been cast aside. A man plays the banjo, while young lovers flirt, the girl paying less attention to her peas than to her suitor. The rundown condition of the house is apparent, but so too is the fact that this is not a cabin, shack, or stereotypical slave quarters. Johnson seems to be suggesting that the house is reparable should its occupants choose to use their spare time at that task, but such intentions would be foreign to these characters. This quaint scene would have been enjoyed by Johnson's mid-nineteenth century audience, as it is by the young white girl in the right foreground. She, like the viewer of the painting, is an intruder, almost a voyeur, who has come upon a scene of domestic tranquility that would have been novel to the majority of her white countrymen, especially the northern patrons whom Johnson was trying to court. It is presumably a contemporary

1 Eastman Johnson, Negro Life in the South, *1859, oil on canvas, 36 x 45¼ in., New York Historical Society*

scene, in all probability inspired during the time that Johnson had spent in Washington, D.C. before his move to New York City in 1859, but it is concurrently nostalgic in that it depicts a way of life, and perhaps even a people, that many white Americans believed had already become anachronistic as the nation entered the second half of the nineteenth century.[9]

By 1867, *Negro Life in the South,* Johnson's vision of apparently contented, studiedly picturesque black people, had become widely known as "My Old Kentucky Home" after the popular song by Stephen Foster; its subject matter and nostalgic tone offered a charming representation of Foster's "summer" when "the darkies are gay."[10] By the end of the nineteenth century, however, another song that invoked similarly nostalgic memories of bygone days, James A. Bland's "Carry Me Back to Old Virginny" (Boston, New York, Chicago, 1906), would also come to be associated with this image. Bland was a free black man, who apparently had never been to Virginia before he penned his most famous song. (In this way he was not unlike Foster, who wrote the majority of his songs about the South from Pittsburgh.) Bland conceived this

piece for the popular minstrel shows of his era, in which white performers in blackface caricatured black characters.[11] Engravers apparently saw the usefulness of using the title of one popular song to attract potential purchasers to another, and so by the turn of the twentieth century Johnson's supposed painting of "My Old Kentucky Home" began to appear on the sheet music for "Old Virginny" (fig. 2).

Such interwoven associations helped lead to the creation of a mythic Old South, which is not completely devoid of currency today. Johnson's "South," Foster's "Kentucky," and Bland's "Virginny" suggested the existence of a harmonious society where there had been amicable relations between the races. Two generations later, the Georgia of Margaret Mitchell's best-selling novel, *Gone With the Wind,* which was quickly transformed into one of the most popular films in Hollywood history, solidified conceptions of the Old South as a romantic, pastoral world of moonlight, magnolias, and mint juleps, of handsome, well-mannered gentlemen and beautiful southern belles, and, perhaps most tellingly, of benevolent masters and contented slaves. (Such representations told a story

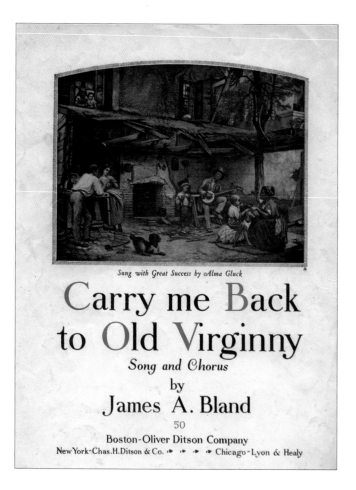

2 *James Bland, "Carry Me Back to Old Virginny" (Boston, New York, Chicago, 1906), sheet music, Virginia Historical Society*

quite different from Frederick Douglass's *Narrative*, Harriet Beecher Stowe's *Uncle Tom's Cabin*, or the other abolitionist writings that purported to expose the realities of plantation life.) These vignettes, narratives, and novels about a specific time and place in the Old South, whether positive or negative, were meant to be exemplary; the writers aimed to crystallize an image of life in the antebellum South in the popular imagination. Audiences came away believing that the lives of the aristocracy somehow reflected the South as a whole.[12] While a study of the great variety of representations of the Old South would be worthwhile, in this exhibition we will largely confine our attention to the diverse history and mythology of Old Virginia, from the beginnings of the oldest colony to the present.

Bland's now well-known melody—"Carry Me Back to Old Virginny"—has occasionally been confused with the much older "Carry Me Back to Old Virginia," which was written in 1847 and quickly became a staple of Christie's Minstrels (fig. 3). Along with the nearly identical titles, both compositions would have been performed by what was purported to be an elderly black man, who longs to return to the Virginia of his youth. Both express a nostalgic view of "Old Virginny" in the days of slavery and a sadness about the passing of the relationships fostered on

the plantation, a sentiment that continued to resonate with white audiences well into the twentieth century. Another cause of this confusion was the action taken by the Virginia Legislature in 1940, which at that point adopted Bland's "Carry Me Back to Old Virginny" as the state song. In doing so, however, they changed the title to "Carry Me Back to Old *Virginia*," a move which seemed in keeping with the dignified position to which the song had been raised.[13]

In 1970, then state Senator L. Douglas Wilder objected to Bland's lyrics, which he felt romanticized the institution of slavery. He suggested that another, more appropriate, state song be found. This debate has continued, on and off, for decades and has inspired powerful feelings on both sides. While agreeing that the song's lyrics are racist, and that "it offends everybody," whites as well as blacks, state Senator Madison E. Mayne made the point that the song is part of Virginia's heritage and should be preserved, perhaps with changes made to the more offensive expressions. Others remarked that Virginia was the only state with an official song penned by a black man, which added weight to the argument for continuance, and that in any case the well-known melody would always be identified with Virginia. The song's opponents stood firm, however, and all attempts to make the song more palatable by modifying the lyrics failed. As Delegate William P. Robinson put it, "There is nothing that can be done to the melody or the lyrics of this song that will engender a feeling of pride in black Virginians."[14]

Intrinsic to this debate was what the Old Virginia of the title connotes. On the one hand, this song suggests that the oppressive aspects of slavery were commingled with feelings of affection between master and slave, and that having traveled far from his former home, the elderly speaker wishes at the end of his life to return to a place where he was born and recalls having been happy. That said, it is inescapable that both versions of "Carry Me Back to Old Virginia" invoke a time when many southern black people were in captivity, imprisoned in a plantation system that by the mid-nineteenth century had held one people in bondage to another for more than two hundred years. Any positive or cathartic emotions that the song's nostalgic tone might engender had to be weighed against its invocation of a time of great suffering and anguish. In the end, Bland's "Carry Me Back to Old Virginia" was relegated to "state song emeritus" in 1997; the search for a new state song for Virginia continues to this day.

Old Virginia, whether viewed in its tragic or nostalgic sense, has often emerged as a counternarrative to the events in the present that have inspired a reminiscence of Virginia's past. For instance, during the 1830s, the challenges to the old society and economy of Virginia inspired a conviction that the old ways were best for the state, this at a time when even some members of the great families were allying with the forces of progress. This hearkening back, while it had little practical effect, had great symbolic meaning for many Virginians, who were looking for an anchor in increasingly turbulent political and economic waters. The recent debates about the state song demonstrate that Old Virginia has long meant different things to different people and remind us that Virginians have ever been willing to fight vigorously to defend their individual interpretations of the term, as well as for the honor of the commonwealth. (It is not surprising that General George Pickett's final words to his men at Gettysburg before the charge for which he became famous invoked their allegiance to "old Virginia.")[15] In this exhibition we will examine both the reality of life during the various periods that would come to be classified as Old Virginia, and the often contrasting associations inherent in historical, literary, and visual representations of those periods.

Whether or not one subscribes to the notion that the history and mythology of New England have triumphed over those of the South in the American historical imagination, it cannot be denied that over the years this thesis has allowed for much lively discussion. Indeed, the first

doubts cast on the veracity of John Smith's narratives in the late 1850s and 1860s by New Englanders John Gorham Palfrey, Charles Deane, and most famously Henry Adams, had an implicit sectionalist agenda; these attacks put pressure on southerners to defend the history of their founding at a moment when patriotic feelings on both sides were running high.[16] After the Civil War, Virginians such as John Esten Cooke and William Wirt Henry rose to the challenge, but they often found themselves in a position of responding to specific aspersions and therefore not in a position to assert the primacy of the histories of the eldest colony.

Although southern historians during the first half of the twentieth century did much to remedy this situation, a debate that took place on the pages of the *Saturday Evening Post* in early 1954 suggests that feelings about what was perceived to be a lack of understanding about the South were still running high. In a piece pointedly entitled, "They Don't Tell the Truth About the South," the eminent southern historian Herbert Ravenal Sass argued that southern history, and especially the southern founding narrative, had long been marginalized, and was ultimately overwhelmed by the constructions of American history put forward by northern commentators:

> In the mass American consciousness, Plymouth Rock and the Pilgrims have simply obliterated Jamestown and the Virginia colonists, who preceded them by thirteen years and whose comparatively liberal philosophy was much nearer ours today than the strong but terrifying zealotry which ruled Massachusetts with an iron hand, the hangman's noose and Beelzebub's brimstone.

In his reply, Bernard DeVoto, representing the northern view, discussed what he called the southern "inferiority complex," which allowed, and perhaps even encouraged, a southern belief that their history has been undervalued, a thesis DeVoto then goes on to argue is simply untrue. As recently as 1999, however, even in the wake of Walt Disney's historically problematic film, *Pocahontas*, Ann Uhry Abrams was able to suggest that the myth of the Pilgrims did indeed triumph over the stories of the Jamestown founding, even though the latter includes the story of John Smith and Pocahontas.[17]

Although we would not go so far as to say that the South in general or Virginia in particular have been left out of either scholarly or popular American history, it is fair to say that modern historians' rightful attention to the institution of slavery has allowed for the formation of gaps regarding our understanding of many of the other factors that influenced life in the colonial and antebellum South. The common heritage of slavery has led in some cases to oversimplifications about southern society and has obliterated state boundaries, to the point where an

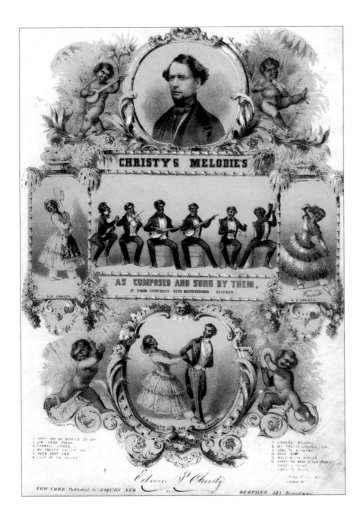

3 E. P. Christy, "Carry Me Back to Old Virginia" (New York, 1847), sheet music, Virginia Historical Society

image of the early South that includes a plantation need not include any other geographic designation—the plantation, and all it connotes, has become of primary importance. In *Old Virginia: The Pursuit of a Pastoral Ideal* we will spend a good deal of time attending to matters having to do with slavery, but we will also look at what the aristocratic, white landowners of the eighteenth and nineteenth centuries were trying to achieve and the agendas of those postbellum apologists and twentieth-century theorists who recalled aspects of those earlier eras with fondness.

Our focus on the gentry means that we will not have the opportunity to examine in any depth the complex lives of the middle- and lower-class Virginians of the plantation era. Falling as they do between the well-known extremes of mansion and slave quarters, whether working small farms that could not compete with the production or mercantile connections of the great houses or plying trades in the emerging towns in a world where much of the menial work was done by non-paid laborers, many members of this population were challenged to make ends meet. Although some few through various types of entrepreneurship were able to make their way into the lower levels of the aristocracy, the lives of most of the "poor whites" in the region were no doubt difficult at best. This does not, however, suggest that there was a lack of pride in their home state. As was proven during the Civil War, most defenders of the commonwealth's honor thought of themselves as sons of Old Virginia, even though in most cases their families had not participated in the type of lifestyle that one associates with that term. While members of the lower classes will enter at times into this study, a thorough inquiry into their existence will await future investigators.

As was true in the case of our previous exhibitions, *Pocahontas: Her Life and Legend* and *George Washington: The Man Behind the Myths*, we were inspired to take on this project in part because of what we perceived to be gaps in our own knowledge about the subject matter. Although the crucial events of Virginia's past are well known, there is much about early Virginia society that has been lost, or, we believe, is worthy of reconsideration. An additional impetus was provided by our similar experiences when giving lectures having to do with George Washington. Inevitably, the initial questions would have to do with his being a slaveholder, which, while certainly an important aspect of his life—as evidenced by his own dwelling upon the subject—is only one of many matters concerning Washington worthy of serious discussion. In short, while it has become common in recent years to see such figures as Washington, Thomas Jefferson, Patrick Henry, and James Madison as slaveholders first and patriots second, we hope to illuminate how such men and their contemporaries in the Virginia hierarchy saw themselves, and

what they believed to be their place in eighteenth and early-nineteenth century American society. In this way we are following in the footsteps of earlier reinterpreters of colonial and antebellum southern life, including the postwar apologists, the Colonial Revivalists, and the modern historians, who have brought to our attention other voices long silenced and issues and events long forgotten.

Our study begins with an examination of the European traditions of the pastoral ideal, which would eventually make their way to a colony that in its early years was in search of an identity. In Chapter II we turn to the eighteenth century, to the attempt by the colonial Virginia gentry to achieve a life based on gentility and the pursuit of virtue, which, because their inspirations were based on classical models and British predecessors, had to be carried out in an appropriately agrarian setting. The country life, which the tobacco-based economy demanded, suited this scheme; it ultimately allowed Virginians to transform the parameters of their existence from simply "rural" to "pastoral" and thereby fit their intention to convince both the doubters in the mother country, and perhaps themselves, of the worthiness of their way of life. In Chapter III we examine the decline of that society during the antebellum years and the resistance to change that inevitably followed. Chapter IV is devoted to the postwar period. We study the ways in which the lost world of antebellum Virginia came to be mourned. Apologists saw Old Virginia not only as the embodiment of a "Lost Cause," but also as a lost world of honor, decency, and refined manners. Our last chapter will focus on the Colonial Revival as it was manifested in Virginia, culminating with the construction of Colonial Williamsburg, which was based in part on the notion that we can both learn from, and be inspired by, a better understanding of the events of the past. We will then briefly consider the new ruralism that would inspire preservationist impulses in many powerful Virginians of the twentieth century. Throughout, our touchstone will be Old Virginia, an imaginative term that at times is used with great specificity, at others with intentional vagueness. Old Virginia is a changing idea, which has often represented changing ideals, both for those who lived through these historical periods and for those who would tell their stories.

Images from the colony's earliest history necessarily included descriptions of the people whom the first Englishmen encountered. Such interactions would prove to be useful to those who wished to argue that the New World as a whole, and Virginia in particular, should be seen as a garden, which was only lacking European cultivation to achieve its divinely destined fruition. While the colony's natural advantages would continue to be noted throughout the seventeenth century, Virginia concurrently came to be characterized as a wasteland, which for all of its potential was thought by some commentators to be an economic and social failure. During this first full century of exploration and settlement, the myriad descriptions of Virginia were sown with the sorts of contradictions that would blossom again at various, often troubled, times throughout its history.

1.1 *Thomas Cole*, The Pastoral or Arcadian State, *1834, oil on canvas,*
39¼ x 63¼ in., New-York Historical Society, from The Course of Empire

I. European Origins of the Pastoral

s the second of the five images in his monumental series *The Course of Empire*, Thomas Cole chose *The Pastoral or Arcadian State* (fig. 1.1). This appealing view of a rural summer landscape at mid-morning, with its clear sky, healthy vegetation, and quiet river, provides a contrast to both *The Savage State*, which preceded it, and the urban magnificence of *The Consummation of Empire*, the next painting in the series.[1] While presenting the expected details of the pastoral world—from a shepherd tending his flock while another plays his pipe under a tree, to a beautiful young woman who approaches an old, blind bard (as many in the period pictured Homer), to the classical temple in the background—Cole also manifests the continuing obsession in nineteenth-century America with the rural life, which as early as 1834 seemed to be in danger of passing away. Indeed, in Cole's series, the idyllic pastoral state inevitably will metamorphize into a great city, a transformation that will at once signal the triumph of the empire and the beginning of its collapse.

The pastoral ideal as it was transported to the New World was based on models that had originated in the Europe of antiquity as they had been filtered through the Italian and English Renaissance, and later through the Neo-Classical Age in Great Britain. This type of imagined utopia, which in its most basic form suggested the possibility for a life of simplicity and virtue in a rural, rustic setting, was extant among the ancient Greeks, with Theocritus its best-known envoy. But the ideal is thought to have come into full flower through the writings of a number of great Romans, the most important of whom, as he was in so many aspects of the life of the imagination, was Virgil. In the *Eclogues* and the *Georgics* Virgil codified and in some cases problematized many of what would come to be seen as the crucial constituents of the pastoral ideal.

Classical and Renaissance Models

Whether identified as the "Mantuan Swain" by James Thomson in *The Seasons* (1730) or simply as the "great poet" in Richard Payne Knight's *The Landscape, A Didactic Poem* (1794), Virgil was viewed as the inspiration, the authority, and the standard when considering the pastoral ideal. His imagery provided the model not only for poets, but for visual artists as well. As early as 1712, in a discussion of the great classical writers, Joseph Addison in *The Spectator* points to the aspect of Virgil's work that would have the greatest effect on those who would consider the pastoral in his own day: "Homer is in his Province, when he is describing a Battel or a Multitude, a Heroe or a God. Virgil is never better pleas'd, than when he is in his Elysium, or copying out an entertaining Picture. . . . Virgil has drawn together, into his *Aeneid*, all the pleasing Scenes [that] his Subject is capable of admitting, and in his *Georgics* has given us a Collection of the most delightful Landskips that can be made out of Fields and Woods, Herds of Cattle, and Swarms of Bees."[2] His ability to create scenery, his insights into human nature, and his manipulation of the philosophical issues raised by his use of pastoral motifs, combined to make Virgil's influence pervasive during the Renaissance and Neo-Classical Age.

The *Eclogues*, Leo Marx suggests, are "the true fountainhead of the pastoral strain in our literature." There Virgil identifies "the solid satisfactions of the pastoral retreat: peace, leisure, and economic self-sufficiency."[3] In the opening poem, however, the rural world of Tityrus is threatened by powers external to this oasis. Meliboeus has been ruined, and although he congratulates Tityrus on the latter's apparent security, the reader cannot but be concerned that reality, the world of unforeseen historical events and potential disasters, is still a presence, even as Tityrus plays his shepherd's pipe under a beech tree. In these early poems, which it has been argued are as much about the evils and temptations of the city as about rural life, Virgil both defines many of the tropes of the literary pastoral and suggests that the difficulty of living in that world—be it an actual rural retreat or a construction of the poetic imagination—is greater than one might believe.

As the poet C. Day Lewis put it in the introduction to his ambitious translation, "The fascination of the *Georgics* for many generations of the English-speaking peoples is not difficult to explain. A century of urban civilization has not yet materially modified the instinct we inherit from ancestors devoted to agriculture and stock-breeding, to the chase, to landscape gardening, to a practical love of Nature. No poem yet written has touched on these subjects with more expert knowledge or more tenderness than the *Georgics*" (fig. 1.2).[4] In this remarkable poem, which has been praised for its beauty and passion and ap-

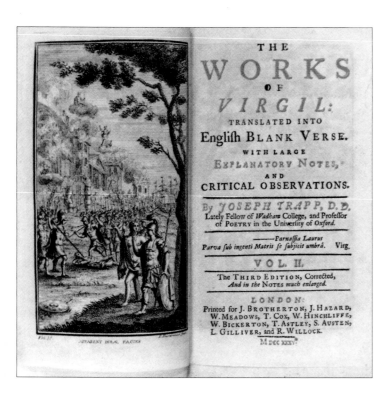

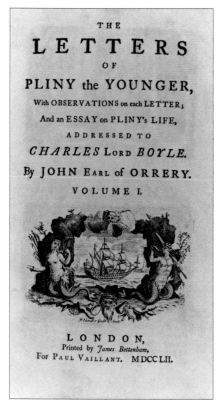

1.2 Above, top Joseph Trapp, ed., The Works of Virgil *(London, 1731), Virginia Historical Society*

1.3 Above The Letters of Pliny the Younger, with . . . an Essay on Pliny's Life, Addressed to Charles, Lord Boyle by John, Earl of Orrery *(London, 1752), Virginia Historical Society*

preciated for the poet's expertise in these rural pursuits (some of which was gleaned from Varro's *Res Rusticae*), Virgil reminded his contemporaries and all readers since of the demands and rewards of the rural life. His beautiful descriptions, and his suggestion that a virtuous existence was more readily attainable outside of the city, provided the most important early impetus toward the urge among urban sophisticates to live at least part of their lives in the country.

In *The Genius of Place*, their edition of commentaries on the English landscape garden from 1620 to 1820, John Dixon Hunt and Peter Willis make clear the period's crucial philosophical instigators toward the quest for a genteel country existence: "The most decisive literary influence was from classical Roman writings about villa and rural life. These contributed to the *topos* of 'beatus ille,' the happy man, whose contentment was attributed to his rural dwelling and (given the elision of Christian and Roman ideas) his virtuous, even pious, appreciation of the harmonious scheme of nature and its benevolent Creator. The classics provided descriptions of villa layouts and lifestyles (above all in the letters of the younger Pliny) and much literary mileage was made out of direct or oblique allusions to Virgil, Martial, Horace, and others."[5] We know that some wealthy Romans built splendid gardens in the city; Plutarch tells us of Lucullus, who after a lifetime of struggle "sought the restful pursuit of philosophy" in his magnificent gardens in the middle of Rome.[6] However, many wealthy citizens had country homes, and because of the carefully written, often detailed accounts that are found in his *Letters* (fig. 1.3), and such texts as Robert Castell's *The Villas of the Ancients* (1728), which made extensive use of them, Europeans had come to know a good deal about the estates of Pliny the Younger. From his villas on Lake Como, which he called Tragedy and Comedy, to his lucrative Tuscan estate, to his beloved seaside villa at Laurentum, Pliny provided many of the models and actual garden plans that would be invoked by architects and landscape designers during the Renaissance and Neo-Classical periods.[7] Also, to those who read his *Letters* the connection between wealth and the ownership of a home (or homes) outside of the city would have been explicit. Men of great means should have the ability to "retire," to seek out leisure and simplicity away from the urban world of political and commercial intrigues where one was often measured by one's pride, ambition, and success in the pursuit of fame and fortune. The concept of *otium*, a life of peace and contentment, could be found in the rustic, humble retreats of pastoral shepherds, but it could also be created in the splendor of an estate, or the less ostentatious charm of a country villa.

There are any number of other writers from the classical period in Rome who could be mentioned in this context, including Horace, who Richard D. Brown has

ROMAN
FARM MANAGEMENT.

THE TREATISES OF

CATO AND VARRO

DONE INTO ENGLISH, WITH NOTES OF MODERN
INSTANCES

BY
A VIRGINIA FARMER

[Fairfax Harrison]

New York
THE MACMILLAN COMPANY
1913

All rights reserved

Virginia Historical Society

1.4 Roman Farm Management; The Treatises of Cato and Varro, . . . with Notes of Modern Instances, by a Virginia Farmer [Fairfax Harrison] (New York, 1913), Virginia Historical Society

pointed out "had contrasted the decadent over-sophistication of urban high society with the moral and natural beauties or rural contentment." But one cannot conclude such a discussion without a mention of Cato. His *Letters* were extremely popular in eighteenth-century America, and Joseph Addison's tragedy *Cato* (1713) had a great vogue among the revolutionary generation. His *De Agri Cultura* (fig. 1.4) provided a good deal of useful advice for those who wished to become a "good husbandman" or a "good farmer," a worthy aspiration to Cato because "one so praised was thought to have received the greatest commendation."[8] And he reintroduced and popularized a personage from Livy's *Roman History*, Cincinnatus, the soldier turned farmer who would further enforce the idea that "retirement" to one's farm was the correct choice after one had completed one's toils in service of the nation. After his retirement from command at the end of the Revolutionary War, George Washington would be seen as the American Cincinnatus, a man who gave up power to return to his home in the country.

Although it would not be fair to say that classical motifs as they related to the pastoral ideal had vanished completely from the Europe of the Middle Ages, many of them were revived in earnest during the Italian Renaissance. An early manifestation of what would become a new vogue for the "villa" was the Villa Madama in Rome (1515–21), designed by Raphael for Giulio de Medici, who would later become Pope Clement VII. Later in the sixteenth century, architects led by Andrea Palladio (1508–1580) built villas in the countryside near such ur-

ban centers as Venice for their wealthy clients. Palladio and his followers had studied Roman architecture; they brought a sense of symmetry and "harmonic proportions" to their designs. The theories of Palladio were published along with drawings of Roman ruins in his *Quattro Libri dell' Architettura* (1570), which found a wide audience. The Palladian villa would ultimately become a popular choice for the country homes of Englishmen in the eighteenth century, in part because of its architectural possibilities, and in part because of what this style suggested about the principles of its owner.

In his examination of the Villa Pisani in Stra (1730), Ehrenfried Kluckert discusses *Villegiatura* (loosely defined as "villa culture"), which he links to "the glorification of country life in Veneto." He notes that it was "based on the Villa books' that had been popular since the sixteenth century. In them, the authors argued for the fusion of agricultural and humanist studies. Their goal was a life lived close to nature and in agreement with the corresponding philosophical principles concerning the conduct of life."[9] The villas near Venice provided for their owners a pleasurable respite from the city, often a productive farm, and a sanctuary from recurrences of the plague. Apart from their practical utility, these estates were built to be expressions of the philosophy of their proprietors, who had studied the classics and wished in a country setting to seek diversion in the life of the mind. Their eighteenth-century English counterparts would move to the countryside for many of the same reasons. Olive Cook goes so far as to state that "The men of this new Golden Age were conscious of kinship with those of the vanished Golden Age of antiquity: each, it seemed to them, inhabited an eminence of light, between which lay the murky gulf of medieval superstition, barbarism and ignorance. It was as natural that classical scholarship should be regarded as proper to the character of a gentleman as that he should live in a house where not only the portico but the proportions, the fireplace designs and the ornaments were derived from the classical temple."[10]

Kluckert argues that in eighteenth-century Italy, "The agricultural aspect soon lost its interest, and the philosophy of life, with its moral approach, gave way to the villa owners' desire to cut a stately figure."[11] In England the move to the villa represented an improvement over the seventeenth-century sense that property should be seen primarily as a source of wealth, more for what it could give its owner financially than spiritually. The idea had been to buy as much land as possible and work it to its fullest; judicious management of one's land and resources was not part of the equation. By contrast, the interest in Neo-Classical architecture that had been inspired by Palladio, with its requisite attention to symmetry and to the relationship between the house and the natural world, brought to the attentive mind the ideas that were thought to be the foundation for such designs in the ancient world. The hope in many cases was that the style of one's rural retreat would suggest the substance beneath. In the *Villa of the Lords Nicolo and Luigi de Foscari* (fig. 1.5) we find the balance, the relationship of parts to the whole, and manipulation of classical motifs that is representative of the architecture of Palladio; in *A House in Twittenham, middlesex near the River Thames* from Colin Campbell's *Vitrivius Britannicus* (fig. 1.6) we see the type of villa that was built along the Thames and other English rivers by Palladio's English disciples, the foremost of whom was Richard Boyle, third earl of Burlington.

As Palladio's writings had ensured the survival of the architectural ideas of the classical period, so traditional literary themes, including the pastoral mode, were revived during the Renaissance on the continent and ultimately transported to the British Isles. The earliest of these manifestations of the pastoral came through English translations of such texts as the *Diana* of Jorge de Montemayor, Tasso's *Aminta*, and Petrarchan poetry as refashioned by Sir Thomas Wyatt. The popularity of this mode can be seen in the explosion of pastoral poetry during the English Renaissance, including Sir Philip Sidney's *Arcadia* and Edmund Spenser's *The Shepheardes Calendar.* Elements of the pastoral can also be found in Spenser's *The Faerie Queen*, Shakespeare's *As You Like It,* and Milton's *Comus.* Christopher Marlowe would famously invoke the pastoral mode in his well-known lyric, "The Passionate Shepherd to His Love," to which a clever response was conceived by Sir Walter Ralegh in his "The Nymph's Reply to the Shepherd."[12] The idealized world of simple country folk, of shepherds and shepherdesses, became a useful vehicle for the love poetry of the period, as well as for writers who had a covert political or social agenda.

The classics came into play in a number of genres. Images of an arcadia became especially important during the Age of Discovery. Howard Mumford Jones reminds us that Captain John Smith's *A Map of Virginia* (1612) was "put together . . . in twelve books" and was therefore "like a prose Aeneid" with Smith, not surprisingly, assuming the role of the hero who would eventually be recognized as the founder of a great empire.[13] Once the conceptual link between the apparently primitive Indian of the New World and the pastoral shepherd of antiquity was forged, and the possibility seemed to exist for the dawn of a new Golden Age in these new lands, the flood of pastoral imagery was unrelenting. As Leo Marx succinctly put it, "In Elizabethan writing the distinction between primitive and pastoral styles of life is often blurred, and devices first used by Theocritus and Virgil appear in many descriptions of the new continent."[14] Familiarity with the colonies bred contempt, however, during the first half of the seventeenth century, and by the Restoration the pastoral was no longer a common motif when writers at home re-

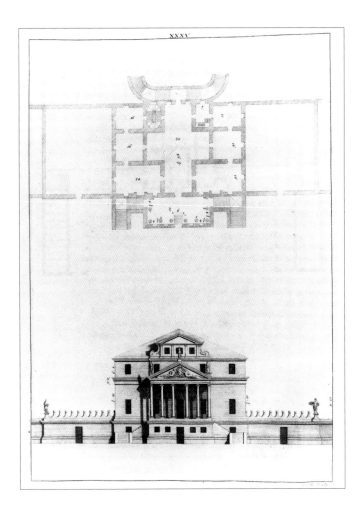

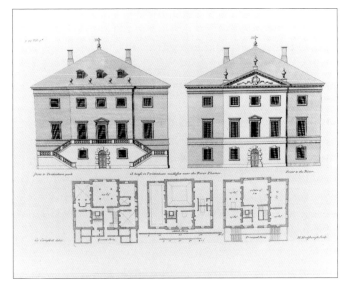

*1.5 **Above, top*** Villa of the Lords Nicolo and Luigi de Foscari (on the Brenta River near Venice), *Plate XXXV in Giacomo Leoni,* The Architecture of A[ndrea] Palladio *(London, 1721), Virginia Historical Society*

*1.6 **Above*** A house in Twittenham middlesex near the River Thames, *Plate 93, Volume III of Colen Campbell*, Vitruvius Britannicus *(London, 1717-71), Virginia Historical Society*

ferred to England's overseas possessions in America.

It should be said that while attention was continuously paid to the ideals that were thought to have their roots in the classical world, the mediators, like Palladio, often left their distinctive touch. For instance, there were, in fact, few surviving models of classical gardens to be seen. Thus, as Hunt and Willis put it, "Englishmen who had been on the Grand Tour extrapolated from Latin written descriptions on the basis of what they knew about Renaissance garden design which it was thought recreated the antique. The classical was thus mediated by the modern, and the translation to England of Italian garden forms endorsed even as it achieved a 'progress of the arts' to its northern climax in the British Isles."[15] Yet, at the same time, we have such texts as Rene Rapin's *Of Gardens* (1666), which was translated from the Latin by John Evelyn in 1673. In this poem, which includes a discussion of the rewards of "rural retirement," we have an example of "offering late Renaissance ideas and themes through the mediating vision and language of the classics."[16] In this case elements of the classics, including the very language of the poem, were the medium; in others, although there were at times some translations and modifications necessary, the voices of the ancients provided the message.

Writing of the era of the younger Pliny, J. H. Westcott first ponders whether the love for the country elucidated by so many Romans writers was authentic or conventional, but then provides his sense of the matter: "[I]t is clear that many Romans of that over-civilized age had a real taste for the enjoyment of country seats during a part of the year, and their literature from Catullus on is full of appreciation of the milder and lovelier aspects of nature. They delighted in a trim garden or well-kept park, in the soft, sweet beauty of a peaceful landscape, reminding us not a little in this respect of the English poets of the eighteenth century."[17] While Westcott might be accused of putting the cart before the horse, his sense of the influence of Roman writers on the many English nature poets of this period is well-founded. Although there was certainly some filtration through the writers of the Renaissance, the number of allusions to the great literary works of ancient Greece and Rome during what becomes known as the Neo-Classical or Augustan period make clear that many of the most important British authors of the late-seventeenth and early eighteenth centuries, from Thomson and Pope to Gray and Goldsmith, were enamored of the ancients. Indeed, the term "Augustan" was derived from Augustus Caesar, whose reign was seen as a period of stability and internal peace following the Civil Wars; it was also an era during which poets wrote for, and sought patrons among, an educated, sophisticated audience. This was the model that aristocratic Englishmen hoped to follow, in both their philosophical and architectural pursuits. Olive Cook points out that, "The eighteenth-century landowners were responsible for the establishment of a situation in which a high level of taste and production was unquestionably accepted throughout society. . . . They were dominated by a noble zeal for building, for laying out gardens, planting avenues and improving their land and (in striking contrast to ourselves) enhanced instead of destroying natural beauty, achieving a deeply satisfying equilibrium between man and his environment."[18] Wendell Garrett reminds us that while these landowners pondered how best to express classical ideals on the grounds of their estates, they had a number of sources to which to refer: "These ideas about the English garden had support from both literature and painting. In fact, the contributions of other arts to gardens were enormously vital: as Walpole would put it, 'Poetry, Painting and Gardening, or the science of Landscape, will forever by men of taste be deemed Three Sisters, or the *Three New Graces* who dress and adorn nature.'"[19] There was no doubt that this new generation of aristocrats were an economic elite; they wanted to be seen as a humanistic elite as well.

Cook goes on to say that the Neo-Classical Period "was an interval of tranquility between the discord and fanaticism of the seventeenth century and the evils of industrialization and class conflict which were soon to fragment and dominate society. Marlborough's great victories at Blenheim, Ramillies, Oudenarde, and Malplaquet, in making Britain one of the leading nations of the world, had fostered a sense of security and, above all, permanence. Perhaps the most impressive manifestations of this were the way in which gardens and trees were planted for the enjoyment of grandchildren not yet conceived. . . ."[20] This stability allowed one to look to the future and see one's own life as part of a continuum from one's ancestors to one's heirs. Pictured together in front of their splendid country seat, Atherton Hall, which fits comfortably into the natural world that it inhabits, are Robert and Elizabeth Gwillym and their family (fig.1.7). In this portrait by Arthur Devis we see three generations of Gwillyms, who exist on the land, in a world of stability and order, properties that are clearly life affirming, as can be judged by both the abundant trees and plants and the abundance of children. Gwillym is rightly as proud of his family as he is of his classically proportioned home, but he chooses to have this picture executed in the natural world, with which he has a harmonious relationship, an affinity that he no doubt hopes will be passed down to his sons and the generations to come. The house exists both as a crucial member of this family portrait and as a literal link between the generations. As Gwillym points toward his children, the viewer's eye must scan the house to get to them; the building should be appreciated for its elegant proportions and for its importance, both practical and psychological, to its owner.

1.7 Left Arthur Devis, Robert and Eliza-beth Gwillym and Their Family, of Atherton Hall, Herefordshire, ca. 1745-47, oil on canvas, 40 x 50 in., Yale Center for British Art, Paul Mellon Collection

1.8 Below Joseph Nicholls, Pope's Villa, Twickenham, ca. 1765, oil on canvas, 17⁵/₁₆ x 32¹/₈ in., Yale Center for British Art, Paul Mellon Collection

The last twenty-five years of one of the period's great men of letters, Alexander Pope, were spent at his countryside retreat. In Joseph Nicholls's view of *Pope's Villa, Twickenham* (fig. 1.8) we see the classical forms inspired by Palladio, and the riverside setting that would inspire both his English contemporaries and Virginians such as William Byrd II to seek out similar sites. Pope was also interested in landscape gardening; he built gardens at Twickenham, which included a "grotto" that became fa-mous in his lifetime. He would ultimately share his thoughts and design principles in his *Epistle to Lord Burlington* (1731). Pope was a Roman Catholic who was

deformed from childhood by tuberculosis of the spine. He did not have open to him the avenues of patronage that were available to other writers, and so he found ways to support himself, which included his translating of Homer and composing his "Imitations of Horace." In his brilliant use of satire, his command of "heroic couplets"—pairs of lines of rhymed iambic pentameter—and his well-known advice to "First follow Nature," Pope showed him-self to be well-versed in the methods and models of the great Classical poets, as well as one of the masters of the English language. At his villa he entertained many of the great men of his day, men who shared Pope's interest in gleaning what clues we might from the ancients about how best to achieve tranquility and follow the path toward virtue.

Ironically, by the middle of the eighteenth century, the rural environs of the English lower classes, and with them the lifestyles of those modern-day farmers and shepherds, were thought by some commentators to be disappearing. As Virgil had suggested in the first of the *Eclogues*, and as had been true because of the machinations of the profit-minded land owners of the seventeenth century, the lifestyles—and in some cases the very lives of the rural poor—were always vulnerable. The coming of agricultural reforms and the impetus to enclose what had been useful farmland into parks had them again under attack. As Oliver Goldsmith points out in *The Deserted Village*, there was little for those who had made a subsistence living on small land holdings to do but seek work in the city or to emigrate to America. In a nation in which the aristocrats were busily setting aside land for private contemplation, Goldsmith's lines suggest that in this process something vital was being lost:

> Even now the devastation has begun,
> And half the business of destruction done;
> Even now, methinks, as pondering here I stand,
> I see the rural Virtues leave the land. (395-98)[21]

The artificial enclosing of land, one might argue, is decidedly unnatural, and with the loss of the rural way of life comes the loss of such virtues as "Piety," "Loyalty," and "faithful Love."[22] Artifice, in the guise of promoting an equilibrium between man and the natural world for a chosen few, has, according to Goldsmith, cast aside the very qualities that embody a life led according to the pastoral ideal.

1.9 William Tombleson, View [of the Thames] from Richmond Hill, *ca. 1830, engraving, 4 x 6⅛ in., Virginia Historical Society*

In his discussion of the relationship between nature and art in *An Analytical Inquiry into the Principles of Taste* (1805), Richard Payne Knight points to the role that what he calls "the spontaneous association of ideas" plays in our appreciative powers:

> The skilful painter, like the skilful poet, passes slightly over those parts of his subject, which neither the compass of his art, nor the nature of his materials, allow him to represent with advantage; and employs all of his labour and attention upon those, which he can adorn and embellish. These are the *picturesque* parts; that is, those which nature has formed in the style and manner appropriate to painting; and the eye, that has been accustomed to see these happily displayed and embellished by art, will relish them more in nature; as a person conversant with the writings of Theocritus and Virgil will relish pastoral scenery more than one unacquainted with such poetry. The spectator, having his mind enriched with the embellishments of the painter and the poet, applies them, by the spontaneous association of ideas, to the natural objects presented to the eye, which thus acquire ideal and imaginary beauties; that is, beauties, which are not felt by the organic sense of vision; but by the intellect and imagination through that sense.[23]

On the one hand, Knight is positing the Romantic notion that our appreciation of art, of poetry, and of nature itself is based in part on the viewer's "inner light." What we bring to the encounter, our preparation, whether based on previous study or life experience, will effect our ability to discern and value the best of what we see; this theory of "Associationism" would remain in vogue well into the nineteenth century. Having an "ideal" in mind, however, be it the poetry of Virgil or the efforts of landscape painters, might actually make more problematic the task of observation, as in reality it is often difficult to live up to imagined expectations. The owners of country estates in England, and ultimately in Virginia, often had a specific ideal in mind when they considered their bucolic rural retreats. The realities of plantation life, however, would ultimately intrude on even the most adaptable pastoral models.

In choosing a site near a river for his retreat, Alexander Pope was in fact following the choice made by Virgil in book 3 of the *Georgics.* The poet will build his "shrine of marble/ Close to the waterside, where the river Mincius wanders/ With lazy loops and fringes the banks with delicate reed."[24] He was also heeding the advice given by Cato at the opening of *De Agri Cultura* that for the purposes of good transportation, when choosing a farm it should be "near the sea or a river where ships go up or a good and well-traveled highway."[25] The scenic advantages of such a choice are evident in William Tombleson's print of 1830, *View [of the Thames] from Richmond Hill* (fig. 1.9). Early Virginians who were interested in marketing their produce had sought such environs for the practical reasons stated by

1.10 *Lefevre Cranstone,* James River, Richmond, Virginia, *1859, watercolor, 6½ x 12 in., Virginia Historical Society*

Cato, but, as the years passed, thoughts of a quiet life alongside a tranquil river on the British model would become more attractive to colonial Virginians as they considered how to transform their rural farms into idyllic retreats.

The view from Richmond Hill, which had long been a favorite gathering spot for those who wished to take respite from the noisy, comparatively crowded, world of London, would ultimately inspire William Byrd II to name his new city on the banks of the James River, Richmond. While Tombleson chose a view of the Thames to the southwest toward Twickenham, Lefevre Cranstone, by looking eastward out of Richmond toward the old plantations of the Tidewater, provides his mid-nineteenth century audience with a similar relationship to the river, if not a similarly bucolic scene (fig. 1.10). Cranstone had to deal with the bland, uninteresting commercial buildings at the eastern end of the city, as well as the fact that many of the hills close to Richmond had been cleared of their native vegetation. His vantage point, however, also allowed him to include a distant vista of the still largely undeveloped Charles City County, and thereby permitted his creation of "the background landscape in such a Claudian manner that it seems to echo with wistful memories of its two centuries of English habitation."[26] By the 1830s

Tombleson's view of the Thames was already nostalgic, the approaching storm symbolizing the assault on the rural countryside by the forces of industrialization. In America, as the Civil War loomed, Cranstone's look down the James in 1859 toward Byrd's Westover and the other great houses of the eighteenth century was also a look back in time. In the distance we see the world that a century before was in the process of being transformed to match the idyllic speculations of Virginia's colonial aristocracy.

The "Contrary Character" of Early Virginia

"In the beginning, all America was Virginia." William Byrd II's now famous paraphrase of John Locke's comment in the *Second Treatise of Government*, "Thus in the beginning all the World was America," reminds us that Virginia was the first and for a time the only English colony in the continental New World, whose boundaries spread as far to the north and west as could be imagined by her sixteenth-century explorers. Tied to that early period in her history was a sense of the colony's purity, her "virginal" status as suggested by her name, which was in honor of Elizabeth, the "Virgin Queen." This designation intimated her readiness to be cultivated by the European

1.11 *Thomas Hariot,* Adam and Eve, *in* A Briefe and True Report of the Newfound Land of Virginia *(London, 1590), engraving, Virginia Historical Society, bequest of Paul Mellon*

males who came to take possession. Virginia was an un-spoiled land, often represented as a garden, as opposed to the howling wilderness that would await the Plymouth and Massachusetts Bay colonists.[27] The frontispiece to the 1590 edition of Thomas Hariot's *A Briefe and True Report of the Newfound Land of Virginia* went so far as to picture Virginia as the Garden of Eden, with a prelapsarian Adam and Eve standing at the foot of the Tree of the Knowledge of Good and Evil and a hermaphroditic Satan entwined in its branches (fig. 1.11). This remarkable image of Virginia as the archetypal Garden of the Judeo-Christian world, which in its crispness and detail far surpassed most of the other engravings of the period, served to support Hariot's intention to convince Elizabeth I not to turn away from these potentially profitable lands after the failure of the "lost" Roanoke colony.

The image breaks neatly into three sections. In the foreground are the featured players: Satan gestures toward the forbidden fruit, Eve's hand is on the apple, and Adam watches her with evident chagrin. We get a sense that the peaceful power that has thus far protected the rabbit and rat from their dangerous neighbors may well be about to adjourn, judging by the look on the face of the male lion. In the background we see the future, what will be wrought by the Fall. To the left a woman and her baby sit inside of a dwelling that is made up both of man-made logs and a deciduous tree. Her curse will be to bring forth children in pain, and to be subject to her husband, who will have to work to provide shelter. In the

right background we see a farmer laboring in the soil, with his domesticated animals nearby; henceforth, mankind will have to toil in order to eat.

The idea of the Garden of Eden, with its apparent possibility for a new beginning for Europeans in this New World, could not be presented to a Judeo-Christian audience without an expectation of the Fall. To a believer, what is beautiful in the foreground must inevitably pass away into the world of the background. And we must also remember that God does not curse Adam; rather, "cursed is the ground because of you."[28] The land itself absorbs the fury of God's wrath. The coming of Europeans to this "Garden" can therefore be equated to the coming of Satan, as with their arrival the native peoples will be cast out of their Eden and forcibly dragged into a world of "thorns and thistles." In fact, native Americans will ultimately be expected to take up the European methods of agriculture and husbandry, which, presumably, had to be developed only after the newcomers' Judeo-Christian forebears had been cast out of their primordial Garden of Eden. The loss of innocence that attended the early European landings in America was not lost on the invaders, even if it could not have been contemplated in those terms by the people whom they encountered.

This New World was not yet thought to be the type of arcadia that would inspire virtue. Rather, its Edenic qualities lay in its abundant—to European eyes untouched—natural resources, and in its apparent readiness to be cultivated by European explorers. The natives whom sixteenth-century Englishmen met in Virginia seemed to support the notion that the Americas would offer a return to a world that could only have been imagined in scripture or mythology. In John White's pictures the Indians of Virginia were often depicted as existing in a simpler time, their partial or total "nakedness"—a crucial term in European descriptions of aboriginal peoples—suggesting their innocence and liberality (fig. 1.12). As Arthur Barlow had suggested in 1584, the Indians were "most gentle, loving and faithfull, void of all guile and treason and such as lived after the manner of the golden age."[29] In a way, however, images such as those by White were immediately nostalgic in that the arrival of Europeans, who brought with them their traditions of the Fall away from Eden and the loss of an imaginative "golden age," cannot but have corrupted the prelapsarian peoples whom they encountered or the lands upon which they lived. Allusions to early Virginia, and more generally to America, that call to mind referents in either the Judeo-Christian scriptures or classical mythology—and sometimes to both simultaneously—would continue to be made during the Age of Discovery, to the point where C. Allan Brown has remarked, "it became commonplace to cast the New World as both Eden and Arcadia, the Promised Land and the Hesperides."[30]

1.12 Above John White, Theire Sitting at Meate, 1585-86, watercolor, 8¼ x 8½ in., British Museum

1.13 Right John White, The Indian Village of Secoton, 1585-86, watercolor, 12¾ x 7¾ in., British Museum

While the emphasis in many early representations of Virginia was on the original state of these primeval lands, at the same time commentators were simultaneously, and perhaps unwittingly, pointing to the fact that the cultures that Europeans had "discovered" were themselves of long duration. In White's *The Indian Village of Secoton* (fig. 1.13) we see not a simple clearing in a forest primeval, but a well-established, orderly hamlet, whose citizens had carefully laid out specific areas for dwelling, eating, and worship, and who clearly had a sense of proper agricultural methods in that they had restricted areas for new, green, and ripe corn. Such villages were, in fact, impermanent; many of the native people of Virginia moved seasonally. White, however, creates the illusion of a settled, relatively civilized people inhabiting a site that would be recognizable as a "village" to his European audience. His portrayal of *One of Their Religious Men* (fig. 1.14) of the settlement, as well as his depiction of *A Chief Herowan* (fig. 1.15) suggest the existence of a priestly caste and an aristocracy before the coming of Europeans. In part these identifications were due to the fact that White could only recognize the members of the Virginia Indian society through the use of the European terminology he had at hand. His need to so differentiate, however, suggests that this stratification was of great importance to the native people, and therefore crucial if one was to produce an accurate account of their persons and culture.

The necessity of describing native Virginians in terms that would be understandable to a European audience was perhaps most famously demonstrated in the portrait of Pocahontas by Simon Van de Passe (fig. 1.16). In this

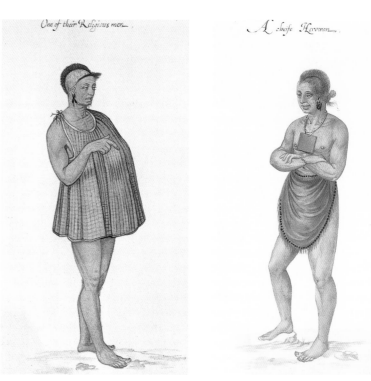

1.14 Above, left John White, One of Their Religious Men, 1585-86, watercolor, 10¼ x 5⅞ in., British Museum

1.15 Above, right John White, A Chiefe Herowan, 1585-86, engraving, 10⅜ x 5¾ in., British Museum

engraving, taken in 1616 during her fateful trip to England with husband John and son Thomas from which she would not return, the twenty-one-year-old former captive is identified not by her now famous nickname, but as "Matoaks als [alias] Rebecka daughter to the mighty Prince Powhatan Emperour of Attanoughkomouck als virginia." Rebecca was the name that she was given at her baptism, which is noted here, as is her marriage to John Rolfe. However, what is most crucial about her, and why she is worthy to carry an ostrich feather, is that she is royal, a princess, the daughter of the "Emperour" of Virginia. That Virginia had an emperor and a princess gave it a hierarchy that the English could understand, which ostensibly must have operated under roughly the same conditions as did the monarchy of Great Britain. The workings of government in the New World were of course quite different from those in Europe, but the necessary reliance of such commentators as John Smith and John Rolfe on common descriptive terminology augmented the already existing mythology about Virginia, which could now include powerful princes and their beautiful daughters, figures who were customary in the myths and legends of many European traditions. The descent of royal blood from a monarch to his child further put these people in line with the established norms of the continent.

Although the conversion of Pocahontas is by far the best-known manifestation, it is fair to say that religion in general, and the propagation of Christianity among the Indians in particular, were important aspects of life in early Virginia. There can be no doubt that the quest for profit was the pre-eminent motive for many of the early adventurers; however, the Church of England was always a presence, as Sydney Ahlstrom put it, "not just because a chaplain had been put aboard, but because the leaders of the Virginia Company were convinced that Englishmen needed the church's ministrations and were dedicated to propagating the gospel in the New World."[31] There would be dissenters—the Reverend Alexander Whitaker himself has been described as a "moderate Puritan"[32]—as well as members of other Protestant denominations in early Virginia, but apparently few non-believers. So, as Perry Miller, Karen Ordahl Kupperman, and other notable historians have pointed out, the traditional differentiation "between the secular outlook of the Virginians and the theological cast of New England thought" is misleading.[33] From the early invocations of the Garden of Eden to the Great Awakening of the mid-eighteenth century, the use in the colonial period of Biblical imagery and allusions in writings about life in Virginia suggest the type of strong familiarity with the scriptures that is often associated only with the New England founders.

In fact, as early as 1616 John Rolfe invoked a Biblical passage that would become a standard figuration for life

1.16 *Simon van de Passe,* Pocahontas, *1616, engraving, 6³⁄₄ x 4³⁄₄ in., published in John Smith's* Generall Historie, *1624, Virginia Historical Society*

in the colony. In his effort to enlist the support of the earl of Pembroke, Rolfe suggested that Virginia was a land in which one could find "every man sitting under his *figtree* in safety, gathering and reaping the fruits of their labors with much joy and comfort."[34] George Washington himself was known to use this expression, particularly after having returned from his public duties to the private life that he enjoyed at his beloved Mount Vernon.[35] The first appearance of this image in the Hebrew Scriptures is in I Kings 4:25. The subject is the peace and prosperity that was attained during the reign of Solomon. It too speaks of both the public and private realms, of the tranquil state of the country that allows for the individual to pursue a contented life. Throughout the history of the colony the "vine and fig tree" was often the trope of choice in moments of political or military calm, between the waves of storm that destroy or remove one from domestic bliss. Alternatively, it could be appealed to as a longed-for refuge from the responsibilities and concerns of one's daily toils. As C. Allan Brown has noted, "the Solomonic metaphor that Rolfe invoked persisted as a familiar refrain among Virginia planters well into the nineteenth century."[36] Its manifestation in Micah 4:3–4, following the famous prophesy (earlier seen in Isaiah 2), "they shall beat their swords into plowshares, and their spears into pruning hooks," looks ahead to the glorious future in store for Israel after the "house of the Lord" has been established: "they shall sit every man under his vine and fig tree, and

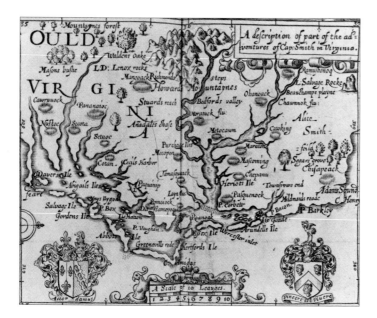

1.17 Robert Vaughan, Ould Virginia, *map published in John Smith,* Generall Historie *(London, 1624), Virginia Historical Society*

none shall make them afraid." A time of peace and prosperity is in the offing, and one can take comfort in that assurance, even in the midst of the turmoil and suffering that for many were fixtures of colonial life.

According to Captain John Smith, one area of Virginia was already "Ould" by 1624. In an effort to differentiate between the patent that had allowed for the founding of the Jamestown colony in 1607 and the earliest attempt at colonization—Sir Walter Ralegh's ultimately failed Roanoke plantation of the late sixteenth century—Smith labeled that earlier territory "Ould Virginia" on a map that was included in his *Generall Historie of Virginia, New-England, and the Summer Isles* (fig. 1.17).[37] This designation had the added advantage of separating "Ould Virginia" from "New England," which Smith had christened in an earlier narrative, and which was clearly thought to be a separate entity by the time of the *Generall Historie*. It also had the perhaps subversive implication that this part of Virginia was no longer as receptive to cultivation, or as potentially fecund, as it had been in Ralegh's day.

Smith had by this time given up his long-held wish to return to the New World, and so he set about composing his monumental *Generall Historie* with an eye toward writing himself in bolder strokes into the narrative of Virginia's success. For instance, it is only here that we find the detailed account of his rescue by Pocahontas, which has since become an important event in America's mythohistoric past. Throughout the book, Smith is often at great pains to call attention to his many contributions to the survival of the colony, for which, he believed, he had not received adequate credit. The year 1624 also marked the end of the Virginia Company, which had been instrumental in marketing the potential of the new lands. In his map, Smith invokes Ralegh and the colony's beginnings, and points to its settlements almost as a proud parent, whose child has come of age.

The early existence of an "Ould" Virginia was supported at mid-century by John Farrer, who differentiates his "Ould Virginia" from such places as the younger English colony, Maryland, and such neighboring lands as "Noua Francia" (fig. 1.18). On his map of 1651, Farrer also looks back to the earliest days of the colony, but he chooses Sir Francis Drake, rather than Ralegh, as his inspiration and link to the colony's formation. This is Drake's "New Albion," which Farrer suggests may yet prove to be a middle ground between England and Asia; "The Sea of China and the Indies" lies somewhere to the near west of his "Ould Virginia." By mid-century there seems to have been no doubt about the primacy of the Virginia founding, and in 1660 Charles II would give Virginia its best-known sobriquet; his reference to the colony as "our auntient dominion" provided an alternative identification that continues in popular usage.[38] By 1666, Thomas Ludwell, secretary of the colony, would refer to Virginia as "this ancientest colony," when complaining that its governor received a salary "less than any other Governor in the West Indies." There are many other such notices, all of which speak to Virginia's age and, often, her importance to the English colonial enterprise.[39]

The establishment of a genteel, pastoral society was not the immediate goal of Virginia's earliest settlers; indeed, its cultivation was actually something of an afterthought, even to the "gentlemen" who had made the voyage. While many of the traditional pastimes of the aristocracy were apparently available to those who would hazard the journey—as was advertised in "What the Gentry and others in Virginia Do for their Entertainment," an engraving published in Theodore de Bry's *America* of 1618 (fig. 1.19)—this image of a land of plenty was more meant to inspire notions of abundance, and therefore potential

1.18 John Farrer, Virginia, *1651, map, 10⅛ x 13⅛ in., Virginia Historical Society*

1.19 *Left Unknown artist,* What the Gentry and others in Virginia Do for their Entertainment, *1618, engraving, 5 1/8 x 6 7/8 in., published in Theodore de Bry's German* America, *Virginia Historical Society*

1.20 *Above James I,* A Counterblaste to Tobacco, *1604, manuscript, Virginia Historical Society, bequest of Paul Mellon*

fortune, than to suggest that one would enjoy the same sport in the same ways as one had at home. Wealth, to be sure, was on most minds, and when it became clear that there would be no bonanza in gold or gems as had been found elsewhere in the New World, those who aspired to economic success in Virginia acquired land and established great "plantations." John Rolfe's experiments had shown that the milder tobacco of the West Indies could be grown successfully in Virginia, and soon that highly profitable export crop became the planting of choice, often taking up acreage that should have been used for subsistence crops. These early Virginia entrepreneurs, who were ignoring the arguments that had been made by James I in his *Counterblaste to Tobacco* of 1604 (fig. 1.20), and the thoughts of Charles I, who in 1630 predicted that those colonies "lingering onely upon Tobacco, are in apparent danger to be utterly ruined," were responding to what Jack Greene has called the most important catalyst toward successful colonization, the opportunity to better one's fortune.[40]

Although some attempts were made to broaden the base of early Virginia's agriculture, including the importation of silkworms and mulberry trees, Virginia never developed the diversified economy that had been envisioned by the Virginia Company. Tobacco remained the rage. It permitted individual settlers to establish plantations wherever they wanted, which led to the creation of a distinctly un-English social landscape; planters decided that "the further [they settled] from their neighbors the

better." According to John Oldmixon, this tendency caused Virginia to become dependent on importation. Through trade they could manage well enough without a diversified economy: Virginians could "provide themselves with any thing which they can fetch elsewhere for Tobacco."[41] Although there were some lean years, many early Virginians built the foundations of great fortunes on this single crop.

While such early commentators as John Smith and John Rolfe had boasted about Virginia's potential, and some planters had actually achieved success, in the opening years of the colony there was a concurrent sense of failure. To some, Virginia seemed less an earthly paradise than a "barren and unprofitable" country. As early as 1610, one reporter struggled to find a way to make his readers accept the fact that the "felicites and miseries" of the colony must be "reconciled together."[42] Jack Greene points out that throughout the period there was in England and its colony "an obsessive fear that Virginia had not yet come close to fulfilling the promise predicted by its earlier proponents."[43] By mid-century, Lionel Gatford, a merchant himself, argued in a pointedly titled account, *Publick Good Without Private Interest or, A Compendious Remonstrance of the present State and Condition of the English Colonie in Virginea,* that Virginia had brought "shame and dishonour" upon England, because self-seeking colonists had gratified their own appetites and ambitions, drinking excessively, living where and how they pleased, and cultivating tobacco to their heart's content—in short, pursu-

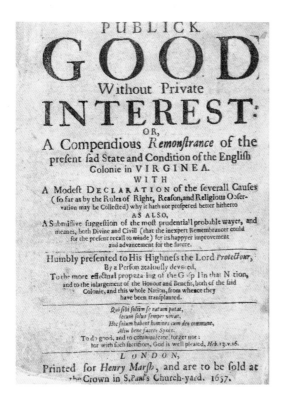

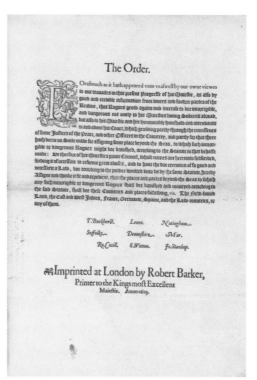

1.21 *Far left* Lionel Gatford, Publick Good Without Private Interest or, A Compendious Remonstrance of the present State and Condition of the English Colonie in Virginea *(London, 1657), Virginia Historical Society, bequest of Paul Mellon*

1.22 *Left* King James I, The Order [banishing rogues to the New Found Lands], *London, 1603, Virginia Historical Society, manuscript, bequest of Paul Mellon*

ing "private interest" instead of "publick good" (fig. 1.21). This negative image of Virginia continued into the eighteenth century. John Oldmixon pointed out that Virginians had made almost "nothing of those Advantages, which would enrich an industrious People," and Robert Beverley famously opined in 1705 that "All the Countries in the World, seated in or near the Latitude of Virginia, are . . . reckon'd Gardens of the World, while Virginia is unjustly neglected by its own Inhabitants, and abus'd by other People."[44]

Complicating matters was the fact that early on Virginia had come to be seen as a place in which to deposit the dregs of English society. Perhaps based on a peculiar interpretation of Virginia as a potential new Eden, where sinful Europeans might be reborn into a state of grace, but more likely because England's leaders simply wanted to find a place to absorb their more troublesome countrymen, King James I's *Order [banishing rogues to the New Found Lands]* of 1603 (fig. 1.22) points to the fact that the newly discovered areas could be used to rid England of her "desperate villianes." The Privy Council decreed that "any such incorrigible or dangerous Rogues shall bee banished and conveyed . . . [to] these Countries and places following, viz. The New-found Land [Virginia], the East and West Indies, France, Germanie, Spaine, and the Low-countries, or any of them."[45] While England's European neighbors no doubt had their own incorrigibles to worry about, the new lands seemed ideal for this purpose. In a 1610 sermon, William Crashaw suggested that only "base and disordered men" would volunteer for service in Virginia, although he allowed that "The basest and worst men trained up in severe discipline, under sharpe laws, a

hard life and much labor, do prove good members of a Commonwealth."[46] John Donne, in a 1622 sermon to the Virginia Company, went further. The colonial enterprise would allow the English to "sweep your streets, and wash your dores, from idle persons, and the children of idle persons, and imploy them: and truly, if the whole Countrey were such a Bridewell, to force idle persons to work, it had a good use."[47] As Peter Linebaugh and Marcus Rediker point out in their illuminating discussion of this tendency in *The Many-Headed Hydra*, for many seventeenth-century Europeans, America came to function like a prison.[48] Although at the outset there were perhaps too many settlers who thought of themselves as "gentlemen" and not enough laborers, by the mid-seventeenth century Virginia had amassed a sizable population of people with no education and few skills, and therefore no clear means of making a living. The practice of sending convicts to Virginia was suspended from 1671 until 1711; by 1722, however, Robert Beverley could complain of these "Newgaters" and their employers: "As for the Malefactors condemn'd to Transportation, tho' the greedy planter will always buy them, yet it is to be fear'd they will be very injurious to the Countrey, which has already suffer'd many Murthers and Robberies. . . ."[49] Beyond their potential to commit actual crimes, these "Malefactors" would have been seen as capable of contributing little to the social or, in the end, the economic stability of the colony.

Mid-seventeenth-century commentators such as William Bullock and John Hammond tried to explain away or excuse the perceived failures of Virginia and pointed again to the immense potential of the colony, but it was apparently difficult to convince many of their country-men. Although it was the rare place where men of small estate could "see themselves in a condition never again to want; but to live like Gentlemen," and where the younger sons of English aristocrats could acquire their own fortunes, the lingering spectre of failure continued to haunt the colony.[50] The paradox that Virginia was both the best and the worst of lands was addressed in 1697 by Henry Hartwell, James Blair, and Edward Chilton in *The Present State of Virginia, and the College.* "It is astonishing to hear what contrary Characters are given to the Country of Virginia, even by those who have often seen it, and know it very well; some of them representing it as the best, others as the worst Country in the World. Perhaps they are both in the Right. For the most general true Character of Virginia is this, That as to the Natural Advantages of a Country, it is one of the best, but as to the Improved Ones, one of the worst of all the English Plantations in America."[51] Although throughout the seventeenth century men of all estates, from servants to gentlemen, from Cavaliers after the Revolution to Roundheads after the Restoration, had emigrated to Virginia, in the eyes of many Englishmen the colony had yet to live up to its potential.

The original hope, as expressed in the charter of 1606, had been that colonists would "have and enjoy all the liberties, franchises, and immunities . . . to all intents and purposes as if they had been abiding and born within this our realm of England." The truth is that the bad press that Virginia received throughout the seventeenth century assured a continuation of a lesser status. The imagery on the first Virginia seal, which suggests that this new region was the "fifth kingdom," on a par with En-

1.24 Seal of Virginia, *1776, Virginia Historical Society*

gland, France, Scotland, and Ireland, was never taken seriously by the colony's detractors (fig. 1.23). As we shall see, the insistence on the part of those in power at home on the colonial nature of both the enterprise and its inhabitants would at the beginning of the eighteenth century cost a great hero of the realm the position that he most coveted, and would, half-a-century later, infuriate a former colonel in the Virginia militia named Washington, a man who in his forties would come to believe that ridding himself and his fellow landowners from economic oppression through revolution would be the only way to make a success of Mount Vernon, the plantation that he had acquired after the death of his elder brother.

A different type of equality is suggested in the seal of Virginia that emerges during the Revolutionary period (fig. 1.24). The motto "Sic semper tyrannis"—"Thus always to tyrants"—appears beneath the powerful goddess of liberty who has defeated the fallen male monarch, points to a demand for benevolent, if not necessarily democratic rule, and the result if one attempted to govern Virginia in a harsh or dishonorable manner. Almost two hundred years after the first landings, this Virgin, a symbol of Virtue who carries a sword and lance and whose raiment allows for the bared left breast often associated with the Amazons of antiquity, is no longer willing to be dominated by "masculine" European powers.

A brief discussion of the lives of two prominent turn-of-the-century Virginians is appropriate here, in that in many ways their experiences exemplify a number of the contradictions that were imbedded in early Virginia society. Such incongruities would ultimately help to shape the often conflicted image of the region. Although each achieved a degree of success, the differences between William Fitzhugh and Daniel Parke II far outweigh any similarities. However, one could go as far as to suggest that their successes and failures provide us with a useful picture of the issues with which even the most important of the early Virginians of the period had to deal.

The British-born William Fitzhugh was among the first Virginia colonists to establish a dynasty on the land. In his portrait he looks like a prominent Londoner, rather than a resident of what was still a backwater colony

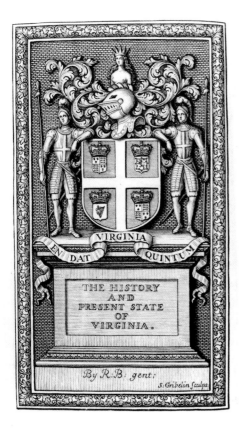

1.23 Early "Stuart" Virginia Coat of Arms, *from Robert Beverley,* The History and Present State of Virginia *(London, 1705), Virginia Historical Society*

not entirely comfortable with his achievements, in part because his newly won wealth and social position were gained in an isolated, largely undeveloped colony. Richard D. Brown points out the problem: "for English settlers . . . especially in Tidewater Virginia, the sense of isolation was so much a part of the colonizing experience from Roanoke and Jamestown onward, that it became prominently imbedded in the region's common culture."[52] In his letterbook he commented extensively on Virginia's shortcomings (fig. 1.26).

Life on Virginia's frontier molded Fitzhugh's cautious philosophy. The colony of the late seventeenth century was, in Fitzhugh's words, " a strange land." Few of the institutional structures that formed the foundation of aristocratic life in England were in place. Further, there was a scarcity of "good & ingenious company" in the sparsely settled countryside, a "want of spiritual help and comforts," suggesting that the rural parishes were not providing the necessary solace to their flocks, and an absence of appropriate schools for the education of one's heirs. As a member of an emerging gentry he would dress the part, build a fine house, and furnish it handsomely with family portraits, tapestries, and fine silver, in an effort to create the "creditable" façade that he believed one needed to live "comfortably" in Virginia. And there can be no doubt that he did enjoy living "very contentedly & well" on his plantation, Eagle's Nest, where he entertained visitors not only with "good wine," but also with "three fiddlers, a jester, a tight-rope dancer, [and] an acrobat who tumbled around."[53] However, Fitzhugh was aware of the fact that Virginia's tobacco-based economy was unstable. Prices could fluctuate wildly, which could lead to disaster for the profligate. He avoided debt when he could; when ordering silver he would "rather leave some out, than bring me a penny in Debt," and his bed curtains were "plain & not very costly." He collected silver, amassing one of the largest collections in the colonies, both because it made a social statement and because it was a sound, highly prudent investment. Silver could be melted down quickly if one needed money in a pinch and was easily transferable to the next generation.[54]

In his portrait, Fitzhugh impresses the viewer as a highly competent, successful, and stylish man. Yet with that success necessarily came a degree of caution. The gentry of Fitzhugh's generation held no illusions that their lifestyle matched that of their models in England, and they were aware of how tenuous was their hold on wealth, the necessity that would allow for the pursuit of the civility to which they aspired. Fitzhugh noted tamely that for those who "desire[d] privacy and retirement" and, as John Rolfe had suggested, wanted only to "sit safely under their own Vines & fig trees," there was no better spot than Virginia.[55] He was one of the colony's most successful entrepreneurs, and yet he makes clear

1.25 Above Unidentified artist, copied by John Hesselius in 1751, William Fitzhugh, 1698, oil on canvas, 30 x 25 in., Virginia Historical Society

1.26 Left William Fitzhugh, letter of 30 January 1686/87 to Nicholas Hayward, Letterbook, Virginia Historical Society

(fig. 1.25). Fitzhugh chose a rural life because that seemed the quickest way to make money; he used slaves to cultivate tobacco on his huge land holdings, which would grow to 54,000 acres. This portrait, one of the most important to survive from so early a date in America, shows him at age forty-six, when his pre-eminent position in Virginia society was well established. He is posed proudly, and clothed in the grandest of wigs and the voluminous robes and cravat that were all the fashion in contemporary London. He was a self-made man, a successful planter and lawyer, who had accomplished much with the opportunities afforded him in Virginia. However, he was that his existence, because it lacked the culture and society that could only be found in England, was at times less than fulfilling.

Daniel Parke II (fig. 1.27) would ultimately leave Virginia in his quest for success. Born in York County to wealthy parents, Parke's early education came in Surrey, England, at the home of his mother's family, the Evelyns. After his mother's death he returned to Virginia and ultimately married Jane Ludwell, the daughter of the powerful Philip Ludwell II of Green Spring. He would return to England, and, after a series of misadventures and bad choices, he came back to Virginia in 1692, with his mistress, who would soon give birth to his illegitimate son. Julius Caesar Parke, as the boy was called, would be left behind, as would Parke's wife and daughters, Frances and Lucy, when he again deserted his Virginia family and left the colony for good in 1697.

After an unsuccessful attempt to buy a seat in the House of Commons, Parke turned to the military for advancement. He fought under the Duke of Marlborough in the War of the Spanish Succession against the armies of Louis XIV of France and proved himself to be a courageous soldier. He rose to the rank of lieutenant-general, and after the crucial Battle of Blenheim it was his good fortune to be sent to present the news of the victory to Queen Anne.[56] This triumph engendered a period of national euphoria, and Parke basked in his moment of

glory. It is this event that is celebrated in John Closterman's ambitious portrait. In the background is the cannon fire at Blenheim. Around his neck Parke wears a miniature of the Queen on a red ribbon, which was one of his rewards for bearing the good news. He was also honored by the allies who fought against Louis; the most prominent of the gold medals in the left foreground is the so-called "Ambassador's Medal" of the States General of the Netherlands, which, although it had traditionally been awarded only to departing ambassadors, was voted to Parke on 21 August 1704. It must have seemed to this native Virginian that he had the world at his feet.

Parke would ultimately seek the governorship of Virginia as a reward for his services to queen and country. Ironically, however, because he had been born in the colony, the crown would not seriously consider awarding him such an important position. Instead, Parke was made governor of the Leeward Islands, a post that he unhappily accepted. After his arrival in Antigua in 1706, Parke, to the chagrin of many of the island's seamen, mercilessly began to enforce acts of trade against smuggling. Worse yet, the new governor debauched the wives and daughters of many of the settlers. Frustrated in their unsuccessful efforts to remove Parke from office, the citizens formed a mob that brutally murdered him at the statehouse of Antigua in 1710.[57] Parke had risen to great heights and become an international hero, but his attainments could not overcome the stigma of his being a colonial.

The lives of Fitzhugh and Parke point to the restrictions that tempered the success that one could achieve if one either lived in Virginia or was a Virginian by birth. While both, by any measure, had grasped more than most men of their age attempted to reach, the limitations imposed by their associations with Virginia left them wanting. The Old Dominion's isolation and oft-sullied reputation in her mother country would allow British politicians to disavow placidly any inroads toward equality. As the eighteenth century progressed and more Virginians began to acquire wealth and, given the time that wealth allows, to articulate more clearly the values upon which they would base their society, these colonials would aspire to create a regional community that rivaled their European models in civility and genteel living. For most, however, this would be impossible, a dream barred from its fruition by what they saw as unfair taxation and other forms of economic and political sanction. From their ensuing contention against long-held British prejudices against colonials in general and Virginians in particular would emerge a number of the most important leaders of the burgeoning revolutionary movement.

1.27 John Closterman, Daniel Parke II, *ca. 1705, oil on canvas, 50¼ x 40½ in., Virginia Historical Society, gift of Mr. and Mrs. D. Tennant Bryan*

2.1 *Unknown artist,* The Plantation, *probably 1ˢᵗ quarter of 19ᵗʰ century, oil on wood, 19¹⁄₈ x 29¹⁄₂ in., Metropolitan Museum of Art, gift of Edgar William and Bernice Chrysler Garbisch*

II. The Pursuit of Gentility in the Virginia Colony

n the 1630s and 1640s people from the English privileged classes began migrating to Virginia in increasing numbers, but gentrification was slow. By mid-century, thanks in part to the encouragement of longtime Governor Sir William Berkeley, an aristocracy had begun to form. As Paul Williams wrote at the time, however, "Though there be here some Gentlemen of Rank and Quality, yet there are but few."[1] The younger sons of noble and gentry-level families soon began to see Virginia as a doorway to opportunity, and thus "many Gentlemen of Virginia," John Oldmixon would be able to assert in 1710, could "boast as good Descents as those in England." Moreover, the achievements of Fitzhugh's generation caused an observer in 1703 to write, "Many of the more Ancient Families" now live "in a State and Equipage equal to that of the best Gentry in England." There was still, however, a degree of defensiveness. William Beverley felt the need to remind his readers that the colony had not been settled only by the "indigent and necessitous." He tells us that once the dangers inherent in the first years of settlement were over, "People of better Condition" had come to Virginia. During the Civil War in England, "several good Cavalier Families went thither with their Effects, to escape the Tyranny of the Usurper." After the Restoration, "many People of the opposite Party took Refuge there, to shelter themselves from the King's Resentment." Through such infusions an upper class began to take shape.[2]

The Flowering of a Colonial Aristocracy

The Virginia patriciate of the seventeenth century had been unstable. The dependence first on the tobacco crop itself, and then on the whims of European consumers and merchants, left even the wealthiest of their number like Fitzhugh fearing for what at any moment could become a precarious financial situation. However, it would be these "proto-aristocrats," to use Wayne Craven's term, who by building fine houses and amassing what fortunes they could, set the stage for the realization of a Virginia aristocracy in the next generation.[3] Their inheritors would still be concerned about making money, but they would have the luxury of concurrently seeking societal stability as well. Guthrie Sayen succinctly describes what was at the heart of this attempt:

Throughout the Anglo-Atlantic world of the eighteenth century, the gentry, regardless of political proclivity, cultivated a distinctive style and set of values, which together may be called the genteel ethos, or gentility. Put another way, the quality of gentility distinguished gentlemen from commoners. The ideal English gentlemen was well-born; possessed of enough landed wealth to be independent; handsome in appearance; graceful in movement; refined in speech, manner, and taste; knowledgeable in the arts, sciences, and languages; acquainted with the world; hospitable, generous, and honorable; deferential to social equals; affable to social inferiors; virtuous in morality; disinterested in public service; and brave in battle.[4]

(It should be noted that disinterest here means an unbiased, unselfish, and impartial approach to public life. While some of the gentry were undoubtedly *uninterested* in politics, those who chose to serve did so *disinterestedly*.) The greatest public servant of his day would spend his entire life in the pursuit of rural virtue. For many, George Washington would come to embody the genteel ethos, and his plantation, Mount Vernon—the most famous home in the nation—would be pictured for generations as exemplary of the American pastoral ideal (fig. 2.1). To become a member of the gentry one had to keep up appearances. Toward that end, Richard Bushman tells us, "In every region, the gentry erected dwellings with spaces and furnishings to stage the occasions of genteel life; they learned appropriate conduct and taught it to their children; they dressed, ate, and carried themselves to suit the part. As they learned manners, the aspiring gentry, in some ways rough and awkward, in other respects elegant and imposing, formed themselves into a polite society." This would not be an easy process, however: "The adoption of gentility could not be accomplished without effort. The colonials had to attend to every aspect of life to achieve even a pale facsimile of English gentility."[5]

In the first two decades of the eighteenth century, as growing sums of money were accumulated through the tobacco trade and the proto-aristocrats were giving way to their heirs, the colony matured dramatically. The new capital at Williamsburg, which had been founded in 1699, gave the scions of the great families a place where they could gather, and a new pride was taken in the colony's antiquity and the life that the early planters had built there. Some hoped that more such cities would rise. In

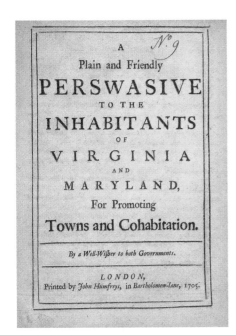

2.2 *Francis Makemie,* A Plain and Friendly Perswasive to the Inhabitants of Virginia and Maryland, For Promoting Towns and Cohabitation *(London, 1705), Virginia Historical Society, bequest of Paul Mellon*

1705, the evangelist Francis Makemie penned *A Plain and Friendly Perswasive to the Inhabitants of Virginia and Maryland, For Promoting Towns and Cohabitation* in the hope that their establishment would encourage "education and vertue" (fig. 2.2).[6] Many towns were in fact laid out at the time that Williamsburg was established, but most would not develop into cities. Instead, there was an explosion of growth along Virginia's rivers, akin to the Thames pattern. By 1732, William Hugh Grove would write that Yorktown was "Like a Black heath or Richmond Hill and Like that Overlooks a fine river Broader than the Thames at Those places"; he found the Mattaponi River to be "Thick seated with gentry on its Banks with in a Mile or at most 2 mile from each other. . . . Most of these have pleasant gardens and the Prospect of the River render them very pleasant [and] equall to the Thames from London to Richmond, supposing the Towns omitted."[7]

As the founding of the Virginia colony had been expressed in both Biblical (Garden of Eden) and classical (Golden Age) terms, so later allusions to scriptural "vines and fig trees" had a corresponding classical referent, the pastoral ideal. It would emerge in the New World as a haven from British disapproval, but would evolve into the lifestyle pattern of choice for the rising colonial aristocracy. While in the late seventeenth century Virginia's society had ironically become increasingly less English—the colony's diffuse settlements and singular economic basis had actually discouraged the development of towns and industries—by its turn a new sensibility was beginning to take shape. In part because of the confidence inspired by their growing wealth, Virginians in the early eighteenth century began to define themselves differently. First and foremost, they accepted the reality of their rural settlement. The absence of an urban society, and the multifaceted economy that would have developed with it, were no longer to be objects of embarrassment. According to Jack

Greene, we can see an early manifestation of this rethinking in Robert Beverley's pivotal study, *The History and Present State of Virginia* (1705). While other commentators were convinced of the importance of bringing what they could of modern English life to the still relatively young settlements, "Beverley's ambivalence about the benefits of Anglicization as well as his pointed admiration for many aspects of the more primitive cultures of the Indians betrayed a powerful tendency, briefly articulated by Rolfe during the first decade of settlement and barely visible in Hammond at mid-century, to retreat into an arcadian self-image, which, in the face of the obvious superiority and complexity of metropolitan culture and the failures of Virginians to recreate much of it in their own society, extolled the virtues of a plain pastoral life. . . ."[8] The tendency to which Greene refers is the ever-present desire to "sit safely" under one's own "Vines and fig trees," the dream of an idyllic pastoral world that had to be pointedly sought out in England but was readily available in Virginia. As the eighteenth century progressed, planters came to believe more firmly than apologetically that their colony should be appreciated rather than deprecated for its rurality. Although writers still emphasized the beauty and climate of the colony, such descriptions now carried additional weight. Virginia's ties to the literary pastoral, which made it akin to the rural society of Augustan Britain as well as to that culture's classical models, should be celebrated. The inference was that the quest for virtue that had been based on Old World conceptions of the pastoral could perhaps be carried out with greater hope of success in the New. The colony's society, economy, and even its settlement patterns, could be reinvented as expressions of this pastoral ideal.

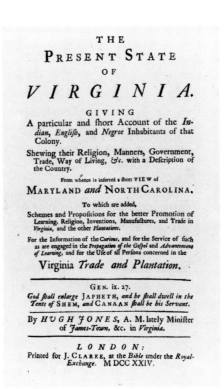

2.3 *Hugh Jones,* The Present State of Virginia *(London, 1724), Virginia Historical Society, bequest of Paul Mellon*

While in England a country home provided a useful, relaxing, and invigorating respite from urban life, no such move was necessary in eighteenth-century Virginia. The aristocrats of the day were already resident in the country. And although the pursuit of wealth certainly occupied their minds much of the time, by mid-century there was also the perceived need for some type of relief from the drudgeries of farm management. The pastoral ideal gave colonial planters the means to philosophically transform their backwater, rural seats into idyllic agrarian retreats, where the quest for wealth could continue, but it would now be in the more agreeable service of the pursuit of contentment, and ultimately virtue. At its height, "the Horatian model of gentility—once employed as an apologia for one's distance from the civilization—became transformed into the rural republican ideal." Virginia could be "viewed less as a retreat than as the center of a polished, learned, and purified society, free of the corruptions of the greatest extremes of wealth."[9] However, the depletion of the land due to negligent tobacco culture, and the moral burdens of slavery, without which plantations were unsustainable, would undermine this imagined arcadia.

Two decades after Beverley, in the wake of the "advances" and "improvements" that were celebrated by the Reverend Hugh Jones in 1724, Virginians would be ready to argue all the more forcefully for the merits of their rural life. By the end of the first half of the century, as Greene puts it, "Virginia society began to appear, to visitors as well as natives, as sufficiently British to make it possible for its inhabitants credibly to think of their society as an American model of that quiet and virtuous pastoral society so much celebrated by contemporary writers in Augustan England."[10]

The Present State of Virginia (1724) by the Reverend Jones was a crucial document toward Virginia's being seen in a new, more advantageous manner (fig. 2.3). This young Anglican clergyman's goal was to combat "very erroneous and monstrous Thoughts" that had long been held in England about the colony. He wrote that in recent years Virginia had "far more advanced and improved in all Respects . . . than in the whole Century before."[11] In many ways Virginia had "altered wonderfully"; the increased adoption of English manners in the early eighteenth century had inevitably led to a greater gentility among her upper classes. Jones also celebrated the remarkable growth of Williamsburg, stating that its public buildings were the best in all the colonies. In addition, he made clear to his largely British audience that many Virginians consider England their home, and "behave themselves exactly as the gentry in London."[12] His generally positive account concluded that Virginia was "the most antient and loyal" and "the most extensive and beneficial Colony belonging to the Crown of Great Britain."[13] In

short, while it might not have seemed to all "the happy retreat of true Britons" that Jones suggested, the Virginia that he described in the early eighteenth century had in many ways evolved to the point where the gentry could at least attempt to claim some level of parity with their counterparts in England.[14] And although Jones is also willing to point out some of the colony's shortcomings, he makes it clear that Virginians are "neither Favourers of Popery nor the Pretender on the one Side, nor of Presbytery nor Anarchy on the Other; but are firm Adherents to the present Constitution in State, the Hanover Succession, and the Episcopal Church of England as by Law established. . . ."[15] This loyalty to English institutions was crucial to any argument concerning the colony's modest attempts toward European-style civility.

Sydney Ahlstrom has pointed to other factors that influenced the early Virginia church, including the tobacco culture and its ultimate reliance on slave labor, and, perhaps surprisingly, Virginia's topography: "Many long and wide river estuaries made the tidewater region a series of peninsulas, and with the rise of immense waterfront plantations, the parish as it had been understood for centuries in western Christendom simply ceased to exist. A Virginia 'parish' was sometimes sixty miles long; a vast, thinly populated territory which had some logical reality on a map, but little actuality for the hapless priest charged with the spiritual care of its scattered population."[16] Although the colony's charter had made clear that the "ecclesiastical laws of England" would govern its religious life, perhaps because of the difficulties in Anglican ministration there was wavering and at times outright dissent throughout Virginia's early history. A number of denominations, including Puritans, Quakers, and Presbyterians, gained footholds in the colony, and there were strong reactions, especially by the middle and lower classes, to such fiery preachers as Samuel Davies and George Whitefield. The latter was one of the leading voices of the Great Awakening, and during visits to Virginia he preached in both Bruton Parish Church and in the pulpit of the Reverend Patrick Henry (the uncle of the Revolutionary firebrand) in Hanover.[17]

While the masses would be open to such influences, the Virginia gentry for the most part remained loyal to the Church of England. And although they would have identified themselves as devout Christians, in practice it was sometimes difficult to attend to all of the traditional theological responsibilities. Their useful knowledge of the Bible, which is suggested by the many invocations of scripture that we see in their writings, points to a solid moral foundation, but their acquaintance with the classics suggests what for the gentry may well have been an ancillary impetus toward a virtuous life. What was sometimes lacking in their Christian practice, based either on the inattentiveness of their ministers or on their own lack of

2.4 William Aitkin, John Campbell, second duke of Argyll and duke of Greenwich, *ca. 1718- 25, oil on canvas, 50 x 40¾ in., Virginia Historical Society*

theological fervor, could be made up by their attending to the precepts of the pastoral ideal.

Responding to Lewis Simpson's suggestion that the colonization of the South was an "errand into an open, prelapsarian, self-yielding paradise, where they would be made regenerate by entering into a redemptive relationship with a new and abounding earth," Samuel S. Hill, Jr. points out "how much affinity" this notion "has with establishmentarianism within Christendom and, to boot, with Anglicanism. This is the language of stability and gradualism, of the affirmation of the world pretty much as it is." This was the Anglicanism of many members of Virginia's rising aristocracy, a religion that helped to allow them to retain the social and political as well as the religious status quo. When it was possible, most no doubt attended church services, in part because membership in a certain church, and seats in particular, forwardly placed pews, helped to maintain one's social standing; church entry also served as a way for the nouveau riche to announce their entry into the aristocracy. As Richard D. Brown suggests, "because churches in Virginia were less intensely preoccupied with conversion and salvation than in New England, . . . participants could make churchgoing into such a communicative social occasion. Participation by gentry in public worship, . . . was not only exemplary for their social inferiors, it also enhanced their images of themselves as true English gentry."[18] As in the mother country, a strong affinity with the Church of En-

gland could be asserted when one needed to maintain societal boundaries—as the Catholic Alexander Pope could attest—but in general it is fair to say that religion in Virginia served as an aid to maintain the structure of its earthly society as well as a path toward one's heavenly reward. In a culture in which power relations were crucial, the Church of England, while open to all, ironically served as yet another method for segregating those with the power from the powerless.

Of the many British noblemen who could have served as models for their colonial contemporaries, one eminent aristocrat would have contact with two of the important Virginians of the period. John Campbell, the duke of Argyle, pictured here in his superb portrait by William Aitkin (fig. 2.4), fought beside Daniel Parke as a commander under the duke of Marlborough in the War of Spanish Succession. Like Parke, Argyle was praised for his gallantry, which almost cost him his life at the victory at Malplaquet. By his mid-twenties Argyle was already highly influential in Scottish politics; he played an important role in swaying the Scottish Parliament to accept the union of 1707 with England, for which he added duke of Greenwich to his ancestral title. His military acumen was showcased in 1715 when he helped to crush the Jacobite uprising in Scotland by outmaneuvering vastly superior forces, yet he managed to maintain a reputation in his homeland as a patriotic statesman, as his role in the denouement of Sir Walter Scott's *The Heart of Midlothian* attests.

In all probability, Argyle met William Byrd II when both young men were completing their educations in the London of the 1690s. Although he may well have been somewhat intimidated by Argyle's power and position, Byrd was attracted to the duke's outgoing personality, and soon the two outsiders—Argyle a Scot and Byrd a Virginian—became friends. They corresponded after Byrd's return to the colony in 1705. The duke would certainly have been interested in Byrd's 1706 marriage to Lucy Parke, the daughter of his former comrade-in-arms, and during the London years after 1714 they were frequent companions at coffeehouses and dinners. Argyle's name appears some sixty times in Byrd's London diary; he notes almost methodically Argyle's "kindness" in receiving him.[19] The duke invited Byrd to his English country house on several occasions, and helped to protect his friend's fragile political standing at the court of George I. On 25 January 1718 Byrd "asked him for his picture, which he promised me."[20] This portrait was the result.

Argyle is pictured by Aitkin proudly wearing the blue velvet mantle and embroidered star of the Order of the Garter. Allusions to his military career can be seen in his

2.5 *Attributed to Hans Hysing,* William Byrd II, *ca. 1724, oil on canvas, 50 x 41 in., Virginia Historical Society*

sword and armor, and his Scottish heritage is suggested by the castle over his left shoulder. His impetuosity, his instinct for passion over prudence that would ultimately undermine what had been a promising political career, is evident in Argyle's pose and attitude, which almost challenges the viewer to match his status and accomplishments. The Aitkin portrait, in combination with Byrd's reminiscences of their friendship, would no doubt have greatly impressed his visitors to Westover, his Virginia estate. This is the sort of man one wanted to be, a leader who had influenced politics at home and the balance of power abroad. Such a personage, who had the wherewithal to live where he pleased, saw the importance of being at the seat of power when necessary, but given the chance would retire to his country estate, where one could attend to more pleasant, if no less cerebral, matters.

Homes had been constructed along Virginia's rivers in the seventeenth century. Thomas Glover in 1676 went so far as to say that houses had been built "all along the sides of the Rivers . . . after the English manner."[21] He mentions in particular Green Spring, Governor Berkeley's mansion near Jamestown, which, although its precise form is unknown, was certainly one of the largest homes of its day. Most of these riverside houses, however, were small, "single-pile" dwellings. They did not presume to be "villas" of the type then becoming popular in Europe, nor did their inhabitants pretend to be philoso-

phers. It would not be until the following century that agricultural prosperity would support the melding of humanistic and agrarian pursuits.

Concurrent with the flowering of a colonial aristocracy and the pursuit of the pastoral ideal in Virginia was the rise to prominence of the Byrd family. And undoubtedly one of the foremost Virginians of his era, who embodied the rise of the newly conceived landed gentry, was Argyle's friend William Byrd II (1674–1744; fig. 2.5). The son of a successful planter and entrepreneur who had provided him with the requisite wealth, Byrd proved to be a worthy scion. In this portrait, which is attributed to Hans Hysing, we see Byrd as a mature man, who apparently still has the bearing, spirit, and sense of fashion of a man half his age. Rarely is a painted portrait accompanied by a literary self-description, but in this case we have Byrd's self assessment of 1722-23 in which he outlines his peculiar experiences, ambitions, and vulnerabilities. This revealing document discloses that the Virginian's path through London society, while not without many successes, was also not without anguish.

Sent to England for an education at the tender age of seven, Byrd would see his father only twice again in his life and his mother only once. Left largely on his own as a youth, he turned to the popular courtesy books of the day that preached the gentlemanly (and classically inspired) virtues of moderation and the stoic acceptance of one's fate. As a young adult, having been stigmatized socially as a "provincial," he developed a character that has been described by a biographer as "brittle."[22] In his self-portrait Byrd confessed a striving for the "highest pitch of achievement," and also admitted sufficient disappointments to be "sorely sensible of Injurys."[23] Like his one-time father-in-law he longed to be named governor of Virginia, but to the Lords of Trade and Plantations such ambition in a colonial was troublesome. They denied his bid, and nearly had him removed from the colony's Council. He was to some a likable, urbane, good-natured person and a loyal friend; concurrently, he was a sensualist, who recorded in his diary incidents of deviant sexual behavior, and a rampant chauvinist. While his strong ambition carried him into the highest circles of London society— where he had friends among the nobility, the theater set, including Congreve and Wycherley, and the circle of Pope, including Teresa Bount (fig. 2.6), whose portrait he brought home to Westover—his complexities would not allow him to revel in his successes.[24] Beneath his proud façade lurked a bruised, self-protective human being. Hysing has managed to catch a number of the multiple facets of Byrd's personality, including his drive, his public front, and his masked but still visible vulnerability.

Byrd made the statement that "he knows the world perfectly well and thinks himself a citizen of it." He described himself in 1723 as neither a colonial nor an En-

2.6 Unidentified English artist, school of Sir Godfrey Kneller, Teresa Blount, *ca. 1710-15, oil on canvas, 50 x 40 in., Virginia Historical Society*

glishman, but a man caught between two worlds.[25] By 1724, however, he seems to have come to some conclusions about his life. He stops courting heiresses and makes a prudent marriage to Maria Taylor, a handsome, intelligent Englishwoman, if one with little fortune. In the Hysing portrait we see a ship over his shoulder, a reminder of his distant holdings in Virginia. This portrait, which he commissioned for his friend Charles Boyle, the earl of Orrery, would be given to Orrery in exchange for one of the earl for Byrd's collection at Westover. Throughout these last years in London he was apparently thinking about the position of social and economic prominence in Virginia to which he would return. It is not until 1726, however, that he actually gets back to Westover. From that moment until his death, Byrd would contribute notably to the social and political development of the colony.

Byrd repeatedly took the position that Virginia was an arcadia reincarnate. He often tried to convince his friends and acquaintances, and quite possibly himself, that life in Virginia was as good as in Great Britain. In a famous letter to Orrery in 1726, Byrd falls back on a traditional motif: "Like one of the patriarchs, I have my flocks and my herds, my bond-men and bond women, and every soart of trade amongst my servants, so that I live in a kind of independance on everyone, but Providence." At times, though, his praises have a rather ambivalent subtext. He

goes on to say that "we sit securely under our vines, and our fig trees, without any danger to our property. We have neither public robbers nor private, which your Lordship will think very strange, when we have often needy governours, and pilfering convicts sent over amongst us."[26] The following February he wrote again to Orrery, again using Biblical metaphors, both lauding Virginia and then tempering his sentiment: "Our ground likewise instead of thorns and thistles, brings forth pleasant fruits and wholesome grain, with little cultivation, and our poor Negroes are free-men in comparison of the slaves who till your ungenerous soil; at least if slavery consists of scarcity, and hard work. Our land produces all the fine things of Paradise, except innocence and the tree of life; and these we should have in some measure, if we had the grace to use our other good things temperatly."[27] Perhaps at this moment, still soon after his return to Virginia, Byrd truly believed that the tranquility of life at Westover was superior to the often wicked society of London that he described in his diaries. He admitted to Orrery that "There are so many temptations in England to inflame the appetite, and charm the senses, that we are constant to run all risques to enjoy them. They always had I must own too strong an influence upon me, as your Lordship will belive when they could keep me so long from the more solid pleasures of innocence, and retirement."[28] Six years later Byrd would write longingly to John Boyle, who had be-

2.7 Attributed to the studio of Sir Godfrey Kneller, Lucy Parke Byrd, *ca. 1716, oil on canvas, 50 x 41 in., privately owned, from the estate of the Misses A.C. and L.W. Stewart*

come earl upon his father's death, of life in England and about his financial problems, which were based largely on the low price of tobacco: "It is that which with-holds me from the pleasure of returning to that enchanted island, which I shall always long to do, so long as your Lordship is there, but I must wait with patience for that, till better times, or better fortune shall re-establish my finances. In the mean while I must make the most of my retirement, and content myself with rural and domestick joys, which have this advantage at least, that they are innocent, and need but little repentance."[29] While on one level he is certainly flattering Orrery, we also get a sense that the "joys" of Virginia are truly pale in comparison to those available in London. However, his Virginia pleasures that needed "little repentance"—either financial or spiritual—would be all that were within his limited means.

Although it would seem logical for a man of his age and varied experiences to seek out the peaceful, presumably contented existence that was available to him in the Virginia countryside, Byrd must be allowed a good deal of license in his praise of colonial life. That said, as he looked back from Westover over his often tumultuous history, he might well have recalled the youthful aspirations that he took with him on an earlier trip from London to Virginia in 1705, when he would both serve as the executor of his father's will and successfully court the daughter of Daniel Parke. William Byrd II and Lucy Parke would be married on 4 May 1706.

Lucy Parke (1687–1716; fig. 2.7) was nineteen—the blush of youth had faded—when she married the highly eligible William Byrd II. However, she is pictured here in a circa 1716 portrait attributed to the school of Sir Godfrey Kneller as a beautiful young woman who is just blossoming into adult life; in fact, the twenty-nine-year-old Lucy would die of smallpox less than a year after this portrait was completed. Her husband recorded their alternately affectionate and tempestuous relationship in the pages of his early diary. Both were young and spirited, and they quarreled over innumerable matters, including William's flirtations with other women, the at times extravagant goods that she ordered from England, and her treatment of their slaves. Although William Byrd was quick to complain when slaves were unproductive, he had to restrain his young wife when she whipped domestic servants or inflicted burns on them as punishment. While that sort of cruelty is not immediately predictable based on this portrait, we certainly see a young woman who was used to getting her way. Her gesture, whether it is for us to look at the highly decorative round box or at something outside the range of the painting, is clearly directive. The exotically dressed slave to her left is at the ready should his mistress need his attention. She is in charge of her sphere, and, Kneller seems to suggest, one would not like to be the person with whom she disagrees.

The unknown surveyor who drew *A Plan of Westover* provides us with an early attempt to create a pastoral estate of the English model in Virginia (fig. 2.8).[30] Geometric gardens flank the plantation house, which almost seems about to be engulfed by the vast, surrounding wilderness. There is a careful accounting of particular topo-

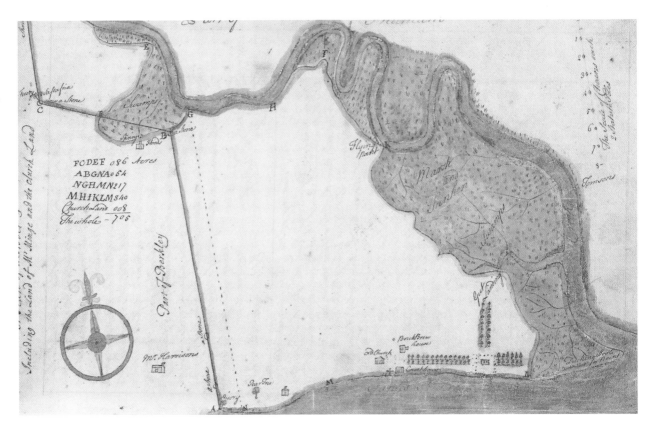

2.8 *Copied after an unidentified surveyor,* A Plan of Westover *(Charles City County), probably after 1731, ink and wash, William Byrd Title Book, Virginia Historical Society*

2.9 *Unidentified artist, probably in London,* Fan, *ca. 1720, painted ivory, Virginia Historical Society*

2.10 *Unidentified artist, probably in London,* Watch, *ca. 1720, gold and enamel, Virginia Historical Society*

graphical features, such as the marsh and "sunken swamps" of the James River, and a use of what must have been well-known flora, such as a particular pear and "hicory" tree, to help orient the viewer. The river would of course be important for practical purposes, but Byrd would have appreciated the vista created by the elbow in the James at the southeastern corner of the property. One "retired" to such an estate to both cultivate nature, as he would do in his arbors, and to be inspired by it. It is the latter relationship that supports his allegiance to the pastoral ideal.

Byrd's interest in things pastoral is evidenced by two presents that he purchased for his daughters. To Evelyn he gave a painted ivory fan on which is pictured a pastoral scene; the temple pediment in the background is meant to suggest ancient Rome (fig. 2.9). The motif of the young man tilling the soil in the presence of a young woman, beyond its inherent attractiveness, perhaps suggests the possibility that a woman might be able to find a suitable mate outside the city. This might have been given to encourage Evelyn, to convince her that she could be happy in the comparatively deserted countryside around Westover. Evelyn Byrd would never marry, however, and would die in Virginia at the age of thirty. To Wilhemina he gave a gold and enamel watch, in which we see a young swain courting a beautiful, young, classically garbed woman (fig. 2.10). The farming implements and the vine upon which pearls rather than grapes appear to be growing look both to the pastoral and to the Biblical vines, both of which promise a life of peace and contentment. The nest of small, presumably young birds that the man offers predicts a union that will bear fruit, while the pair of birds to the right suggests his faithfulness. Perhaps Byrd is allowing for the fact that one day a man will come and take Wilhemina away from the idyllic life that he has created on his Virginia estate. This scene depicted on a watch might well have suggested to his daughter that the time was coming. Such purchases tell us both of Byrd's sense of what would have been stylish in the early eighteenth century, and of his ability to adapt the motifs of the pastoral to suit his purpose of the moment.

The invocation of the pastoral in Augustan England and colonial Virginia did not mean, however, a complete

2.11 *Attributed to John Hesselius,* Landon Carter, *ca. 1755, oil on canvas, Beverley R. Wellford and R. Carter Wellford IV*

ment from the outside world. Richard D. Brown writes, "in their enthusiasm for occasions like weddings, christenings, and funerals, for horse races, fox hunts, and balls, for the festivities that accompanied the installation of a new governor or the proclamation of a new monarch. . . . the great gentry had succeeded in creating a polite Anglo-Virginian society. . . . " Further, the isolation of the "man of letters"—be he poet, philosopher, or parvenu landowner—was "meaningful only because it is in relation to the community of men of letters and learning." Lewis P. Simpson goes on to say that, "The library in the garden—e.g., Pope's grotto at Twickenham—is a pastoral image supporting the concept of the independent, secular, eighteenth-century mind following the pursuits of literature and knowledge. Byrd among his thirty-six hundred books at Westover, engaged in his correspondence with other men of letters, is a figure in the community of the eighteenth-century mind." Although he suggests that some of Byrd's allusions to the felicities of the pastoral might be less than convincing, Simpson concludes, "in the context of the adaptation of the pastoral convention in America, William Byrd of Westover is the first full-fledged embodiment of a singular figure in American and, you might say, Western literature: the pa-

triarch-philosophe—the slave master and man of letters—of the Southern plantation world."[31] Byrd had seen great houses and country villas in England, and he understood their significance to their owners and to the aristocratic society at large. He also understood the difficulties of creating such a society in the colony, but he went forward, and ultimately provided a prototype to which all who had dreams of recreating the European pastoral ideal in Virginia could aspire.

Another of the other great landowners of the period who was well acquainted with the precepts of the pastoral ideal was Landon Carter (1710–1778; fig. 2.11), son of the great Robert "King" Carter of Corotoman. (Landon's second wife, until her untimely death, was Maria Byrd, another of the daughters of William Byrd II.)[32] As captured in this portrait attributed to John Hesselius, "Colonel" Carter is unquestionably a man of means. He gazes confidently at the viewer in appropriately aristocratic attire, with his hand jauntily placed on his hip, his hunting dog in attendance, and his great land holdings alluded to in the distance. Robert Carter had been one of the wealthiest men in the colonies, and he provided well for all of his children. Landon owned tens of thousands of acres in the Northern Neck, and would be left "eight fully equipped and working plantations."[33]

When it became time for Carter to build his country estate he named it "Sabine Hall," after the Sabine Villa of Horace. The poet had been enamored of his rural retreat, where he was free from the "doubled wealth and doubled care" of Rome and could live undisturbed by "fame" and "worth."[34] Carter had been in England from 1720 to 1727, completing his formal education and learning what would have been expected from a young man of wealth and privilege. He then learned the subtleties of plantation management from his father, living at Corotoman until soon after Robert Carter's death in 1732. The next year he determined to build a country retreat for himself on a charming location that his father had patented for him along the Rappahannock River in Richmond County.

Pictured here, as the house would have looked in the eighteenth century, we see in Sabine Hall the classical lines and features that would have been familiar to the landed Englishmen of the day (fig. 2.12). Carter's decision to build his Richmond County estate not on the bank of the river, but on the hillside above it, away from the potentially unhealthy, low-lying marshes, made the design of his house and garden a bit more difficult, although such arrangements were not uncommon in the Chesapeake. Not surprisingly, he turned to a European source for advice. The sixty-fourth chapter of Sebastiano Serlio's *Architectura* (1600) is pointedly entitled "A Proposition for Building on a Hillside" (fig. 2.13). Serlio, a near-contemporary of Palladio, had considered that some

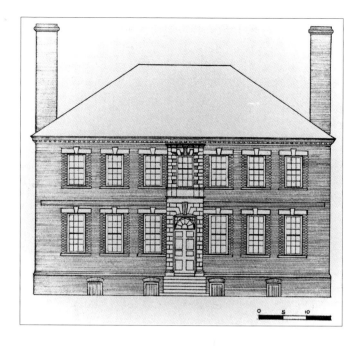

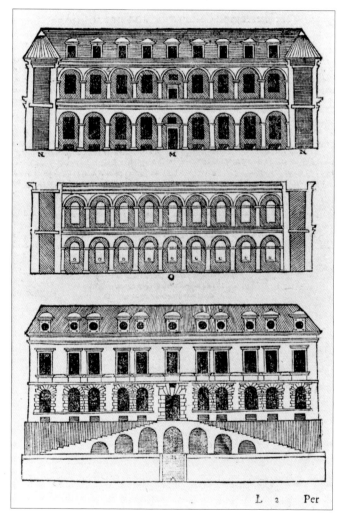

2.12 Above, top Sabine Hall, *1733-42, Richmond County, reconstruction of the initial appearance of the house prior to alterations in the early nineteenth century*

2.13 Above A Proposition for Building on a Hillside, *Chapter 64 in Sebastiano Serlio,* Architettura *(Venegia, 1600), Virginia Historical Society*

members of the local aristocracy might not have access to what would have been considered an ideal site on a river, especially in the hills and valleys that were ubiquitous in the Italian countryside. He attempted to provide both ideas about how to build the house itself, including the appropriate architectural elements, such as bold door and window treatments, and how to gain the best advantage in terms of its vista. The garden at Sabine Hall sloped down the hillside in six terraces toward the Rappahannock, which is visible three miles in the distance. The picturesque views would no doubt have encouraged the Carters and their guests toward contemplation, and therefore toward contentment.

Landon Carter, however, was a man who sought but rarely found such satisfaction. Although his life had been a series of accomplishments and successes in the public and private spheres, Carter was not gratified. Jack Greene writes that "a sense of bitter disappointment . . . nagged Carter throughout his final years. For some reason he had failed—and he knew he had failed—to make any lasting impression upon his generation, to achieve that recognition among his contemporaries that would assure him of a place in history."[35] Throughout his life he had contemplated the weaknesses and imperfections of his contemporaries, which "manifested itself in a pronounced reserve and caution in his personal relationships, an almost total cynicism about the motives and actions of his fellow men, a profound skepticism that made it impossible for him to accept anything not confirmed by his own experience, and a constant and thorough scrutiny of his own behavior."[36] He strove to lead a virtuous life and to achieve a personal piety, while attempting to keep at bay a fiery temper, and his advice to others often mirrored his own sense of mankind's innate weaknesses. In 1755 Carter advised the young George Washington to "regard the inner Man," and he praised the soon-to-be commandant of the Continental Army in May of 1776: "I only wish that every one was, as you have shown yourself to be, not so much in quest of praise and emolument to yourself as of *real* good to your fellow-creatures."[37] Like Washington, Carter retired at various times from his public life to the serenity of his country estate. Unlike the general, who relished his rural life, Carter's personal demons often accompanied him to the idyllic confines of Sabine Hall.

In the case of Mount Airy, the Tayloe family home and immediate neighbor of the Carters of Sabine Hall, one again sees many of the architectural and design elements recommended by Palladio and his followers (fig. 2.14). Here, the ideas of the Italian masters were mediated by a contemporary Englishman, James Gibbs. In his *A Book of Architecture* (1728) we find "A Design Made for a Gentleman in Dorsetshire" (fig. 2.15), a plate that clearly served as the inspiration for a number of the features at Mount Airy.[38] The architect said in his Introduction that

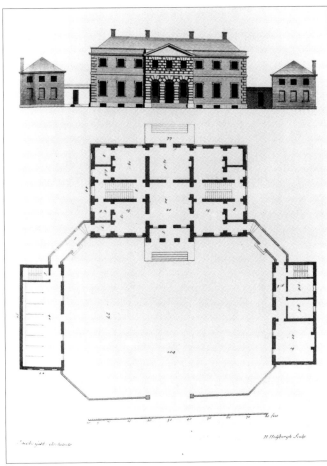

2.14 *Above, top* Mount Airy, *ca. 1754-64, Richmond County, Virginia Historical Society photograph*

2.15 *Above* A Design made for a Gentleman in Dorsetshire, *Plate LVIII in James Gibbs,* A Book of Architecture *(London, 1728), Virginia Historical Society*

this book would be useful "especially in the remote part of the country," where such matters as the accumulation of the necessary materials and the lack of experienced builders might be of greater concern than in the immediate environs of a settlement.[39] The fact that Mount Airy would be built using largely local brown sandstone suggests that a solution was found early for at least one of these concerns. However, the logistics of constructing one's idyllic retreat in the countryside would continue to plague all but the wealthiest Virginians of the period. For most, the tranquility afforded by such estates must have seemed like a fitting reward for the monumental efforts that it took to build them.

These great houses make clear the fact that it was important to the Virginians of the day to model their country retreats on those of their contemporaries in England. From the classical design elements, to the location—which, for philosophical as well as practical reasons, had at the least to be in the vicinity of a tranquil river—there was a real attempt to bring the best of English style to the colony, which, it was hoped, would no longer be considered a backwater outpost in a wilderness, but rather a remote part of England itself. The new gentry pursued other traditional accoutrements of the aristocracy as well, such as decorative objects, silver, books, and paintings—Byrd had an impressive library and would assemble the largest and best portrait collection that would hang in colonial America. To the Carters, Tayloes, Byrds, and their contemporaries, such objects identified both themselves and their heirs as members of the gentry, and pointed to the cultural and social advancements in the colony as a whole. In some cases, such as that of William Fitzhugh's silver, no trace of the treasure has been found; in others, such as Byrd's portrait collection or the dozen wonderful "Stamp Act Spoons" ordered by Landon Carter, we can now contemplate both the objects and the intentions of the men who designed and crafted them (fig. 2.16).

Richard Bushman suggests that the style, if not the size, of the great houses eventually worked its way down to the lower levels of the burgeoning aristocracy: "This new wave of mansion building was not reserved for the uppermost provincial elite. . . . The Georgian style spread widely among the colonial gentry as the [seventeenth-century] porch design had never done. In Virginia few planters could raise a huge pile like Thomas Lee's Stratford or William Byrd's Westover or Mann Page's Rosewell. . . . But vernacular builders sensed the essence of the great houses and copied the fundamental elements for a much wider segment of well-off planters."[40] Ambition was in the air, and as models for the great houses had migrated from England, models for the homes of the lesser elite had meandered up the major rivers to the tributaries, allowing for young men on-the-make to aspire to the positions and pursuits of the landed. If one prepared himself early in life for success, learned what he could from the existing gentry, and made calculated decisions about his short- and long-range future, then there was wealth and success to be had. With the increase in public building, the establishment of private schools and industrial enterprises, the emergence of Norfolk and other trading centers, and the improvement in the colony's agriculture with the cultivation of grain and other crops to augment the ever-present tobacco, anything must have seemed possible in mid-century Virginia.[41] Without this atmosphere, which must have been invigorating for those willing to accept the challenge, it is doubtful that the third son of an upper-middle class couple would have paid such close attention to his betters, married so well, or ultimately created so impressive a country seat at Mount Vernon, thereby fashioning himself into the George Washington who would one day lead the nation.[42]

The first map to document effectively the settlement boom along Virginia's rivers appeared at mid-century. It was produced by two historically significant figures: Joshua Fry, the Albemarle County surveyor, who on the eve of the French and Indian War would precede Washington as commander of the Virginia Regiment, and his deputy, Peter Jefferson, the father of the future president. In their effort, *A Map of the most Inhabited part of Virginia containing the whole Province of Maryland with Part of Pennsylvania, New Jersey, and North Carolina* (1751), we see that plantations line many of the main rivers (fig. 2.17). We can contrast this with Captain John Smith's map of 1624,

2.16 *Unidentified English silversmith (undecipherable mark), Spoon, 1767, silver, 8 in., engraved "LC / 1767 / the REPEAL of the AMERICAN Stamp Act," Virginia Historical Society*

in which almost all of the land is in the possession of the Indians, and almost all of the identifications are derived from native words. From the density of settlement, particularly in the Tidewater region, we learn that Virginia in the early eighteenth century had enjoyed a dramatic increase in population and wealth, and that the settlement of the colony had remained predominantly rural. This is not a land of cities or counties—the latter are not even designated on the map—rather, it is a series of large plantations, many of which line the banks of the Tidewater rivers. From this map we also get a sense of the extension of Virginia to the north and west. The colony must have seemed, as it appears here, to be limitless. The map, we should remember, is specifically "of the most Inhabited part" of the state. The Ohio River in the northwest corner does not seem as though it will be an impediment to future settlement; indeed, the "Bounty Lands" awarded to Washington and his officers after the French and Indian War will be in this region. These western lands would ultimately be of great importance to the gentry. However, unlike in England, where great landowners rented acreage to working farmers, in the colony there would be much land speculation, which as it turned out was a far less reliable road toward financial success. Finally, in the cartouche we see the source of most of Virginia's wealth—a dock-side negotiation concerning barrels of tobacco, and the slave labor that allowed for the colony's commercial prosperity.

English ideas about gentility had been more easily transported to Virginia than to other American colonies because of its close ties to the mother country. These affinities contributed to the colony's success but at the same time made the harsh treatment that Virginia landholders received at the hands of their religious and ideological brethren at home all the more difficult to understand. By the 1760s it was judged by many colonials to be both unfair and insulting, an affront to both their pocketbooks and their honor, a characteristic of great importance to the post-French and Indian War Virginia gentry.[43] Indeed, the pride in what they and their forefathers had accomplished on the land can be seen as an important factor in

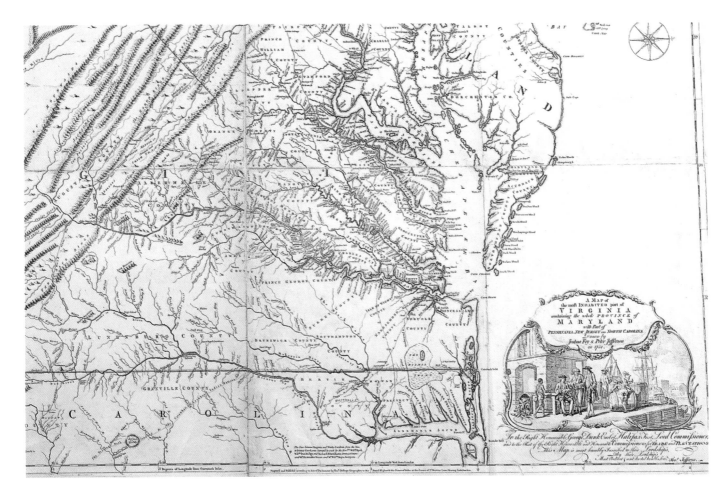

2.17 *Joshua Fry and Peter Jefferson,* A Map of the most Inhabited part of Virginia containing the whole Province of Maryland with Part of Pensilvania, New Jersey and North Carolina, *1751, London, detail, Virginia Historical Society*

the process that would turn what had been loyal Englishmen into nascent Americans. As tensions between colonists and colonizers mounted, an article in the *Virginia Gazette* in 1771 would proclaim that Virginians were "the happiest and most free People upon Earth."[44] They believed themselves to be, in Jack Greene's words, "a humane, hospitable, and polished people," who deserved the respect and the admiration of their counterparts in Britain.[45]

Elusive Virtue

The Africans pictured in the cartouche of the Fry/Jefferson map are wearing loincloths; a contemporary who consulted this resource, which would become the "preeminent map of Virginia for the remainder of the eighteenth century," would have seen them performing the sorts of menial tasks considered appropriate, in attire reminiscent of their African origins.[46] The inclusion of these slaves can be explained in a number of ways: it speaks of the importance of the young, well-dressed planter who grows and sells the tobacco; it reminds the viewer of who actually does the physical work to complete the transaction, and thereby perhaps encourages other

young men of means to take part in the apparently lucrative, less than laborious (for the trader) tobacco business; and it suggests the pervasiveness of slaves in Virginia, in that they are at work not only in the fields, but also in personal service (the young black man to the left offers a cup of wine) and commercial enterprise. In the mid-eighteenth century this would have pointed to the affluence of the colony, which was based almost wholly on tobacco, which spills out of the large barrel on the left as if it were a horn of plenty.

In 1770, John Henry, the father of Patrick, produced *A New and Accurate Map of Virginia* (fig. 2.18). As counties had been omitted in the Fry/Jefferson map, Henry makes the point that his effort includes "most of the COUNTIES" which are drawn from "ACTUAL SURVEYS." Henry also provides information concerning population and agriculture. By defining the wealth and attainments of high-born Virginians in his notes, Henry offered a measure of the success of their pursuit of gentility. The prosperity of the region's tobacco industry, which by this time was possible only through the use of slave labor, had made Virginia the largest, most populous, and wealthiest of England's colonies. The limitless expanse to the northwest is similar to that pictured in Fry/Jefferson, but

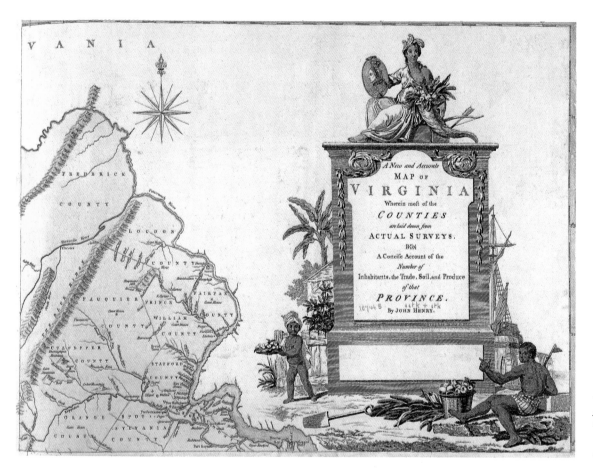

2.18 John Henry, cartouche from A new and accurate map of Virginia, *1770, London, Virginia Historical Society, bequest of Paul Mellon*

Henry adds that a treaty between the English and the Six Nations (Iroquois) will cede nine or ten million acres in this area to Great Britain. Because of its errors and omissions, and the death of John Henry only three years after it was published, this later map did not replace the Fry/Jefferson map as the standard. Nor did Henry's closing sentiment—"that upon the whole it is much the richest as well as of the greatest Importance to Great Britain and therefore well deserves its Encouragement and Protection"— keep prominent Virginians like John Henry's son from agitating for a more potent voice in the political decisions that would effect the colony.

The cartouche of Henry's map, while similar in some respects to Fry/Jefferson, makes a far more provocative statement. At the top we have a young Indian woman; such figures had long been used to symbolize America and had special significance in Virginia because of the role that Pocahontas had played in the founding of the colony. She holds a portrait of her sovereign, George III, in her right hand and a cornucopia in her left. A bow and arrow, the traditional weapons of Native Americans, are present, but they have been put aside and are only partially visible behind the pedestal upon which she sits. The presence of the English king might be explained by the fact that the engraver of this map, Thomas Jeffreys, identifies himself as "Geographer to the King," but Jeffreys had also produced the Fry/Jefferson map in which there is no such overt tribute. More probably, the Indian woman serves to remind viewers both that the presence of the English, as symbolized by their king, was necessary for Virginia to be transformed from its primitive state into

the prosperous colony it had become, and of Virginia's continuing allegiance to the crown. Below we again have Africans dressed in exotic but seemingly appropriate costumes. The basket and the small boy's tray, which are overflowing with fruit, and the randomly fallen corn plants and tobacco leaves assert the fertility of the new lands, while the ship and barrels remind viewers of the importance of the trade in tobacco, fruits, and slaves.

Henry purports to tell those who consult his map the complete story of Virginia, from the geography of the entire region, to the parameters of the counties, to how Virginia attained its great wealth, to the actual numbers relating to population and commerce. In a gesture that strikes a modern viewer as amazingly subtle for the late eighteenth century, Henry also points out that one group of stories has yet to be told. The older of the two slaves points to the bottom, the foundation of the classically configured monument, upon which all that Virginia has become was built. It is blank. His history, the stories of the slaves whose labor led to Virginia's affluence, is still unknown to the white populations of Europe and the colony. Henry might well be admitting that he does not have the knowledge or capability to represent the African population fairly. However, by explicitly manifesting that an important factor in the story of Virginia's rise to power is missing, in tandem with the subjugation of the Indians suggested above, Henry seems to be artfully asking his viewers to consider the relationship between the colony's affluence and the suppression of its non-white races.

The arrival of slaves in Virginia in 1619 did not initiate a large-scale importation of field hands. As in many colonies, indentured servants formed an important part of the labor force in seventeenth-century Virginia. Such workers often proved to be less than dependable, however, and when they disappeared before the length of their indenture had expired they were difficult to track down. This circumstance, coupled with the colonists' early conclusion that the Native Americans would not provide adequate labor for their expanding plantations, made an increase in the importation of Africans necessary. The Virginia economy began to flourish as the tobacco crop boomed, and this growth demanded even more slaves for both field and domestic work. A statute supporting slavery had been passed in 1662, after which various strategies were employed in the effort to bring additional slaves to the New World. The inevitable increase in captives was explained in an early broadside, *The Case of the Separate Traders to Africa* (fig. 2.19). Between 1672 and 1698 the African Company had a monopoly on such trade. When the plantations, including those in the English Caribbean islands, complained that they did not have "a sufficient Number of Negroes," an act of Parliament in 1698 had opened up the trade beyond the existing African Company, "to all Subjects of England," with the result that "5 times the Number of Ships" were employed, and "the Plantations were supplied with 5 times the Number of Negroes as by the Company. . . ."[47] As the eighteenth century progressed, the need for slaves continued to increase in the colonies, while in England, as Enlightenment ideals began to take hold, there was increasing opposition to its continuance; a motion to abolish slavery was introduced in Parliament in 1788, although the slave trade would not actually be abolished until 1807.[48] It is ironic that the continuing dependence on slave-grown, health-impairing tobacco as the foundation of Virginia's economy was evidence that the colony was deficient in the very virtues that its patriarchy were trying to attain.

On the eve of the American Revolution, however, many prominent Virginians believed that their recreation of English country life did indeed lead to a virtuous society. "The prevailing principle of our government is *virtue*," proclaimed a contributor to the *Virginia Gazette* in 1769.[49] The vigorous role of Virginia's political leaders in taking a stand against British taxation, and later in championing independence, was put forward as evidence of this rectitude. Benjamin Franklin wrote at the time that Virginians were justified to "claim the Honour of having taken this Lead."[50] Such accomplishments, writes historian Jack Greene, "appeared powerfully to give the lie to any suspicions that the free inhabitants of Virginia were in the process of succumbing to luxury and degeneracy."[51]

Slavery, however, would discredit even the most persuasive arguments that a version of the pastoral ideal had

[1]

The CASE of the *Separate Traders* to *Africa*.

BEtween the Years 1672, and 1698. the present *African* Company enjoyed the Trade to *Guinea* by Patent from King *Charles*, exclusive of all others; but on the repeated Complaints from the Plantations, of their not being supplied by the said Company with a sufficient Number of Negroes, the Trade was laid open by Act of Parliament in 1698, to all the Subjects of *England* to trade to alike, on paying 10 *per Cent.* on Exports, for supporting Forts, &c. who improved it to such a Height in a Year or two, that there were employed 5 times the Number of Ships, and the Plantations were supplied with 5 times the Number of Negroes as by the Company, when exclusive, as appears by an Account lately sent from *Barbades*, of the Numbers delivered into that Island in 10 Years past, being 7000 and odd by the Company, and 27000 and odd by Separate Traders, and in proportion to all the other Plantations, supplying the Spaniards with great Numbers besides.

2.19 The Case of the Separate Traders to Africa *(London, 1709), broadside, Virginia Historical Society, bequest of Paul Mellon*

been attained in Virginia. The institution was firmly locked into place by the time that the first arguments about rural bliss were put forward. According to Hugh Jones, some planters by 1724 already owned hundreds of slaves. The Swiss promoter Samuel Jenner wrote that slaves simply were "required" by those who sought "to carry on planting and trade." In 1757 Peter Fontaine observed that "to live in Virginia without slaves" was "impossible." By the 1770s slaves made up forty percent of the population, and the wealthiest Virginia families had vast sums invested in slave labor.[52]

In defense of a system that was critical to their economy, colonial Virginians attempted various strategies in their effort to justify slavery. In some cases the approach was to insist on the savagery of these forced laborers. Hugh Jones wrote that blacks were "naturally of a barbarous and cruel temper." In 1764 Arthur Lee quoted writers on Africa to argue that "cruelty, cunning, perfidy, and cowardice" were their chief "characteristics" in their home continent, and that they had a "stubborn, stupid, and untractable disposition."[53] A few Virginians, however, recognized that slavery was evil and that its effects on society were pernicious. In 1771, in the early days of the struggle for liberty, a writer who called himself "Associator Humanus" declared in the *Virginia Gazette* that "we should have . . . manifested a more genuine Abhorrence of Slavery"; this might have happened "had we not been too familiar with it, or had we not been conscious that we ourselves were absolute Tyrants, and held Numbers of poor Souls in the most abject and endless State of Slavery." Even Arthur Lee admitted that slavery was "danger-

2.20 *Virginia House of Burgesses,* Petition to King George III, *1772, manuscript, vellum, 13³/4 x 26¹/2 in., Virginia Historical Society, bequest of Paul Mellon*

ous to the safety," "destructive to the growth of arts & Sciences," and productive of "a numerous & very fatal train of Vices, both in the Slave and in his Master." While what Quaker John Woolman had called a "dark gloominess" hung over the landscape of colonial Virginia because of slavery, the institution would remain in place because white Virginians knew of no practical way to end the system that afforded them ease and affluence. Recalling the Adam and Eve analogy that was popular at the time of the first settlement of Virginia, Peter Fontaine reported in 1757 that each generation was drawn "into the original sin and curse of the country of purchasing slaves." This institution would prove to be the poisonous fruit in the garden.[54]

In 1772 colonial Virginians went so far as to ask for a ban on the further importation of slaves from Africa (fig. 2.20). This petition—which in all likelihood was drafted by Richard Henry Lee and was signed by Peyton Randolph, the House speaker who would soon preside over the Continental Congress in Philadelphia—seemed to arise primarily from humanitarian motives: "The Importation of Slaves into the Colonies from the Coast of Africa hath long been considered as a Trade of great Inhuman-

ity, and . . . we have too much Reason to fear will endanger the very Existence of your Majesty's American Dominions." They also claimed, however, that the trade "greatly retards the Settlement of the Colonies, with more useful Inhabitants, and may, in Time, have the most destructive Influence."[55] This comment hints at the true root of their concerns. The burgesses anticipated that the hindering of the foreign slave trade with high import duties might reduce the number of laborers in the colony, thus driving up the price of tobacco. This would trim the flow of cash out of the colony, eliminate competition to the domestic slave trade, perhaps encourage the immigration of artisans and craftsmen, and decrease the potential for slave insurrections. Not surprisingly, George III and his ministers rejected the proposal, leading Thomas Jefferson to include the monarch's "suppressing every legislative attempt to prohibit or to restrain this execrable commerce" as one of the charges against the king in his draft of the "Declaration of Independence."[56]

The economic "misfortunes" that had been inflicted on the colony by Britain were seen by by some Virginians in 1769 as "an opportunity given us by indulgent Providence to save ourselves" from "a general depravation of manners" that had set them "loose from all the restraints of private and public virtue." Such misfortunes would awaken them to the need to "promote and encourage Industry and Frugality, and discourage all Manner of Luxury and Extravagance."[57] However, instead of simply promoting industry and frugality, the economic crisis eventually became so severe as to encourage a revolution.

The irony is that slavery, which was the greatest of the obstacles on the path to virtue in the colony, had freed the leaders of Virginia society from toiling away their energies as active farmers; they were positioned to read and theorize, in the manner of the ancients and their European disciples, about matters of state. Thus, such prominent Virginians as Thomas Jefferson, James Madison, and George Mason were able to answer the colony's British critics by creating, at least on paper, a more perfect, more enlightened system of government than that known in the mother country.

As we look back on the era of the founders, it becomes clear that considerations of slavery and matters attendant to it were pervasive in the Virginia society. To invoke the most famous example, George Washington pondered the moral and economic effects of slavery throughout his adult life, even as he vigorously pursued his own incarnation of the pastoral ideal. Washington had been born into the colony as notions of the pastoral were being carried from Augustan England to the banks of Virginia's rivers by such planters as William Byrd II. In his youth he had observed the hierarchy of Virginia society, including the slave-holding Fairfaxes of Belvoir, and had learned that chief among the necessities for entrance into their

2.21 *John Trumbull*, George Washington, *1780, oil on canvas, 36 x 28 in., Metropolitan Museum of Art, bequest of Charles Allen Munn, 1924*

company was wealth, which could be manifested in fine dress, expensive decorative objects, impressive horses, and, most importantly, a splendid country estate. He took note of architecture during his travels and he consulted the architecture and garden design books of the day in his quest to transform Mount Vernon into the type of seat that would impress his guests and provide himself and his family with the appropriate sort of rural retreat.[58] As he matured, however, the problems inherent in the slave system came more regularly to his mind. Although he was often troubled about this institution, about the solvency of his plantation, and about the survival of the new nation, Washington's portraits consistently embody the traits of dignity, honor, and virtue to which aristocratic eighteenth-century Virginians aspired.

By keeping an army in the field and winning the occasional skirmish, Washington had been surprisingly suc-

cessful in the years leading up to 1780 when John Trumbull, in London, painted his full-length portrait (fig. 2.21). This image of the famous general would have looked right to European eyes. Washington stands with his horse and servant, like the subjects in a succession of portraits that date back to Anthony Van Dyck's famous 1635 painting of *Charles I à la Chasse*.[59] Trumbull's *Washington* was engraved the following year by the London printmaker Valentine Green, and soon afterwards copies became available to a curious audience in England and on the continent who wanted to get a look at this already famous general who had somehow held off the most powerful armed force in the world. As Trumbull produced this portrait in London, much of Washington's army was still positioned on the lower Hudson River; a fort under attack is the scene in the background. Although no major battle was won there by the colonials, the "fox," as

2.22 *Sebastian Bauman (major of the New York or 2nd Regt of Artillery), engraved by Robert Scot,* Plan of Yorktown *"taken 22-28 October 1781" and dedicated "To His Excellency Genl. Washington, Commander in Chief of the armies of the United States of America," 1782, Philadelphia, 25 x 17 in., Virginia Historical Society, gift of Edmund Ruffin of Prince George County in 1833*

Lord Cornwallis called the man he could not trap, remained in the suburbs of New York doing his best to wear down the will of the enemy, until his climactic journey to Yorktown in 1781.[60]

The convention of including a black support figure in the portrait of a notable subject was adapted here by Trumbull without pretension. Washington was accompanied in the field by William or "Billy" Lee, a slave who had become his personal servant.[61] (Such a figure is also present in the portrait of Lucy Parke Byrd, fig. 2.7, page 42.) The artist had seen Lee on a daily basis when he served as Washington's aide-de-camp, but it is not known how much he remembered about Lee's actual appearance. To modern eyes, it is of course ironic that the champion of American freedom would be depicted as a slaveholder. But the hypocrisy that is raised by this double portrait would not have occurred to the artist, to the subject, or to the patrons for the painting and the prints that were derived from it.

Trumbull's Washington appealed not only to Americans, but to champions of liberty throughout the world as

well. He is invincible, and perhaps an American victory is therefore inevitable, a sentiment that might have chilled some of Trumbull's London viewers. The general's stoic public persona, however, masked his often deep-seated fears. In a letter to his brother, Washington invoked what was already a well-known trope in his desire to be at Mount Vernon rather than in the field: "God grant you all health & happiness—nothing in this world would contribute so much to mine as to be once more fixed among you in the peaceable enjoymt of my own Vine, & fig Tree."[62] However, because it was his home, his "own Vine, & fig Tree" that he was fighting for, the general had to carry out his martial duties. Washington often expressed such sentiments; there can be no doubt that his wish to preserve the idyllic, if at times worrisome, life that he had created for himself and Martha at Mount Vernon was a major impetus toward his accepting his military and political offices.[63]

Washington was hailed, even venerated, after his military successes in the Revolutionary War. Sebastian Bauman, a major in the Second Regiment of Artillery who had participated in the siege, dedicated a plan of Yorktown "To His Excellency Genl. Washington, Commander in Chief of the armies of the United States of America" (fig. 2.22). Washington's greatest victory, which had put an end to British resolve to hold on to the thirteen rebellious American colonies, inflated his already lofty reputation. When he surrendered power, on the model of the great Roman Cincinnatus with whom he was immediately compared, Washington reached heights of acclaim perhaps never before imagined. About his relinquishing his position and returning to his farm, George III was reputed to have said, "If he does that, sir, he will be the greatest man in the world."[64] By the time the king would have made such a statement, Washington was already the most famous man in the Atlantic rim, and he would retain his formidable reputation as a leader and freedom fighter throughout his later public and private lives.

This esteem did not save him from occasional disparagement. In a letter of 1796 (fig. 2.23), Edward Rushton, a self-described "Liverpool poet" and former slave trader, criticized the president for remaining a holder of slaves: "But it is not to the commander in chief of the American forces, nor to the president of the united states, that I have aught to address, my business is with George Washington, of Mount Vernon, in Virginia, a man who, notwithstanding his hatred of oppression and his ardent love of liberty, holds at this moment hundreds of his fellow beings in a state of abject bondage. . . . that you, I say, should continue to be a slave-holder, a proprietor of human flesh and blood, creates in many of your British friends both astonishment and regret."[65] In his powerful conclusion, after talking about the American fight for liberty, Washington's role as the leader of a free people, and the president's reputation for religious piety, Rushton exclaims, "yet you are a slaveholder!" He had hoped to encourage the general to free his slaves. Such a manumission by a man of Washington's position and reputation might well have inspired his countrymen to do the same. However, it is unknown whether this missive ever reached its intended recipient; it is known today largely because after its return Rushton had it published in a pamphlet. Washington's struggles with the morality and efficacy of holding slaves would not be settled until his death, when he provided for the liberation and care of the slaves that he owned (not the "dower slaves" who had come to Mount Vernon through Martha's family) at his wife's death.

The irony forever present when we think of those who conceptualized and articulated America's quest for freedom while still in the position of slavemaster is perhaps most tellingly illustrated in the case of Thomas Jefferson. Jefferson was the product of a rural upbringing, for which he would be a staunch advocate throughout his career. In a slave society, however, Jefferson's vision of rural virtue could never truly be realized. In his writings he pointed out the evils of slavery, yet like Washington he could find no way to bring this institution to an end.

One of the practicalities that had to be attended to by slaveholders was the recapturing of runaways. In an advertisement that he placed in the 14 September 1769 issue of the *Virginia Gazette*, the twenty-six-year-old Jefferson makes it clear that he is serious about bringing back "Sandy," even though, for all of his abilities, "he is greatly addicted to drink, and when drunk is insolent and disorderly, in his conversation he swears much, and in his behaviour is artful and knavish"[66] (fig. 2.24). It is somewhat surprising to see who subscribed this advertisement, but it should not be. Landowners who counted on the income from their farms to allow them to pursue other occupations—Jefferson was admitted to the bar in 1767 and became a member of the House of Burgesses in 1769—had to maintain discipline and order among their servants and to make what efforts they could to assure the return of their property. In his later career Jefferson would have much to say about liberty and about the deleterious effects of slavery for both slave and master, but at this point he simply needed to get his shoemaker and part-time carpenter back.

Perhaps the best known of Jefferson's comments about slavery appear in *Notes on the State of Virginia* (fig. 2.25): "There must doubtless be an unhappy influence on the manners of our people produced by the existence of slavery among us."[67] After pointing out that slavery is pernicious for the slave, for the master, who has difficulty "restraining the intemperance of passion toward his

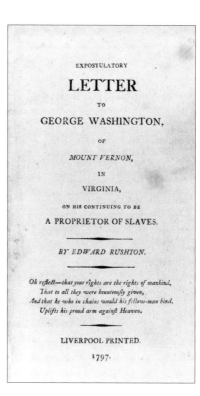

2.23 **Left** *Edward Rushton,* Expostulatory Letter to George Washington, of Mount Vernon, in Virginia, on His Continuing to Be a Proprietor of Slaves *(Liverpool, 1797), Virginia Historical Society*

2.24 **Below** Run Away From the Subscriber . . . Thomas Jefferson, *advertisement,* Virginia Gazette, *14 September 1769, Virginia Historical Society*

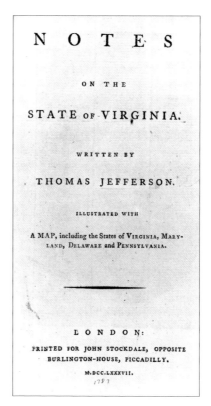

2.25 *Thomas Jefferson,* Notes on the State of Virginia *(London, 1787), Virginia Historical Society*

A PHILOSOPHIC COCK

2.26 *Attributed to James Akin, Newburyport, Massachusetts,* A Philosophic Cock, *ca. 1804, engraving, American Antiquarian Society*

newspapers about the affair, the image reminds us of the often wide discrepancies between words and works where slavery was concerned. Many of the great Virginians of the day, from Washington and Jefferson to Patrick Henry, James Madison, and George Mason were slaveholders. Mason would call slavery "disgraceful to mankind," yet a perusal of his will of 1792 mentions many slaves.[69] And while prominent Virginians spoke out against the institution during the Constitutional debates, Joseph Ellis suggests that for many a degree of ambivalence was not far beneath the surface:

> Upon closer examination, however, Virginia turned out to resemble the fuzzier and more equivocal picture that best describes the nation at large and that the Constitution was designed to mirror. For beneath their apparent commitment to antislavery and their accustomed place in the vanguard of revolutionary principles, the Virginians were overwhelmingly opposed to relinquishing one iota of control over their own slave population to any federal authority. Whether they were living a paradox or a lie is an interesting question. What is undeniably clear is that the Virginia leadership found itself in the peculiar position of acknowledging that slavery was an evil and then proceeding to insist that there was nothing the federal government could do about it.[70]

Slaves were, put simply, a necessity for those aristocrats who needed to derive an income from the land. It is difficult for us to fathom why the founders left in place this institution, which would haunt their antebellum successors as much as their words concerning personal liberty and the rights of states would inspire them. But to the great Virginians of the late colonial and early national periods, it may well have been poignantly clear that the time available for them to speculate on such matters was only made free because their laborers were not.

Cynthia A. Kierner points out some of the problems that would face the heirs of many prominent Virginia families:

> Beginning in the 1760s, the great planters of Virginia sank ever deeper into debt; taxes, soil exhaustion, and continuing troubles in the tobacco market compounded their financial difficulties in the postrevolutionary decades. At the same time, political revolution and evangelical religion gradually undermined the legitimacy of the social hierarchy that the old planter elite had dominated.[71]

The abolition of primogeniture, which thereby allowed for the subdividing of estates among all heirs, put further

slave," and for the master's children, who will copy what they learn from observing the exchanges between master and slave and thereby perpetuate the problem, Jefferson famously looks ahead to what could be the fate of the new nation: "Indeed I tremble for my country when I reflect that God is just; that his justice cannot sleep forever; that considering numbers, nature and natural means only, a revolution of the wheel of fortune, an exchange of situation is among possible events; that it may become probable by supernatural interference!" Such a consummation, which reverses the roles then played by the black and white races, was no doubt a frightful notion in Jefferson's day. Yet, although there was much consideration of the subject, slavery continued to exist and after the Missouri Compromise of 1820 would be carried to the new states to the South and West. Jefferson's hope in *Notes* for a "total emancipation . . . with the consent of the masters" would never come to pass.[68]

The recent speculations about Jefferson's relationship with Sally Hemings had precursors in his lifetime. In one of the earliest allegations of sexual relations, we see Jefferson as "A Philosophic Cock" and Hemings as a hen in this 1804 print attributed to James Akin of Newburyport, Massachusetts (fig. 2.26). While there was certainly contemporary political capital to be gained by such a representation, which supported assertions in Federalist

2.27 *Attributed to John Hesselius,* William Byrd III, *ca. early 1750s, oil on canvas, 49 x 39¾ in., Virginia Historical Society, bequest of Mrs. James Walter Carter*

pressure on the great families and their dwindling fortunes and led to a decentralization if not always a decline in economic power. The tobacco economy imposed rural settlement and thereby discouraged the development of any sort of traditional manufactures; in part because of what Charles J. Farmer has called the "persistence of country trade," towns did not form, and without a middle class that would have emerged in towns, there was a sizable economic gap between the rich and poor.[72] And although cutting-edge planters—such as the "first farmer of the nation," George Washington—experimented with different crops and a melding of animal husbandry and floriculture in an effort to counteract the soil exhaustion, their efforts met with as much failure as success.[73] The difficulties of British taxation before the war, the hardships brought on by the war itself, and the political uncertainty of the 1780s put an additional economic and psychological strain on Virginia's elite.

Kierner goes on to note that "Gentility at home and on public occasions masked the extent to which the economic and political fortunes of many of Virginia's leading planters were declining by the revolutionary era."[74] If the genteel ethos could be maintained, so could the illusions of both prosperity and the virtuous, humanistic lifestyle that had been its reward. And if the generation of William Byrd II can be seen as the culmination of the

gentrification process, the trials of three scions of the great families can be seen as evidence of the difficulty in achieving and maintaining the type of existence imagined by their forebears: William Byrd III would ultimately commit suicide; Robert Carter III would reject his fortune and social position; and Fernandino Fairfax, heir to George William and Sally Fairfax of Belvoir, would spend most of his adult life dissolving the enormous fortune he had inherited.

In a portrait presumed to be by John Hesselius, we see William Byrd III (1728–1777; fig. 2.27). The elegant clothes, genteel deportment, and appropriate pose of this heir to the Westover fortune show him to be a man of wealth and good breeding. At this point he is an affluent, confident young aristocrat, who had no idea of the direction his life would take. He had spent one year in England, in theory gaining an abbreviated version of the grooming that his father had attained during his own long residencies, but in practice learning as many bad habits as good, and gambling away large sums of money. Byrd III was a contemporary of George Washington and shared a number of his diversions. His pride in his life as a landed aristocrat and his interest in fine horses are both depicted by Hesselius; the latter inclusion hints at a vice that would contribute to Byrd's downfall.

Although the history of the building projects at Westover is uncertain, it is clear that Byrd III had an interest in architecture. He no doubt participated in the restoration and rebuilding efforts that took place after the fire of 1749, and he showed his knowledge of current building trends when he erected an elegant mansion that he named Belvidere a few miles up the James River from Richmond. On his inheritance of Westover in 1771, the younger Byrd was master of two of the grandest estates on the James. However, in the midst of his building projects his marriage of 1748 to Elizabeth Hill Carter of neighboring Shirley plantation deteriorated. It soon became a burden to his already wayward lifestyle. The relationship was sufficiently strained by 1756 for Byrd to send their oldest children to England to be raised by cousins, while he abandoned his wife for five years' service in the French and Indian War. He never fought in a battle, but he expended large sums of money providing for the soldiers in his care. After the war he returned to his life of extravagant spending and gambling, primarily on horse races. By the 1770s he was hopelessly in debt, and the coming of the Revolutionary War "greatly disturb[ed]" the "Peace of Mind" of a man with Loyalist sympathies.[75] On New Year's Day, 1777, William Byrd III committed suicide.

Robert Carter III would not lose his fortune in the same way. The son of Robert II, grandson of Robert "King" Carter, the wealthiest Virginian of the early eighteenth century, and nephew of Landon Carter, Robert III (1728–1804) would, however, ultimately withdraw from

2.28 *Thomas Hudson,* Robert Carter III, *1753, oil on canvas, 50 x 40 in., Virginia Historical Society, bequest of Louise Patten*

the life of a Virginia landowner. As depicted here (fig. 2.28), in a beautifully rendered portrait that he commissioned during his stay in England from Thomas Hudson, perhaps London's finest portraitist at mid-century, we see a confident young man who was at ease in British social circles. Carter is dressed for a masquerade ball in an elegant "Van Dyck" costume from a century earlier, the grand era of Charles I. He holds a mask in his left hand as if he had just removed it to reveal the privileged young gentleman beneath, a role that Carter the colonial heir played well in England. That said, if we can believe his cousin John Page, the future governor, the sojourn in London actually provided little useful training for Carter, who was left "inconceivably illiterate, and also corrupted and vicious."[76]

After his return to the colony, Carter was ultimately chosen in 1758 to serve on the Council. At the age of thirty he probably had more power in Virginia than anyone but Governor Dinwiddie himself. For more than a decade Carter lived in the still relatively small town of Williamsburg, but in 1772 he abruptly retired to Nomini Hall, the plantation that his father had built on the Potomac River in Westmoreland County. As time went by he repudiated the major institutions of colonial gentry society. Although he had been a willing participant in the aristocratic pursuit of politics, he abandoned public life; although his family's fortune had been made on the land, he gave up life as a planter; and although he had been a

lifelong member of the Church of England, he deserted the Anglican Church, becoming a Baptist in 1778. He was ambivalent about many aspects of Virginia life, including slavery, at times defending it and at others calling it a depravity; he eventually freed his nearly 500 slaves. In the end, Carter escaped rural Virginia for residence in the city of Baltimore, the family home of his wife Frances Ann Tasker. There he became a Swedenborgian disciple. Nomini Hall, as well as his other holdings, were willed to heirs.

The demands of the colonial plantation society on its prominent scions, who would have been expected to shoulder the burdens of public life in town and to live up to a generalized set of expectations based on the rural society of England in the country, may have been too much for Carter to bear. Hudson's wonderful portrait, in which we see the "unmasking" of the young Carter to reveal a more subtle mask beneath, is a provocative manifestation of a phenomenon inherent in the lives of many members of the late colonial gentry in Virginia—the difficult search for personal, colonial, and ultimately national identity in a society that had been created as an attempt to mirror the life led by aristocrats in Great Britain. The rural escape, without the cosmopolitan metropolis that commentators from Virgil to Pope had lauded the escape from, may have proven too isolated and confining, and therefore less than satisfying for Carter and many of his contemporaries.

Although George William and Sally Fairfax had quit Virginia, other members of the family remained. Among them was Ferdinando Fairfax, the son of George William's younger brother, the minister Bryan Fairfax. Ferdinando (1769–1820) was heir to the sizable estates of his uncle in both Virginia and England. He spent much of his adult life in Jefferson County (later West Virginia) on lands granted from the original proprietary. His major pastime appears to have been disposing of his fortune. On the one hand he fathered sixteen children, which certainly contributed to his spending, but he also maintained a lifestyle reminiscent of the mid- century elite, which led to the pointed comment in his obituary that "more money escaped from him than from any other man."[77]

As pictured here at the turn of the century (fig. 2.29), we see something of a falling away from the opulence and elegance of eighteenth-century portraits. Some of the confidence manifested by previous generations of Anglo-American aristocrats seems drained from his face, which looks far older than that of a man in his thirties. He wears a handsome cravat, as would have been expected, but he also is pictured in his own hair. Late-century planters faced a hard life on exhausted soil during times of political upheaval, when they could not be sure of markets for their dwindling produce. These heirs of the wealthiest colonial Virginians were inevitably less prosperous, if not

2.29 *Unidentified artist,* Ferdinando Fairfax, *ca. 1800, oil on canvas, 18 x 14³/₄ in., Virginia Historical Society*

Despite the conscientious pursuit of virtue carried on by many members of the gentry, there was as well a moral decline in late eighteenth-century Virginia. This was tied largely to the colony's peculiar slave-driven economy, but other factors came into play as well. If we are to believe some visitors to the region, amusements that had existed in the days of William Byrd II were revived during this period, and latter-day Virginians exhibited a predilection for these vices, which further undermined any aspirations toward virtue.

From William Byrd III's losses at horse racing, to Landon Carter's displeasure at the gambling of his sons Robert Wormeley and John, to the numerous billiard tables that had apparently sprung up in the colony-turned-state, there was a renaissance in gaming in the region that caught the attention of a number of travelers. As early as 1769, Alexander Cluny had suggested that in Virginia "the want of Variety of internal Employments having weakened the Spirit of Industry, and of course introduced a Turn to Dissipation and Expence to the Inhabitants, of all Degrees, that must instantly affect, and if not corrected, in the Course of Time totally overturn the Prosperity of any Country."[79] At the end of the century, Benjamin Henry Latrobe took the time to sketch *Billiards in Hanover Town, Virginia* (fig. 2.30), a place where other than a few "very agreeable and most respectable men," the townsmen were "void of rational employment and sentiments. . . . It is evidence enough against them, that they support two Billiard tables, at which it is impossible for the mind to catch the most distant entertainment or

in every case more profligate, than their ancestors. A landed aristocrat like Ferdinando Fairfax, who was still collecting rents on the proprietary, could ride out such periods by spending his fortune. Other Virginians from all walks of life, more than a million strong, would migrate from the state during the first half of the nineteenth century.[78]

2.30 *Benjamin Henry Latrobe,* Billiards in Hanover Town, Virginia, *1797, pencil, pen and ink, wash, 7 x 10¹/₄ in., Maryland Historical Society*

improvement."[80] Isaac Weld went farther: "Perhaps in no place of the same size in the world is there more gambling going forward than in Richmond. . . . Indeed, throughout the lower parts of the country in Virginia, and also in that part of Maryland next to it, there is scarcely a petty tavern without a billiard room, and this is always full of a set of idle, low lived fellows, drinking spirits or playing cards, if not engaged at the table."[81] Although it would have been surprising to find a young scion associating with these types of common people, idle white gentlemen, if the activities of Byrd III and the Carter sons are exemplary, had their own ways of ridding themselves of their hereditary wealth. That said, the fact that "At horse races and fox hunts, at cockfights and boxing matches, at militia musters and at elections, some gentleman descended to drunkenness and brawling unbecoming their station" suggests that such contacts with rustics did indeed take place, and were having a debilitating effect on some impressionable members of the gentry.[82]

An idealized visualization of the popular "vine and fig tree" motif can be found in the anonymous, untitled painting that is now generally known as *The Plantation* (page 36, fig. 2.1). Although little is recorded about the circumstances that inspired this vibrant work, the stripes and field of the American flag on the passing warship assure the viewer that it was fashioned after the conclusion of the Revolutionary War.[83] The general shape and color of the large mansion on the hill, with the river flowing beneath, suggest Mount Vernon, the best known house of the period. The presence of ample grape vines and fig leaves allude to the well known Biblical passages and remind the viewer that this was Washington's retreat, where he was able to find refuge from the cares of the outside world. The willow, however, the tree of mourning, tells us that the general has gone to his reward; he has achieved a more permanent degree of peace and contentment than was possible even here.

No human beings can be seen near the mansion or any of the smaller houses or outbuildings, but a lone fisherman, dressed in black, is evident in the right foreground, reminding us that life goes on at the estate, even as the household is now mourning. Serene in full sail on Washington's beloved Potomac, the warship still has its guns at the ready. If Mount Vernon represents the sort of idyllic pastoral retreat that was sought by many eighteenth-century Virginians, the frigate reminds us that such ideals must be defended. Peace and contentment always have a price. The ship prompts as well memories of the distinguished military career of the general, whose gallantry and iron will had allowed for the continuing

pursuit of gentility and virtue in the fledgling republic, of which in his lifetime Washington had already been declared the "father." It also reminds us that, Cincinnatus-like, Washington had given up the glory of command to return to the sylvan landscape of Mount Vernon. While we will probably never know for certain, it is a good possibility that *The Plantation* was conceived and executed as a tribute to Washington, a subtle memorial to the man who had launched and kept afloat the American "ship of state."

In his early nineteenth-century view, *Mount Vernon, Virginia, the Seat of the late Gen. G. Washington* (fig. 2.31), William Birch provides a slightly different but still idealized representation of the quintessential plantation. He chooses an angle of the east façade, which with a bit of manipulation allows for the inclusion of the Potomac River below. The riderless white horse—the color mount preferred by Washington—reminds us of the passing of the general, while the frolicking youngster suggests the youthful nation that he had brought into being; he is powerful and energetic, but still immature. A strangely dressed servant holds the general's mount, whose lively step indicates that he can still perform his martial duties. The clouds clearing off the river suggest that the storms of war through which the general had led his nation are over. At the left we see golden light, a gentle hill, carefully placed trees, and water—all commonplace elements of the picturesque—which help to recall the idyllic setting where Washington had made his home.

While it does not seem as though Birch intended the man in the scene to be a slave, servants of all types supported the attempt by prominent Virginians like Washington to create a lifestyle based on European and ultimately classical models. It is perhaps not surprising that the presence of slaves is not overt in either *The Plantation* or Birch's *Mount Vernon* in that both are tributes to Washington. The presence of people who were unambiguously slaves might well have served to undermine the elegiac tone of both of these works, although one could certainly argue that among the many outbuildings evident in *The Plantation* are slave quarters. As we have seen, the slave system both supported the creation of an idyllic lifestyle and simultaneously undermined that attempt, in that the existence of human bondage on such estates would make the virtue that aristocratic Virginians sought all the more difficult to achieve.

Birch included *Mount Vernon* in *The Country Seats of North America*. Although by 1808 both the architecture and the garden design of Washington's home were out-of-date, it would have been imprudent to leave this house out of such a collection, in part because Washington had been the most famous man in the world, and because his house epitomized a particular kind of retreat, and therefore served as a useful exemplar for Birch. While his es-

2.31 *William Russell Birch,* Mount Vernon, Virginia, the Seat of the late Genl. G. Washington, from The Country Seats of North America *(Bristol, Pennsylvania, 1808-09), copper plate engraving with hand coloring, 4 x 5³/₈ in., Virginia Historical Society*

tate had served the general well in its guise as a country seat, Washington inevitably spent a great deal of time thinking about how he could increase the income from his lands. The troubling economic system and exhausted soils would make this pursuit precarious for most Virginia landholders of the antebellum era, which would lead to either deferred maintenance or the actual abandoning of many of the great mansions; even Mount Vernon itself would fall into disrepair.

As the nineteenth century began, anti-slavery agitation was a growing annoyance, although it would not blossom into "abolitionism" until the mid-1830s. The founding of the nation's capital on the banks of the Potomac, which at first was believed would provide an economic boost for the region, did not lead to the hoped-for prosperity, nor did the trouble-laden Potomac Canal project. If things were not difficult enough, the Indian wars in the West and the second war with the British, while ending successfully for the newly united states, put

further pressure on those who sought to sell their agricultural products. All of these problematic factors made the pastoral life that the ancestors of the old Virginia families had hoped to attain, with its combination of selfless public-spiritedness and private contemplation, difficult for many of their early nineteenth-century descendants to conceptualize and, as it turned out, impossible for them to achieve.

3.1 Jean-Julien Deltil, for Jean Zuber et Cie, Mulhouse, France, Virginia, 1833, wallpaper, 88½ x 93¾ in., Virginia Historical Society, Lora Robins Collection of Virginia Art

III. Decline and Resistance in Antebellum Society

I n a hand-printed wallpaper mural designed in 1833 by Jean-Julien Deltil for the French firm of Jean Zuber et Cie (fig. 3.1), Virginia is shown to be characterized by a resident aristocracy—of which to French observers Thomas Jefferson had been the consummate exemplar—Native and African American populations, and great natural wonders, the most famous being Natural Bridge. Deltil depicted the bridge in a peculiar manner; its towering height and distinctly unnatural tilt aided in the artist's attempt to create a unique vision of the sublime. Deltil's source was a lithograph published in 1828 by the French scientist and artist Jacques Gèrard Milbert in his *Itinèraire Pittoresque du Fleuve Hudson et des Parties Latèrales de l'Amèrique du Nord* (Paris).[1] The wallpaper's vibrant colors and lively characters—who represent "The Three Races that Inhabit the United States" that Tocqueville would discuss at length in *Democracy in America* later in the decade—suggest that by the early nineteenth century Virginia had attained a distinct, if skewed, identity in the minds of many Europeans. The Virginia view was conceived by Zuber as one section in a series of five *Vues d'Amèrique du Nord* that when pieced together run a remarkable thirty-two feet. The other four sections picture famous views in the North—Boston Harbor, New York Bay, West Point, and Niagara Falls. The paper is rare; only six impressions are known to exist from the original printing. One set was installed in the White House by Jacqueline Kennedy in 1961.

Although several of the other Virginia Founding Fathers were revered in France, particularly George Washington who was renowned throughout Europe, Jefferson had the greatest popularity. This stemmed in part from his service as ambassador there in the 1780s, when he was accepted as a cultivated, aristocratic gentleman, rather than ostracized as a provincial as William Byrd II had been on occasion in eighteenth-century London. Jefferson's *Notes on the State of Virginia* was first published in French in 1784–85. It had been written in response to a request from the Marquis de Barbè-Marbois, the secretary of the French legation in Philadelphia, who was interested in the geography, flora, fauna, and social history of Virginia. In this book, Jefferson refuted the notion held by many European naturalists, especially the Comte de Buffon, that North American species had degenerated

and were therefore inferior to their European counterparts. He also took the opportunity to comment on Virginia's Indian population, as well as on slavery. He invited his French readers to make the pilgrimage to Natural Bridge, which was one of the wonders of America, and unpretentiously provided other statistical and anecdotal information that he thought would be of interest to his audience. In later years Jefferson kept up his allegiance to France in the face of the British-leaning Federalists, led by Alexander Hamilton, and so maintained his popularity there, which no doubt was important during the negotiations carried out by James Monroe and Robert Livingston during Jefferson's first term as president that resulted in the Louisiana Purchase of 1803.

French interest in Virginia is further explained by events of the Revolution. Aid that had been provided to the Continental Army by generals Lafayette and Rochambeau and Admiral the comte de Grasse during the Yorktown campaign in 1781 had played a large part in ending the war. France had nurtured the struggling colonials in their fight for independence, and so not surprisingly the French paid attention, even through their own tumultuous revolution, to the goings on in the young nation across the Atlantic.

In Deltil's view, America had begun as an arcadia. The Indians who stand are pictured in Roman-like togas, an idea that was probably derived from earlier illustrations of South American Indians, while the dancers are dressed in cloth with leather straps rather than in the simple animal skins that they actually wore. Here is Rousseau's natural man in a natural setting, as appealing a myth to European eyes as that of Virgil's shepherds in their pastoral simplicity, as can be gleaned by the looks of enjoyment on the faces of the white viewers of the spectacle. The African Americans are not slaves in this mythologized view of Virginia, but instead are shown to be free, well dressed, and cosmopolitan as blacks might have appeared in Paris at that time. The Caucasian Virginians are shown to be similarly well appointed; the carriage that speeds off to the right on rails suggests the state of New World technology.

The French wallpaper scene is an idealization of what in the second quarter of the nineteenth century would have been referred to as Old Virginia. At that time, however, the region's old society was in fact being threatened by massive change. Natural Bridge would soon become a travel destination for trainloads of tourists from Europe and the North. Internal improvements in the form of roads, canals, and railroads would establish a transportation network that would carry newcomers and the products of their industry across the state. In contrast to the fictional residents shown by Zuber to be enjoying a leisurely, carefree outing, their real life counterparts were concerned about Virginia's loss of political preeminence on the national stage. The impoverished soil of the Tidewater had shifted large populations westward, where many would try to reconstruct the life that they had abandoned, or had hoped to achieve, in the East. Most African Americans in Old Virginia were slaves. The well-dressed group presented by Deltil masks the reality of slavery and the frustration of Virginians that grew out of their inability either to phase out the institution or to make slave labor more efficient and less troublesome. They also had abolitionists to worry about—radical, often militant thinkers who might ultimately find the political support to overturn their system. These concerns shook the very core of Virginia society. Robert P. Sutton has written that consequently "The planter aristocracy, which had so ably guided the state with reason and optimism in its days of glory, now, in the years of decline, became imbued with a deepening nostalgia, pessimism, and malaise."[2]

In their efforts to resist such formidable forces, and as a means to counter the pessimism and to preserve the status that was a legacy from colonial Virginia, Virginians created what amounts to a mythology about their past. In the years after 1830 residents from the old school began again to celebrate the established ways of life that had been initiated by the English colonists but now seemed in danger of extinction. The term Old Virginia was put into widespread use for the first time to identify that portion of antebellum society that was made up of the descendants of the ancient plantation families. "Old" was equated with "good." The old ways, after all, had produced the Founding Fathers. The rural society of the Tidewater was again said to have been idyllic. Americans who longed for an aristocracy on the model of those in Europe as a component that was missing in the national identity eagerly accepted such ideas. They read novels that transformed contemporary Virginia planters into honorable, virtuous knights, that venerated the plantation mistress, and that portrayed the slave as loyal, contented, and even happy in his bondage. Antebellum planters also continued the eighteenth-century tradition of breeding pedigreed horses, with long bloodlines that rivaled their own, in an attempt to recreate what was essentially the life of the English country squire. Many came to believe that the culture of Old Virginia could be carried westward to the Valley of Virginia and revitalized there. The old ways seemed to live again at the thermal and mineral springs, many of which were built to re-

3.2 Title Page *of Edward Beyer,* Album of Virginia, *1858, lithograph, 13 x 19 in., Virginia Historical Society*

semble plantations. And finally, the region's colonial history was recalled as evidence that the old ways, and the leadership provided by the posterity of the old English families, were best for Virginia and ultimately for the nation.

The idea of Old Virginia was seemingly endorsed by all of these descendants, be they rich or poor. This was because most Virginians felt a nostalgia for the plantation traditions that had produced the region's illustrious Founding Fathers; they were proud to be conceptually associated with the likes of George Washington and Patrick Henry. Middle- and even lower-class Virginians of the antebellum era bought into the idea that Old Virginia was their past, and that the idyllic lifestyle that was a legacy of that tradition was available to everyone in the region. This is not to say that in later years a Confederate soldier willing to die for Old Virginia saw the term as describing anything other than his homeland, nor had the simple Virginia farmer—who was determined to hold on to the status quo in the face of challenges from newcomers to the region—read Virgil. As had happened in eighteenth-century England, a common person could be thought by the elite to be living a life no less virtuous than did his wealthiest neighbor, although he himself would have been oblivious to the intellectual traditions of western civilization that celebrated pastoral bliss. We can say, however, that in the process of its revival, the pastoral ideal got intertwined with a nostalgia for the old ways. From this entanglement emerged a figuration of Old Virginia that would serve the state well in the disquieting decades before the Civil War.

Challenges to the Old Order

In the mid-1850s the German artist Edward Beyer and his wife lingered in the Valley of Virginia enjoying the companionship that they found there in the German communities. While there he painted the landscape in town views that served his patrons as expressions of pride of place. In 1858 he published his sketches of landscapes, spas, and various internal improvements as a collection of lithographs that he labeled *Album of Virginia.* On the title page (fig. 3.2) we find visual evidence of both the old and the new, of a society that was in transition.

Immediately recognizable in Beyer's composite picture are depictions of Mount Vernon and Monticello, which were actually in disrepair in 1858, as were the farming operations that surrounded them. While these images served to identify the region and no doubt bolstered Virginians' pride, at the same time viewers could not help but be reminded that during the first half of the nineteenth century the political stature of Virginia had declined on the national stage when no successors of equal stature had replaced the Founding Fathers. With the retirement and then the passing of the nation's first, third, fourth, and fifth presidents (Washington, Jefferson, Madison, and Monroe), Virginians saw a diminution of their ability to influence federal policy.

In addition to what was perceived to be a political decline was an agricultural failure in the Tidewater, where the soil was exhausted from the overproduction of tobacco. Beyer alludes to both the agricultural tradition and the pastoral ideal by encircling his depictions of the two plantations with vines, grapes, and leaves that reference the Old Testament image of the vine and fig tree that had long been associated with early Virginia. By showing the old architecture, the artist suggests that agrarian plantation life was a fundamental component of Virginia's past. He also pictures a factory, a railroad, and

a steamship, which were symbols of new industrial progress, and its counterpart urbanization, which challenged what had been rural dominance in Virginia.

Many of these industries had been developed by Germans like Beyer. Immigrants to the region had grown in numbers and prominence; their increase instigated what the heirs of the old, established families in rural Virginia feared would be a problematic future. As to the slave system that underpinned both the old farming society and the new industries, not only was the institution inefficient, but it was increasingly condemned both nationally and internationally. Slavery proved to be a great political liability because it stigmatized Virginia society as uncivilized and lacking in humanistic virtue. To counter what had become a persistently negative image, Beyer borrowed for the focus of his page the figure of virtue that viewers would recognize from the state seal (page 33, fig. 1.24). The goddess of liberty holds an American flag to suggest Virginia's tenuous position of national prominence as well as her patriotism, both of which were in jeopardy by 1858.

Political and Agricultural Decline

Political perceptions in Virginia in the early years of the nineteenth century were measured by a cousin of the fourth president. In 1807 Bishop James Madison published what became known as the "Bishop Madison" map of the region (fig. 3.3). Then president of the College of William and Mary, Madison compiled this document in collaboration with William Prentis, who carried the preliminary surveys to local authorities for review.[3] This first map of the region to be produced locally was an ambi-

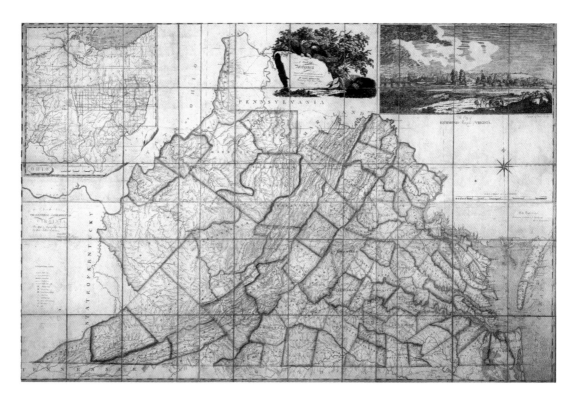

3.3 *James Madison,* A Map of Virginia Formed from Actual Surveys, *1807, Richmond: James Madison, William Prentis, and William Davis; engraved by Frederick Bossler, Virginia Historical Society*

tious project; it exemplifies the high aspirations of well-placed Virginians as they entered the new century.

Instead of a traditional cartouche that referenced slaves and tobacco as identifying symbols of a subservient colony, Madison presents an American eagle so boldly perched as to seem proud not only of the extreme accuracy that is said to underlie the details of the map, but also of the importance of Virginia to the nation. The political prominence of the region at this early date is further suggested by the unusual inclusion next to the cartouche of a sizable view of the landscape of the new capital, Richmond, as seen from the river (fig. 3.4, detail). This burgeoning urban center, labeled a "metropolis" on the map, is shown to be equal in significance to the Ohio lands that had long held an important place in the psyches of Virginians, which are plotted in the map's opposite corner. As Thomas Jefferson had intended, the Capitol that he designed to resemble a classical temple dominates the skyline of the emerging city.

The counties are neatly delineated in Bishop Madison's map, but much of the land, particularly in the Tidewater, was by his time exhausted. The rural nature of this society—and perhaps even a hint of its agricultural decline—is suggested in the foreground of the Richmond view, where, partly in concession to the traditional imagery in Virginia maps, slaves are pictured hauling tobacco to indicate the survival of the old ways of the plantation society. This foreground, however, is a remarkably quiet and empty place. The pace there is slow; the energy of business is elsewhere.

In hindsight we now can suggest that the dark clouds to the west in the Richmond scene should be viewed ominously. Virginians had every reason to be politically optimistic at the start of the century. One of their own, Thomas Jefferson, held the presidency. In less than two years after the publication of his map, the bishop's cousin would succeed Jefferson for two terms, to be followed by James Monroe for the same duration, so that Virginians would occupy the White House from 1801 until 1825. The political future of the state would soon darken, however. Washington and Henry had both died in 1799, and as the careers of Madison, Monroe, and John Marshall drew to a close, the shadow cast by the Revolutionary era giants served to emphasize what younger Virginians increasingly came to perceive as a political decline. Mason Locke Weems seems to have anticipated this eventuality. He feared that the rising generation of Americans could actually be harmed by contemplating the greatness of Washington: "To be constantly placing [Washington] before our children, in this high character, what is it but like springing in the clouds a golden Phoenix, which no mortal calibre can ever hope to reach? Or like setting pictures of the Mammoth before the *mice* whom 'not all the manna of Heaven' can ever raise to equality?"[4] William Wirt questioned, "How little does any House [of Delegates] that we have had for some years past resemble the House in which Jefferson, Pendleton, Henry, Richard H. Lee, Wythe, Bland, and others were members?"[5] Such comparisons, if not always fair, were inevitable; the bar had been placed so high by the Revolutionary fathers that

3.4 *(detail)* The City of Richmond, Metropolis of Virginia, *illustration from James Madison,* A Map of Virginia Formed from Actual Surveys, *1807*

3.5 *E. B. & E. C. Kellogg after William Henry Brown,* John Randolph of Roanoke, *1846, lithograph, 13¼ x 10 in., Virginia Historical Society*

it would be impossible for any Virginian in succeeding cadres to clear.

Through the first quarter of the nineteenth century, the sole Virginia statesman of the rising generation who seemed to possess the talents that would earn him a national stature equivalent to that of the Founding Fathers has been described by Dumas Malone as "one of the most pathetic as well as one of the most brilliant figures that ever strutted and fretted his hour upon the American public stage."[6] John Randolph of Roanoke (fig. 3.5) was a peculiar figure who to many elicited fear rather than admiration. Because his inclination was to object and defend rather than to conciliate and then lead, Randolph came to epitomize the doomed Virginia politician who clung to old ways and outdated expectations in the face of the commonwealth's political decline.

Randolph was born with the right pedigree and most of the right credentials. He was descended from a quintessential Old Virginia family, and through voracious reading and innate intelligence he had prepared himself for leadership. As a congressman during Jefferson's first term Randolph successfully promoted the policies of the president, using his abilities as a master parliamentarian to manipulate the discussion toward his own ends. During this same period, however, because of his poor health, his frail and diminutive figure, and his pale, boylike counte-

nance and soprano voice—not to mention his periods of dementia or his appearance on the floor of Congress wearing boots and carrying a whip in his hand—Randolph established a reputation as eccentric. His political method was to browbeat opponents into silence by terrifying them with lengthy, venomous, often brilliant oratory. Henry Adams labeled him the "Virginian Saint Michael—almost terrible in his contempt for whatever seemed to him base or untrue."[7] Randolph's eight-thousand-acre plantation in the Virginia Southside, from which he took his popular epithet, was seat to some four hundred slaves and to stables of pedigreed horses, but the congressman resided there in only two modest buildings, one of logs. Rather than detract from the odd image that Randolph had established in Washington, Roanoke only added to it.

Randolph was instinctively a champion of lost causes. When political inertia within Virginia caused a transition around 1825 from a climate of constructive self-examination to one of increasing defensiveness, Randolph easily shifted his stance to become an ardent sectionalist. He played that role at the Virginia convention of 1829–30, where he was more visible than the aging Madison, Monroe, and Marshall. There he defended eastern interests against those of the western counties, and vociferously opposed any change to the state constitution ("This is the mother which has reared all our great men.").[8] Consequently, he was credited with much of the responsibility for the conservative victory.

The 1829 convention was called in response to pleas from the western counties for better representation in the state legislature, and, in turn, more governmental attention. But the convention considered other problems as well—the political and agricultural decline, the shift of populations within and beyond Virginia's borders, and the region's economic transition. (At that point truly half of the counties had few or no slave residents.) The conclusion, however, was that the state constitution was not to blame. Decline was a subject of considerable concern, and the conservative delegates feared further regression if laws were altered. (For instance, if the vote was given to the masses, including the new immigrants in the cities and in the Valley who were not landowners, then members of the old families might no longer be elected to officiate over the government.) To those of the old order it seemed that even more change, no doubt for the worse, would result from such manipulations.

The artist George Catlin traveled to Richmond from New York to record this unprecedented gathering of Virginia's old and new politicians (fig. 3.6). Predictably, he emphasized the former in his canvas, picturing Monroe as presiding, with Madison speaking and Marshall seated directly to his rear. But as it turned out, it was the younger voices that best addressed the issue of decline. On the far side of Monroe, in the middle row, three over

3.6 Left *George Catlin,* The Virginia Convention of 1829, *1829-30, oil on canvas, 24½ x 33 in., Virginia Historical Society*

3.7 Below, left John Randolph of Roanoke to John Randolph Bryan, *7 April 1830, letter, Virginia Historical Society*

is Benjamin Watkins Leigh of Richmond; two over is John Randolph. Leigh defined a tripartite decline—a loss of "Genius," a loss of wealth, and a loss in population. He saw the three as interrelated, the last being the cause of the first two. Leigh asked, "What has become of our political rank and eminence in the Union? Whither, in the language of Henry, whither has the Genius of Virginia fled? . . . Virginia has declined, and is declining—she was once the first State in the Union—now she has sunk to be the third, and will soon sink lower in the scale . . . in wealth and population." The explanation, as Leigh saw it, was the exodus of Virginians to the West: "none has contributed more to the peopling of the new States, than Virginia. . . . This is the reason of what gentlemen call the decline of Virginia."[9] Randolph defined Virginia's decline differently, in terms of the state's loss of political power in Washington. Virginia no longer held the votes to control

Congress because of "King Numbers." He argued, "Sir, the all-prevailing principle, that Numbers and Numbers alone, are to regulate all things in political society" has resulted in "monstrous tyranny." For more than thirty years Virginia alone had checked "the mad and unconstitutional usurpations of the Federal Government," which were "intended to be charged only with the external relations of the country." With the loss of Virginia's political might, however, the federal government "has become the regulator of the interior of the country" as well, so that "we can't take a step without breaking our shins over some Federal obstacle." The result, Randolph complained, was that "We are now little better than the trustees of slave-labour for the nabobs of the East, and of the North, . . . and to the speculators of the West."[10]

Randolph did not blame Virginia's decline on emigration; however, he readily acknowledged the phenomenon. The congressman closed his lengthy plea for the rejection of changes to the state's constitution by eloquently comparing Virginia to Shakespeare's King Lear, "an old and feeble monarch" who had been deserted by his offspring.[11] As early as 1813 Randolph had noted "the rage for emigration" to "*Kaintuck,* or the *Massissippi,*" where produce could be grown "for one-fifth of the labor" required in Virginia.[12] In a letter of 1830 advising a young relative to think twice about buying property in Virginia, where nearly two centuries of planting tobacco had exhausted the soil, Randolph described his state as a landscape where "soil and staples [were] both worn out . . . [and] the country is in a gallopping consumption" (fig. 3.7).

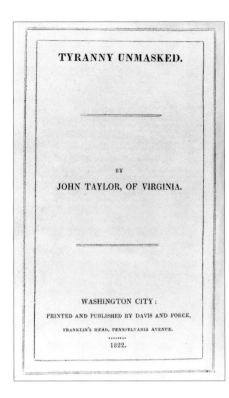

3.8 *John Taylor of Caroline,* Tyranny Unmasked *(Washington City, 1822), Virginia Historical Society*

In *Away, I'm Bound Away, Virginia and the Westward Movement,* David Hackett Fischer and James C. Kelly examine how the failure of the state's agricultural base prompted the migration of "nearly a million men and women out of the commonwealth to points farther west or south." They explain that "A long period of agricultural depression devastated Virginia's planters. . . . Soil exhaustion in the Tidewater became chronic. . . . The decline began not later than 1770. Thereafter the Tidewater could not support a growing population. Families saw the nation's future, and their own in the West."[13] Innumerable letters document the agricultural failure. John J. Ambler, Jr., whose family had long been established at Jamestown, described the setting of eastern Virginia as "one wide waste of desolation."[14] After a two-month tour of the state in 1827 James Mercer Garnett of Essex County complained that "We have made ourselves a tributary to the North and East." He then lamented, "Virginia—poor Virginia furnishes a spectacle at present, which is enough to make the heart of her real Friends sick to the very core. . . . her Agriculture nearly gone to ruin from a course of policy which could not well have been worse destructive if destruction had been its sole objective . . . I will would [sic] hope for better things, but hope is nearly dead."[15] Many who left the state looked back with few regrets, at least with respect to the issue of farming. In his descriptively titled book, *Flush Times of Alabama and Mississippi* (1853), Joseph G. Baldwin argued about the difficulty of prospering in Virginia. The habitual losses suffered by those who attempted to make a living from the land had made some husbandmen skeptical of the possibilities for agricultural success anywhere. By contrast, Dr. James Somerville had reported in 1837

that "there are opportunities for making money in the S. West which though not so great as a few years ago are still astonishing to Virginians."[16]

Fischer and Kelly explore what contemporaries saw as the causes of the agricultural failure. Some blamed ineffectual and antiquated farming techniques, principally the neglect of Virginia farmers to rotate crops, rest fields, and restore soil with fertilizers. Others faulted the absence of an adequate support system to transport and market crops that could no longer be rolled to river landings and shipped to England. To many, the principal culprits were a slave force that was unproductive, and Yankee merchants whose first impulse was always toward greed.[17] This rapacity became evident with the passage of protective tariffs that benefitted the northern factory owner at the expense of the farmer, whose very way of life was thereby threatened.

Southern sentiment regarding the mercantilist policies of the federal government was perhaps best expressed by John Taylor of Caroline County, who practiced scientific methods of agriculture in the Tidewater and wrote about them in a treatise that he titled *Arator* (1813). In his book *Tyranny Unmasked* (fig. 3.8), Taylor defended the rights of the farmer against a government that he attacked for its unconstitutional support of special interests. He strongly advocated states' rights and the limitation of federal powers. Otherwise, he warned, sectional strife will escalate and destroy the republic. A Jeffersonian, Taylor advocated an agrarian republicanism that was derived from the eighteenth-century English belief in the virtue of simple farm life.[18]

The agricultural decline extended from the fields to the plantation houses. Sizable portions of the landscape, particularly in the Tidewater, were strewn with the architectural ruins of a decaying society. In George Tucker's *Valley of the Shenandoah* (1824), Edward Grayson, whose father was compelled by debt to move westward from the Tidewater, returns to "Easton, the place of his nativity in Charles City [County]"; "the sight of this venerable seat of his ancestors, reminded him of the fall of his family from their former opulence and consequence to the most absolute poverty; and the tender and not unpleasing melancholy he had formerly experienced, was exchanged for a bitterness of feeling, and soreness of the heart, which had nothing in it consolatory or agreeable." Tucker goes on to describe broken windows, rotted thresholds and sills, and moss-covered stone steps "moved . . . by frost and vegetation" to become "an asylum for lizards, frogs, and toads."[19]

A number of the mansions of colonial Virginia had become as run-down as the fictional Easton. Nomini Hall (fig. 3.9) had been abandoned by its owner Robert Carter III (page 58, fig. 2.28) when he relocated to Baltimore to live in the family home of his wife. He had willed the opu-

3.9 Nomini Hall, *Westmoreland County, mid-nineteenth century drawing (unlocated), photograph of the drawing, Virginia Historical Society*

lent Westmoreland County plantation to heirs, but by the early nineteenth century, prior to its destruction by fire in 1850, Nomini Hall had deteriorated. A mid-century sketch of the exterior shows that large areas of once-fashionable white stucco had fallen away to expose the brick beneath. Rosewell (page 147, fig. 4.35), the great Page mansion in Gloucester County, managed to survive until it burned in 1916, but it was in such sad condition even before the Revolution that John Page, a friend of Thomas Jefferson and later a governor of Virginia, described it in 1771 as "very much out of repair." Following Page's death in 1808, Rosewell was largely uninhabited for the next thirty years. An English visitor would later record that "rats had eaten holes in the paneling, plaster was falling, the roof was leaking, windows were broken, and there had been other destruction by vandals. The yard was badly overgrown and many of the shade trees [were] dead."[20] Then as now, the lack of attendance to routine maintenance matters had left many great houses in near ruin.

Contrary to the images provided by Edward Beyer in 1858, even the well-known homes of the nation's third and first presidents had fallen into decay. Nothing better symbolized the agricultural decline of the state than did the physical demise of Monticello and Mount Vernon. In 1832 William Barry, the postmaster general of the United States, made the pilgrimage to Jefferson's home: "All is

dilapidation and ruin," he wrote. In the same year John Latrobe, the son of architect Benjamin Henry Latrobe, recorded that "the first thing that strikes you is the utter ruin and desolation of everything."[21] The farming operation at Monticello had failed earlier, leaving the president in debt at his death in 1826. Two years later the house had to be offered for sale "for the payment of the testator's debts."[22]

Visitors to the home of the "Father of his Country" were appalled to find it in disrepair. Horace Greely reported in 1856 that fences, shrubbery, and Negro huts and barns were "in the last stage of decay" or "fallen away," adding that "the whole place has an aspect of forlorn neediness which no description can adequately paint."[23] In 1849 a correspondent for the Boston *Atlas* left a lengthy account that picks up themes now familiar to us. He noted the "worn and exhausted" land that "is the fact in this part of Old Virginia," on account of "the tobacco plant" and the land's treatment "by dull unintelligent slave labor." The ruinous condition of the estate moved him to despair: "Decay appeared impressed every where and on every thing. . . . Even the tomb of this great man bore the same evidence of neglect. . . . Everything was wild, and rude, and neglected, and I turned away with a melancholy frame of mind, and sat for half an hour by the shore of the Patomac, listening to the ripple of the waters upon the beach, and the sighing of the winds amid the forests that lined its banks." The Bostonian critically concluded, "If we had Mount Vernon in Old Massachusetts, . . . how the spot would be treasured in our hearts, and beautified by our hands!"[24] A photograph taken in 1855 that shows a decaying piazza supported by old ships's masts confirms such written accounts (fig. 3.10).

With George Washington gone and his house in disrepair, a number of antebellum artists painted Mount Vernon with a gloomy palette, to suggest not just the passing of an era but also a fall from the greatness and enlightenment that Americans associated with the Founding Fathers. In a sand-painted canvas that probably dates to the 1850s (fig. 3.11), the estate—even nature itself—is shown to be almost in mourning for the general who rests in his tomb in the foreground. The sectional differences that Washington had so valiantly struggled to eradicate now clouded the national horizon. The sand-painting technique, which was often taught to young girls in school, must have seemed an appropriate medium for the moment. The dark colors give a somber air to this view of what once had been a lively estate.

Many of the large plantations had been broken apart into smaller units. This was an inevitable consequence of inheritance, population increase, and economic decline. Joan Cashin explains that because there were no mandatory entails, which in England left a family's entire estate to the eldest son for multiple generations, "By the 1830s . . . the old grandees, owners of 5,000- and 10,000-acre estates, had all but disappeared" in Virginia.[25] The effects of such subdivisions were to be seen everywhere in the Tidewater.

Also changed on the landscape was the architecture of the region's early churches, many of which were as ruinous as were the mansions. Most of the old wooden structures, a number of which dated to the seventeenth century, had become dilapidated because of their age and building material. But even the brick churches of the colony had fallen into disrepair. A number of these had been abandoned to the weather due to the withdrawal of financial support from the state following independence, when the Church of England was disestablished. John Gadsby Chapman's painting of *The Ruins at Jamestown* (page 116, fig. 3.72) is evidence of the decay of one of those buildings. Some became shells that were eventually repaired, either by Anglicans or by members of the newer denominations who took them over. Others were left to deteriorate on their abandoned rural sites.

In the eighteenth century, Englishmen and in turn Anglo-Americans had found satisfaction in the domestic landscape when it was cultivated with crops in the fields and gardens near the house. They were also pleased to enjoy peaceful scenery that was picturesque or to contem-

3.10 Mount Vernon, 1855, *photograph courtesy of the Mount Vernon Ladies' Association*

3.11 *Unidentified artist,* Mount Vernon, *ca. 1850-60, charcoal, paint, and marble dust on board, 12 x 19 in., courtesy of Mrs. Clare Edwards*

3.12 *John Gadsby Chapman,* Lake of the Dismal Swamp, *1830s, engraving, 4¹⁄₂ x 6¹⁄₄ in., Virginia Historical Society, Lora Robins Collection of Virginia Art*

THE FALL OF THE HOUSE OF USHER.

BY EDGAR A. POE.

DURING the whole of a dull, dark, and soundless day in the autumn of the year, when the clouds hung oppressively low in the heavens, I had been passing alone, on horseback, through a singularly dreary tract of country ; and at length found myself, as the shades of the evening drew on, within view of the melancholy House of Usher. I know not how it was—but, with the first glimpse of the building, a sense of insufferable gloom pervaded my spirit. I say insufferable ; for the feeling was unrelieved by any of that half-pleasurable, because poetic, sentiment, with which the mind usually receives even the sternest natural images of the desolate or terrible. I looked upon the scene before me—upon the mere house, and the simple landscape features of the domain—upon the bleak walls—upon the vacant eye-like windows—upon a few rank sedges—and upon a few white trunks of decayed trees—with an utter depression of soul which I can compare to no earthly sensation more properly than to the after-dream of the reveller upon opium—the bitter lapse into common life—the hideous dropping off of the veil. There was an iciness, a sinking, a sickening of the heart—an unredeemed dreariness of thought which no goading of the imagination could torture into aught of the sublime. What was it—I paused to think—what was it that so unnerved me in the contemplation of the House of Usher ? It was a mystery all insoluble ; nor could I grapple with the shadowy fancies that crowded upon me as I pondered. I was forced to fall back upon the unsatisfactory conclusion, that while, beyond doubt, there are combinations of very simple natural objects which have the power of thus affecting us, still the reason, and the analysis, of this power, lie among considerations beyond our depth. It was possible, I reflected, that a mere different arrangement of the particulars of the scene, of the details of the picture, would be sufficient to modify, or perhaps to annihilate its capacity for sorrowful impression ; and, acting upon this idea, I reined my horse to the precipitous brink of a black and lurid tarn that lay in unruffled lustre by the dwelling, and gazed down—but with a shudder even more thrilling than before—upon the re-modelled and inverted images of the gray sedge, and the ghastly tree-stems, and the vacant and eye-like windows.

3.13 *Edgar Allan Poe, The Fall of the House of Usher (1839), published in Burton's Gentleman's Magazine, Philadelphia, September 1839, Virginia Historical Society*

plate wild nature that was so powerful as to seem sublime. But in antebellum Virginia, much of the Tidewater landscape was being transformed into none of these traditional categories. Rather, it was returning to a wilderness that was broken only by what John Dickinson critiqued at the time as the "eyesores" of ruined farms. Accordingly, by the 1830s and 1840s, the traditional English aesthetics of the beautiful, the picturesque, and the sublime had begun to go through a radical shift in Virginia. Joan Cashin points out that "a handful of writers began to portray the commonwealth's deserted ruins and worn land as attractive rather than ugly. Its abandoned churches inspired a pleasant 'melancholy feeling' in one writer, and the older and more desolate a place was, the better. . . . Edgar Allan Poe . . . was not the only Virginian who found an elegiac beauty in dereliction, impermanence, and decay."[26]

In coming to grips with their new self-image as doomed aristocrats, Virginians began to interpret the physical decay of their environment as mirroring the situation of man. A lost paradise was seen to be a fitting environment for a lost culture. In the 1830s John Gadsby Chapman pictured the Dismal Swamp, which seemed to symbolize the state's political and agricultural operations gone awry, with a perched vulture that served to amplify the mood of melancholy in the landscape (fig. 3.12).[27] Edgar Allan Poe was attracted to the print, which he said was the sort of image that would adorn his ideal room. The Great Dismal had long intrigued Poe for its elements of stagnation and disintegration, which he often created in his literary landscapes.[28]

In his famous short story "The Fall of the House of Usher" (fig. 3.13), the region where the Usher family resides is not established, but the reader is inclined to think about Old Virginia, where the author lived, particularly the Tidewater where the old families had been established for two centuries. (Poe served briefly in Richmond as editor of the *Southern Literary Messenger.*) The desolate and decaying house in this tale of terror could be easily associated with the broken-down structures of eastern Virginia and the malaise of the antebellum Virginia gentry. "The Fall of the House of Usher" can be seen as an allegory of the upshot of the over-indulgences of an ancient "house," which must finally reap what the previous generations have sown. Once the small "fissure" had become visible, the inevitable collapse of the "house" had to follow. While we do not know if Poe meant to suggest the fall of southern society based on its history of self-gratification—Poe's views on slavery are debated by scholars to this day—he certainly means us to think about our ability to perceive reality when it seems to undermine all that we have long believed to be true.

As with the agricultural failure in the Tidewater, Virginia's political decline would persist through the end of the nineteenth century. In the 1830s, in his novel *The Partisan Leader,* Beverley Tucker lamented the passing of Virginia's giants: "From that time the land of Washington, and Henry, and Mason, of Jefferson, Madison, and Randolph, sunk to the rank of a province, administered and managed by the Rives and Ritchies, the Barbours and Stevensons, the Watkinses and Wilsons, whose chance to be remembered in history depends . . . on the glories of that temple of liberty which they first desecrated and then destroyed."[29] In 1841, however, the Virginian John Tyler, the back half of the famous "Tippicanoe and Tyler Too" campaign slogan, did assume the presidency on the death of "Old Tippicanoe," William Henry Harrison. (Harrison was himself a Virginian by birth and rearing, but decades earlier he had abandoned the state for military fame in the Northwest Territory.) Harrison's Whig cabinet, however, quickly resigned when the new president refused to compromise on issues relating to the National Bank and its branches in the states, and so Tyler became a president without a party—a president with lofty and consistent political ideals but with little of the power that his Virginia predecessors in the office had enjoyed.[30]

Slavery Under Fire

When the New York artist John William Hill traveled to Virginia at mid-century to sketch a panoramic view of Richmond that would be one in a series of prints of American cities, he produced as well a watercolor that focuses as much on the slave family in the foreground as it does on the urban landscape in the distance (fig. 3.14).

3.14 *John William Hill,* View of Richmond, *1847, watercolor,*
8 x 26½ in., Virginia Historical Society

Without overemphasizing the point, Hill suggests that Richmond and Virginia are perhaps better identified by their large African American populations than by an admittedly picturesque city view, which was dominated by Thomas Jefferson's Capitol. A decade earlier Michael Chevalier had written, "There is something in Richmond which offends me more than its bottomless mudholes, and shocks me more than the rudeness of the western Virginians, whom I met here during the session of the legislature; it is slavery. Half of the population is black or mulatto." He added, "they are treated as if they did not belong to the human race."[31] Brissot de Warville had seen the black presence even on the landscape: "Pass into Maryland and Virginia, and . . . you are in another world;—you find not there those cultivated plains, those neat country-houses, barns well distributed, and numerous herds of cattle, fat and vigorous. No: every thing in Maryland and Virginia wears the print of slavery."[32] At least to the eye of the outsider, Virginia remained throughout the antebellum years a landscape dominated by blacks. The image of the region seemed inseparable from slavery.

Like their predecessors of the late colonial era, antebellum Virginians of the Tidewater and Piedmont inherited a system that many of them found both morally wrong and economically inefficient. During the first decades of the century, slavery was often criticized by Virginia's plantation heirs, who looked to end or at least to reform the institution. But if they recognized the problems with slavery, they could find no solutions. In time, however, as slavery came under attack from outside the state, many Virginians reversed themselves and defended the practice that they had once faulted. They were the experts on this subject, and they would be the ones to put an end to slavery, in their own way and time.

For decades southern slavery had been acceptable to most Americans. Some northerners, including James Kirke Paulding in *Letters from the South* (1817) and *Slavery*

in the United States (1836), actually defended the institution: "How it would mortify the pride of the white man . . . if it were indeed found, that these poor fellows were happier than those who affect to pity their miseries. . . . They certainly are exempt from many of the cares that beset their masters."[33] Northerners were likewise willing to tolerate slavery for the sake of maintaining both the Union and the commercial markets in the South that were critical outlets for the products of their manufacturing interests. Also, it was widely believed that southerners had attained a cultural maturity that had eluded other Americans, which must have been attributable to their social system. There can be no doubt that white Americans from all regions looked down upon blacks. The French observer de Tocqueville thought racial prejudice to be greatest in those states where slavery had been abolished.[34] Finally, many of the antebellum churches—the Presbyterians, Methodists, and Baptists among them— were bitterly divided on the subject of slavery.[35]

By mid-century, however, the stance taken by many European observers, the rise of abolitionism—which began in earnest with the emergence of William Lloyd Garrison's weekly, *The Liberator* in 1831—and the publication of key anti-slavery texts by Frederick Douglass and Harriet Beecher Stowe, bolstered the effectiveness of those who opposed the very nature of Virginia's rural society. Their movement fueled sectionalism and thereby would ultimately inflame the southern inclination to secede. It should also be noted that in their often virulent attacks, the abolitionists would unwittingly encourage the mythology that had been created to defend the traditional way of life in the Old Dominion.

John William Hill was tolerant of slavery; his bucolic view notes a fact of life in the South without much comment. By contrast, many European travelers to antebellum Virginia, troubled by the scenes that daily met one's eye, horrified by the spectacle of slave auctions, and frightened by the evidence of runaways and the potential

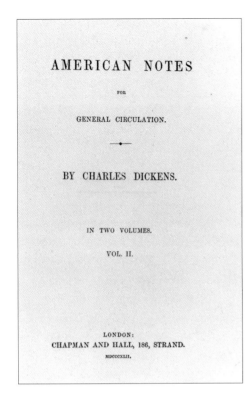

AMERICAN NOTES

FOR

GENERAL CIRCULATION.

BY CHARLES DICKENS.

IN TWO VOLUMES.

VOL. II.

LONDON:
CHAPMAN AND HALL, 186, STRAND.
MDCCCXLII.

3.15 Charles Dickens, American Notes for General Circulation *(London, 1842), Virginia Historical Society*

of slave insurrection, strongly condemned the institution. In 1818 Francis Hall "expressed [his] horror" on hearing of the traffic in Virginia of slave traders.[36] Frances Trollope complained in 1832 that the "brutal" treatment of blacks by "the poorer class of landowners" was "the most disgusting moral spectacle I ever witnessed."[37] Her invocation of the differences between the classes of slaveholders is interesting when we look ahead to *Uncle Tom's Cabin,* in which the treatment of slaves is related to the class and economic condition of their owners. Brissot de Warville defined what he termed "the print of slavery"; it was visible in "a starved soil, bad cultivation, houses falling to ruin, cattle small and few, and black walking skeletons; in a word, you see real misery, and apparent luxury, insulting each other."[38]

Charles Dickens was both the best known of these observers and perhaps the most effective in describing a landscape of "ruin and decay" that he attributed to a "horrible institution"(fig. 3.15):

> The tract of country . . . was once productive; but the soil has been exhausted by the system of employing a great amount of slave labour in forcing crops, without strengthening the land: and it is now little better than a sandy desert overgrown with trees. Dreary and uninteresting as its aspect is, I was glad to the heart to find anything on which one of the curses of this horrible institution has fallen; and had greater pleasure in contemplating the withered ground, than the richest and most thriving cultivation in the same place could possibly have afforded me . . . .

In this district, as in all others where slavery sits

brooding, (I have frequently heard this admitted, even by those who are its warmest advocates:) there is an air of ruin and decay abroad, which is inseparable from the system. The barns and outhouses are mouldering away; the sheds are patched and half roofless; the log cabins (built in Virginia with external chimneys made of clay or wood) are squalid in the last degree. There is no look of decent comfort anywhere. The miserable stations by the railway side; the great wild wood-yards, whence the engine is supplied with fuel; the negro children rolling on the ground before the cabin doors, with dogs and pigs; the biped beasts of burden slinking past: gloom and dejection are upon them all.[39]

Dickens carried his feelings of malaise to the capital city, which he saw entirely differently than did Hill: "The same decay and gloom that overhang the way by which it is approached, hover above the town of Richmond." The English novelist looked away from "the pretty villas and cheerful houses " of the city to search out instead the "deplorable tenements, fences unrepaired, walls crumbling into ruinous heaps," so that these could be "remembered with depressing influence, when livelier features [were] forgotten."[40]

Even Dickens, however, had to admit that at least some of the slaveholders whom he met in Virginia were not evil. As the defenders of slavery often claimed, these planters had inherited a system that they did not know how to change and that they tried to administer with as much benevolence as they could. Dickens described one such slaveholder in Manchester, now a part of Richmond:

> On the following day, I visited a plantation or farm, of about twelve hundred acres, on the opposite bank of the river. Here again, although I went down with the owner of the estate, to "the quarter," as that part of it in which the slaves live is called, I was not invited to enter into any of their huts. All I saw of them, was, that they were very crazy, wretched cabins, near to which groups of half-naked children basked in the sun, or wallowed on the dusty ground. But I believe that this gentleman is a considerate and excellent master, who inherited his fifty slaves, and is neither a buyer nor a seller of human stock; and I am sure, from my own observation and conviction, that he is a kind-hearted, worthy man. [41]

Such masters, who did not abuse their workers and did not participate in the slave trade, seemed a cut above those who bought and sold their human chattel.

In viewing a landscape cluttered with the signs of slavery—from broken-down buildings and posted notices to an idle white population and a prominent black presence—most travelers were appalled. Of all such sights, however, the one that most distressed them was the slave auction. Broadsides and newspaper ads, which reduced black people to the status of property, publicized such

Commissioner's
SALE OF
NEGROES.

BY virtue of a decree of the Circuit Superior Court of Law and Chancery of Fauquier County, at *May Term, 1845,* in the suit of *Carter vs. Carter,* the undersigned *Commissioner's,* will proceed on Wednesday, the 2d day of July, 1845, in the town of Upperville, in the County of Fauquier, before the tavern of *Thompson Ashby,* to sell at Public Auction, for Cash, eight or ten likely slaves.

INMAN HORNER, }Com's.
SAMUEL CHILTON. }

May, 28, 1845.

3.16 Commissioner's sale of Negroes . . . in the suit of Carter vs. Carter . . . on Wednesday, the 2nd day of July, 1845, in the town of Upperville, in the county of Fauquier . . . , *broadside, 15 x 11 in., Virginia Historical Society*

sales (fig. 3.16). By the eve of the Civil War such auctions actually attracted painters and writers who opposed slavery. Eyre Crowe and Lefevre Cranstone were English artists who visited Virginia in the 1850s and brought their heartrending depictions of slave auctions in Richmond, which had become a leading center in the nation for such commerce, to awaiting northern and European audiences (figs. 3.17 and 3.18). (Crowe was in service as secretary to William Makepeace Thackeray, who was on an American lecture tour and preparing his novel *The Virginians.*) Shocked by slavery, and especially by slave auctions and the consequences of such sales, they expressed a hatred of the institution akin to that of Dickens and the other English writers whom they had read prior to their visit.

In his novel *Valley of the Shenandoah* (1824), George Tucker had given a white Virginian's perception of the same episode, which he too found despicable. His account, however, is coupled with a less-than-enlightened acceptance of slavery as tolerable if it is administered properly:

One not accustomed to this spectacle, is extremely shocked to see beings, of the same species with himself, set up for sale to the highest bidder, like horses or cattle; and even to those who have been accustomed to it, it is disagreeable, from their sympathy with the humbled and anxious slave. The weight of his fetters, the negro, who has been born and bred on a well regulated estate, hardly feels. His simple wants are abundantly supplied, and whatever of coercion there is on his will, it is so moderate and reasonable in itself, and, above all, he has been so habituated to it, that it appears to be all right, or rather, he does not feel it to be wrong. He is, in fact, a member of a sort of patriarchal family. But when hoisted up to public sale, where every man has a right to purchase him, and he may be the property of one whom he

never saw before, or of the worst man in the community, then the delusion vanishes, and he feels the bitterness of his lot, and his utter insignificance as a member of civilized society.[42]

The issue of whether the South was in fact a "civilized society," and whether or not blacks were actually members of it, would re-emerge as abolitionism began to take a stronger hold on northern sensibilities.

In another episode in *Valley of the Shenandoah,* some of the slaves that the insolvent Grayson family is forced to sell are purchased by a benevolent master, Mr. Stokes, who grew cotton in Georgia, where he had moved from Tidewater Virginia: "Although there was no separation of husbands from wives, or mothers from young children, yet, in some instances, those who were going to Georgia, were very near relations to many of those who remained behind. . . ."[43] Many of the slaves who were sold in Virginia were destined for the deep South, where a thriving cotton economy fueled a demand for field laborers. This ability to sell slaves "down the river" as it would be called in the West, made voluntary abolition, for financial reasons alone, an unattainable goal. Charles Dickens described the tragic aftermath of an actual slave auction that he saw as he traveled near Richmond:

In the negro car belonging to the train in which we made this journey, were a mother and her children who had just been purchased; the husband and father being left behind with their old owner. The children cried the whole way, and the mother was misery's picture. The champion of Life, Liberty, and the Pursuit of Happiness, who had bought them, rode in the same train; and, every time we stopped, got down to see that they were safe. The black in Sinbad's Travels with one eye in the middle of his forehead which shone like a burning coal, was nature's aristocrat compared with this white gentleman.[44]

Dickens no doubt hoped that the words from the "Declaration" would ring in the ears of his American readers. A decade later, after witnessing slave auctions and their aftermath in Richmond, Eyre Crowe painted the beginning of such a journey (fig. 3.19).

As Thomas Jefferson and the other Founding Fathers from Virginia had learned from personal experience, some slaves were so discontented that they attempted to escape. The region's newspapers, and the southern landscape itself, were littered with advertisements, posters, and broadsides that offered rewards for the return of those who had run off (fig. 3.20). Much was made by the abolitionists of the plight of those who attempted in this way to find their freedom. The so-called "underground railroad," which offered support to those in flight, became a celebrated institution.[45]

3.17 *Eyre Crowe,* Slaves Waiting for Sale, Richmond, Virginia, *ca. 1853-61, oil on fabric, 29 x 39 in., Mrs. H. John Heinz III*

3.18 *Lefevre James Cranstone,* Slave Auction, Virginia, *ca. 1859, oil on fabric, 13 x 21 in., Virginia Historical Society*

3.19 Above, top *Eyre Crowe,* Slaves Going South after Being Sold at Richmond, *1853-54, oil on fabric, 32 x 41 in., Chicago Historical Society*

3.20 Above $50 reward! Ran away from the subscriber . . . May 15th, a Negro, calls himself John Butler . . . Richard K. Lee, *1856, broadside, 10³/₅ x 9²/₅ in., Virginia Historical Society*

Virginia's famed Dismal Swamp became associated with these fugitives because some actually took refuge there. Henry Wadsworth Longfellow wrote a poem in 1855 entitled "The Slave in the Dismal Swamp," and the next year Harriet Beecher Stowe's produced her second novel, *Dred: A Tale of the Dismal Swamp.* Both tell of runaways who even out of bondage are deprived of their freedom because the landscape itself entraps them. In 1864, while Union troops patrolled the swamp, Thomas Moran painted a version of his *Slave Hunt* to raise money in Philadelphia for the northern army. This picture makes a powerful abolitionist statement (fig. 3.21). In Moran's nightmarish vision of a hellish Eden, figures that call to mind Adam and Eve are chased by bloodhounds. Their "fall" seems imminent.

The slave's viewpoint was clearly expressed when he or she ran away. Owners, however, were inclined to argue that most slaves were content with their status. It is perhaps surprising today to read that in 1838 Harriet Martineau concluded that the truth lay somewhere in between:

> The traveller in America hears on every hand of the fondness of slaves for slavery. If he points to the little picture of a runaway prefixed to advertise-

ments of fugitives, and repeated down whole columns of the first newspaper that comes to hand, he is met with anecdotes of slaves who have been offered their freedom, and prefer remaining in bondage. Both aspects of the question are true, and yet more may be said on both sides. The traveller finds, as he proceeds, that suicides are very frequent among slaves, and that there is a race of Africans who will not endure bondage at all. . . . On the other hand, the traveller may meet with a few Negroes who have returned into slave land from a state of freedom, and besought their masters to take them back.[46]

The ultimate crisis imagined by the slave owner was the uprising. Despite Jefferson's premonitions on the subject, the danger had seemed remote to most whites.[47] In 1831, however, in the Tidewater county of Southampton, Nat Turner led about sixty of his compatriots in a 48-hour rampage of brutality that left dead some sixty white men, women, and children; the perpetrators then fled to the nearby Dismal Swamp. A broadside published in New York provides evidence of the horror that this rebellion inspired throughout America (fig. 3.22).

Because Turner's former master was reputedly just, every slaveholder in Virginia suddenly felt threatened.

3.21 *Above, top* Thomas Moran, The Slave Hunt [Dismal Swamp, Virginia], *1864, oil on paper on board, 7 x 9⅛ in., Virginia Historical Society, Lora Robins Collection of Virginia Art*

3.22 *Above* Horrid Massacre in Virginia, *1831, broadside, 14 x 11 in., Virginia Historical Society*

Virginius Dabney has described the insurrection as "an alarm bell which roused the entire South."[48] Travelers recognized the resultant tension that thereafter characterized the antebellum environment. Martineau reported that "The white man . . . knows that in secret the Negro broods over hopes and schemes of vengeance, . . . The precautionary measures which this knowledge has induced the whites to adopt, are such as freeze the heart of a stranger with horror."[49]

Slavery in Virginia had first come under fire from the very people who maintained the institution. They attacked ineffectually, however, and often with some ambivalence. Washington and Jefferson had recognized the evils of slavery but could find no solutions. The Marquis de Chastellux, who moved in their circle as he toured the region in the 1780s, had written that Virginians "seem grieved at having slaves, and are constantly talking of abolishing slavery and of seeking other means of exploiting their lands."[50] In the 1830s, shortly before his death, James Madison discoursed at some length about slavery with Harriet Martineau when she visited Montpelier. In the presence of slaves who "lounged about in the room" during their conversation, the former president "owned himself to be almost in despair" with regard to the situation and "talked more on [this] subject than on any other, acknowledging, without limitations or hesitation, all the evils with which it has ever been charged." Madison worried that "the black population in Virginia increases far faster than the white," and admitted that he "had parted with some of his best land to feed the increasing numbers, and had yet been obliged to sell a dozen of his slaves the preceding week." Madison also "observed that the whole Bible is against slavery," "spoke with deep feeling of the sufferings of the [white] ladies [of the plantation] under the system," and "mentioned the astonishment of some strangers, who had an idea that slaves were always whipped all day long, at seeing his Negroes go to church one Sunday."[51] Martineau makes clear that this vexing subject was much on the mind of one of the architects of the American system of government in his final years.

Other Virginia heirs of slavery were also willing to criticize the system that they inherited. George Tucker was shocked by a scene in Portsmouth, where thirty slaves, "some of them loaded with chains," followed their driver "in funeral procession" to be sold out of state. "Is it not strange," the author questions, "that a people of common humanity, should tolerate an abuse of this horrible character? . . . Surely the Virginians are not barbarians. . . . Many of the spectators appeared to be deeply afflicted at the scene. For myself, it has made an impression upon me that nothing will ever efface."[52] In *Valley of the Shenandoah* he summed up what he believed to be the prevailing sentiment among Virginians: "We, of the present generation, find domestic slavery established among us, and the evil, for I freely admit it to be an evil, both moral and political, admits of no remedy that is not worse than the disease. No thinking man supposes that we could emancipate them, and safely let them remain in the country. . . . We are fully aware of its disadvantages—that it checks the growth of our wealth—is repugnant to its justice—inconsistent with its principles—injurious to its morals—and dangerous to its peace."[53]

One possible solution seemed to be to ship the African Americans to Africa. Tucker complained in 1824 that no "practical scheme as yet [has] been devised for sending them abroad."[54] Soon, however, the American Colonization Society came into being, in which Virginians assumed the leading roles. Bushrod Washington, the nephew of the former president, was a leader, and John Hartwell Cocke was an active member. Madison was optimistic about the Society, although Martineau wondered about its plausibility: "How such a mind as his [Madison's] could derive any alleviation to its anxiety from that source is surprising."[55]

Other Virginians argued for a more radical solution: the ending of slavery altogether. The Nat Turner rebellion inspired a number of proposals for emancipation; among the contributors were Thomas Jefferson's grandson, Thomas Jefferson Randolph, and John Marshall's son, Thomas.[56] In his *Review of the Slave Question* (fig. 3.23), Jessie Burton Harrison proposed to take the whole labor of the state out of the hands of the enslaved. He argued that the institution was the essential hindrance to the prosperity of the slave-holding states. Similarly, in an

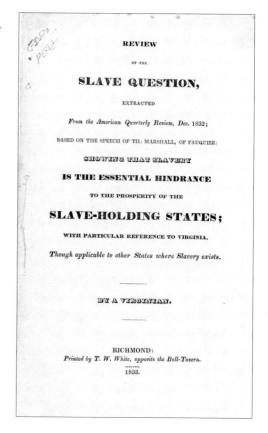

3.23 *Jessie Burton Harrison,* Review of the Slave Question, *1833, pamphlet, Virginia Historical Society*

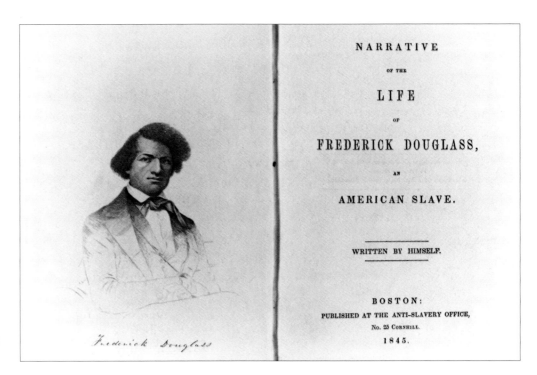

NARRATIVE

OF THE

LIFE

OF

FREDERICK DOUGLASS,

AN

AMERICAN SLAVE.

WRITTEN BY HIMSELF.

BOSTON:
PUBLISHED AT THE ANTI-SLAVERY OFFICE,
No. 25 CORNHILL.
1845.

3.24 *Frederick Douglass,* Narrative of the Life of Frederick Douglass, an American Slave *(Boston, 1845), Virginia Historical Society*

Address to the People of West Virginia; Shewing that Slavery is Injurious to the Public Welfare, and that It may be gradually Abolished (1847), Henry Ruffner, the president of Washington College, expressed a viewpoint prevalent west of the Blue Ridge. Slavery should be abolished because it was the cause of the decline of Virginia farming and manufacturing.

At the Convention of 1829 the slavery issue inspired earnest debate, but in the end it was accepted by the legislators as appropriate for Virginia. From that point forward, despite the pleas of the likes of Harrison and Ruffner, the majority of Virginians decided to approve the practice of slavery and to defend it when attacked. Considering the investments made by many plantation owners, James Fenimore Cooper asserted, "I think no candid man will deny the difficulty of making two or three millions of people, under any circumstances, strip themselves, generally of half their possessions, and, in many instances, of all."[57]

Thomas R. Dew, a professor at the College of William and Mary, wrote the most well- received and influential of several texts that appeared in defense of the institution that was the very bedrock of Old Virginia. His *Essay on Slavery* (first published in 1832) put forward an idea that at the time did not seem preposterous: slavery was "perhaps the principal means for impelling forward the civilization of mankind."[58] In 1837 William Gilmore Simms of South Carolina argued in a similar vein in *The Morals of Slavery*: "Every primitive nation . . . in the world's history, has been subjected to long periods of bondage" that have "elevated and improved" it; "God himself . . . placed a favorite people [the Israelites] in foreign slavery," so that they could "work out their own moral deliverance"; "Negro Slavery [is] the destined agent for the civilization of all the states of Mexico, and all the American states beyond." Simms surmised that "Providence has placed [the

Negro slave] in our hands, for his good, and has paid us from his labor for our guardianship."[59] In a remarkable extrapolation, Simms added that the continent of Africa was undeveloped in his day because slavery was not imposed there to force labor, and that the North American Indian, now "a raw and naked skeleton of what was once a numerous and various people," would have fared better if he too had been enslaved.[60] Even George Tucker, who had pointed to many of the problems with slavery, was able to convince himself that the "situation" of slaves is not "so bad": "They are perhaps better supplied with the necessaries of life than the laboring class of any country out of America. They . . . probably enjoy as much happiness, with as few drawbacks, as any other class of our population."[61]

It would take the publication of two highly influential anti-slavery tracts to turn the tide of public sentiment toward the abolitionist movement. These were the first widely known slave autobiography, Frederick Douglass's *Narrative of the Life of Frederick Douglass, an American Slave* (fig. 3.24), and what would become the best-selling American novel of the nineteenth century, Harriet Beecher Stowe's *Uncle Tom's Cabin*. Douglass, a former slave in Maryland who escaped to freedom in New England and soon enjoyed notoriety as an abolitionist lecturer, published the story of his indignities and sufferings in bondage in 1845. Douglass's description of his enthusiasm for William Lloyd Garrison's *The Liberator* mirrors the effect that his autobiography had on abolitionist readers: "My soul was set all on fire. [The paper's] sympathy for my brethren in bonds—its scathing denunciations of slaveholders—its faithful exposures of slavery—and its powerful attacks upon the upholders of the institution—sent a thrill of joy through my soul, such as I had never felt before!" In a Preface written for the *Narrative*, Garrison applauded the emergence of Douglass into the na-

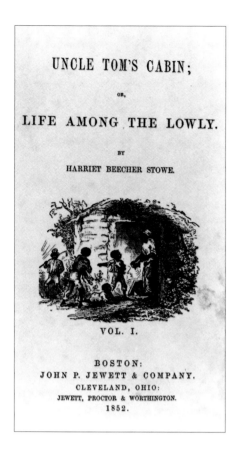

3.25 *Harriet Beecher Stowe,* Uncle Tom's Cabin; Or, Life Among the Lowly *(Boston and Cleveland, 1852), Virginia Historical Society*

tional spotlight as "fortunate for the multitudes, in various parts of our republic, whose minds he has enlightened on the subject of slavery, and who have been melted to tears by his pathos, or roused to virtuous indignation by his stirring eloquence against the enslavers of men!" [62]

Nothing brought slavery more under fire than did *Uncle Tom's Cabin* (fig. 3.25). After first appearing serialized in the *National Era*, a Washington anti-slavery newspaper, Stowe's novel sold a remarkable 300,000 copies in its first year alone. In this tale, which made use of many of the conventions of the popular sentimental novels of the day, the slaves George and Eliza and their son ultimately escape to freedom, but the ever-faithful and devoutly religious Tom, after being sold from the Shelby family of Kentucky to the St. Clares of Louisiana, whose daughter, the angelic Little Eva he would save from drowning, is ultimately sold again to the brutal Simon Legree, on whose Texas plantation Tom finally beaten to death. Stowe's stated purpose was "to awaken sympathy and feeling for the African race, as they exist among us; to show their wrongs and sorrows, under a system . . . necessarily cruel and unjust." [63] She wrote the book out of indignation about southerners' demands that fugitive slaves be returned, which was reaffirmed by the passage of the "Omnibus Act" (the Fugitive Slave Law) of 1850: "when she heard . . . Christian and humane people [in Congress] actually recommending the remanding escaped fugitives into slavery, . . . she could only think, These men and Christians cannot know what slavery is." She claimed to have "given only a faint shadow, a dim picture, of the anguish and despair that are, at this very moment, rival-ing thousands of hearts, shattering thousands of families, and driving a helpless and sensitive race to frenzy and despair. . . . Nothing of tragedy can be written, can be spoken, can be conceived, that equals the frightful reality of scenes daily and hourly acting on our shores, beneath the shadow of American law, and the shadow of the cross of Christ." [64]

Stowe's effective use of melodrama and appeals to piety made *Uncle Tom's Cabin* a sensation. Thomas Nelson Page, the most widely read of the postwar apologists for the old ways of Virginia, affirmed that *Uncle Tom's Cabin* was "one of the most powerful [arguments] ever penned" and that it put forward "the most renowned picture of Southern life," one that was often factually erroneous, but that a decade later brought triumph to the abolitionist movement. "Mrs. Stowe did more to free the slave than all the politicians." [65] On meeting Stowe, Abraham Lincoln reputedly remarked, "So you're the little woman who wrote the book that made this great war." It is difficult to summarize the effect that this novel had on the American consciousness. It is certain that it gave us the most widely known impression of life in the Old South until the next blockbuster novel on the subject, Margaret Mitchell's *Gone With the Wind* of 1936.

Both anti-slavery and pro-slavery novels followed in the wake of *Uncle Tom's Cabin*, but none came close to matching its impact. Emily Clemens Pearson's abolitionist novel about Virginia, *Cousin Franck's Household; or, Scenes in the Old Dominion* (Boston, 1852), detailed the abuses to be found in that state, and subtly pointed to the hypocrisy of the Virginia slaveholder who took pride in his descent from the interracial union of John Rolfe and his Powhatan bride. The story is told through the letters of "Pocahontas," a young white woman from Connecticut who travels to the Virginia plantation of her relations and is horrified by the barbarity of the slave system. Opposed to *Cousin Franck's Household* was Mary H. Eastman's *Aunt Phillis's Cabin, or Southern Life As It Is* (Philadelphia, 1852), which was a southern attempt to answer *Uncle Tom's Cabin*. Eastman represents plantation life in Virginia as blissful. The author was a southerner; her husband, the painter Colonel Seth Eastman, sketched the setting for the novel (fig. 3.26). In a lengthy preface that is remarkable to the modern reader, Mary Eastman defends slavery on biblical grounds, beginning with the "curse" placed by the Creator on the African descendants of the Old Testament figure Ham. She concludes that in nineteenth-century America the matter remains beyond mortal hands: "Slavery, authorized by God, permitted by Jesus Christ, sanctioned by the apostles, maintained by good men of all ages, is still existing in a portion of our beloved country. How long it will continue, or whether it will ever cease, the Almighty Ruler of the universe can alone determine." [66] In her "Concluding Remarks," the author gives

3.26 *Seth Eastman,* Aunt Phillis's Cabin, *1852, drawing, 4½ x 8 in.,* *collection of Calder Loth*

fifteen pages to rebuttals of specifics in *Uncle Tom's Cabin,* arguing that "Mrs. Stowe's horrors can be accounted for satisfactorily" and suggesting, "Let the people of the North take care of their own poor. Let the people of the South take care of theirs."[67]

The attacks on slavery by abolitionists would spark a philosophical—and ultimately a military—defense of an institution that many of its defenders found to be morally objectionable. Yet, they would not be coerced into freeing their slaves, and therefore themselves, from the life that this institution inflicted upon them both. Thomas Jefferson had suggested in *Notes on the State of Virginia* that slavery was in some ways worse for the master than for the slave, a sentiment with which many antebellum southerners would have agreed. This was especially true in Virginia, where slavery had demanded an allegiance to agriculture on lands that had long been drained of their fecundity. Yet, as things got worse for the planters, they seemed to be looking up for the burgeoning industrialists of the state's emerging urban centers. Investments by wealthy Virginians, by northerners, and by the growing immigrant population, who brought their capital and their sweat to the task, had expanded the economy. Other immigrants, who found their way to the western part of the state through Pennsylvania, had more success in agriculture than could the planters in the Tidewater or Piedmont. Both of these apparent success stories, however, would work against the continuation of the society that the heirs of the Revolution had hoped to preserve.

Urban Growth, Internal Improvements, and Social Change

As Virginia was facing political and agricultural decline and abolitionists were gathering at the door, the survival of the traditional way of life on the Anglo-Virginian plantations of the Tidewater was further threatened by the development of towns into mercantile centers like those of the North, by internal transportation improvements that would link these urban hubs and thereby support their manufacturing and merchandising interests, and by the increasing prosperity and prominence of the state's non-English populations. Germans, Scotch-Irish, and Quakers living in the bountiful countryside west of the Blue Ridge, many of whom were agrarians like the old-school planters, led lifestyles so different as to cause concern among the planters of the east, who maintained their customary aristocratic pursuits and continued to own slaves. Concurrently, immigrants in the cities seized upon commercial opportunities that had long been underappreciated by the existing gentry.

In his popular novel *Swallow Barn, or A Sojourn in the Old Dominion* (1832), as well as in his private letters of this period, John Pendleton Kennedy gave expression to the old society's concerns regarding all three of these pressing developments. In *Swallow Barn* Kennedy's Mark Littleton reports that Virginia has "no large towns where men may meet and devise improvements or changes in the arts of life"; the perhaps surprising point being made is that the state is much better off without cities and the uncultivated society they breed. The novel's protagonist, Frank Meriwether, "thinks lightly of the mercantile interest, and, in fact, undervalues the manners of the large cities generally."[68] As to internal improvements, even the yeomanry in Meriwether's neighborhood object to the right of Congress to "take a road of theirn any where they have a mind to, through any man's land." They ask, "What does Congress care about your state rights?" and "What's the use of states if they are all to be cut up with canals and railroads and tariffs?"[69] Concerning those outsiders who had migrated to the Valley in search of available land, Kennedy complained to his fiancée in a letter of 1828 that the Germans and Scotch-Irish were so vulgar and parsimonious in their lifestyles, so democratic and ignorant, as to jeopardize the culture of the English:

> [In the northern portion of the Valley] how completely the elegancies of society and the best points of a luxurious mode of living have been invaded by a stiff, awkward and *churchly* morality, that seems to have attacked every seat of grace and gesture, speech, 'affections of delight' (as Shakespeare calls them), every thing that made Old Virginia once the seat of noblemen, but now of penny-saving presbyterians. I think he would say a fair land is spoiled by that very distemper which, to my eyes, makes New England so odious—perhaps, I should use another word—so distasteful.

In *Swallow Barn* the representative of the German population in the Tidewater is Hafen Blok, who is poor, of the lowest class of society, and dismissed as "a well-meaning, worthless, idle stroller."[70]

In general, the city was the bane of existence for the southern planter, in part because the urban centers of the North were at the root of the federal government's policies to establish tariffs, which would protect the manufacturer, and to finance internal improvements, which would facilitate his commerce. These policies lessened and then taxed the profits of the planter. Cities additionally bred undesirables, a class of merchants and industrialists whose greed might supplant the enlightened values of a rural gentry.[71] There was a lingering feeling in the state that to give in to Yankee-style urbanization would incur a cost that many Virginians were not prepared to pay. As late as 1854, the speaker who delivered the Fourth of July Address at the Virginia Military Institute feared the loss of a "peculiar type of Virginia character" that could be "blotted out forever" should the state give in to what Richard N. Current calls "a wave of commercialism and industrialism sweeping down from the North."[72] The move to more modern employments would necessarily mean a move away from the land, which translated to an abandoning of the life and culture of which generations of Virginians had been proud. Although a few planters chose to move

ahead, and others took a fateful glance toward the future, the hesitancy on the part of many antebellum Virginians of the old school to look to what appeared to be northern ways and means as a solution to their economic woes can be explained by the weight of their agrarian past, which they would shoulder in defiance rather than abandon in despair.

There were additionally issues of ethnic prejudice in cities akin to those that Kennedy had described in the Valley. In his description of the emerging society of Richmond in *Letters from Virginia* (1816), George Tucker, who was himself of old English stock, complains that he found the newer inhabitants "not exactly to my taste." The author also makes the telling point that at this early date the higher classes were "chiefly of foreign extraction" and therefore unlike "the true old Virginia breed, frank, generous, and hospitable, whom it is a real pleasure to shake by the hand." Such outsiders "live in a state of ambitious rivalry with one another, each endeavouring to surpass his neighbour in fashion and folly, a very unprofitable contest at best."[73]

Although strongly biased against cities, the Virginia planter allowed one exception. In *Swallow Barn*, Frank Meriwether "makes now and then a winter excursion to Richmond, which, I rather think, he considers as the centre of civilization."[74] With its capitol sitting high above the James River, Richmond had become a symbol for the old-school legacy of which it was most proud, Virginia's political importance to the colony and early republic. Brissot de Warville had stated in 1792 that "this capitol turns the head of Virginians; they imagine, that from this, like the old Romans, they shall one day give law to the whole north."[75]

In 1834 George Cooke and William James Bennett provided one of the best in a series of views by a half-dozen artists that celebrate the development of the city into Meriwether's "center of civilization" (fig. 3.27). They picture controlled urban growth, coupled with the progress that was embodied in the building of a canal alongside the James River. Richmond is presented as a governmental rather than a mercantile center. The buildings that are prominently pictured are civic: the Capitol, which towers over the less important industrial and business district, the new prison, City Hall, and the governor's house are all easily recognizable, in part because the artists exaggerated their size. The city is shown to have its idyllic aspects as well, in that cows graze and members of the gentry enjoy unspoiled nature. The suggestion was thereby made that the development of this seat of government has been advantageous, and has posed no threat to the rural lifestyle of the Tidewater and Piedmont.

In 1837, however, Michael Chevalier noted that "ambition" was in the air to make Richmond an industrial as well as a political center: "it aspires to be a metropolis,

3.27 *William James Bennett after George Cooke,* Richmond from the Hill above the Waterworks, *1834, aquatint, 17⁷/₈ x 25 in., Virginia Historical Society*

and it is making the due preparations to assume that character by the great works which it is executing or aiding to execute, canals, railroads, water-works, huge mills, workshops, for which the fall in the river affords an almost unlimited motive power."[76] The old school would have to watch carefully any such transformation; too much growth would inevitably threaten the rural lifestyle that was at the heart of Old Virginia.

In 1839 Chevalier's ambitious city leaders formed a stock company to fund the building of a palatial hotel to stimulate the city's development. New Englander Isaiah Rogers, then the nation's premier figure in the genre of hotel architecture, was awarded the commission. His Exchange Hotel (fig. 3.28), designed in the so-called Greek Revival style, was soon celebrated as one of the great buildings in the nation. In the year of the hotel's opening, Charles Dickens judged it "very large and elegant" and reported that he was "well entertained" there.[77] The Exchange Hotel became a symbol of Richmond's progress and potential for further expansion.

By this time the capital had become the center of a prospering flour industry that enjoyed an international market. As early as the 1780s, while profits from tobacco dwindled, wheat production in the region had surged,

3.28 *Isaiah Rogers,* Exchange Hotel, *southeast corner of Franklin and Fourteenth Streets, Richmond (the Exchange Hotel is to the right), 1840-41, albumen print of ca. 1870s, photograph, Virginia Historical Society*

prompting the pioneering in the Shenandoah Valley of machinery for harvesting that crop, as well as the building of new mills throughout the state. Richmond was particularly well situated; mills could harness the hydraulic force of the falls of the James, below which the river was navigable to ocean vessels. By mid-century the Richmond mills had surpassed all competitors in the annual volume of flour produced. The largest complex had been established at the turn of the century by a Spanish immigrant, Joseph Gallego (1758– 1818, fig, 3.29), one of the new-

comers to the city who were noted disparagingly by Tucker. The Gallego complex (fig. 3.30) would help to transform the landscape of Richmond's waterfront into an industrial center that by the 1830s contained some of the largest structures then standing in America. By their size—and despite their importance to the agrarian economy that gave birth to them—these buildings signaled more progress, commercial success, and urban growth than many of the old guard cared to see.

Richmond's tobacco processors had long ago given Virginia the national lead in that manufacture, and the city's Tredegar Iron Works became the foremost southern industrial complex of that type. It was one of seventy-seven iron manufacturers in the city. Thus by 1851, when J. P. Kennedy published the second edition of *Swallow Barn*, Richmond had changed from the quiet governmental complex pictured by Cooke; its continuing commercial and manufacturing growth would ultimately make it the natural choice to serve as the capital of the Confederacy. Kennedy lamented that "[Time] and what is called 'the progress,' have made many innovations [in Virginia], as they have done every where else." When he added that "The country now apes the city in what is supposed to be the elegancies of life," he could only be referring to Richmond, the one Virginia city large enough to concern the old-school planters.[78]

The proponents of the old ways who endorsed the concept of a single governmental center had also hoped for the development of small market towns to meet the needs of a plantation society, not for cities that were ever expanding with new industries. By mid-century, however, Norfolk, Petersburg, Lynchburg, Wheeling, and other formerly quiet settlements seemed poised for further growth. Numerous factories were established during these

*3.29 **Above** Unidentified artist,* Joseph Gallego, *ca. 1800-10, oil on canvas, 30 x 25 in., Virginia Historical Society*

*3.30 **Right** Gallego Mills, Twelfth Street between Cary and Canal Streets (at the former James River and Kanawha Canal Turning Basin), Richmond, 1835, rebuilt or expanded 1848, 1860, photographed after the evacuation fire of 1865, photograph courtesy of The Valentine Museum*

years, until by the late 1850s Virginia could claim 4,841 manufacturing establishments, making it fifth among all the states in this category and first in the South.[79] For all of its urban growth and industrialization, however, Virginia in fact lagged far behind the more progressive North in industry and commerce. In 1841 a reporter for the *New York Express*, in recounting his "Trip to Richmond–Old Virginia," complained that despite the state's great natural resources of climate and landscape, and despite a remarkable legacy of "a succession of men [who were] the most illustrious in history," the Old Dominion had for thirty years been "standing still" in economic matters. Since "the peace of 1815, when America started on a new race of material and business enthusiasm," he wrote, "Virginia has not of herself, advanced a step. . . . The whirlwind of events sweeps over them and they are buried in the sand." This disparaging point of view was reaffirmed in 1855 when Governor Joseph Johnson, a westerner from Harrison County, reported to the General Assembly that "Virginia has greatly the advantage over any portion of the North in all the elements requisite to constitute a commercial and prosperous community," but "like the unfaithful servant, she has failed to improve the talent entrusted to her care."[80] Virginius Dabney concludes that the state simply "failed to advance commercially and industrially with anything like the speed that might reasonably have been expected. The same is true of the port of Norfolk, which never came close to realizing its potential in the antebellum years."[81] The talents of Virginians, whether in the guise of coins or abilities, had not been invested wisely, and so any potential rewards would be forfeited. The New York reporter of 1841 placed the blame on Thomas Ritchie, the powerful editor of the Richmond *Enquirer*, for opposing the new ways of progress: "He has discouraged mostly all enterprise. . . . His *summun bonum* is to make the world stand still."[82] Ritchie was indeed an able spokesman for the old school of Tidewater planters who opposed change. Even though Richmond continued to grow, proponents of the old ways could take pride in their success in holding back much unwanted progress, which allowed for the continuation of their agrarian culture.

The inference in *Swallow Barn* is that the old families *en masse* were emphatically opposed to internal improvements. Some planters, however, supported the canal schemes. This is evident in the biographies of many of the board members of the James River and Kanawha Canal Company. For instance, the president from 1835 to 1846, Joseph Carrington Cabell (fig. 3.31) was from an old Virginia family, he owned a large plantation, and he voted in the Virginia Assembly in favor of bills to improve agricultural conditions in the state. To his thinking, a canal to the west would help to perpetuate the plantation system and to extend it west of the Blue Ridge. Such a

3.31 Joseph Carrington Cabell, *ca. 1850, daguerreotype, Virginia Historical Society*

canal was in fact essential for the survival of the old ways. Cabell, who has been described as Thomas Jefferson's right-hand man in the founding of the University of Virginia, and John Hartwell Cocke—another board member and friend of both Jefferson and the University, whose plantation house Bremo was modeled after Monticello—were among many plantation-born men who supported the canal. While some saw such improvements as the beginning of the end of Old Virginia, those like Cabell and Cocke saw canals as the possible means for its perpetuation.

The transportation improvements that Frank Meriwether's neighbors in *Swallow Barn* feared would traverse the state had done so by mid-century. This progress is charted in a series of maps published by Colonel Claudius Crozet in 1838, 1848, and 1853 (fig. 3.32). An immigrant who had been born and trained in France and was a veteran of Napoleon's army, Crozet served as the principal engineer of the state's Board of Public Works. With the 1848 map he published a 67-page report entitled *Outline of the Improvements in the State of Virginia*. These documents suggest that Virginia's efforts at building lines of transportation, which on a national level were among the broad objectives of the Whig party during the

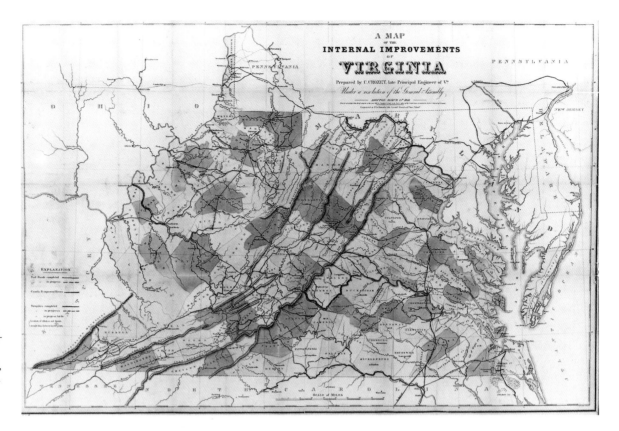

3.32 *Claudius Crozet,* A Map of the Internal Improvements of Virginia, *Philadelphia: P. S. Duval, lithographer, 1848, 21³/₄ x 33 in., Virginia Historical Society*

1830s and 1840s, were not without some vigor. Pictured on Crozet's maps are the Dismal Swamp Canal, various railroad projects, and the James River and Kanawha Canal. The latter project would tie up the capital, manpower, and imaginations of Virginians for decades.

The movement to modernize with canals, turnpikes, railroads, and bridges received additional impetus from the state's western residents, whose physical isolation was a source of political, economic, and social constraint. In 1812 the westerners had instigated the appointment of commissioners to examine river traffic; in 1816 they prompted the creation of both a small Fund for Internal Improvements and the Board of Public Works that Crozet would head. This body soon set the state on a course to make the James and Kanawha rivers the principal commercial arteries of the region. The idea was first to improve navigation on those rivers and then to connect them with a turnpike.

Many old-school Virginians were not opposed to canals. Water traffic had been integral to the plantation system of the Tidewater from the start. Canals did nothing to change the topography of the state, nor did they necessarily encourage the building of towns; they only enhanced the effectiveness of existing waterways. Further, canal building had been sanctioned by Virginia's greatest son. In 1770 George Washington had been one of the earliest proponents to open the inland navigation of the Potomac River by means of a canal that would link the Ohio lands to the Tidewater. He owned stock in the James River Canal Company, which was awarded to him in the 1790s by an appreciative state legislature. A decade

earlier he had written about the "practicability of opening a communication between the rivers which empty into Albemarle Sound . . . and the waters of Elizabeth or Nansemond Rivers."[83] The twenty-two mile canal that would connect the waterways of North Carolina and Norfolk was begun in 1787, the year that Washington presided over the Constitutional Convention. When this artery, now called the Dismal Swamp Canal, finally opened in 1828, this engineering feat attracted so much national attention that a Boston painter, Robert Salmon, celebrated the accomplishment (fig. 3.33). Governor John Tyler, a champion of the old school, shared the northerner's enthusiasm; two years earlier he had actually anticipated the "immense advantages to the citizens of North Carolina and Virginia" that this canal would bring.[84] The success of the Dismal Swamp project, the legacy of George Washington's endorsement of water traffic, and the potential for expanding the old ways westward, would account for the interest of many old-school Virginians in the ill-fated James River and Kanawha Canal project.

Virginians held great expectations for this western artery, as is evident from the ambitious title given to one publication that looked for "the Speedy Completion of the Water Line of Virginia, . . . which will reach from the wharves of Norfolk, far into Kansas, and eventually to the very bases of the Rocky Mountains" (fig. 3.34). In fact, the canal never carried even to the western counties of Virginia. By 1855, the time that Edward Beyer arrived, it had reached its unanticipated stopping point of Buchanan in Botetourt County (3.35). Even at its heyday at mid-century, the James River and Kanawha Canal never rivaled the commercial

3.33 *Robert Salmon,* Dismal Swamp Canal, *1831, oil on canvas, 10 x 14³/₁₆ in., Virginia Museum of Fine Arts, Richmond, gift of Eugene B. Sydnor, Jr.*

success of New York's Erie Canal. The undertaking proved to be disastrous for the state financially, in terms of both the revenues that were poured into it and the anticipated gains from trade that never materialized. In fact, in hindsight it is possible to surmise that one reason that the lifestyle of Old Virginia survived little scathed until the Civil War was that the state's grand canal project deterred the development of railroads.

In terms of land traffic in Virginia, progress had been made in the 1830s with turnpikes in the west: perhaps the most famous was the Valley Turnpike from Winchester to Staunton, while another linked Harrisonburg to Warm Springs. Sections of railroad were also completed, but the Baltimore & Ohio Railroad, which had been incorporated in 1827, was initially barred from the state by hardline Virginians who did not live in either Norfolk or the western counties, the two areas that would have benefitted from the rail lines. Railroads were different from canals. They would literally "cut up" a man's property, and worse, they would give rise to new, urban transportation centers, and thereby to new manufacturing and greatly increased commerce. Many of the Old Virginia planters vigorously opposed railroads because they could conceiv-

ably change the state into a mercantile region like New England. The commercial and industrial development of much of Virginia was thereby necessarily curtailed. "Lower Tidewater [was] seething," Virginius Dabney writes, and "the far western part of the state remained in near-revolt."[85] But Old Virginia had won at least a temporary victory by delaying the construction of these lines of progress.

While the James River and Kanawha Canal was still under construction, railroads became dominant as the most cost-effective method of transportation. The railroad was soon recognized to be the most efficient way to cross the Virginia mountains; thus it was essential to the further development of the far-western counties. In his *Viaduct on Cheat River Near B. & O. Railroad* (fig. 3.36), Edward Beyer celebrates one of the many remarkable engineering feats that were required to traverse the rugged terrain of what would become West Virginia. As indicated by the title of this image, the Baltimore & Ohio Railroad eventually gained control of many of the significant lines in Virginia, not only this one over the Cheat River, but also those in the Valley, over which produce from the western counties soon enough made its way to Baltimore,

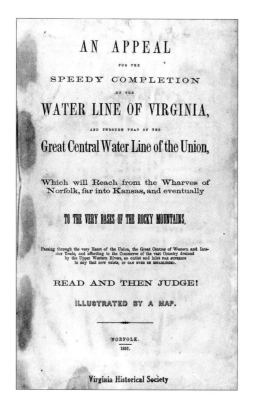

Virginia Historical Society

3.34 *D. T. Bisbie,* An Appeal for the Speedy Completion of the Water Line of Virginia, . . . which will reach from the wharves of Norfolk, far into Kansas, and eventually to the very bases of the Rocky Mountains, *Norfolk and Richmond, 1857, Virginia Historical Society*

a port that developed into a metropolis at the expense of Norfolk. The economy of Old Virginia to the east was therefore left essentially unchanged, while the far-western counties were linked in commercial allegiance with the North. Their ultimate political allegiance, which led to the creation of the state of West Virginia, was not, therefore, surprising.

Beyer also points here to the power of technology. The train tracks tower over the river and agricultural landscape below. The future is in the now easily reachable western counties, and it is a future based on mechanized motion. The old agricultural society, with its traditional employments and water-based modes of transportation, which had held sway in Virginia since the seventeenth century, was to Beyer's eye being left behind. While the heirs of the colonists would put up a good fight, the Civil War, with its destruction of the plantation culture, only brought to a quicker end a society that's demise was inevitable.

In the end, the newly-built canals, turnpikes, and railroads pleased neither the progressives, who bankrupted the state and in many cases themselves in the effort to complete the James River and Kanawha Canal, nor the members of the old school, including J. P. Kennedy, who bristled at the sight of the governmental and entrepre-

3.35 *Edward Beyer,* The James River Canal Near the Mouth of the North River, *from the* Album of Virginia, *1858, lithograph, 9 x 13¾ in., Virginia Historical Society*

3.36 *Edward Beyer,* Viaduct on Cheat River, B. & O. Railroad, *from the* Album of Virginia, *1858, lithograph, 11 x 17³/₄ in.,* Virginia Historical Society

neurial meddling that so changed their landscape. Although such improvements often did not provide the hoped-for economic successes, they ironically contributed to the survival of Old Virginia. The failure of the new projects served to encourage those who wished to recall and recapture the region's older agrarian past.

The Valley of Virginia had been settled in the eighteenth century principally by pioneers of English descent moving westward from the Tidewater and Piedmont, and Germans and Scotch-Irish emigrating southward from Pennsylvania and Maryland. These were the people whom George Washington had defended from the French and Indians in the 1750s, when the region was sparsely settled. By the antebellum era a large enough population was in place for the Anglo-Virginians to make more careful observation of their neighbors, as George Tucker did in his novel *Valley of the Shenandoah* (1824). Tucker goes on at some length about the immigrants, offering unabashedly prejudiced opinions about both ethnic groups that to modern eyes stand as glaring evidence of a mounting concern in the old camp about the rising power and visibility of the state's non-English inhabitants. The Germans, he writes, are "a pains-taking, plodding, frugal people; and sober more in consequence of their

industrious pursuits, their slight relish for social pleasures, and their habits of thrift, than indifference to liquor"; they are, however, a "useful class of citizens in their place." He goes on, "The Irish character presents . . . a strong contrast to that which I have placed before you—as ardent and impassioned as the others are cold and phlegmatic." As to the Scotch, "When bent on the pursuits of gain or ambition, they manifest great enterprise and perseverance; but are often idle, indolent, and improvident. . . . If the German settler may be compared to the dray-horse, the Scotch-Irish resembles the light and spirited riding-horse, a noble animal by nature; and, when free from defect, destined for worthier purposes, but more liable to accident."[86] If Tucker admired the Scotch-Irish more than the Germans, he recognized the flaws in both, as well as the distinctiveness in their cultures that set them apart from the old school of Virginia. And it should be noted that one reason that the Germans and Scotch-Irish troubled the Anglo-Virginian planters was the immigrants' disenchantment with slavery, the system that was at the heart of the Old Virginia economy. (The Quakers, who had been present in Virginia since the early eighteenth century, were also strong, often vocal, opponents of slavery.)

The Scotch-Irish and British borderers were the most numerous of the immigrants. They settled primarily in the southern end of the Shenandoah Valley in Augusta

3.37 *Lefevre Cranstone*, Negro Shanty, Virginia, *ca. 1859, watercolor,*
6½ x 12 in., Virginia Historical Society, bequest of Paul Mellon

County, where they made up three-fourths of the population. About half were descendants of Scottish and English
settlers in northern Ireland—and therefore were called
Scotch-Irish in America, a name that they disliked—while
the other half came from the borderlands of northern
England and Scotland, an area that had been contested
by the two nations for hundreds of years. They shared a
common border culture that was adaptable to the American frontier, which was identifiable by distinct architecture, dialect, food ways, and social structuring around the
family clan.[87] To Kennedy, these crude customs were an
anathema to the nobility of Old Virginia.

The most distinct of all the Old World settlers in Virginia were the rural Germans. These immigrants had begun to arrive in the colony as early as the 1730s, venturing
through Pennsylvania and western Maryland to the northern end of the Shenandoah Valley, as well as to the Piedmont, the Roanoke Valley, and Southwest Virginia. By
1790, twenty-eight percent of Virginia's white population
was of German ancestry. These people inevitably attracted
notice because they maintained Old World traditions of
dress, diet, decorative arts, and architecture. They also
upheld their traditional gender roles and language; many
spoke and published in German. They were hard workers, who appeared to their Anglo-Virginian contemporaries to be thrifty and withdrawn, and were deeply religious.[88]

Admittedly, once in Virginia the German immigrants
abandoned the village arrangements that many had
known at home for isolated farmsteads akin to the English model. Although their architecture, as it was
adapted to its new setting, would begin to exhibit some
English influences, their houses were more notable for
their continuance of the spatial arrangements of the traditional German three-room floor plan, which incorpo-
rates both work and storage spaces. The English artist
Lefevre Cranstone pictured one of their banked houses,
which served as part residence and part barn, as the background in a mid-century watercolor (fig. 3.37). While
many Anglo-Virginian houses had the kitchen in a separate dependency, the German *Flurküchenhause* had its
kitchen on the ground floor. The multiple doors, want of
end chimneys, and general lack of bilateral symmetri-
cality were also features of the Rhenish-American house.

Cranstone labeled this sketch *Negro Shanty* in reference to both the small but sturdy house in the foreground—although "shanty" is probably not the word we
would use to describe it—and to the resident who is pictured before it. The visual evidence suggests that this neat
and tidy woman was free; a gazetteer of 1832 lists 6,323
free blacks in the western counties (as opposed to 53,465
slaves). The interrelation of Cranstone's two buildings,
and by implication, these two cultures, would have been
inconceivable to the Old Virginia gentry. For more ways

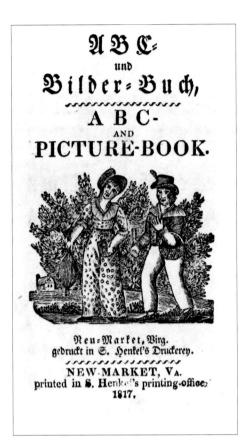

3.38 ABC=und Bilder Buch [ABC and Picture Book], *New Market, published by Solomon Henkel, 1817 (first edition, 1808), Virginia Historical Society*

than one, this scene would have represented a jarring element in the rural landscape.

When these emigrants from the European mainland established German-speaking schools and German-speaking publications, they threatened the dominance in the region of the English language, which was another reason for dismay in the Anglo-Virginia camp. One example of a publication that was used as an educational aid is the illustrated *ABC Buch* (fig. 3.38), the earliest children's primer published in any language in the South. It was first printed in 1808 by the New Market Press, which was in operation from 1806 until 1854. If by mid-century the use of the German language was in decline, many of the old cultural usages survived. The decorative arts tradition, for one, persisted; this was characterized by the use of lavishly applied designs on furniture and on *Fraktur*, certificates of important life events such as birth, baptism, and marriage.[89]

Evidence of German prosperity, even at an early date, is found in a stove plate (fig. 3.39) produced in 1773 by the Marlboro Furnace, which was located in the northern end of the Valley. It was run by Isaac Zane, a Quaker outcast who became a slaveholder in order to keep his blast furnace running. With the same practicality, Zane recognized the emerging economic presence of his German neighbors, and so he made it his business to be ready to supply any items that they might need. The inscription on this plate reads, "Ein ieclicher wird unter seinem Weinstock und Feigenbaum wohnen ohne Scheu." If Zane's Anglo-Virginian patrons could have recognized

this phrase as a translation of a now familiar verse from the Bible ("Every one shall under his own vine and fig tree live without fear"), they would have realized that, as was true of many English immigrants, it was the search for a life of contentment, free from persecution, that had lured the Germans to the New World in the first place. In rural Virginia they found the same security and prosperity that the long-standing Anglo-Virginians enjoyed.

Throughout the antebellum era developers encouraged immigrants to relocate to the western part of the state because the landscape and climate there allowed for the production of Old World grain crops. An undated nineteenth-century broadside states that "The soil is . . . adapted to the cultivation of Corn, Wheat, Tobacco, Vine, Flax and all the different kinds of fruits and vegetables usually raised in temperate climates" and "is admirably adapted for grazing farms" (fig. 3.40). This broadside also explains that the region that is now West Virginia had been "little settled," due to the poor "convenience of communication" and "the existence of slavery in Virginia." Those issues are then purported to have been resolved: "new routes of communication are now being constructed" and "The slaves there are exceedingly few in number, and those are found employed in Hotels or are in domestic service." As the century progressed, Virginia's western reaches increasingly became home to a variety of ethnic groups, many of whom lived, built, dressed, and worshiped in ways that differed from the Anglo-Virgin-

3.39 *Isaac Zane*, Stove Plate, *Marlboro Furnace, Frederick County, 1773-92, cast iron, 20³/₄ x 17¹/₂ in., Bucks County Historical Society, Doylestown, Pennsylvania*

TO EMIGRANTS.
COLONIES IN WESTERN VIRGINIA.
200,000 ACRES.

3.40 To Emigrants. Colonies in Western Virginia. 200,000 Acres, *broadside, pre-Civil War (n. d.), 9½ x 12 in., Virginia Historical Society*

ians. In time, such differences became irreconcilable; by the eve of the Civil War the far-western counties, because they saw themselves as sharing too few commonalties with the Tuckahoes of Old Virginia, decided not to support the slaveholders and secede with them from the Union.

The cultural diversity that characterized the western counties of Virginia had seemed a threat as early as the 1820s to the defenders of the plantation system. At mid-century J. P. Kennedy concluded that the fears that he had expressed more than two decades earlier had sadly been prophetic. In the second edition of *Swallow Barn* the author lamented the passing of the "luxuriance" and "hospitality" that characterized Old Virginia, a lifestyle that he identified as "American," which had now fallen victim to the impact of the non-English cultures. Kennedy would not go so far as to assert that those cultures were flawed—at least not in print. He would only assert that they were different, and were the catalysts for change:

> The Old Dominion is losing somewhat of the raciness of her once peculiar, and— speaking in reference to the locality described in these volumes— insulated cast of manners. The mellow, bland and sunny luxuriance of her old-time society—its good fellowship, its hearty and constitutional *companionableness*, the thrifty gayety of the people, their dogged but amiable invincibility of opinion, and that overflowing hospitality which knew no ebb,— these traits, though far from being impaired, are modified at the present day by circumstances which have been gradually attaining a marked influence over social life as well as political relation. An observer cannot fail to note that the manners of our country have been tending towards a uniformity which is visibly effacing all local differences. The old states, especially, are losing their original dis-

tinctive habits and modes of life, and in the same degree, I fear, are losing their exclusive American character. . . . There is much good sense in that opinion which ascribes a wholesome influence to those homebred customs, which are said to strengthen local attachments and expand them into a love of country. What belonged to us as characteristically American, seems already to be dissolving into a mixture which affects us unpleasantly as a tame and cosmopolitan substitute for the old warmth and salient vivacity of our ancestors.[90]

What in the early twentieth century would be characterized as the American "melting pot" was already boiling in antebellum Virginia, to the chagrin of its ancient families and their spokesmen.

Other proponents of Old Virginia took a different tack than did Kennedy, interpreting the "uniformity" in the region at mid-century as evidence of a victory of the old ways, an indication that eastern traditions had finally been adopted by the non-English populations west of the Blue Ridge. A new state constitution passed in 1851 removed property qualifications for voting and allowed for the popular election of the governor; the state's first chief executive from the western counties, Joseph Johnson, was almost immediately placed in office. This legislation answered western demands well enough to aid in the process of making some westerners feel that they too were a part of Old Virginia. The state was also brought together by the attacks on the South in general and Virginia in particular by northern abolitionists. A new camaraderie emerged, in which to attack one Virginian was to attack all. The far-western counties, however, so geographically distant and with mountainous topography so different from the Tidewater as to be foreign to the plantation system, would never be convinced to join the fold.

"Old Virginia For Ever": The Pastoral Ideal Revived

In 1858 the Maryland artist Francis Mayer painted a provocative canvas entitled *Leisure and Labor* (fig. 3.41). This image raised a question about American society that had been in the air for the previous half-century, and that soon would be answered by the Civil War. Should the nation be led by members of an aristocratic fellowship, modeled on the gentility of the South, and particularly of Virginia, or should the work-a-day lifestyle of the merchants and industrialists of the North become the norm? Maryland was a slave state; travelers for decades had equated the region with Virginia, so similar did they seem after leaving the free soil of Pennsylvania. Mayer's image, then, reminds us of the pressures that were being brought to bear on the scions of the old families of the South, many

3.41 *Francis Blackwell Mayer,* Leisure and Labor, *1858, oil on canvas, 15⅝ x 23 in., Corcoran Museum of Art*

of whom seemed ill-equipped to handle roles of sectional, much less national leadership.

To the right, the artist presents an elegantly dressed aristocrat who is identified by the accouterments of his leisurely way of life. His fine riding boots, sleek hunting dog, and well-bred steed, who is in the process of being shod, remind us that the southern gentleman of the plantation was free to enjoy the pursuit of hunting, that most genteel of sports. Harvested crops in the distant background suggest that farming is the source of his wealth. The broken plow in the right foreground, however, points to the agricultural decline that differentiated the antebellum era from the more productive colonial years when tobacco was king. A poster above it apparently depicts a fugitive slave—the running figure is akin to those in newspaper ads. "Stop Theif!!" (sic) is the graphic beneath the image of a man who appears to carry both a scythe, a tool used for harvesting and a symbol of both the passage of time and death, and what seems to be a goblet, like the one served by a slave in the cartouche of the Fry-Jefferson map of 1751 (see page 49, fig. 2.17). This figure, who runs toward the right edge of the canvas, away from the young man on whom the light directly falls, invites the viewer to question who is the thief, the planter or the runaway slave? We fur-

ther wonder whether leisure time built on such a despicable foundation breeds a true aristocracy or simply leads to idleness and vice.

To the left is an industrious figure, a version of a character well known to Americans from Henry Wadsworth Longfellow's popular and nostalgic poem of 1841 "The Village Blacksmith."[91] This is the symbol of the proper conduct of life labors; his "brow is wet with honest sweat" from the effort of his "mighty hands." We all, including the planter and his coursing dog, stop to watch him work. The blacksmith and his helper labor tirelessly, in a setting that is neat and plain but far from luxurious. The blacksmith is free of vice—in Longfellow's poem he "owes not any man"—but is he too absorbed in work, in the affairs of the moment, to be able to grasp more complex issues? It would appear that Mayer admired honest labor but saw its limitations, and found the gentry lifestyle appealing but was aware of its overindulgences. (Perhaps he preferred the American way of life to be somewhere in between, as his painting of the same year of a poor but dignified *Squire Jack Porter* (page 160, fig. 4.54) seems to suggest.) Marylanders were divided on the matter of leisure versus labor. In a letter of 1828 to his fiancee, J. P. Kennedy, the author of *Swallow Barn* and a Baltimore resident who revered the old leisurely lifestyle, writes about her father, "You know his prejudice . . . against Virginia, for its loose manners and thriftless mode of life."[92]

In 1837 Michael Chevalier examined the nature of the American lifestyle in his *Society, Manners and Politics in the United States.* "The physical labour of colonization is now nearly brought to an end; the physical basis of society is laid," he wrote. "On this base it becomes necessary to raise a social structure of yet unknown form. . . . which of the two races—the Yankee or the Virginian—is best suited to execute this new task?" The still comparatively young nation dearly needed an aristocracy, he reasoned, because "recently, scenes of murder, outrage, and destruction . . . have been exhibited throughout the United States." Chevalier went on, "The period has come, when it will be necessary for authority to be organized" that will "preserve and perpetuate traditions, give system and stability to policy, and devote itself to the most difficult of the arts, . . . that of governing." In terms of who might be suited for this task, "The Southern States are already organized on the principle of hereditary aristocracy"; the establishment of a hierarchy with stability, he predicted, "would be most difficult in the States without slaves."[93]

Chevalier found the two races, the Yankee and the Virginian, to be "very unlike each other; they have no great love for each other, and are often at variance." In what would be an allusion often made during this period, he reminded his readers that "They are the same men who cut each other's throats in England, under the name of Roundheads and Cavaliers." The Yankee is:

> reserved, cautious, distrustful; he is thoughtful and pensive, but equable; his manners are without grace, modest but dignified, cold, and often unprepossessing; he is narrow in his ideas, but practical, and possessing the idea of the proper, he never rises to the grand. He has nothing chivalric about him. . . . His imagination is active and original, producing, however, not poetry, but drollery. The Yankee is the industrious ant; he is industrious and sober, frugal, and, on the sterile soil of New England, niggardly . . . . For a statesman, he wants that greatness of mind and soul which enables a man to enter into and love another's nature. . . . But if he is not a great statesman, he is an able administrator, an unrivalled man of business."[94]

The Virginian, by contrast, had much about him that was appealing:

> The Virginian of pure race is frank, hearty, open, cordial in his manners, noble in his sentiments, elevated in his notions, he is a worthy descendant of the English gentleman. Surrounded, from infancy, by his slaves, who relieve him from all personal exertion, he is rather indisposed to activity, and is even indolent. He is generous and profuse. . . . To him, the practice

of hospitality is at once a duty, a pleasure, and a happiness. . . . there is no place in the world in which he would not appear to advantage, no destiny too high for him to reach; he is one of those, whom a man is glad to have as a companion, and desires as a friend. Ardent and warm-hearted, he is of the block from which great orators are made. . . . he has all the qualities needful to form a great statesman.[95]

In this case "leisure," even with its attendant potential for indolence, seems better suited to provide the necessary leadership for the nation than would "labor"; the administrator must bow before the statesman.

If Chevalier's discourse about the value of an aristocracy seems peculiar, his attention to this component of society was not extraordinary in the aftermath of Jacksonian democracy in America and the revolutions in Europe. In 1839 Francis Grund noted, "I have heard more talk about aristocracy and family in the United States than during my whole previous life in Europe." In his *Aristocracy in America, From the Sketch-Book of a German Nobleman*, this author acknowledged the need for a ruling class in the new nation, and located the most qualified models in the South: "The mere moneyed aristocracy which is establishing itself in this country [in the North] . . . *hates* the industrious masses over whom it strives to elevate itself"; the result is "a continual jarring: the rich claiming a rank which the poor are unwilling to grant; and the poor provoked by the *unprofitable* arrogance of the rich, opposing to them a species of insolence which a labouring man in Europe would hardly dare to offer his equals." This lack of "good-will towards the inferior classes," which can only lead to no good end, is a problem that "does not exist at the South," where people "are infinitely more amiable in their manners" perhaps because they are "not continually in contact with the labouring classes":

> There the veriest fault of the people is generosity. The slaves, who enable them to be aristocratic without being mean, stand to them in the relation of vassals to their lords; and the planters, not fearing the power and political influence of their slaves, but, on the contrary, having an interest in their physical well-being, treat them generally with humanity and kindness. There never was a great moral evil, without producing also some good; and thus it is that the very relation between master and slave engenders ties and affection. . . .
> If the tendency of wealth in the Northern States is towards an aristocracy of money, the aristocracy of the Southern States, founded on birth and education, is a sort of offset to it,—a means of preventing the degeneration of the high-minded democracy which once swayed the country, into a vulgar oligarchy of calculating machines without poetry, without arts, and without generosity. . . . If aristocracy, the original sin of society, must be entailed upon man in every climate, then let me at once have that of the

South. Give me an aristocracy above the cares and toils of ordinary life. . . . I would rather live surrounded by negroes, and, in the society of their aristocratic but high-minded and generous masters [than in the North].[96]

The "prevailing seriousness and melancholy air of business" outside the South also "oppressed" Charles Dickens, who in 1842 complained that "the graces of life [had been rejected in the North] as undeserving of attention."[97]

Virginia had been aristocratic from the start. As the Marquis de Chastellux noted in the 1780s, this was because the colony had been founded by gentlemen who carried "prejudices of nobility"; he predicted that Virginia "will always be aristocratic" because slavery would perpetuate such a lifestyle.[98] The state's reputation in Europe, as suggested by the French wallpaper scene of the 1830s (page 62, fig.3.1), was that it was a land of aristocrats. Frances Trollope wrote in 1832, "In Virginia I heard that I was come to the land of gentlemen."[99] In 1838 James Fenimore Cooper stated, "I am of the opinion, that in proportion to the population, there are more men who belong to what is termed the class of gentlemen, in the old southern States of America than in any other country of the world. . . . I do not know where to find gentlemen of better air or better breeding throughout, than most of those I have met in the southern *Atlantic* States."[100]

Chastellux had also worried, however, that slavery "nourishes vanity and sloth," and the Italian traveler Luigi Castiglioni described "the Virginian way of life" as one of "indolence and barbarity." Castiglioni republished an account that had appeared in the *American Museum*, a Philadelphia periodical, in which the Virginia planter is said to sleep and drink most of the day, while his slaves perform hard work from dawn to dusk and live under miserable conditions.[101] Francis Hall wrote in 1818, "Of the Virginian character, generally, my impressions were not favourable. They seem, especially the plantation-bred Virginians, to have more pretension than good sense."[102] Brissot de Warville found "objection in the character, the manners and habits of the Virginians" because "They seem to enjoy the sweat of slaves. They . . . love the display of luxury, and disdain the idea of labour." He would "banish slavery; which infallibly produces those great scourges of society, laziness and vice, in one class of men; unindustrious labour and degrading misery in another."[103] In *Valley of the Shenandoah*, George Tucker similarly linked leisure, slavery, and vice: "As our whites who can command the labour of slaves, are not permitted to work by their prejudices and their pride, for want of other employment, they are very much exposed to the seductions of gaming and drinking."[104]

The Virginia model of aristocracy, as Frances Mayer seems to suggest in *Leisure and Labor*, was acknowledged to be far from perfect because of its reliance on slavery. The

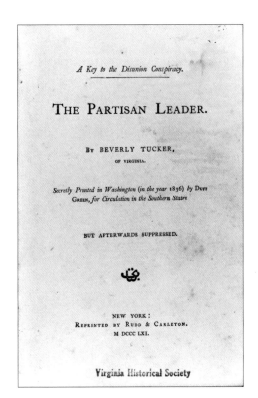

3.42 Nathaniel Beverley Tucker, The Partisan Leader, A Tale of the Future (Washington, 1836), Virginia Historical Society

choice, then, as to which of the social models would provide the best leadership for the nation, the laboring North or the leisurely South, was difficult because each society had its drawbacks. The failure of Virginia to produce the type of high-quality leaders that it had in previous generations seemed to argue for the lessening of its power on the national stage. In the 1830s, the rising tide of abolitionism would begin to make inroads in both the North, where many came to feel that slavery should be abolished, and the South, which saw its society in need of defense. In the years before the battle would be joined in the field, southerners mounted an ideological defense of their way of life. Progressivism offered little use, and so attention turned again to the past; concurrently, the time period represented by Old Virginia slid forward. There was still an interest in the events of the colonial past, but the term also had to encompass the plantation life that was being lived in the present, the life that was under attack. Such immediacy did not allow for the development of a sophisticated platform. As Lewis Simpson put it, "The imperative quest of the South was for a basis on which firmly to establish itself as a novel civilization. But the quest was so constricted by the pressure of historical expediency—by the South's need to defend its singular institution—that the quest had little time to develop philosophical amplitude or depth."[105] The most advantageous solution seemed to be to revive the notion that the Virginia plantation lifestyle was pastoral, rather than simply rural, and therefore allowed for the pursuit of humanistic virtue in a manner that would have been inconceivable in the North.

In Nathaniel Beverley Tucker's prophetic novel *The Partisan Leader, A Tale of the Future* (fig. 3.42), the war cry "Old Virginia for ever" was used by those who so opposed

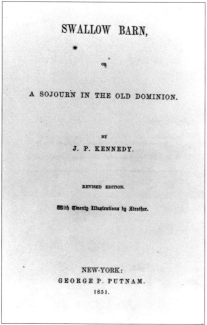

SWALLOW BARN,

OR

A SOJOURN IN THE OLD DOMINION.

BY
J. P. KENNEDY.

REVISED EDITION.

With Twenty Illustrations by Strother.

NEW-YORK:
GEORGE P. PUTNAM.
1851.

3.43 Left *John Pendleton Kennedy,* Swallow Barn, or, A Sojourn in the Old Dominion *(New York, 1851), Virginia Historical Society*

3.44 Above *David Hunter Strother,* Joe Crane's Barn, Jefferson Co. Virginia, *1847, retouched in 1850, pen, pencil, white, 9¼ x 12⅛ in., West Virginia University; used as the frontispiece to the 1851 edition of* Swallow Barn

and once more vindicated her proud motto, . . . SIC SEMPER TYRANNIS! AMEN. SO MOTE IT BE."[106] To many in the South the whims of tyrants now emerged from Washington, D.C. and Congress, rather than from London and Parliament, but the affect on the agrarian lifestyle was little different from what George Washington had complained about in the 1770s. The region had to reassert itself, and as ever, Virginia would have to take the lead.

The Antebellum Plantation

John Pendleton Kennedy's *Swallow Barn, or, A Sojourn in the Old Dominion* (1832) did much to shape antebellum conceptions about southern plantation life (figs. 3.43 and 3.44). Remembering his boyhood experiences in the Valley, and making use of his knowledge of the Tidewater, Kennedy imagined an arcadia characterized by a slow-paced and constant lifestyle, by prosperity, with allowances for some decay, and by harmonious relations between the races. In this novel many of the various personalities on a Virginia plantation are brought to life. Readers, who included many northerners and Europeans, view this world through the eyes of Mark Littleton, a New Yorker, who is paying a visit to Swallow Barn plantation in the Tidewater.

At the start it is noted that "Virginia has the sentiments and opinion of an independent nation," and a "temper" that is "aristocratic." Much is made of the camaraderie of rural Virginia life: "You will never know your

the political agenda of northern interests, which favored the support of industry at the expense of agriculture, that they would secede from the Union. The setting is the future, 1856; the states of the deep South have already peaceably seceded and being free from tariffs enjoy a new prosperity. Virginia, which is still under Federal control, is engaged in guerrilla warfare against the regime of Martin Van Buren, who remains president in his fourth term of office. In the end "Virginia achieved her independence; lifted the soiled banner of her sovereignty from the dust,

friend so well, nor enjoy him so heartily in the city as you may in one of those large, bountiful mansions, whose horizon is filled with green fields and woodland slopes and broad blue heavens." Isolated on his plantation, and lord over dozens of dependents, squire Frank Meriwether has become opinionated: "The solitary elevation of a country gentleman . . . begets some magnificent notions. He becomes as infallible as the Pope; gradually acquires a habit of making long speeches; is apt to be impatient of contradiction, and is always very touchy on the point of honor."[107]

Honor was in fact a guiding principle of the southern lifestyle. Initially it helped to fill a void left by the failure of organized religion either to establish a strong value system or to give sufficient structure to Virginia society.[108] According to Bertram Wyatt-Brown, honor was the "keystone of the slaveholding South's morality," a "means to holding fast to the social order that they so deeply cherished" by "prevent[ing] unjustified violence, unpredictability, and anarchy." Honor "provided a means to restrict human choices, to point a way out of chaos. Thus it helped southern whites to make life somewhat more predictable than it would have been otherwise. It established signposts of appropriate conduct."[109] It was therefore important for Kennedy to emphasize the importance of honor to Meriwether, who was imbued with a characteristic that tied him to his forebears. Whether defending one's position in a discussion, or defending one's life in a duel, which remained an option always open to the gentleman, this code served to separate, for good or ill, the southern aristocrat from his northern equivalents.[110]

Squire Meriwether is benevolent to his slaves: "Frank's kind and considerate bearing towards his servants and dependents" is "appreciate[d]": they "hold him in most affectionate reverence, and, therefore, are not only contented, but happy under his dominion."[111] Much is said concerning Meriwether's holding of "servants and dependents." The institution yields an "air of contentment and good humor and kind family attachment." On the subject of manumission, Meriwether, speaking for his fellow plantation owners, states that southerners do not have a "right, in the desire to free ourselves, to whelm them in greater evils than their present bondage." Littleton's soliloquy about the blacks that he has observed seems to support the behavior of his host:

> I came here as a stranger . . . to the negro character, . . . indeed, from prepossessions, to look upon them as severely dealt with, and expecting to have my sympathies excited towards them as objects of commiseration. I have had, therefore, rather a special interest in observing them. The contrast between my preconceptions of their condition and the reality which I have witnessed, has brought me a most agreeable surprise. . . .

> Perhaps . . . this is a transition state in which we see them in Virginia. If it be so, no tribe of people have ever passed from barbarism to civilization whose middle stage of progress has been more secure from harm, more genial to their character, or better supplied with mild and beneficent guardianship. . . . Having but few and simple wants, they seem to me to be provided with every comfort which falls within the ordinary compass of their wishes, and . . . they find even more enjoyment . . . than any other laboring people I am acquainted with.[112]

Meriwether concludes that "A violent removal of [the slaves], or a general emancipation, would . . . produce . . . calamities." He goes on to state emphatically what would be a constant southern position on the matter: "the question of emancipation is exclusively our own, and every intermeddling from abroad will but mar its chance of success."[113]

In the end, *Swallow Barn, or, A Sojourn in the Old Dominion* does not fully achieve what it was apparently meant to become, what Lewis Simpson has called "a highly effective rendition of the nostalgic mode of the pastoral." The problem has to do with the rendering of slavery, especially in the final quarter of the book, when, aside from the comments of Meriwether and Littleton, we also hear from "Old Lucy," a slave who tells the heartrending story of her youngest child, Abe. Simpson sees the novel as manifesting "a pathos of pastoral order which occurs in the effort of the Southern literary imagination to institutionalize chattel slavery in the name of the pastoral."[114] Kennedy's effort earned mixed reviews in the North. The book—and in essence the rural slave society of Old Virginia that it describes—was well received in Philadelphia and New York; it even won praise in London. But the reception was hostile in New England, where readers found the white males of Virginia insipid: "the gentlemen of Swallow Barn are the most ordinary, trifling, useless generation the world ever saw," wrote one reviewer.[115]

Anyone who would have doubted the actual existence of such fictional types as Frank Meriwether could have found any number of living examples in the Old Dominion. Many of these heirs to the old English estates fought those challenges that threatened to alter their lifestyle, which survived little changed until the Civil War overturned Virginia society. William Byrd Harrison of Upper Brandon in Prince George County (1800–1876, fig. 3.45) typifies the group. He was of the sixth generation of Virginia Harrisons. Resident on the south bank of the James River across from Westover, Harrison was a son of Evelyn Taylor Byrd and a neighbor of both John Tyler and Edmund Ruffin. The former would become president; the latter, who would soon enough be famed as a secessionist, was significant in his earlier years as a pioneer in progressive farming. Harrison's estate of Upper Brandon

3.45 *William James Hubard,* William Byrd Harrison of Upper Brandon, *1835, oil on canvas, 30 x 25 in., Virginia Historical Society*

had been carved from that of Brandon, which was inherited by his brother George. Despite this division, the Brandons were both huge plantations.

In 1834 the traveler Charles Augustus Murray, second son of George Murray, the fifth earl of Dunmore and Virginia's last royal governor, said that Harrison's "hospitality to strangers is not surpassed in any country that I have seen."[116] His "rich" and "varied" entertainments were also noted by David Hunter Strother in a travel journal in 1849.[117] Harrison could entertain freely because like Kennedy's fictional Swallow Barn, Upper Brandon was well stocked with cattle (79), sheep (79), hogs (165), and enough slaves (105) to take care of so large an operation.[118] Like Meriwether, Harrison argued that slavery was entrenched, beneficent, and that he saw no way to end it; his brother George, the master of the contiguous plantation, wrote that "the difficulty of removing it is felt and acknowledged by all save the fanatics." Harrison differed from Frank Meriwether, however, in his progressive approach to farming. Harvard-educated and well traveled in England, where he observed modern agricultural practices, the master of Upper Brandon published articles on such subjects as crop rotation and the use of lime in the *Farmer's Register*, a magazine edited by Ruffin. In the process he made Upper Brandon a highly productive farm.

George and William Harrison did "not regard negro slavery, however mitigated, as a Utopian system." Unlike

the relationships imagined in the fictional *Swallow Barn*, their overseers would "constantly . . . use the lash, both to men and women;" George Harrison freely admitted that "vicious and idle servants are punished with stripes, moderately inflicted." In the wake of the Nat Turner insurrection, which is ignored in *Swallow Barn*, the Harrisons placed restrictions on their servants: slaves were forbidden "to preach except to their fellow-slaves, the property of the same owner [Turner had been a preacher]; to have public funerals, unless a white person officiates; or to be taught to read and write." William wrote, "There is so much excitement and alarm in consequence of the [Nat Turner] insurrection . . . felt here that I do not like to leave my family."[119] This was the type of reality that was hidden in many of the romances produced by southern writers during the period. The lack of attention in these books to the abuses of slavery would make the cruelties catalogued by Frederick Douglass all the more shocking to northern audiences.

In Lucretia Meriwether readers found an exemplary plantation wife. Since the early years of settlement, the mistress of the Virginia plantation had been the supervisor of its domestic affairs. In 1785 the Englishman Joseph Hadfield marveled at the magnitude of this responsibility and at the effectiveness of Virginia women in fulfilling it:

> Here I must do justice to the American ladies who certainly had an extraordinary personality, for they had not only all the elegancies of their own families with many strangers on a visit to attend to, but they had the whole negro establishment, provisions, clothes, and every other want to superintend. I have accompanied them in the morning and followed them during their arduous task, and nothing could equal their judgment and patient examination into everything. They delivered from their stores to each servant all that was necessary for the day, and gave instructions what they were to do. They then proceeded to the workhouse where all the negro sempstresses were employed in making the clothes for the slaves. . . .
>
> All was method and regularity and I must say that no women are better wives or managers.

"Fortunately they are so," Hadfield added, "for with a few exceptions the men are dissipated and gamesters."[120]

Partly because of the burden of their workload on a sizeable estate, which included the demands of time and attention made by the slave system, many plantation wives detested the role that was assigned to them. Mary Chestnut wrote in her diary that southern women "hate slavery worse than Mrs. Stowe does."[121] Virginia Cary, in *Letters on Female Character*, which was published in Richmond in 1838 (fig. 3.46), described the institution as "a fearful evil" that has "its effect on the female temper": "I acknowledge it is hard to bear with patience, the trials inci-

3.46 *Mrs. Virginia Cary,* Letters on Female Character *(Richmond, 1838), Virginia Historical Society*

3.47 *Unknown artist,* Julia Gardiner Tyler, *ca. 1845, oil on canvas, 41½ x 35 in., privately owned, on extended loan to the Virginia Historical Society*

dent to domestic life in Virginia, but I sincerely wish my countrywomen were aware, that they *may* and *must* be borne. The obligation to bear them is imperative, because it involves the eternal happiness of every individual. Awful indeed will be the condition of those slaveholders, who have abused the trust reposed in them, and ill treated the creatures committed to their charge."[122]

At least one highly prominent Virginia plantation mistress of this period actually championed the opposing argument. According to Julia Gardiner Tyler (1820–1899, fig. 3.47)—wife of the former president and resident in 1845 at Sherwood Forest, their Charles City County plantation on the James River where some seventy field hands raised corn and wheat—slavery was neither an evil nor a burden to the southern woman. Formerly a New York socialite, the beautiful Julia had become at age twenty-four the young second wife of John Tyler, who was fifty-four at their marriage in 1844. In 1853, in response to an antislavery petition issued by the duchess of Sutherland and signed by a half-million English women, Mrs. Tyler penned a defense that was quickly reprinted and sensationalized in newspapers in both nations. She was, after all, a former first lady, as well as a northerner, who had traveled throughout Europe observing the laboring classes there. Her experiences having made her a somewhat unique slaveholder, Julia Tyler informed her readers about the free black population in her adopted state and the efforts by Virginians to resettle freed slaves in Liberia, while she criticized the English for fostering slavery on the American colonies in the first place, and the duchess for intruding into American domestic affairs. She then pointed to what she saw as the greater mistreatment of workers in Victorian England.[123]

While Julia Tyler's purpose had been to justify the institution of slavery, in doing so she also perpetuated the tradition that the plantation mistress epitomized virtue and benevolence. In identifying the personal characteristics of the Virginia lady, Tyler echoed ideas that had been passed down in the region since the late seventeenth century. "The vestments" that southern women "wear," she wrote, "are those of meekness and charity, their diamonds are gems of the heart, and their splendor the neatness and order and contentment which everywhere greets the eye."[124] "Meekness" and "charity" are virtues long celebrated in English courtesy books, such as Richard Allestree's *The Lady's Calling* (London, 1673), which were found in nearly every library in colonial Virginia.[125]

In her portrait, Julia Tyler plays the role of Virginia plantation mistress to the fullest. Her facial expression suggests the presence of such expected virtues as mercy, compassion, piety, and devotion. The glove on one hand suggests her modesty. But there is also a sensual nature to the still luminous Julia; this is the young woman who would give her middle-aged husband seven children. A

3.48 Robert Matthew Sully, Rose Bradwardine (from Sir Walter Scott's Waverley), ca. 1850, oil on canvas, 29¹/₂ x 24¹/₂ in., privately owned, from the estate of the Misses A. C. and L. W. Stewart

jeweled headband pulls back her hair, but long tresses drip provocatively on satiny shoulders. She is presented almost as another of the exotic plants that surround her in the lush southern landscape. The hairstyle and gown, both of the latest fashion, border on excessiveness, almost on coquetry, in defiance of the advice of such prudish defenders of southern virtue as Virginia Cary. Evelyn Pugh writes that when Julia Tyler became first lady "White House social life was once again as lively as it had been in Dolley Madison's day," and that at Sherwood Forest "Mrs. Tyler maintained a life-style reminiscent of former glory. Mrs. Tyler was hard pressed to pay for the extravagant wardrobe which she needed for visits to fashionable resorts."[126] Her beauty and lifestyle, when added to the tradition of virtue that was the hallmark of the plantation mistress, as well as her willingness to step into the public sphere to defend her adopted society, gave Julia Tyler a mystique that few women of her time could match.

It was perhaps only in the realm of fiction that equivalent characters could be found. The Virginia lady, as had ladies in Great Britain for centuries, would "continue in contented subordination to [man's] authority"[127] because she would be conversely honored by him under a cult of chivalry that had swept the state as quickly as the romantic novels of Sir Walter Scott could reach their eager readers. The first, *Waverley*, was published in 1814, and as each new romance appeared, Scott's popularity, which would

inspire the great American romancer of the North, James Fenimore Cooper, and of the South, William Gilmore Simms, would continue to grow. His representations of medieval English and recent Scottish history, as imagined with pageantry, clan and nationalistic loyalty, and bold, larger-than-life figures, became particularly popular in antebellum Virginia because chivalric notions reinforced traditions that were at the very core of the old plantation ways. Highly visible in Scott's world was a landed aristocracy that could be seen as akin to that of Virginia. The attention there to manners and appearance, the celebration of feminine virtue, the focus on horsemanship, and the strict code of honor could all be seen as rooted in Old World chivalry. Also, the author tended to side with the underdog in the clash of cultures, and Virginians saw themselves as newly in that role as they struggled against Yankee dominance. Five million copies—an unheard of figure—of the novels of Sir Walter Scott were printed in America before 1824.[128]

The popularity of *Waverley* is evident in the commission awarded to a Virginia artist, Robert Matthew Sully, to paint a portrait of the heroine of the novel, Rose Bradwardine (fig. 3.48); to this day the canvas hangs in a nineteenth-century Richmond house. This historical novel is the story of Edward Waverley, a romantic young English army officer stationed in Scotland in 1745, the time of the Jacobite rebellion, when Scottish forces under Prince Charles Stuart, son of the pretender to the British throne, challenged the union with England and rule by the Hanoverian monarchy. Waverley first sides with the rebel Highlanders, who have persisted in maintaining their old ways long after the union of 1707. When he visits the baron of Bradwardine, a family friend, Waverley meets Rose, the baron's daughter, who in some ways is a product of the county where she resides. Perthshire is situated on the border between the tamed Lowlands and the wild Highlands, and spans this divide by allowing for the survival of the values of each culture. Waverley is tempted by the charms of Flora MacIvor, the sister of the Jacobite chieftain Fergus, but in the end Flora rejects his suit, the Jacobites are crushed at the battle of Culloden, Fergus MacIvor is hanged, and Waverley marries Rose, symbolically bringing together two worlds.

Scott's purpose was to honor the heroic, and ultimately doomed, culture of the Highlanders; Robert Matthew Sully has left us evidence that he was successful with his Virginia audience. Rose Bradwardine, by bridging the highland and lowland cultures of Scotland, was appealing to Virginians as a woman who was not simply beautiful, but who by her probity could rise above regional differences. The fair Rose is the antithesis of the fiery, freedom-fighting Flora. In her we see a budding lady, who will fulfill her role as a wife and will be a paradigm of the domestic virtues so honored by many southerners.

A number of the other aspects of the chivalric world became popular subjects in the fiction and visual arts of the period. David Hunter Strother chose to sketch a scene from *Swallow Barn* in which a young damsel, Bel Tracy, goes hawking on a neighboring plantation (fig. 3.49). Kennedy writes that Bel "is a little given to romantic fancies, such as country ladies who want excitement and read novels are apt to engender." She has trained "a beautiful marsh-hawk" and "By an intimacy of one year she had rendered this bird so docile, that, at her summons, he would leave a large wicker cage . . . to perch upon her wrist. The picturesque association of falconry with the stories of an age that Walter Scott has rendered so bewitching to the fancy of meditative maidens, had inspired Bel with an especial ardor in the attempt to reclaim her bird [from the wild]." The hawk was dressed in leather leggings and silver bells, and on one leg on a silver ring "was engraved the name of her favorite, copied from some old tale, 'Fairbourne,' with the legend attached, 'I live in my lady's grace.'" Fairbourne is soon lost, but Ned Hazard, in his quest for the hand of Bel, retrieves the bird. In the end, they "regained Swallow Barn: returning like knights to a bannered castle from a successful inroad,—flushed with heat and victory,—and covered with dust and glory."[129] The flight of the hawk is a useful devise, in that we are reminded of the romantic world of knights and fair ladies, but are also asked to consider whether beings who are held in thrall, even when they are pampered, truly wish to be free.

The Virginian's breeding and racing of fine horses was another connection to a mythologized past. As in the colonial era, this elitist pastime tied the gentry of antebellum Virginia to their counterparts in Augustan England. Racing lost the favor of many aristocrats following the revolution; Brissot de Warville observed in 1788 that the racetracks had "fallen into disuse" and "were all abandoned."[130] But the sport was revived in the antebellum era, when Virginians again came to the fore as turfmen. This rejuvenation was enhanced when thoroughbred horses like Tobacconist (fig. 3.50), owned by John Minor Botts of Half Sink Plantation in Henrico County, became renowned for their racing exploits. He was painted in 1833 by Edward Troye, along with the slave trainer and jockey who cared for him. Tobacconist is shown to be a remarkably sleek, powerful, and athletic creature, who did honor to his bloodline. His father Gohanna was so fine a specimen that in 1826 the state legislature adjourned for half an hour so that its members could view the horse as it passed through Richmond. Gohanna was a son of the even more famous racehorse Sir Archy.[131]

3.49 *David Hunter Strother,* Hawk in Flight, *illustration in* Swallow Barn *(1851), Virginia Historical Society*

3.50 *Above, top* Edward Troye, *J. M. Botts' Tobacconist, with Botts'* *Manuel and Botts' Ben,* *1833, oil on canvas, 24³/₈ x 29¹/₈ in., Virginia Museum of Fine Arts, Richmond, Paul Mellon Collection*

3.51 *Above* Contention will stand . . . at Warrenton, Fauquier County . . . *1829, broadside, 20⁷/₈ x 10¹/₄ in., Virginia Historical Society*

The cult of the horse was exaggerated with characteristic humor by Kennedy, whose Frank Meriwether "is somewhat distinguished as a breeder of blooded horses; and [following some highly publicized races between northern and southern horses] has taken to this occupation with a renewed zeal, as a matter affecting the reputation of the state. It is delightful to hear him expatiate upon the value, importance, and patriotic bearing of this employment, and to listen to all his technical lore touching the mystery of horse-craft." As John Minor Botts entrusted the care and training of his horses to his slave Manuel, so Meriwether depended on "a pragmatical old negro, named Carey, who, in his reverence for the occupation, is the perfect shadow of his master. He and Frank hold grave and momentous consultations upon the affairs of the stable, in such a sagacious strain of equal debate, that it would puzzle a spectator to tell which was the leading member in the council." Meriwether shows Littleton his herds of "blooded colts, which, it is not vanity to affirm, are of the finest breed in Virginia; and when I say that,—it is equivalent to telling you that there is nothing better in the world. . . . I have nothing better to show you

THIRD DAY'S RACE,
OVER THE
Tree-Hill Course.

Jockey Club Purse, $1000....Four Mile Heats.
ENTRIES.

William R. Johnson enters ch. h. Havoc, by Sir Charles, 4 years old, weight 100 lbs. Dress, blue jacket and blue cap.
John M. Botts enters br. m. Mischief, by Virginian, 4 years old, weight 97 lbs. Dress, orange jacket and black cap.
William Wynn enters b. m. Kate Kearney, by Sir Archie, 5 years old, weight 107 lbs. Dress, red jacket and red cap.
Hector Davis enters b. m. Sally Hornet, by Sir Charles, 4 years old, weight 97 lbs. Dress, yellow jacket and blue cap.

J. M. SELDEN,
Proprietor.

Thursday, April 29th, 1830.

3.52 Third day's race, over the Tree-Hill course. Jockey Club purse $1000, four mile heats. Entries . . . *(Henrico County), broadside, 1830, 9 x 12 in., Virginia Historical Society*

at Swallow Barn. You see, on yonder meadow, some of the most unquestioned nobility of Virginia. Not a hoof stays on that pasture, that is not warmed by as pure blood as belongs to any potentate in the world." Carey adds, "I call them my children, master Littleton," and he explains that almost all are descended from old Diomed, one of whose sons was the celebrated racehorse Sir Archy. Diomed won the Derby in England and "is as famous amongst us, almost, as Christopher Columbus" in that he "founded a new empire here." As was perhaps the case with many northern readers, Meriwether's discussion of "points of symmetry" is "lost" on the visitor, as is the discussion of equine genealogy, which "might as profitably have been delivered in Greek." But Littleton concedes what Troye suggests: "in the movements of these quadrupeds [there was] a charm that I could not fail to recognize."[132]

The importance of breeding to the turfman is made clear by the frequent appearance in antebellum Virginia of broadsides and notices in newspapers that advertised blooded horses for stud. For example, in 1829 in Fauquier County, the availability of the horse Contention is announced (fig. 3.51). His potential value as a sire was measured by his pedigree, which is described at great length, and by his successful "performances on the turf," which are then enumerated in similar detail. Such races, which were held with some frequency in antebellum Virginia, were also advertised on broadsides. Figure 3.52 gives notice of a contest in Henrico County in 1830 that offered the huge purse of $1,000. Four leading turfmen, including Botts, provided the entries; one of the horses was sired by Sir Archy.

The perceived relationship of bloodlines to the creation of both fine horses and fine people has a long his-

tory in Virginia. This belief in the power of pedigree survived well into the twentieth century, and some would hold that it has not been completely abandoned to this day. To choose a well-known example, in 1934 Douglas Southall Freeman explained Robert E. Lee's remarkable character in these terms: "Back to Richard [Lee] the immigrant, . . . there is not one instance in which a direct progenitor of Lee mated with a woman of blood and of station below his own. . . . If blood means anything, he was entitled to be what he fundamentally was, a gentleman."[133] While bloodlines are not always foolproof, in horses or in people, there was a real sense during the antebellum period among those who could trace their lineage back to the colonial period that they were better suited for leadership because of their ancestry than were newcomers or the nouveau riche.

The breeding and racing of fine horses was a diversion and a challenge for the wealthiest Virginians, who managed to preserve their fortunes in an environment that was generally unfriendly to the old agrarian way of life. The soil in the east was not producing as it had for their forefathers, and neither the Potomac nor the James had become great corridors for merchandise. For those heirs who wanted to become country squires in their own right, for those of the middle class who aspired to the lifestyles of the great landed families, or for those who simply wanted to make a living on the land, the move was clear. The West and South seemed ready to provide opportunities that were no longer available in the Tidewater or Piedmont. These areas would be colonized by multitudes from Old Virginia, who in some cases would attempt to recreate what they could of the good old days.

"Westward Ho!": The Old Ways Beyond the Tidewater

By early in the nineteenth century, the Tidewater way of life had been exported across the Blue Ridge to the state's western counties, and to the new states and territories beyond. The emigrants from Virginia took with them not only their prized possessions, but often the styles of architecture that had defined the landscape back home as well. They also brought along a positive, at times arrogant, attitude that was shaped by their pride in their heritage. In *Away, I'm Bound Away: Virginia and the Westward Movement*, David Hackett Fischer and James C. Kelly examine the accomplishments of these figures who migrated outside the state; their successes generally served to enhance the mystique of the place from whence they came.[134] Although Virginia's shortcomings had spurred the exodus, the Old Dominion was awarded the credit for a stupendous achievement, the settling of a large portion of America. James Kirke Paulding wrote of Virginians in

3.53 *Lefevre James Cranstone*, Rippon [Ripon] Hall, York River, Va., *1860, watercolor, 6 x 11¾ in., Virginia Historical Society, bequest of Paul Mellon*

3.54 *Edward Beyer*, Bellevue, The Lewis Homestead, Salem, Virginia, *1855, oil on canvas, 38 x 50 in., private collection*

Kentucky in *Westward Ho!* (1832); Michael Chevalier wrote in 1838 that "Virginia, after having settled her western part . . . has sent forth to the Gulf of Mexico those numerous swarms that have invaded the southwest."[135] The matter of how she "settled her western part" is what concerns us here.

In *Letters from South* (1817), Paulding describes a "snug little rivalry [that] is beginning to bud vigorously in Virginia" between the populations east and west of the Blue Ridge. This is not unusual, he points out. It was happening in "all the considerable states, to the south of New-York inclusive." The result, however, might be surprising; because "the west is generally the most extensive, as well as fruitful, it is gradually getting the upper hand of the other, and removing the seat of power farther into the interior." In Virginia such forces would prompt the calling of the state convention in 1829. Paulding explains that the westerners in the Old Dominion "call those east of the mountain *Tuckahoes*, and their country Old Virginia. They themselves are the *Cohees*, and their country New Virginia."[136] The author, of course, had oversimplified the settlement pattern of the Valley, where Anglo-Virginians had been co-existing with other ethnic groups for a century. The old families of the East, however, under pressure from northern industrialism and abolitionism and eager to reassert a regional identity, soon reimagined the entire state to be Old Virginia and attempted to recall the pastoral ideal when they moved to or even simply visited the pristine lands in the western counties.

As the old ways were carried beyond the Tidewater they were revitalized by the bountiful landscape of the Valley. In 1760 Andrew Burnaby had described the Shenandoah as having "the most delightful climate, and richest soil imaginable."[137] Much of the landscape of western Virginia was thought to be idyllic, as William Gilmore Simms noted in 1854 when he characterized the Valley of the Shenandoah as the "most perfect idea of Arcadia. . . . Here the farmer may become the poet."[138] The small size of the slave population also made the western counties appealing to some observers; Brissot de Warville wrote in 1797 that "you see free labor introduced there in a part of Virginia, in that part bordered by the beautiful river Shenandoah. In travelling here, you will think yourself in Pennsylvania."[139]

Although the population in the Shenandoah Valley was but fifteen percent enslaved, eastern traditionalists recognized that the plantation lifestyle could not be successfully perpetuated west of the Blue Ridge without this institution.[140] Scenes painted at mid-century by two European visitors, Lefevre Cranstone and Edward Beyer, manifest the differences between the exhausted east and the fertile west. Cranstone, in a view of the Rippon Hall plantation on the York River (fig. 3.53), shows the Tidewater to still offer a pastoral beauty, but the setting is notably

quiet and empty. The decline in agricultural productivity is evident. Once the plantation of a prominent statesman, Edmund Jenings, who had served as attorney general, president of the Governor's Council, and twice lieutenant governor of the colony, Rippon Hall in 1850 was no longer a thriving tobacco producer. The fields are still well cared for, but this is hardly a scene of intense farm activity.[141] In Beyer's view of the agricultural operation at Bellevue, the Lewis homestead west of the Blue Ridge (near modern Roanoke) that was designed to resembled a Tidewater plantation, slaves are pictured prominently, busily at work in what are highly productive fields (fig. 3.54). This productivity explains how, despite the undeniable decline of farming in the Tidewater, antebellum Virginia enjoyed something of an agricultural revival, holding its own as the leading agricultural state in the South and positioned among the leaders in the nation in producing corn and wheat.[142] Cultivation of the latter is pictured at Bellevue, which would then be sent to feed the giant flour mills in Richmond.

In the far distance of the painting of Bellevue we see the market town of Salem, which Colonel Lewis had founded. There neighboring planters sold their produce and purchased hard and soft goods, equipment, seed, and feed. When Thomas Jefferson envisioned a virtuous rural society for Virginia that would be free from the vices of the large European cities, he considered the market town to be integral to such an arcadia. In the antebellum era these centers did in fact spring up, in the Piedmont, the Valley, and beyond.[143] Beyer painted a series of Virginia market towns including Salem (fig. 3.55). These hamlets, and such operations as that at Bellevue, testified to the fact that Old Virginia, as it had been imagined by its founders, had experienced something of a rebirth in the far-flung new counties. And as goods moved toward the markets and processing centers of the East, many denizens of the coast and the North began to visit western Virginia for physical and psychological, rather than economic, replenishment.

In *Swallow Barn* Frank Meriwether "is not much of a traveller," but "towards autumn, it is his custom to journey over the mountain to the Springs." This he is "obliged to do to avoid the unhealthy season in the tide-water region."[144] Virginia's world-famous mineral and thermal springs were in fact valued for both their perceived medicinal worth and as a social setting. As early as 1787 Luigi Castiglioni wrote that "In lower Virginia the ladies, since they do not in general get much exercise . . . they go to places well known for mineral waters, where, spending their nights at gambling and dancing, they insist upon living methodically as convalescents."[145] In 1817 Paulding found Berkeley Springs (fig. 3.56) to be "a famous place, where the beau monde resort from all the country around." When he arrived "at least a hundred gay people

3.55 *Above, top* Edward Beyer, Churches, Blacksmith Shop, and College: A View of Salem of Virginia in 1855, *oil on canvas, 29 x 48 in., Virginia Historical Society, gift of Lora Robins, E. Claiborne Robins, Jr., Bruce C. Gottwald, Paul Mellon, D. Tennant Bryant, Henry F. Stern, Mrs. E. Schneider, and Thomas Towers.*

3.56 *Above* J. E. Magruder, Berkeley Springs Schottisch (Baltimore, 1857), *sheet music, Virginia Historical Society*

of both sexes were rambling among the trees, just in the twilight of a mild summer evening . . . . My philosophy shook in the wind at the view of so many fair damsels, every one of whom, dressed in white, put me in mind of white fringe upon a green petticoat." Paulding, a well-traveled New Yorker, reported that these springs were as "fashionable . . . as any I have ever visited," including "Long-Branch [New Jersey]". At Berkeley "You meet with every distinct variety among the belles and beaux," the types of which he then went on to enumerate. Further, there was "a pleasant drawing-room" at Berkeley, and "Every night or two there is a ball, in a very splendid room appropriated to that purpose." Also, there are "many pleasant rides on horseback in its neighbourhood." Paulding jested that such establishments are "set apart for people who don't know what to do with themselves."[146]

To be so famous and at so early a date (1816), Berkeley Springs had to be a special place. Situated near the Potomac River, about one hundred miles northwest of the nation's capital, Berkeley lies almost in Maryland, and Pennsylvania is but a short distance away. The springs were given to the people of Virginia in 1756 by Lord Fairfax, who owned the land as part of his Northern Neck Proprietary. The town that was founded in 1776 was ambitiously entitled Bath after the renowned watering spot in England. (The official name of the town is still Bath.) The proximity to the river and to these populous states

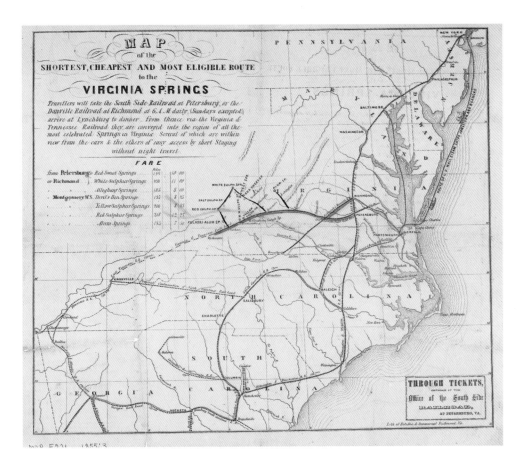

3.57 Map of the springs, *picturing routes from Charleston, S.C. and New York, and the "cheapest fares," 1855, Virginia Historical Society*

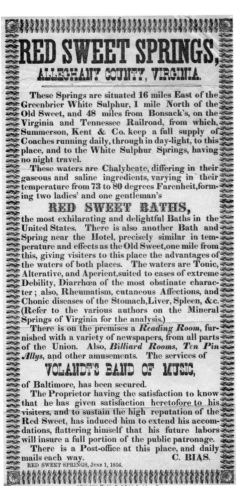

3.58 Red Sweet Springs, Alleghany County, Virginia, *1856, broadside, Virginia Historical Society*

had almost guaranteed the success of Berkeley once this idyllic spot was discovered.

While their remoteness had caused many antebellum springs to fail, by the 1850s travel to the western resorts had become feasible from almost anywhere on the east coast. A guide of 1849 states, "There are now numerous routes and modes of conveyance to these celebrated Springs, all of which have been, within a few years, greatly improved."[147] A map of 1855 (fig. 3.57) shows the routes to be taken from as far away as New York and South Carolina. By the end of the decade, the springs had become meeting places for the high society of the nation. In 1856 Red Sweet Springs was advertised as only "48 miles from . . . the Virginia and Tennessee Railroad" and easily accessible by "a full supply of Coaches running daily, through in day-light" (fig. 3.58). By 1857 the railroad from the east had extended past Lexington to the village of Goshen, within only a few dozen miles of many of the springs.[148]

In response to the increase in visitation, the complexes at the various springs began to be developed with much more thought to their architectural merit than had previous models. Buildings with the large drawing rooms and ball rooms that Paulding had said "would add infinitely to the pleasures of these fashionable resorts" were soon constructed.[149] The architecture at the springs tended to replicate that of an Old Virginia plantation. Many, including Berkeley Springs and Fauquier White Sulphur Springs (fig. 3.59), followed Mount Vernon in design by featuring a giant piazza. They were given as well other elements of classical detailing around doors, win-

3.59 *Edward Beyer,* Fauquier White Sulphur Springs, *from the*
Album of Virginia, *1858, lithograph, 11¹/₄ x 17 in., Virginia Historical Society*

3.60 *Edward Beyer,* Greenbrier White Sulphur Springs, *1853,
oil on canvas, 26 x 50 in., The Greenbrier, White Sulphur Springs*

THE

WHITE SULPHUR SPRINGS,

GREENBRIER COUNTY,

VIRGINIA;

THEIR LOCALITY,

AND THE

VARIOUS ROUTES BY WHICH THEY ARE REACHED;

CHARACTER AND EXTENT OF THEIR ACCOMMODATIONS,

WITH THE

ANALYSES OF THEIR WATERS,

THE

DISEASES TO WHICH THEY ARE APPLICABLE.

WITH SOME ACCOUNT OF

SOCIETY AND ITS AMUSEMENTS AT THE SPRINGS.

PHILADELPHIA:
J. B. LIPPINCOTT & CO.
1860.

3.61 *Above Edward Beyer,* White Sulphur Springs, Greenbrier County, *from the* Album of Virginia, *1858, lithograph, 11 1/8 x 19 1/8 in., Virginia Historical Society*

3.62 *Left* The White Sulphur Springs, Greenbrier County, Virginia; their locality, and the various routes by which they are reached; character and extent of their accommodations, with the analyses of their waters, the diseases to which they are applicable; with some account of society and its amusements at the Springs *(Philadelphia, 1860), Virginia Historical Society*

dows, and eaves that were taken directly from domestic architecture. The pavilions built around the actual spring sites were often small classical temples. It was then logical to arrange the buildings of such a complex in the manner of those of a plantation, with a main hall at the center and support structures positioned before it to form a forecourt. The scale was increased, but the image of most of these springs could be easily associated by contemporary viewers with the plantation tradition.

White Sulphur was the "favorite" of the Virginia springs. According to Appleton's travel guides that were published at mid-century, "the most celebrated and most generally visited are the White Sulphur Springs. . . . These are to the South what the Saratoga Springs are to the North. Thousands annually resort to them, either in

search of recreation and amusement, or to enjoy the benefit of their waters."[150] Edward Beyer pictured White Sulphur on two occasions, before and after a major building program begun on the eve of the war (figs. 3.60 and 3.61). In his painting of "the White" rendered in 1853, the artist presents the scene described by *Appleton's* four years later: "The cottages are built of wood, brick, and of logs, one story high; and, altogether, the social arrangement and spirit here, as at all the surrounding Springs, has a pleasant, quiet, home sentiment, very much more desirable than the metropolitan temper of more accessible and more thronged resorts." To achieve a more "metropolitan temper," as well as to more closely recall the ideal of plantation architecture, were the purposes of the improvements that are described in Beyer's *Album of Virginia*: "Many of the cabins have been removed, and magnificent buildings and handsome cottages have been erected in their stead." The new, sizeable hotel that is pictured in the later scene was celebrated as "the largest in the mountains." Its first floor was given over to the sorts of spaces that Paulding had found lacking at the Virginia springs a half-century earlier— "reception rooms, a dining room sufficient in dimensions to seat 1,000 persons, [and] a ball room sixty feet square."[151] A Philadelphia publication of 1860 (fig. 3.62) that advertises the improved resort is evidence of the popularity of White Sulphur at a pivotal moment in Virginia's history.

Servants, mostly slaves, and the services that they provided, were as abundant at the Virginia spas as on the plantations; their presence in fact had much to do with

3.63 *Christian Mayr,*
Kitchen Ball, *1838, oil*
on canvas, 24 x 29½ in.,
North Carolina Museum
of Art

the attraction of these resorts. In a painting of 1838 they are shown to be as contented as the people whom they serve (fig. 3.63). Christian Mayr, a German emigrant to America, passed through the region in that year and at White Sulphur encountered a scene of well-dressed and refined African Americans that he reimagined on canvas. These servants—some of whom may have been free blacks—are engaged in joyous yet dignified revelry. According to Mayr, lavish entertainment and graceful living extend even into the domestic population in western Virginia. Visitors to White Sulphur were no doubt encouraged to fantasize about the contentment of the servants, who saw to it that every desire of their guests was fulfilled.

By the eve of the Civil War, the springs had become outposts in an arcadian wilderness where flourished the best of the old ways of the Anglo-Virginian plantations. The lifestyle was aristocratic, and the rural setting allowed for the contemplation of the virtues of the pastoral landscape between social engagements. As much as the stereotypical plantation house upon which many of them were modeled, the springs by mid-century had come to symbolize the glories and in some cases the excesses of Old Virginia.

Recollections of Virginia's Heritage

As the Old Dominion came under attack, memories of the greatest heroes of the state's colonial past would

increasingly be invoked in defense. Although the lifestyle of the agrarian plantation was the idea most closely associated with the term Old Virginia, during the prewar years remembrances of the region's Founding Fathers retained their potency as a part of the state's legacy. Both George Washington, who lived the life of an aristocrat on a Tidewater plantation, and Patrick Henry, who proclaimed himself to be a man of the people, served as inspirations for their antebellum heirs.

The death in 1799 of George Washington, Virginia's most famous and accomplished son, had elicited a national outpouring of sentiment that was without precedent: some 1,800 memorial services were held in almost 200 localities; the general's name was given to towns, counties, and natural landmarks; and the first of literally hundreds of biographical studies were published.[152] In 1802, in the best known of the prints issued after his death, John James Barralet depicted an apotheosis, with angels assisting in Washington's journey to heaven (fig. 3.64). In his popular biography Mason Locke Weems, following Barralet, imagined that "Swift on angels' wings the brightening saint ascended." He opened his *Life of Washington* with the claim that the renown of "Columbia's first and greatest Son" was so great that it could "awaken the sigh even of Bonaparte." The parson relates how Napoleon reportedly said to American travelers, "The measure of his fame is full—Posterity shall talk of him with reverence as the founder of a great empire,

112

3.64 *John James Barralet,* Commemoration of Washington, *1802, stipple engraving, 25³/₄ x 19¹/₄ in, National Museum of American History*

the series of images about his life that were conceived at mid-century by Junius Brutus Stearns. The popular engravings that were derived by Stearns from these paintings mark a high point in the cult of the general. The artist re-created four episodes that he thought representative of a well-spent public and private life: Washington is shown as a captain during the French and Indian War at the Battle of Monongahela, at his wedding, as a planter, and as heroic even on his deathbed. In *Washington as a Farmer at Mount Vernon* (fig. 3.67), the general is pictured on his daily rounds, inspecting the agricultural operation of his plantation. The mansion house is to the rear; Washington confers with an overseer, slaves take a break from the harvesting of wheat, and Martha Washington's grandchildren, Nelly and Washington Custis, share in this scene of rural bliss. In his effort to present the greatest American in the private role that he so enjoyed, Stearns painted a quintessential image of the Virginian's achievement of the pastoral ideal.[155] He pictures Washington as the premier exemplar of the state's hereditary aristocracy, which

3.65 *Horatio Greenough,* George Washington, *1832-41, marble, National Museum of American Art, Smithsonian Institution, transfer from the U. S. Capitol*

when my name shall be lost in the vortex of Revolutions!"[153] John Marshall, another great Virginian, who in 1804-07 drafted the biography that was authorized by Washington's family, called his subject one of "those exalted characters which are produced in every age," "the favourite son of America," and a man whose history "is so much that of his country" that the two are inseparable.[154]

Washington would continue to be honored throughout the antebellum period. In 1832, the centennial of the general's birth, Congress awarded the most sought after commission of the era to the sculptor Horatio Greenough to create a new likeness of the general for display in the city that had been named after him. This American artist, who was resident in Italy and knew the great sculptures of antiquity, reinvented the Father of his Country as a bare-chested Greek god, the all powerful Zeus (fig. 3.65). This remarkable effort was not well received. In 1834 John Gadsby Chapman painted sites in Virginia associated with Washington's life. And on the eve of the Civil War Richmond school girls were producing needlework pictures that celebrated the general; Nora T. Mahoney's *General Washington at Trenton* (fig. 3.66) is derived from a print after John Trumbull's much earlier (1792) painting of the subject.

The national interest in Washington during the antebellum period was nowhere better demonstrated than in

113

3.66 *Below Nora T. Mahoney, after John Trumbull,* General Washington at Trenton, *1860, needlework, 48 x 38½ in., reverse-glass inscription, "St. Joseph's Academy, Nora T. Mahoney, Richmond, Va., 1860," Virginia Historical Society*

3.67 *Right Junius Brutus Stearns,* Washington as a Farmer at Mount Vernon, *1851, oil on canvas, 37½ x 54 in., Virginia Museum of Fine Arts, Richmond, gift of Edgar William and Bernice Chrysler Garbisch*

was so much admired by contemporary political thinkers like Michael Chevalier and Francis Grund. The artist also manages to diffuse somewhat the issue of Washington's having been a slaveholder, in that he is shown to take good care of all of those in his charge. He is still serious—there is no hint of a smile on his stoic countenance—but neither is there the suggestion that mistreatment would ever be allowed by the general. He is paternal to all on his estate, as he was to all of his countrymen.

The death of Patrick Henry earlier in 1799 had elicited a similar outpouring of reverence. One eulogist declared that Henry's example will be emulated "as long as our rivers flow and mountains stand" (fig. 3.68).[156] The first biography of Henry, which was written in 1817 by an admiring attorney general of the United States, mixed facts with unsubstantiated tradition and excessive praise to create a mythology about the patriot akin to Parson Weems's treatment of the Father of his Country (fig. 3.69). In his *Sketches of the Life and Character of Patrick Henry*, William Wirt set Henry apart from nearly all of his contemporaries and successors, paraphrasing Hamlet's description of his father in the process: "In a word, he was one of those perfect prodigies of Nature, of whom very few have been produced since the foundations of the earth were laid; and of *him* may it be said, as truly as of any one that ever existed:—'He was a man, take him all in all, *We ne'er shall look upon his like again.'*"[157] For use as the frontispiece of Wirt's book, Thomas Sully created a posthumous image that also served to meet a growing interest in Henry's memory (fig. 3.70). Sully's source was a miniature painting taken during Henry's life in 1795 by the artist's brother Lawrence. The patriot is shown in the scar-

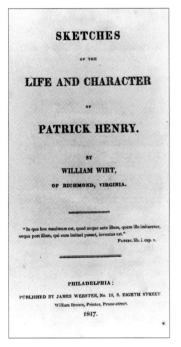

3.68 **Above** *Unidentified author*, Eulogy for Patrick Henry, *ca. 1799, Lee Family Papers, Virginia Historical Society*

3.69 **Below, left** *William Wirt*, Sketches of the Life and Character of Patrick Henry *(Philadelphia, 1817), Virginia Historical Society*

3.70 **Left** *Thomas Sully*, Patrick Henry, *1851 (replica of the 1815 painting that was frontispiece for Wirt's biography of Henry), oil on canvas, 30 x 24³/₄ in., Virginia Historical Society, gift from the artist*

3.71 **Right** *George Cooke,* Patrick Henry Arguing the Parson's Cause at the Hanover County Courthouse, *ca. 1834, oil on canvas, 28 x 36 in., Virginia Historical Society*

let cloak and black clothes for which he became famous, but gone is the ungainly frontier appearance that had shocked aristocrats in Williamsburg on Henry's first arrival there. To create a handsome figure, one more amiable than the Henry who was said to have "never uttered or laughed at a joke," Sully had taken some liberties with the earlier, graver image.

During the 1830s, George Cooke, a Maryland artist who had married into a Richmond family, painted *Patrick Henry Arguing the Parson's Cause at the Hanover County Courthouse* (fig. 3.71), which was based on the incident in which Henry held forth on the subject of King George III's interference concerning the salary set by the Virginia legislature for state-supported ministers. Of

3.72 *John Gadsby Chapman,* Ruins of Jamestown, Virginia, America, *1834, oil on board, 11 x 14 in., Virginia Historical Society*

Henry's three most famous speeches—the "parson's cause," his protest of the Stamp Act, and his call for liberty—this was the most particularly Virginian in scope. In this harangue, Henry argued against the power of the king to encroach on Virginia's rights; in 1830 these same rights seemed threatened by the American North. Henry would continue to be viewed nationally as a crucial spokesman for freedom. In the 1850s the Philadelphia artist Peter Rothermel painted a monumental canvas of *Patrick Henry in the House of Burgesses of Virginia, Delivering His Celebrated Speech against the Stamp Act,* which is now owned by the Patrick Henry Memorial Foundation of Brookneal, Virginia. Henry's veneration in his home state was incalculable, second only to that of Washington. The sculptor Thomas Crawford's grand equestrian *Washington Monument* in Richmond's Capitol Square (begun 1849) features Henry prominently, although one tier below the general.

It was easy for Virginians to celebrate the aristocratic Golden Age that had produced the Founding Fathers. The idea of Old Virginia as demarcating the era of the

Revolution, as well as its continuing use to differentiate the state from its contemporary political opponents, maintained currency throughout the antebellum era. The one period that had escaped public appreciation was the oldest Virginia, the era of the foundings, which, even though its marquee players, Pocahontas and Captain John Smith, had remained popular, had largely slid from the national consciousness. Some commentators in the antebellum era mentioned Jamestown, but without recognizing its true significance as the birthplace of the nation.

George Tucker in *Letters from Virginia* (1816) provided a romantic narrative about Jamestown that verbally anticipates John Gadsby Chapman's 1834 painting of the site (fig. 3.72). Tucker claimed to be interested in "scenes of the state's history," but he admittedly saw these only "with the eyes of a patriotic lover":

> A thousand ideas and emotions, too rapid to be remembered or described, rushed thro' my mind in an instant. I thought upon [John] Smith. . . . I thought upon Pocahontas. . . .

Two or three old houses, the ruin of an old steeple, a church yard, and faint marks of rude fortifications, are now the only memorials of its former inhabitants, amply sufficient however to consecrate the scene, and endear it to fancy and the heart. It was, indeed, with a sort of religious awe, that I drew near to these venerable relicks of antiquity, now sinking into the dust. The old steeple, which stands facing the beautiful expanse of water to the West, drew my eyes to it as by a charm. There it rises in the midst of sycamores and poplars, which have sprung up around it; covered on its north side, even to its summit, with a fanciful wild running vine of ivy and smilax. . . . It was, indeed, a most affecting spectacle for my heart, to see the ancient settlers of this town, of all ranks and conditions in life. . . . all lying together on a level, and mingling their dust in one common mass. O! How frivolous are all the vain pursuits of wealth, honour and pleasure, by which their lives were probably tormented![158]

In a similar vein, at the opening of *Swallow Barn* when Mark Littleton arrives in the state, he has "eagerness to get a peep at Jamestown, with all my effervescence of romance kindled up by the renown of the unmatchable Smith."[159]

The adventures of John Smith and Pocahontas provided the sort of imaginative escape that audiences that thrilled by the romances of Sir Walter Scott so enjoyed. In 1836–40 Chapman painted a giant mural of *The Baptism of Pocahontas* for the rotunda of the U.S. Capitol (fig. 3.73).

3.73 Above, top John Gadsby Chapman, The Baptism of Pocahontas, *1836-40, oil on canvas, 144 x 216 in., U. S. Capitol Rotunda, courtesy of the Architect of the Capitol*

3.74 Above Thomas Sinclair, Captain Smith Rescued by Pocahontas, *1841, lithograph, 11 x 12 in., published in James Wimer, Events of Indian History, 1841, Library of Virginia*

In this same period, her well-known rescue of Smith was rendered by Thomas Sinclair, who makes Smith a young, handsome man, puts him in nineteenth-century attire, and, as was traditional, makes Pocahontas somewhat more Caucasian than the other Indians in the picture (3.74). The New England born artist Edwin White would

117

3.75 *Edwin White,* Pocahontas Informing John Smith of A Conspiracy of the Indians, *1850s, oil on canvas, 44 x 36 in., Mr. and Mrs. William Maury Hill*

later paint the second, lesser-known of her rescues of Smith, her warning in 1609 of her father's plans to kill him at dinner (fig. 3.75). White had studied in Düsseldorf where the vogue was to replicate the style of Rembrandt's paintings of biblical scenes by using chiaroscuro, the dramatic contrast of light and dark. To this artist the Smith/Pocahontas story was a national legacy that was worthy to be depicted in a similar style.[160]

The interest in the colonial era in Virginia did not stop at the Atlantic. At the end of the 1850s, one of England's premier novelists, William Makepeace Thackeray, published in twenty-four serial numbers *The Virginians; A Tale of the Last Century*, which is set in London and colonial Virginia in the years between the French and Indian War and the Revolution (fig. 3.76). In this tale, George and Henry Warrington of Castlewood in Virginia are heirs to Colonel Henry Esmond of England; "to distinguish themselves from other personages" of the family they are known as "the Virginians." These "natives of America and children of the Old Dominion," Thackeray writes, "found themselves engaged on different sides in the quarrel [of the Revolution], coming together peaceably at the conclusion."[161] But the story of *The Virginians* is more about the earlier years, when George Warrington served with Braddock at Monongahela and Harry with Wolfe at Quebec. Crucial to this com-

plicated tale, and the vehicle for much of Thackeray's brand of cultural criticism, is the fact that the twin brothers "both passed much time in Europe." Harry, who appears to be heir to the family's Virginia property when George is thought lost in the French war, sinks into a life of dissipation in London, only to be rescued by his brother who had in fact survived. As the novelist examines the rakish, often unprincipled society of eighteenth-century London, the society of Old Virginia is shown to have a degree of appeal.

Such renditions of Virginia's early history, whether concerned with the founding, the late-colonial period, or the revolution, served as a means to divert attention from the problems that antebellum Virginians faced in the present. The great figures could be imaginatively resurrected, and their deeds rehashed, when the losses of wealth, status, and political influence became intolerable. To aid in this process, and to preserve the greatness of the past for the perusal of the future, the Virginia Historical Society was founded in 1831 to collect the documents and objects that recorded the region's history. Prominent Virginians remembered their great heritage by making gifts to the fledgling institution. For instance, John Page of Williamsburg donated an etymological manuscript in Greek and Latin of part of Homer's *Iliad* that was kept by the eminent jurist George Wythe; the Society's president, Chief Justice John Marshall, provided an inscribed copy of his biography of Washington; and Edmund Ruffin presented an engraved map of the investment of Yorktown (page 54, fig. 2.22).

One of the most important objects to come into the new collection was a copy of "Light-Horse Harry" Lee's funeral oration following the death of George Washington, which was published in 1800 (fig. 3.77). Of the many eulogies delivered in memory of Washington, the oration presented in Congress by Henry Lee is the best remembered, perhaps because of the simplicity of his evaluation of the general and president as "first in war, first in peace, and first in the hearts of his countrymen." In 1800, Lee, a distinguished veteran of the Revolutionary War and a former governor of Virginia, had won election to Congress from Fairfax County. His eulogy, because it was written by one great Virginian to honor another, became a source of pride to their antebellum posterity.

The copy of the Washington eulogy that is presented here is unique. Henry Lee was the father of Robert E. Lee, the future Confederate general, who as a young man owned this volume and boldly placed his signature on its front cover. By signing this book the son made it his own, and through his illustrious life, much of which was modeled on that of Washington, transformed it into an object worthy of veneration. Like his father's commander, Robert E. Lee led the defense of his native region against those who invaded it, a decision that would lead to com-

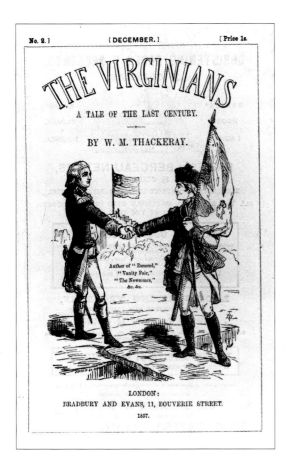

mendation is his own day and criticism in our own. To Virginians, this book will forever serve as a link between the state's greatest sons, and as a reminder of how the past can have a powerful influence on the future.

Fifteen years after its founding, when the Virginia Historical Society was still struggling to survive, a supporter justified its mission to a Richmond newspaper. In so speaking, he identified the importance of recollecting Virginia's history:

> Was there ever yet a Romeo who was indifferent to the history of his Juliet? A lock of hair, a flower which once dark[en]ed her bosom or a scrap of writing traced by her fingers, are invested with a secret charm for the lover. To a true Virginian, nothing Virginian can be uninteresting. He will find a melancholy charm in the mossy tombstone, the dilapidated church, the deserted seat, the patriarchal oaks. Many a scene barren to others, to him teems with associations, and by a sort of necromantic spell, he recalls to life the shadowy forms of those departed worthies, whose genius and virtues have made us proud to say "I, too, am a Virginian."[162]

As the state declined in national prominence and was confronted by internal and external challenges, residents needed to find touchstones that would remind them that they had a past to be proud of and a present worth defending. Old Virginia in its colonial guise provided an imaginative harbor from abolitionists and crop failures, and from tariffs and treacherous Yankee traders. It hearkened back both to a time of prominence for the state, and a time when the joys of the rural plantation life had yet to be undermined. When the decision would be made to fight, it would not be to defend the state's burgeoning industries. As much as for any other reason, the war would come because the land, the ultimate source of Virginia's wealth and pride, would be threatened. Ironically, it would be the war that would end the plantation era forever.

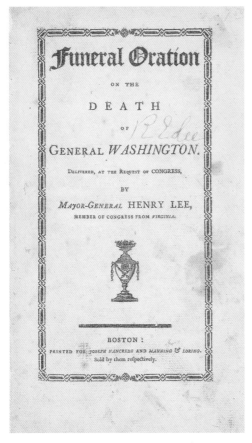

3.76 Above, top *William Makepeace Thackeray,* The Virginians; A Tale of the Last Century *(London, 1857-59), Virginia Historical Society*

3.77 Above *Henry "Light-Horse Harry" Lee,* Funeral Oration on the Death of General Washington *(Boston, 1800), Virginia Historical Society, formerly owned by Robert E. Lee*

4.1 *William Edward West,* Robert E. Lee in the Dress Uniform of
a Lieutenant of Engineers, *1838, oil on canvas, 30 x 25 in., Washington and Lee University*

IV. The Resurgence of the Old Order

Douglas Southall Freeman, his Pulitzer prize-winning biographer, states that in all matters in which Robert E. Lee expressed himself, he was regarded by southerners as the final authority.[1] Freeman was speaking, of course, of the famed Confederate commander, Lee, after 1861. But the younger man, perhaps the most outstanding product of antebellum Virginia, can also serve as a prewar representative of the region, in part because he thought longer and harder than did many of his contemporaries about the pressing issues of the day. In 1838, when he posed for the portraitist William Edward West (fig. 4.1), Lee was a handsome, charismatic young officer, who had the bulk of his promising career in front of him. West manages to capture an innate military nature; at age thirty-one Lee was a lieutenant of engineers who was soon to be promoted to captain. He was accomplished in his chosen profession as an officer in the Army of the United States, with a deportment that even at this early date speaks as much of his character as of his attainments.

Lee took pride in his Virginia lineage; his father's family had long been distinguished in Westmoreland County. Robert Edward Lee had been born in 1807 at Stratford Hall, the colonial mansion of Thomas Lee, once acting governor and a member of the governor's council. Robert's mother, Ann Hill Lee, was a Carter from a no less distinguished seat, Shirley plantation in Charles City County. Lee was firmly linked to George Washington not only because of "Light-Horse Harry" Lee's well-known military and political activities, but also through marriage. Robert E. Lee's wife was Mary Randolph Custis, the only daughter of George Washington Parke Custis, the grandson of Martha Washington. Freeman has written that his "association with Custis and with the Washington family traditions at 'Arlington' [the Custis home] made his father's old commander Lee's ideal, whom he seems consciously to have emulated in his bearing and in his conception of duty."[2]

By the advent of the Civil War, Lee in many ways personified all that was noble and much that was troubling about the aristocracy of Old Virginia. This slaveholder by inheritance held well-considered opinions about that subject, and he was able to articulate clearly the viewpoint of many of the gentry of his native state. Lee owned some half-dozen slaves, who probably came to him from his wife's father, G. W. P. Custis. He advocated gradual emancipation, and in fact released to Liberia several of his servants who chose to go there.[3] In 1856, after reading a newspaper account, Lee wrote to his wife that President Franklin Pierce had stated to Congress his opposition to "the Systematic & progressive efforts of certain people in the North, to interfere with & change the domestic institutions of the South" (fig. 4.2).[4] Stationed with the army at Fort Brown, Texas, Lee offered a reaction to Pierce's speech and to the mounting sectionalist controversy over slavery. He admitted to the evils in the slave system, but as a Virginian caught in the middle of this problematic situation, his criticism was tempered.

Lee believed slavery to be "a moral & political evil in any Country," one that oppressed owners and slaves alike, but it was a problem to be solved not by man but by God. In this way he rejected the dogma-based arguments of the abolitionists. Today his views about racial inequality, which he elaborated here to his wife, seem less than enlightened:

> I think it . . . a greater evil to the white than to the black race, & while my feelings are strongly enlisted in behalf of the latter, my sympathies are more strong for the former. The blacks are immeasurably better off here than in Africa, morally, socially & physically. The painful discipline they are undergoing is necessary for their instruction as a race, & I hope will prepare & lead them to better things. How long their subjugation may be necessary is known & ordered by a wise, Merciful Providence. Their emancipation will sooner result from the mild & melting influence of Christianity, than the storms & tempests of fiery Controversy. This influence though slow is sure. . . . While we see the Course of the final abolition of human Slavery is onward, . . . we must leave the progress as well as the result in his hands who sees the end. . . . The abolitionist must know this. . . . Still I fear he will persevere in his evil Course. Is it not strange that the descendants of those pilgrim fathers who Crossed the Atlantic to preserve their own freedom of opinion, have always proved themselves intolerant of the Spiritual liberty of others?[5]

Lee's theological justification for slavery was a prevailing view. Freeman writes that "most religious people of Lee's class in the border states believed that slavery existed because God willed it and they thought it would end when God so ruled. The time and the means were not theirs to decide, conscious though they were of the ill-effects of Ne-

4.2 Robert E. Lee, Letter to Mary Lee, 27 December 1856, Virginia Historical Society

gro slavery on both races."[6] On the eve of the Civil War many southerners recognized that there were problems, both humanitarian and economic, caused by slavery, but at the same time they needed to rationalize the necessity of the institution. They had tired of the "evil" anti-slavery movement that was led by "the descendants of the pilgrim fathers," partly because it seemed an affront to their honor. Bertram Wyatt-Brown has written that "vindicating an intense if not fanatical sense of honor was uppermost in the minds of disunionists" who "argued that failure to answer the insult of Northern moral criticism and especially the election of an antislavery president [Lincoln] meant a loss of collective manhood and a feminization of the Southern spirit."[7] This sense of honor, of pride in one's family and one's accomplishments, should not be underestimated. As we have seen, honor was a vital component of the Old Virginia mentality. Such affronts, combined with their economic setbacks, had propelled the Virginia gentry of the mid-eighteenth century toward revolution. Their antebellum descendants, many of whom had deeply felt reservations about slavery, would not be moved by those who attacked their reputations under the guise of abolitionism. Secession and civil war, it seemed to many, were therefore inevitable.

On 18 April 1861 Lee was offered field command of the United States army. He declined, putting aside a highly promising career in favor of his allegiance to Virginia. Although he was loath to quit the national military that he had served with distinction since his graduation from West Point in 1829, and was anxious to see the Union preserved, Lee could not bear arms against his native state. He said as much in his personal letters of April 1861 and in his remarks when he accepted the appointment as major general of the military and naval forces of Virginia (fig. 4.3). In a ceremony at the Richmond Capitol, Lee was humble and devout, as George Washington

had been when given command of the Continental Army in 1775:

> Mr. President and Gentlemen of the Convention,—Profoundly impressed with the solemnity of the occasion, for which I must say I was not prepared, I accept the position assigned me by your partiality. I would have much preferred had your choice fallen on an abler man. Trusting in Almighty God, an approving conscience, and the aid of my fellow-citizens, I devote myself to the service of my native State, in whose behalf alone will I ever again draw my sword.[8]

To the president of the Virginia Convention of 1861, John Janney—who like Lee had been a unionist prior to the attack on Fort Sumter and Lincoln's call for troops—the connections between the new commander, George Washington, and the heritage of Old Virginia were obvious. The occasion of introducing Lee to the convention was an opportunity for Janney to elaborate:

> When the necessity became apparent of having a leader for our forces, all hearts and all eyes . . . turned to the old county of Westmoreland. We knew how prolific she had been in other days of heroes and statesmen. We knew she had given birth to the Father of his Country; to Richard Henry Lee, to Monroe, and last, though not least, to your own gallant father, and knew well, by your own deeds, that her productive power was not yet exhausted. . . . Sir, we have . . . expressed our conviction that you are at this day, among the living citizens of Virginia, 'first in war.' We pray God most fervently that . . . it will soon be said of you, that you are 'first in peace,' and when that time comes you will have earned the still prouder distinction of being 'first in the hearts of your countrymen.' I will close with one more re-

4.3 Robert E. Lee, Speech Delivered before the Virginia Convention of 1861, 23 April 1861, Virginia Historical Society

mark. When the Father of his Country made his last will and testament, he gave his swords to his nephews with an injunction that they should never be drawn from their scabbards, except in self-defense, or in defense of the rights and liberties of their country, and that, if drawn for the latter purpose, they should fall with them in their hands, rather than relinquish them. Yesterday, your mother, Virginia, placed her sword in your hand upon the implied condition that . . . you will draw it only in her defense, and that you will fall with it in your hand rather than that the object for which it was placed there shall fail.[9]

Lee was a Whig who had been devoted to the Union. The man who had commanded the troops at Harpers Ferry when they put down the uprising led by John Brown had no sympathy with the secessionist movement. His stand on that issue, however, would ultimately be decided by the question of to whom his first allegiance was due. The answer, Freeman writes, required no great mental disputation by the now middle-aged officer, because "the traditions of his family and its long association with Virginia" were what "instinctively determined [Lee] to cast in his lot with her."[10]

Robert E. Lee accepted the position of commander of the Virginia forces on 23 April 1861. Julia Tyler witnessed the convention that both voted for secession and selected the man who would defend the rights of southerners. Her comment at the time provides an indication of Lee's charisma: "Col. Lee, a splendid man every inch of him, is in command of the Virginia forces."[11] Photographers who recorded Lee's image in these years corroborated her assessment that the man cut a striking figure. It is easy to imagine from the photographs how Lee came to be revered as Douglas Southall Freeman's "finest figure" of the Confederacy and George Bagby's "last Virginia gentleman."[12]

In 1864 a Richmond photographer produced one of the best-known portraits of Lee (fig. 4.4). At the urging of several women then resident in the Confederate capital, Julian Vannerson photographed the general so that a young Virginia sculptor in Berlin, Edward Valentine, could create a statuette of the general from the image; copies of the sculpture would be sold in Liverpool to benefit disabled Confederate soldiers. Lee is posed proudly by Vannerson, in a full dress uniform that presents a splendid appearance. His left arm is brazenly cocked as in any number of colonial portraits, including the image of Daniel Parke at Arlington House that Lee knew well. (page 35, fig. 1.27). The general rests his hand on his sword in a manner that recalls the posturing with hand and cane in Houdon's famous sculpture of George Washington in the Richmond Capitol, just steps away from the room where three years earlier Lee had accepted the Virginia command. In this image Vannerson transformed

Lee from beloved general to saintly champion. He is a gentleman, to be sure, but he is more than that. The figure seems almost to be a man from some glorious era of the past. The pose, sword, and sash resemble those of a knight. This is an image of Freeman's "Southern [King] Arthur," the gallant chevalier who on the afternoon that he proposed marriage to his wife read to her and her mother from a romance by Sir Walter Scott.[13] Although in 1864 the outcome of the Civil War was all but decided, Vannerson's Lee seems as heroic as the Virginians who had won the Revolutionary War against long odds. This is a man who will be capable of restoring glory to Old Virginia, first on the battlefield, and, should that effort fail, in the collective consciousness of its people. Thomas Connelly argues that Lee was so venerated by southerners after the war that by the turn of the twentieth century this general had surpassed even George Washington as the region's greatest hero.[14]

4.4 *Julian Vannerson*, Robert E. Lee, *1864, cartes de visite by Selden & Co., Richmond, Virginia Historical Society*

Because of his accomplishments as the leader of the Confederate forces, his gentlemanly manner, and his seemingly flawless behavior in all situations, Robert E. Lee was idolized in the South both during, and even moreso after, the Civil War. The era following Appomattox was for whites a dark period in southern history, in which the memory of the Confederate cause provided the only existing beacon; it became "the most glamorous memory" of the Old South.[15] Of all of its generals, Lee had been the unquestioned leader, the master strategist, and the model for gentlemanly deportment. As evidence, Freeman points to the response of his Confederate brethren after Lee's death: "In his military achievement, Southern people saw the flowering of their racial stock; in his social graces they beheld their ideals embodied; in the honors paid his memory, every one of Lee's former soldiers felt that he had himself received the accolade."[16] This almost superhuman figure came to symbolize not only the best that the Confederacy had to offer, but also the Virginia society from which he had emerged, and which the Confederacy had destroyed itself in trying to preserve.

The post-war sanctification of the general began early. In 1866 John Esten Cooke elevated Lee high above his contemporaries:

> I have seen the noblest figures of the war, but none can be compared to that of our old captain. In every movement of his person, every tone of his voice, every glance of his honest eye, was the perfect grace, the sweet yet stately courtesy of the old Virginia gentleman. Health, happiness, and length of days to our old hero! His glory is beyond the reach of hostile hands; and to-day, the thousand and ten thousand, who would have died with him, take off their hats and salute him as the flower of truth and honor![17]

Connolly writes that the mythification of Lee gained such momentum in the years after the war that in the popular American mind that conflict became identified solely with Virginia, the general's home state and the setting for many of his military exploits.[18] Freeman states that the South found in Lee "the embodiment of all its best ideals." Emory Thomas, author of a more recent biography of the general, has added that "people usually venerate as a hero someone who exemplifies (or who they believe exemplifies) virtues which they admire or to which they aspire."[19] These virtues, in Lee's case, were the values that had long been associated with both chivalry and the pastoral way of life, two ideals that had a great deal of currency throughout nineteenth-century Virginia.

Vannerson reminds us that the general was a man of good looks and a fine physique. In his eye and expression the viewer can see Lee's great intelligence, his power of critical analysis, and his desire to excel at any task as-signed to him. This was a man who strove to do everything as perfectly as was possible. Added to this was a drive toward public service and a will to fulfill his duties. In discharging his responsibilities he demonstrated self-control and patience in adversity. Never would he utter an oath or be vulgar, in public or in private. Lee's domestic existence was characterized by his love of family life, his devotion to kin, and his proverbial kindness. He met everyone with a smile and a bow, and he sought as a gentleman should to make every right-minded person comfortable in his presence. As to what constitutes the consummate behavior of a gentleman, Lee reminded himself in a note that he wrote during the war:

> The forbearing use of power does not only form a touchstone, but the manner in which an individual enjoys certain advantages over others is a test of a true gentleman. The power which the strong have over the weak . . . —the forbearing or inoffensive use of all this power or authority, or a total abstinence from it when the case admits it, will show the gentleman in a plain light. The gentleman does not needlessly and unnecessarily remind an offender of a wrong he may have committed against him. He can not only forgive, he can forget; and he strives for that nobleness of self and mildness of character which impart sufficient strength to let the past be but the past. A true man of honor feels humbled himself when he cannot help humbling others.[20]

His obsession about manners recalls the *Rules of Civility and Decent Behaviour in Company and Conversation* that the young George Washington had taken great care to master. Such civility had long ago formed a bedrock of the society of Old Virginia.

Freeman argues that the kindness, sense of duty, humility, and spirit of self-denial that characterized Lee were all inspired by his strong religious code. It enabled Lee to resolve every problem into questions of what is right and what is wrong. In the general's creed, a man has a duty to his Maker and to his neighbors. "There is," he jotted down for his own guidance, "a true glory and a true honor: the glory of duty done—the honor of the integrity of principle."[21] His submission to the Divine will explains his calmness in hours of trial, and his spirit of self-denial prepared him for the hardships of the war and for the destitution that followed.[22]

The general's principal biographer contends that his subject's detractors stood in disbelief about him only because of their own personal shortcomings. Lee, Freeman argues, was not a complex man; rather, he is easily understood:

> Because he was calm when others were frenzied, loving when they hated, and silent when they spoke with bitter tongue, they shook their heads and said he was a superman or a mysterious man. Beneath

that untroubled exterior, they said, deep storms must rage; his dignity, his reserve, and his few words concealed sombre thoughts, repressed ambitions, livid repressions. They were mistaken. Robert Lee was one of the small company of great men in whom there is no inconsistency to be explained, no enigma to be solved. What he seemed, he was—a wholly human gentleman, the essential elements of whose positive character were two and only two, simplicity and spirituality.[23]

Not everyone, however, has accepted Freeman's thesis about Lee's greatness. In his 1977 study, *The Marble Man: Robert E. Lee and His Image in American Society*, Thomas L. Connelly contends that Freeman's image of "a Virginia gentleman, guided in life by the simple concepts of devotion to God and duty" is flawed, and that Freeman shaped Lee into "something that he never was." Connelly contends that instead the general was "an extremely complex individual," and that he was "neither serene nor simple":

> His life was replete with frustration, self doubt, and a feeling of failure. All these were hidden behind his legendary reserve and his credo of duty and self-control. He was actually a troubled man, convinced that he had failed as a prewar career officer, parent, and moral individual. He suffered the hardships of an unsatisfactory marriage, long absences from his family, and chronic homesickness for his beloved Virginia. He distrusted his own conduct. . . .
>
> By the 1850s, Lee, disturbed by these inner problems, evidently made some conscious decisions about his life. . . . He would adopt a creed of life that later affected his generalship in the Civil War. The Lee code—duty, self-control, and self-denial—has often been described and praised. Overlooked is the fact that the code was an almost mechanical device that suppressed his naturally strong temper and vibrant personality.[24]

Emory M. Thomas strikes something of a middle ground in his *Robert E. Lee, A Biography* (1995). Lee achieved successes, Thomas writes, but in his mind those triumphs always seemed tainted. Lee himself admitted late in life that he was "always wanting [lacking] something." He accepted the various regulations and conventions that constrained him, to the point where his life was almost tragic. Thomas points out that Lee spent much of his time in pursuit of what he perceived to be his duty to other people. Thus it is to Lee's credit, according to this biographer, that he endured, that he maintained his self-control, and that he followed the rules and repressed his desire to break free from his many social, moral, professional, and cultural shackles. He concludes that Lee was a great human being, perhaps as great as Freeman believed, but great in different ways than Freeman described:

Afflicted with many, though surely not all, of the frustrations and frailties that Connelly and others discerned, Lee was great in his response to his tribulations and to his life in general. He redeemed many moments and brought grace to otherwise grim circumstances. Lee was a great person, not so much because of what he did (although his accomplishments were extraordinary); he was great because of the way he lived, because of what he was.[25]

Thomas explains that Lee is, as well, an enigma, the poet Stephen Vincent Benèt's "marble man" who eludes all biographers. Even his wife, his children, and his staff never felt that they understood him, because he lived so much within himself, so much under control.[26] As Mary Chesnut famously remarked, "Can *anybody* say they know the General? I doubt it, he looks so cold, so quiet, so grand."[27]

In June of 1999 the most recent chapter in the reimagining of Lee unfolded in downtown Richmond. There, along a portion of the city's newly restored Kanawha and Haxall Canals, as part of an outdoor history museum an enlargement of the head and shoulders of the Vannerson photograph of Lee was hung, the first of a group of nearly thirty such banners. This image of Lee ignited nearly as intense a controversy as had the song "Carry Me Back to Old Virginny." City Council member Sa'ad El-Amin protested his inclusion by equating the Confederacy with slavery and saying that those who seek to glorify its soldiers and symbols are nostalgic for the rigid racial boundaries of Richmond's not-too-distant past. El-Amin compared Lee to Adolf Hitler and contended that Richmond's abundance of Confederate memorials offends many African Americans in the majority-black city.[28] Members of the Virginia Division of the Sons of Confederate Veterans responded by rallying at the state Capitol, where they cheered Lee as "the greatest American who has ever walked the face of this Earth." They paraded portraits of the general with the caption "Carry Me Back!" A black scholar, Edward C. Smith, director of the American Studies Program at American University in Washington, D.C., suggested that "Robert E. Lee's name has been defiled," and that the comparison of Lee to Hitler and the removal of a portrait of Lee in Richmond were both "absolutely absurd."[29]

This incident reaffirmed that the mythologized Lee had become too much a symbol of Old Virginia, and therefore of the old ways of the Virginia plantation, to be palatable to many members of contemporary society. Just as "Carry Me Back to Old Virginny" is, according to the song's opponents, forever to be associated with slavery, so Lee seems to have been similarly tarnished. As protestor Barbara Ingram explained when the city council opened public hearings, "No amount of pretty words can change the cause for which Robert E. Lee stood."[30] Former Governor L. Douglas Wilder added, "What purpose is served by continuing to flaunt those images?"[31] The "cause" for which Lee fought, of course, and for which even his enemies thought him a patriot, was the defense of Virginia and the South. He was defending Virginia's railroads, its manufacturing interests, and its mercantile houses, as well as its plantations, its poor, many of whom made up his army, as well as its rich. And he was defending the land, which had nourished some of the greatest Americans who had ever lived. While the matter is far more complex than we have time to discuss here, it is fair to say that characterizing Lee simply as the man who fought for slavery, without any further consideration of what he saw as his honor-bound duty to his state, leaves a large, crucial part of his fascinating story untold.

In *The Old Virginia Gentleman* (1877), the apologist George Bagby decreed that the way of life that in his era was defined by the term Old Virginia had ended with the death of Robert E. Lee in 1870. When Lee, "the last Virginia gentleman was laid to sleep," Bagby wrote, "the heroic age of Virginia ended."[32] What could not have been predicted was that Lee's death ironically spurred the consolidation and ultimate rise of Old Virginia as an imaginative construct. To some postbellum southerners, the immediate, incredibly painful past was quietly remembered; in Virginia it was glorified. The many catastrophic episodes of the Civil War that were fought on the soil of the Old Dominion demanded remembrance, and the attempted restructuring of the society by outsiders demanded resistance. The old ways were thus kept in the minds and hearts of postwar Virginians. Their loyalty to their fallen brethren, and their pride in their own survival, built an imaginative Elysium from the ashes of the Confederacy.

No generation of Americans experienced more societal upheavals than did the Virginians of the Civil War era. The war had ended in defeat, emancipation had reconfigured their social order, and reconstruction had set in motion a democratic movement that bred Readjusters and Populists who threatened to change forever what had been America's most aristocratic society. As convincingly explained by James Lindgren in *Preserving the Old Dominion, Historic Preservation and Virginia Traditionalism*, these calamities inspired tradition-minded Virginians to celebrate their past as a means to control the present and the future. They would convince blacks, populists, and workers to accept an elitist past and power structure as "our history."[33]

Traditionalists memorialized the Confederacy and its fallen sons who had defended their way of life. They reimagined antebellum Virginia as having been an arcadia, a rural society governed by gentlemen, graced by the most virtuous of ladies, and characterized by a refined and lavish lifestyle. They denied to newly liberated African Americans the respect and opportunity that would have allowed those people economic and social advancement. Only in this way could they perpetuate the fiction that antebellum life, including the slave system, had been idyllic. This consciously constructed society of the past proved to be a powerful tool in maintaining the status quo.

During these same decades a New Virginia emerged from the ruins of war. This society was characterized by a more urbanized and industrialized economy. It evolved out of the movement for progress initiated during the antebellum years, and it threatened to transform the state and thereby remove it far from its agricultural base. In the light of the perceived threat signified by New Virginia, the lost rural society of Old Virginia and the ideal of blissful pastoral living seemed all the more poignant and appealing. Ironically, progressivism, which had much to do with the decline of the historical Old Virginia before the war, would contribute to the rise of the mythological Old Virginia after it.

The Cult of the "Lost Cause"

The defeat in the Civil War overturned Virginia society and left a powerful legacy that shaped postwar attitudes. Not only did families face economic ruin in the wake of the war's destructive path, but Virginia's fathers and sons had been killed and wounded in combat. Following Appomattox the white population that had experienced the war, either in the field or at home, would not forget the valor of the state's Confederate soldiers. In the postbellum battle of ideas, they were determined not to lose a second time. White Virginians, like white southerners in general, obsessed about what they called the "Lost Cause," their valiant stand as Confederates against an evil invader. Those writers and artists who were apologists for the old ways felt compelled to proclaim as honorable the Confederate resistance to northern aggression.

The men who had fought in the southern armies were remembered as having upheld such values as honor, virtue, and courage in the face of an overwhelming enemy in defense of their homeland. Their behavior was nothing if not chivalrous. Lee was the greatest of these modern knights, but his generals, especially J. E. B. Stuart and Stonewall Jackson, and their cavalrymen were also thought of as chevaliers. With every Confederate celebration in the region, the memory of Old Virginia was invigorated and, in turn, allegiance to the old order became more firmly entrenched. The idea of the Lost Cause would prevail for decades after Appomattox. Confederate ghosts would linger on the stage of Virginia well into the twentieth century.

Because large portions of the state—especially in the Tidewater, the Piedmont, and the Valley—were ravaged by the armies of both sides, the association of Old Virginia with the Confederate effort was inevitable. Walt Whitman, who had left Brooklyn in 1862 to locate his brother George, who had been wounded at Fredericksburg, wrote in 1864 from near the battlefront at Culpeper about a region that was "dilapidated, fenceless, and trodden with war," so much so that he said the term "Old Dominion" had become a "mockery." Ironically, he saw instead in the landscape a great "capacity for products, improvements, human life, nourishment and expansion," sentiments that would fuel the progressivist movement in Virginia in future decades.[34] The effects of shelling and incineration startled every visitor to the front. A more typical response was that of an assistant surgeon in the Union army, Henry Chester Parry, whose 1864 description of the ruins of a nearby resort hotel, Fauquier White Sulphur Springs (page 110, fig. 3.59), reads like a passage from an antebellum romance:

> It was a handsome structure in its time built of brick covered with yellow plaster—ten doric columns stood among the ruins like great sentinels keeping their watch. I felt like restoring the place as the wind and rain howled through the grounds and made leafles[s] trees sigh for the departed glory of the place.[35] (See page 110, fig. 3.59.)

In the devastation Parry saw vestiges of Old Virginia, which the Confederacy was fighting hard but failing to preserve. There are any number of visual images that parallel his evocative description. Many of these romantic photographs and paintings are poignant records of a noble and seemingly ancient civilization in ruin. As the years passed, they would come to be viewed with nostalgia, and often with affection.

If the northern troops who invaded the region had envisioned Virginia society in its antebellum phase based on their readings of the popular literature of the day, they were quickly reminded by the old houses of Virginia's deep roots in the colonial past. One early and significant victim of the war was the second White House in New Kent County, a structure that Federal troops burned during the Peninsular Campaign of 1862 (fig. 4.5, a. and b.). The White House was rich with the history of Old Virginia. It was a Washington-Custis property that had been the setting for the wedding of the Father of His Country. The first house on the site was Martha Custis's residence, where she had lived with her first husband, Daniel Parke Custis, until his untimely death in 1757; she married George Washington there two years later. This White House was rebuilt in the early nineteenth century by George Washington Parke Custis, Martha Washington's grandson, who inherited the plantation in 1798 and would not allow so historic a landmark to disappear completely. G. W. P. Custis's second building may have closely resembled the first, although there were obvious changes,

such as the treatment of the land-front porch and the addition of the bay window pictured here. At his death in 1857 Custis willed the plantation to his grandsons and appointed his son-in-law, Robert E. Lee, as executor. Union General George McClellan used the White House as a base of supplies. A note reportedly left on the door by Custis's daughter, Mrs. Mary Custis Lee, the wife of Robert E. Lee, is said to have read, "Northern Soldiers who profess to revere Washington forbear to desecrate the home of his first married life."[36] Her entreaty to save the house, however, was to no avail.

The Union topographer and diarist Robert Knox Sneden was present with McClellan's army in New Kent County, although his journal for this period, May of 1862, was lost in a fire. Sneden's sketch of the community of New Kent Court House does survive, however, with notations that "the Rebels burnt the jail" and "the Union soldiers looted the court house and records office."[37] His sketches and account of the spectacular destruction of the Cole House in Prince George County are among the most memorable records of the demise of Old Virginia (fig. 4.6). Sneden's rendering of this house in flames recalls the British painter J. M. W. Turner's vision of the burning of the Houses of Parliament in London in 1834–35, and it prefigures images of the burning of the Confederate capital in 1865. Parliament and the city of Richmond would be rebuilt, but the Italianate mansion of the Cole family was a landmark of the past that would remain lost forever. The story of Confederate lookouts positioned in the tower of this antebellum structure is vividly recounted by the diarist, as is the subsequent burning of so strategic a citadel:

> This was set on fire, and soon the flames streamed out of every window and wrapt the fine dwelling in sheets of fire. The sun had just set, and the scene was grand.
>
> I made a sketch on the spot. The axe men now felled the trees, destroyed the outbuildings, and the fire caught in the dry timber and brush, and at 6:30 p.m. the whole opposite bluff was a sheet of fire and smoke, which burnt clean over twenty acres of ground before morning. . . . The river was lit up for miles, and the rigging of the vessels shone like gold. Many officers and men came from their camps to see the fine sight.[38]

The Cole House lay almost directly across the James River from Westover, the eighteenth-century Byrd family mansion that to this day is a premier symbol of the grandeur of early Virginia. Sneden instantly recognized the aura that surrounds this regal property, and he saw as well its rapid deterioration during the encampment of Union troops there. This northerner was there in July of 1862 and noted Abraham Lincoln's visit at that time. He had much to say about this grand house:

4.5 (Second) White House, *rebuilt early 19ᵗʰ century (burned 1862) on the Pamunkey River, courthouse vicinity, New Kent County, photographs, pre-1862 and ca. 1862, from Benson J. Lossing,* A History of the Civil War, *1912*

I . . . visited General McClellan's headquarters at the old house at Westover. I made a sketch. . . . A signal station had been erected on the roof, and all the fences had been used for firewood. Trees had been cut down for bough houses along the river bank. Quartermaster's tents were pitched. . . . The landing was crowded with wagons and teams. . . .

The mansion was of brick, with white marble quoins and trimmings. Shutters were on the two stories, which wanted a coat of paint badly. Everything outside denoted neglect; and several old slaves yet occupied the quarters adjoining. The mansion has much interest as having been the residence of a family, who, for three generations were representatives of royalty in the colonial times. It still bears evidence of wealth and high standing of its former occupants. . . . All the rooms on the first floor were twelve feet high. The rooms were all paneled and wainscoted throughout, with elaborately carved cornices. But a few articles of furniture remained, no carpets, or books in the library. . . . There was a very handsome chimney piece in the parlor . . . The mirror was smashed, and the pieces were being taken away by relic hunters piece by piece. Soon it will all be gone. . . . Opposite the back door was a large gateway, with ornate wrought iron gates. The brick pillars were square, but most of the stucco on them had fallen off. They were about ten feet high, and were each surmounted by an eagle standing on a ball (the crest of the Byrd family). A cavalryman was trying to wrench one of these off, but I told the officer of the guard, and it was replaced with much unwillingness. After dark, probably this fellow would secure the relic unopposed.[39]

4.6 Robert Knox Sneden, U. S. Troops Burning the Cole House and Plantation, *James River, 1862, pencil, pen, and watercolor, 3½ x 5¼ in., Virginia Historical Society*

4.7 Robert K. Sneden, The Westover Mansion, Harrison's Landing, James River, Va., *1862, pencil, pen, and watercolor, 4 x 6 in., Virginia Historical Society*

Sneden's sketch of Westover provides the viewer with a rare glimpse of the land façade (fig. 4.7). The fact that he gets a number of the details wrong, such as the dormers, the doorway, and the kitchen, which Sneden omits but which exists to this day, suggests that he made a quick sketch on the spot and then finished it at a later date. What is perhaps even more telling is his inclusion of what appear to be the slave quarters, which he describes in his text as adjoining the house. There never were any such buildings so near the house, but Sneden, perhaps because he had seen slaves about and wanted to make a point about their presence, or perhaps because he simply misremembered, creates what are little more than sheds and places them where they never existed. It is not a

4.8 E. L. Henry, The Old Westover Mansion, *1869-70, oil on panel,*
11¼ x 14⅝ in., from a drawing made in October 1864, Corcoran Gallery of Art

stretch to say that Sneden depicted Westover as he wanted it to look, as symbolic of a society characterized by a peculiar mix of grandeur and oppression.

Two years later, Edward Lamson Henry, who accompanied the Union Army on the James River in 1864 as a captain's clerk, provided a representation of the more traditional riverside view of the house. Henry titled his painting "The Old Westover Mansion," to make the point that the Byrd plantation symbolized, if not epitomized, the English traditions of Old Virginia (fig. 4.8). In 1870, about the time that he converted his on-site drawing into the formal image pictured here, Henry wrote to the sculptor Edward Valentine that he had painted and sold several views of "these gorgeous old Manors on the James River. . . . Old Westover is one, that place set me nearly crazy."[40] A native of Charleston, South Carolina, Henry certainly knew grand architecture. Presumably he meant that the sight of so spectacular a house in near ruin was a striking, and probably somewhat romantic, experience for him. His rendering of the spectacle of Westover in decay seems to suggest that while the actual state would emerge from the conflict, Old Virginia would not survive the Civil War.

The corridor between Washington and Richmond saw years of maneuvering between the Union and Confederate armies, often resulting in fierce combat that exacted a toll on the plantation settings of central and Piedmont Virginia. One example of a significant Old Virginia seat in this region that was lost during the war is Mannsfield, a home of the prominent Page and Tayloe families and one of the largest and most formal of the mansions built in the colony. It was obliterated by artillery fire when military campaigns swept through the Fredericksburg area in 1863 (fig.4.9). Late nineteenth-century photographs of the site show only the proud dependencies that then flanked the meager ruins of what had been a massive center house.[41]

Melrose Castle also endured the intrusion of Federal troops, but it survived. An unknown Union photographer's record of the bivouac at Melrose (fig. 4.10) is remarkably similar to Henry's painting of Westover. The castle is located in Fauquier County, in the northern Piedmont, where military activities culminated in the first and second battles of Manassas. A Gothic Revival mansion, Melrose had been designed in 1857 for a Maryland patron by Edmund George Land, a Baltimore architect who was born and trained in England. The architecture of this residence fit neatly with the cult in antebellum Virginia for the Gothic. The war-time photograph is an evocative image that juxtaposes the baggage of the new military with what might seem at first glance to be a medieval fortress.

After the war, the Gothic architecture of Melrose made it a setting easily associated with the Lost Cause, rather than with the Union army that had invaded Fauquier County. The reason is that the interest in things Gothic, which had survived from antebellum Virginia, became intertwined with ideas about the nobility and chivalry of the soldiers of the Confederacy. In particular, the dashing Confederate cavalrymen who had fought so valiantly were easily reimagined as modern knights who

had defended their realm. For those Virginians who before the war had imagined that medieval England had been recreated on New World soil, the knight-like figures who appeared on the Virginia stage would have seemed appropriate. And because the Confederate knights were successful against greater numbers, presumably because they were fighting from the moral highground, they were venerated as heroes of the Lost Cause by those who clearly remembered the old rural society that had produced them.

Medieval jousting or tilting tournaments, and the festive balls that followed, had been staged with some frequency in antebellum Virginia. The tradition was continued during the war, at times simply to fill periods of inactivity, but more often to boost Confederate pride in the southern cavalry, which in prowess surpassed the horse soldiers of the North. Many examples of such festivities could be cited. For instance, in April of 1863 an artillery battalion stationed near Petersburg, commanded by Major James Dearing, hosted a tournament for modern knights that was followed in the evening by a coronation ball to honor current damsels (fig. 4.11). The affair must have been a major event of a season that would become grim three months later with the Confederate defeats at Gettysburg and Vicksburg.

Appomattox brought little interruption to the staging of these events, which after the war were held almost in defiance of the fall of Virginia to the armies of the Union. In September of 1865 at Fairfax Court House, on behalf of the Fairfax Agricultural Society, Captain George A. Armes invited his gentry neighbors to a tournament where some thirty participants were identified as specific

*4.9 **Above**, left Mannsfield, built ca. 1770s, Spotsylvania County (east of Fredericksburg), destroyed by shelling 1863, albumen print, late nineteenth century, Virginia Historical Society*

*4.10 **Left** Unidentified photographer, Melrose Castle, Fauquier County, in 1862, albumen print, Virginia Historical Society.*

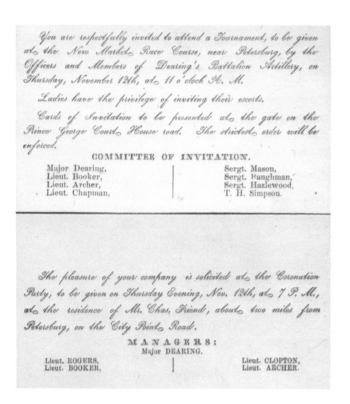

You are respectfully invited to attend a Tournament, to be given at the New Market Race Course, near Petersburg, by the Officers and Members of Dearing's Battalion Artillery, on Thursday, November 12th, at 11 o'clock A. M.

Ladies have the privilege of inviting their escorts.

Cards of Invitation to be presented at the gate on the Prince George Court House road. The strictest order will be enforced.

COMMITTEE OF INVITATION.

Major Dearing,	Sergt. Mason,
Lieut. Booker,	Sergt. Haughman,
Lieut. Archer,	Sergt. Hazlewood,
Lieut. Chapman,	T. H. Simpson.

The pleasure of your company is solicited at the Coronation Party, to be given on Thursday Evening, Nov. 12th, at 7 P. M., at the residence of Mr. Chas. Friend, about two miles from Petersburg, on the City Point Road.

MANAGERS:
Major DEARING.

| Lieut. ROGERS, | | Lieut. CLOPTON, |
| Lieut. BOOKER, | | Lieut. ARCHER, |

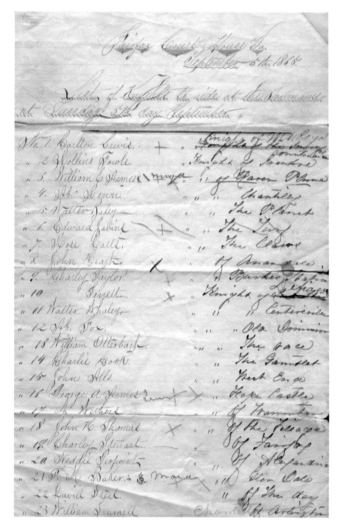

4.11 *Above, top* Major James Dearing, C.S.A., Invitation to Attend a Medieval Tournament and Coronation Party, *Prince George County, 1863, organized by Dearing's Artillery Battalion, Virginia Historical Society*

4.12 *Above* Captain George A. Armes, List of Knights to Participate in a Tournament, *to be held 5 September 1865 at Fairfax Court House, Virginia, Virginia Historical Society, bequest of Paul Mellon*

knights, such as the "Knight of Ivanhoe," the "Knight of the Old Dominion," the "Knight of Chimborazo," the "Knight of Bull Run," and the "Knight of the Pines" (fig. 4.12). The chivalric theme, with references to specific Civil War battle sites, is evidence that the Gothic tradition and the nascent cult of the Lost Cause had quickly merged.[42] Invitation cards that survive in the Virginia Historical Society to tournaments and balls—such as those at Surry Court House, 1872, Lunenburg Courthouse, 1876, Lawrenceville, 1877, and Oral Oaks, 1887—suggest that these occasions were not rare during the postwar period. They provided a means "to keep up the chivalrous spirit of the F. F. V's" and "to revive the grand spirit of our fathers," according to an "Address to the Knights" that was given by the tournament host at a postwar event held in Berkeley County, newly a part of West Virginia.[43]

An unidentified photograph in the Cook Collection illustrates a Virginia jousting tournament (fig. 4.13). A modern knight at full gallop, with a long lance in hand, attempts to engage a small ring suspended from a cross arm. This sport was a less violent alternative to the more traditional competition of unhorsing a combatant, but was still a demanding test of one of the aptitudes of knighthood. Such postwar demonstrations of chivalry would continue to be held during celebrations of the Lost Cause well into the twentieth century. An annual tournament held at Mount Solon in the Shenandoah Valley, which had begun in 1821, was said to be staged there in 1954.[44]

In the year after Appomattox, John Esten Cooke set out to convince a national audience of the chivalry of Confederate officers in his Civil War novel *Surry of Eagle's Nest; or The Memoirs of a Staff-Officer Serving in Virginia, Edited, from the Mss. Of Colonel Surry.* This book was described at publication as a "thrilling and sometimes startling love story" that "will be read by every southern man and woman with a proud, if not aching heart; and no northern man, who has an intelligent soul in him, will be able, after reading one chapter, to put the book aside."[45] Cooke writes in the first person as the Colonel Surry of the title; the novel was meant to be seen as partly autobiographical. It celebrates the actual activities of the Confederate cavalry, which the author intersperses with fictional episodes, such as Surry's eventually successful courtship of the lovely May Beverley of The Oaks. Cooke as Surry begins with the suggestion that his own "adventures" during "the late Revolution" will interest readers because he is able to recount "how Lee looked, and Stuart spoke—how Jackson lived that wondrous life of his, and Ashby charged upon his mild-white steed." Cooke romanticized the Confederacy, a course that he rightly predicted would interest the coming generations more than "the most brilliant arguments about secession."[46]

One of the actual Confederate knights whom Cooke

*4.13 **Above, top** Huestis Cook,* Jousting Tournament, *ca. 1890s, photograph courtesy of The Valentine Museum*

*4.14 **Above** Winslow Homer,* Ashby's Feat of Horsemanship, *wood engraving, in John Esten Cooke,* Surry of Eagle's Nest *(New York, 1866), Virginia Historical Society*

wove into his narrative was Turner Ashby of Fauquier County, who in 1861 had gathered a troop of horse soldiers that became the Seventh Virginia Cavalry. In 1862 Ashby led Jackson's cavalry in the Shenandoah campaign until he was killed in action near Harrisonburg. To Cooke, Ashby "was truly the flower of chivalry, and was as winning by the campfire as he was utterly fearless in the field." A line drawing by Winslow Homer that recreates "Ashby's Feat of Horsemanship" (fig. 4.14) illustrates an incident in 1862 described by Cooke in which Ashby en-

countered Federal cavalry in Winchester at the time that Jackson was evacuating the city. As Union forces entered the town, Ashby "waved his hat around his head, uttered a cheer, and then, drawing his revolver, galloped off, firing as he went." He charged two horseman, "a glow of unmistakable pleasure upon his features":

> One fell, shot through the heart; then, his barrels being all emptied, he seized the second by the throat.
>
> I then witnessed one of those spectacles which are supposed to be confined to romances. Borne on at furious speed upon his powerful white horse, Ashby dragged his adversary clear out of the saddle, never relaxed his clutch, and in a moment was beyond pursuit, still dragging his prisoner by the side of his horse.
>
> A cheer rose from his men as Ashby released the prisoner, and coolly looked to the disposition of his command.[47]

Later in *Surry,* Cooke tells of Ashby's rear guard action at the Shenandoah River near Newmarket, where the general attempted to destroy a bridge before Union cavalry crossed it.

> Ashby now fell slowly back with the rear-guard, obstinately contesting every step; and never shall I forget the chivalric spectacle which he presented, mounted on his superb white horse, as fearless and defiant as himself. The swarthy face, with its heavy black beard, glowed with martial ardor; in the flashing eyes might be read the joy of conflict; and, with drawn sabre, on his spirited animal, he resembled

4.15 *Charles Hoffbauer,* Autumn, *from the* Four Seasons of the Confederacy *murals, 1919-21, Virginia Historical Society*

some knight of the Middle Ages, asking nothing better than an opportunity to meet all comers.

A few days later, Ashby confides to Surry, "I have carried on hostilities, in this struggle which my whole heart approves, as a Virginia gentleman should." He adds, "I have no self-reproach—no regrets. If I could have done more for old Virginia, I would." On the next day, Surry tells us, the general was killed in action. Cooke adds, "Such was the death of Ashby, 'the Knight of the Valley.'"[48]

John Esten Cooke had actually served during the war on the staff of another cavalry legend, the preeminent Confederate knight who was called "the last cavalier." This was General J. E. B. Stuart, who both during the war and even moreso afterwards, because of his gallantry and success in the field, epitomized the chivalric ideal as it was transferred to the Confederate officer. If Lee stood for stoic virtue, Stuart was the epitome of swashbuckling heroism. In *Surry*, Cooke describes the general at length, cautioning his reader "to listen to every detail" because "I am drawing the portrait of one of the immortals":

> He was a man of twenty-five or thirty, of low stature, athletic figure, and with the air of a born cavalryman. There was no mistaking his arm of the service. He was the cavalier all over. His boot-tips covered

the knee; his brass spurs were models of neatness; his sabre was light, flexible, and "handy;" his gauntlets reached to the elbows. The young cavalier was evidently at home in the saddle, and asked nothing better than "a fight or a frolic." He wore the blue undress uniform coat of the United States Army, gathered at the waist by his sword-belt; an old brown pair of velveteen pantaloons, rusty from long use, and his bold face was surmounted by a Zouave cap, from which depended a white "havelock," giving him the appearance of a mediaeval knight with a chain-helmet. Upon that proud head, indeed, a helmet, with its flowing plume, seemed the fittest covering.[49]

With the exception of the coloring of his outfit, Cooke provides the figure of Stuart that was painted a half century later in one of four giant murals in the Confederate Memorial Institute in Richmond (fig. 4.15). Cooke had predicted that in fifty years, "Stuart will then rank with Harry of Navarre and Prince Rupert," great nobles of the past who had fought against long odds in worthy causes.[50]

The Confederate Memorial Institute was the premier monument to the Lost Cause; initially it had even been labeled the "Temple to the Lost Cause." The Institute was conceived in 1894 as a monument to venerate southern history at a time when the Union army was being honored by the Grant Monument (1888–97, popularly known today as Grant's Tomb). Plagued by delays, the Institute was eventually built in 1912–13, perhaps somewhat in defiance of the contemporary congressional vote to remember the former northern commander-in-chief, Abraham Lincoln, with a national memorial. The Institute is little remembered today, in part because it was deeded to the Virginia Historical Society in 1946 and now stands as the core of the Society's greatly-expanded museum structure. Both the Institute and its murals were commissioned by the Confederate Memorial Association, whose membership was drawn from the entire South and beyond. The two principal funders of this project, Charles B. Rouss and Thomas F. Ryan, were New York City capitalists as well as former Confederates.

The mural program, *The Four Seasons of the Confederacy,* was commissioned to decorate the interior of the Institute. It is the most important large-scale paintings cycle that has ever been produced in the American South. The imposing murals, each some thirteen feet tall and twenty-two to twenty-five feet across, were painted in 1913–21 by the French artist Charles Hoffbauer, a prize-winner at the Paris Salon of 1906. They celebrate Virginia campaigns of the Civil War, equating the seasons of the year with the emergence, maturity, fall, and demise of the Confederacy. By its charter the Association had set out to define and honor "the character, life, spirit, and motives of the South and her people." The artist stated that his purpose was to illustrate the "spirit" of the South.[51] Overall, the murals suggest that the Confederates were guided by honor, gallantry, and chivalry, values that remained part of the intellectual heritage of the South well into the twentieth century. They stir the visitor to reconsider his opinions about the Confederacy and the period of reconstruction.

The existence of these murals suggests that the myth of the Lost Cause was not driven by extremists. Southerners were determined to establish for their contemporaries and for future generations of Americans that the average Confederate soldier and civilian, who had nothing to do with the political decision to secede and who almost certainly was not a slaveholder, had acted with valor during an era of crisis out of loyalty to his region. The *Autumn* scene is a tribute to both Stuart and his cavalry, whose chivalric ideals, as much as their achievements, had stirred Virginia's pride when the fortunes of the Confederacy began to wane.

If Hoffbauer presented a figure who is different in some particulars from the J. E. B. Stuart recounted by Cooke, it was because he was advised to do so by historian Douglas Southall Freeman, who took the artist into his own home when the murals were painted to provide historical guidance as well as room and board. Freeman later wrote that Stuart's spectacular achievements with the Confederate cavalry—such as his famous ride around McClellan's troops during the Peninsular Campaign with the loss of only one man, his raiding of Pope's headquarters at Catlett's Station, and his raid into Pennsylvania—gave the general considerable popularity, which was augmented by his own love of the spotlight:

> For while his patriotism was above challenge, and his private life clean and beautiful, he had a lingering adolescent love of being dramatically conspicuous. He always rode a splendid horse—and rode so hard that no animal could long survive his galloping. His gray cloak was lined with red; in the lapel of his jacket was a red flower or ribbon love-knot; his hat was cocked on one side with a star of gilt that held a peacock's plume. In his camp there was music and dancing and much jollity, but never any swearing in his presence, or any discoverable loose living. . . . Lee regarded him almost as a son and remarked after the war that Stuart was his ideal of a soldier.[52]

That lone Confederate casualty of Stuart's ride around McClellan in 1862 was Captain William Latane, a young doctor and officer whose death and dramatic burial were adopted as an embodiment of the losses suffered in this war of rebellion. Several valiant women of eastern Virginia, isolated by the position of the Union army during the Peninsular Campaign, were forced to conduct Latane's burial virtually alone, with help only from faithful slaves who had remained at their home plantations. Having carried much of the burden of the administration of antebellum plantations, Virginia women were shown to be fully capable of completing even such taxing tasks.

The death and burial of Latane, which took place near Old Church north of Richmond, is well documented. John Latane, the deceased's brother, had managed to carry the body to Westwood Plantation, the home of Catherine Brockenbrough. She returned John to the front with assurances that a proper burial would be conducted. The interment took place at neighboring Summer Hill plantation, the seat of Mrs. William B. Newton. When Union troops refused to allow an Episcopal priest passage through their lines, Mrs. Willoughby Newton, the sister-in-law of Catherine Brockenbrough, read the service, in the company of the other two women, her daughter-in-law, and a few children and slaves.

In 1864, two years after the event, the burial of Latane was reimagined by the Richmond artist William D. Washington, who was inspired by a poem about the event. John Reuben Thompson tells the story of "The Burial of Latane" in verse; he also takes this opportunity to predict Virginia's eventual victory against the North and the immortality that is assured for "our early-lost, lamented Latane."[53] Washington exhibited his canvas to Richmond crowds, reputedly beside a bucket that collected contribu-

4.16 A. G. Campbell, New York, after William D. Washington, Burial of Latane, *after 1868, engraving, 23½ x 32 in., Virginia Historical Society*

4.17 John Smith, Lee and His Generals, *after a sketch by Charles P. Tholey, Philadelphia, 1867, lithograph, 17¾ x 23¾ in., Virginia Historical Society*

tions for the Confederate cause. After 1868 an engraving of the painting was reproduced in New York (fig. 4.16). For years the publisher, A. G. Campbell, marketed this iconic image of the Lost Cause with great success; in the 1870s, subscribers to *The Southern Magazine* were offered copies. In this way the print became widely circulated.

Through the story of Latane's burial the Lost Cause found additional heroes in the virtuous and capable women of Old Virginia. To those who had read the classics, the women pictured by Washington would have re-

called other mourning women, including those whom the tyrant Creon would not allow to bury their dead at Thebes, or the women and children accompanying Agrippina as she brought home the ashes of Germanicus. The fact that Latane's name was pronounced "Lat-a-ney" made it conveniently homonymic with words associated with the race that Aeneas had to conquer before the marriage of the Trojan prince to Lavinia, daughter of King Latinus of Latium, which would begin the line that would lead to the founding of Rome. Perhaps as the conquered

4.18 Above Charles Hoffbauer,
Summer, *from the* Four Seasons
of the Confederacy *murals,
1919-21, Virginia Historical
Society*

*4.19 Left George Bagby
Matthews,* Lee and His Generals, *1907, lithograph, 11 x 22½
in., published by A. B. Graham
Co., Washington, Virginia Historical Society*

of Latium had to be joined to their conquerors in order
for the destined empire to emerge, one might argue that
by 1864 there was a sense that the conquered of the South
would have to rejoin with their conquerors before the destiny of America could be fulfilled.

The Burial of Latane was one of two remarkably popular images that many postbellum southerners had in their
homes. The other was "Lee and His Generals," which was
issued in a number of versions in the decades following
the Civil War. One of the earliest, by John Smith, is close
to two feet in length and depicts Lee and twenty-one generals on horseback (fig. 4.17).[54] Another print, *The Generals of the Confederate Army*, was copyrighted in 1881 and enjoyed a wide circulation because it was "published for presentation to each subscriber for *Stephens' History of the
United States.*" In that image, President Jefferson Davis is
included with the fifteen generals who accompany Lee.

For the *Summer* mural of the Richmond cycle, Charles
Hoffbauer was instructed to picture Lee with twelve of his
Virginia generals (fig. 4.18).

It mattered little that these groupings were imaginary. Many of the figures portrayed had never gathered
together during the war and a number of the generals
were dead by its end. More relevant was that such fanciful
groupings presented the hierarchy of the Confederate
military as akin to King Arthur's Knights of the Round
Table. These images served to tighten the association of
the Lost Cause with the chivalric traditions of Old Virginia.

The most widely circulated of the group of Lee prints
was by George Bagby Matthews. His version of *Lee and His
Generals* was published in 1907, the year of the Jamestown
tercentennial but also the centennial of the birth of the
Confederate commander (fig. 4.19). A Virginian from the

Tidewater region, Matthews had studied in Paris in the early 1880s with Carolus Duran before he set up shop, first in Richmond and then in Washington, D.C., where he issued his version of this icon of the Lost Cause. Matthews's image, which pictures Lee with twenty-five generals, is in color, and is perhaps more successful aesthetically than those that preceded it. Such representations of Lee and his commanders lingered on the walls of Virginia parlors well after the last Confederate veteran had died, and many survive to this day.

Near the close of *Surry of Eagles-Nest*, John Esten Cooke looks to Stonewall Jackson. If Lee was the inheritor of the cavalier tradition—English and Episcopalian in character—Jackson was the Confederacy's Calvinist Cromwell, from a Scotch-Irish and Presbyterian heritage. In remembrances of the Confederacy these traditions were fused, providing a measure of pride for every white southerner regardless of his origins, class, or religion. Cooke attributes to Jackson a soliloquy that justifies the Lost Cause in terms of honor and duty, those chivalric values that were at the heart of Old Virginia society. Surry worries that Virginians will "have lost all" in the war and "gained nothing." Jackson, however, quickly interjects "But honor!" and then continues:

> "No, Colonel! You are wrong—a thousand times wrong! Suppose we are conquered— suppose the South does fall—I declare to you that, should I live, I will not regret for one instant this struggle; not the blood, the treasure, the failure—nothing! There may be persons who fight for fame or success—I fight for my principles! I appeal to God for the purity of my motives—and whether I live or die— whether the South falls or conquers—I shall be able to say, 'I did my duty.'"[55]

A few pages later, at the very end of the book, Cooke states that "the Past comes into the Present, and possesses it." Only a year after Appomattox, it was clear to this veteran and to many in Virginia that the Lost Cause of the past would consume the present, which, as we consider it today, seems to leave no room for the future.[56]

In *Surry of Eagles-Nest* and his other Civil War novels, Cooke helped to mythologize the chivalric legacy of the Confederacy. In 1877, in the preface to *The Old Virginia Gentleman*, an essay that lauds the lost society of Old Virginia, George W. Bagby worked in a similar vein. He confesses to offering "a most exaggerated estimate of my State and its people." This is acceptable, he argues, because "our Mother is dead, and much may be pardoned in a eulogy which would be inexcusable were the subject living." On the one hand, both Cooke and Bagby had realized that a lost cause can be highly appealing. The losing participants can be ennobled in part *because* they lost their struggle. The reader, because he knows the inevitable ending, is accepting of exaggeration. Sir Walter

4.20 *Unidentified artist, for William Cameron & Brothers, Virginia,* Our Chief. Lochiel, *1876, lithograph (tobacco label), 10 x 10 in., Virginia Historical Society*

Scott had celebrated the Highlanders of Scotland, whose support of the House of Stuart and whose longing for an independent Scotland had by the early nineteenth century become an exemplary literary lost cause. (Mark Twain would humorously accuse Scott of causing the Civil War.) Similarly, James Fenimore Cooper's romances that included noble Indians like Chingochgook were appealing to an American society that had driven the Native American population from the eastern seaboard. Cooke and Bagby, while tapping into the still rampant patriotism of postwar Virginians, also understood that their readers would identify with, and be attracted to, what we might call Lost Cause propaganda.

Many tapped into such feelings. William Cameron was a Scottish immigrant to Petersburg on the eve of the Civil War who prospered in the tobacco business. He transformed his house, Mount Erin, into a crenellated structure that became known as Cameron's Castle. He then selected a seemingly obscure hero from Scottish history, *Our Chief Lochiel* (fig. 4.20) to provide the name and image for one of his products. In part, Cameron's Scottish ancestry explains his interest in the chieftain. But the larger cultural significance of his celebration of this unusual hero, one who would fight to the death for a Lost Cause, would not have been lost on Cameron's prospective postbellum customers.

In Scotland, the Camerons of Lochiel were for two centuries loyal supporters of the Jacobite cause, which upheld the claims of the Stuart pretenders to the throne. Sir Ewen Cameron of Lochiel had rallied behind Charles II in the 1650s to help undo the Puritan ascendancy. This first significant Cameron had reportedly sunk his teeth into the throat of a Cromwellian to kill him, thus furnishing Sir Walter Scott with an episode for *The Lady of the Lake*, the fight between Roderick Dhu and James Fitz-James. Donald Cameron of Lochiel was a Jacobite leader in 1746 at the disastrous battle of Culloden in which the Highlanders were foiled in their attempt to restore the House of Stuart to the British throne. In 1802 he was immortalized in Thomas Campbell's "Lochiel's Warning," which the poet personally read to Sir Walter Scott, who reputedly memorized the eighty-seven lines on the spot. Cameron's tobacco label quotes passages from this poem, wherein Lochiel rebukes a wizard who tells him that "Culloden [and the Jacobite cause] is lost." Lochiel answers that his men are "true to the last of their blood and their breath":

> Down, soothless insulter! I trust not the tale . . .
> Lochiel, untainted by flight or by chains,
> While the kindling of life in his bosom remains,
> Shall victor exult, or in death be laid low,
> With his back to the field, and his feet to the foe![57]

As defiant and proud as Stonewall Jackson, whom he even resembles physically in the Cameron logo, Lochiel will never surrender, even when all seems lost. In a sense, such Scottish Highlanders as Lochiel were medieval figures, survivors from an age that had supposedly ended several centuries earlier. Lochiel followed the code of a knight and, as a Highlander, dressed in a way that denied the advent of the modern era.

The cult of the medieval that had been so revered in Old Virginia, and that culminated in the veneration of Confederate knights, was perpetuated in a number of peculiar ways throughout the postbellum South, most notably in the formation of the knights of the Ku Klux Klan. This social fraternity, which had been organized in 1866 in Pulaski, Tennessee, was soon controlled by the former Confederate soldiers of that state, including the great cavalryman General Nathan Bedford Forrest. Membership quickly spread throughout the South. These clansmen were like indignant Highlanders with their "feet to the foe"; in burning crosses they borrowed from the Highland clans the signal to muster for a fight. They rejected the Confederate defeat and looked to block the resultant social change. With a vision of reconstruction that was entirely different from that of the federal government, this American Klan avowed to return, as much as was possible, to the old ways of the plantation era.

In *Red Rock, A Chronicle of Reconstruction*, 1899, Thomas Nelson Page complained, "It is the fashion nowadays to have only words of condemnation [for the antebellum South]. Every ass that passes by kicks at the dead lion." Page and other contemporary Virginians felt a bitterness about Reconstruction in general, and in particular about the way that the old plantation system had been dishonored. He defended the southerner's response to the catastrophic results of the war, including the deployment of the Klan:

> If [Southerners] shone in prosperity, much more they shone in adversity; if they bore themselves haughtily in their day of triumph, they have borne defeat with splendid fortitude. Their old family seats, with everything else in the world, were lost to them—their dignity became grandeur. Their entire system crumbled and fell about them in ruins—they remained unmoved. They were subjected to the greatest humiliation of modern times: their slaves were put over them—they reconquered their section and preserved the civilization of the Anglo-Saxon.[58]

The "Ku Klux" is prominent in Page's novel, which is set "in the South, somewhere" that has "blue mountain-spurs"; most readers would thereby imagine that the setting is western Virginia. When a villainous carpet-bagger named Jonadab Leech, who had become "one of the leading men in the State," organizes a black militia unit whose members "absolutely abandoned" their work in the fields and became so "indolent and swaggering" that "the

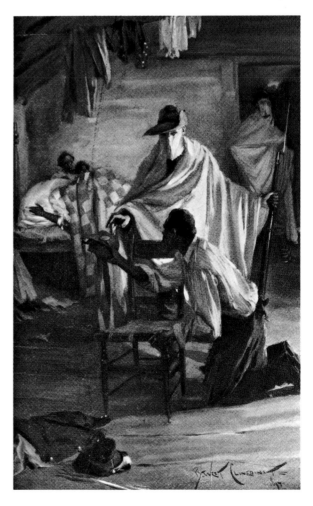

4.21 B. West Clinedinst, Ku Klux—"Awful Forms Wrapped like Ghosts in Winding-Sheets," *illustration in Thomas Nelson Page,* Red Rock, A Chronicle of Reconstruction, *1899, Virginia Historical Society*

whites disappeared almost wholly from the streets," the Klan was called into action. The black leader of the unit tells his men that "we are goin' to raise [taxes] . . . till we bankrupt 'em every one, and then the land will go to the ones as ought to have it, and if anybody interferes with you, you've got guns and you know how to use 'em."[59] In response to so grave a threat to civilization, "a new force" arises, "a force composed of ghostly night-riders" known as the "Invisible Empire." The "Ku Klux" mobilizes "in the dead of night, . . . passing through the county from settlement to settlement and from cabin to cabin, in silence." B. West Clinedinst illustrated the episode for Page's readers (fig. 4.21), which is missing the expected violence:

> All that the dejected warriors could tell next day was that there had been a noise outside, the door had been opened; the yard had been found full of awful forms wrapped like ghosts in winding-sheets, some of whom had entered the houses, picked up the guns and ammunition, and without a word walked out and disappeared.[60]

Elsewhere Page admits in his fictional account that "in some few places there had been force exerted and violence used." To his thinking, however, the means justified the end. "The negroes were paralyzed with terror" and thus a crisis passed.[61]

Later in the novel, through the figure of Captain Steve Allen, a Confederate veteran and heroic leader of the white community, Page makes an effort to justify the Klan to his northern readers. In addressing a young lady from the North, Captain Allen dismisses the evils that by 1899 were associated with the Klan as simply the work of imposters, not the doing of the true southern aristocrats who had established the organization:

> I organized it and led it, because I deemed it absolutely necessary for our protection at the time—for our salvation. No one was seriously hurt. . . . Under the excitement of such an occasion, where there were hundreds of young men, some full of fun, others wild and reckless, some unauthorized acts were committed. . . . but no lives were taken and no great violence was done. The reports you have heard of it were untrue. . . . But I found that the blackguards and sneaks could take advantage of the disguise, and under the disguise wreak their private spite, and by common consent the den was disbanded soon after that night. There have been ruffianly acts committed since that time by men disguised as Ku Klux. . . .[62]

The southern versions of the war, of Reconstruction, and of the Klan were made manifest to an even larger audience in the epic film *The Birth of a Nation*, which was released in 1915. The southerner D. W. Griffith based his film on two overtly racist novels by the Reverend Thomas Dixon, Jr., *The Leopard's Spots* (1902) and *The Clansman*

(1905); the latter had been a best seller. In *The Birth of a Nation* Griffith argues that the Klan redeemed the error of emancipation by reconciling former wartime enemies to save the South from the anarchy of black rule. Griffith toned down the bias in *The Clansman* and eliminated much of the history of the Klan that Dixon provided his readers, but he retained the violence and enough of the racism that the film, while being acclaimed in the South, was picketed when it was presented in such northern cities as Boston, New York, and Chicago.

In the early years after the war, the Klan had seemed a logical means to assure the continuance of the culture that Confederates had fought so bravely to defend. The postwar period seemed a time when extra-legal means were necessary to defend a white population that apparently was no longer being served by governmental power. As in medieval England, when such outlaw/heroes as Robin Hood emerged to protect the oppressed, so in the Reconstructed South, when proper legal action was disallowed, the Ku Klux Klan could fill the breach. It called its members knights, and it vowed to uphold the codes of honor and decency that had been the foundation of the antebellum South. While many of the clansmen may initially have had noble intentions concerning the defense of the helpless, too often they took part in the abusive treatment of former slaves. In many instances the Klan became the instrument of evil. Through their use of violence and disregard for the very justice that they claimed to seek, the knights of the Klan severely tarnished the image of all of those who sought a return to what they perceived to be the morals, if not the methods, of the antebellum South.

Reimagining the Antebellum Past: The Plantation Society Defended

Interest in the rural lifestyle of antebellum Virginia intensified after Appomattox. Despite the problems with the old plantation society that had been evident well before the start of the war—the economic and social deterioration, the exhaustion of the soil, and the injustice of slavery and the perceived indolence of many slaveholders—the way of life during that period came to be seen as superior to the current condition of many postwar Virginians, particularly when the old days were reimagined without those faults. Equally important to the emerging cult of Old Virginia was the fact that postbellum northerners also chose to recall that past. Looking from afar, idyllic ruralism suddenly seemed appealing; the virtues of the region, many of which had always elicited a sympathetic response above the Mason-Dixon line, could now be savored freely, without fear that Virginia's agricultural, slave-driven society posed a threat to either northern mercantile interests or northern morality. The bucolic world of Old Virginia that was but a memory in 1865 would soon rise again in the popular consciousness.

European visitors to postwar Virginia presented varied accounts of the Old Dominion. To some, like Alex Rivington, "Virginia . . . has been able to this day to maintain and propagate its aristocratic traditions, handed down from Raleigh and the men of noble families who accompanied him . . . to found another England in the New World." However, the instrument that had been used to do this was "that most degrading institution, slavery."[63] On the other hand, C. B. Berry encountered what he judged to be a deflated Virginia aristocracy. He saw no evidence of a once idyllic society, only a population of "idle" planters who seemed to have always lacked energy. The southerner, he concluded, was not "the true sort" of gentleman, one who would pursue refinement to the point that he would elevate the people around him.[64]

By the 1870s many Virginians of the old school were oblivious to their shortcomings and denied any such criticism of their society. When they turned their attention to the past, they looked not to what had been lacking before Appomattox, but only to what had been lost there. On traveling through postwar Virginia, the northern journalist Edward King concluded that the former slaveholder wanted only to return to the bygone days:

> He flies to the farthest corner of the lands that have been spared to him out of the wrecks caused by the war, and strives to forget the present, and to live as he did "before the surrender," like a country squire in England two hundred years ago.[65]

King, a proponent of modernism and industrial growth, ridicules what he sees as the planter's attempt to retreat into the rural past. His affront, however, points to the postwar reawakening of the philosophical stance that we have identified as the pastoral ideal. It was revived by the planters as best they could given the collapse of the old order, and by Virginia's apologists, who were effective in reivigorating the entity that has come down to us as Old Virginia. There is a degree of poignancy in these real and imaginary attempts to re-create a rural lifestyle that was conducive to the pursuit of virtue. Writers from Virgil to Goldsmith to twenty-first-century environmentalists have feared, and then lamented, the loss of idyllic spaces, in part because of the concurrent loss of the inspiration that such spaces can provide. The ravages of the late war had laid waste to much of rural Virginia; the best chance for its restoration lay in the mind's eye of the apologists and their many readers.

We have already encountered the three arch-apologists—George Esten Cooke, George Bagby, and Thomas Nelson Page (figs. 4.22, 4.23, and 4.24)—through their association with the Lost Cause. All were Virginians, and

*4.22 **Above, top, left** John Esten Cooke, photograph, Virginia Historical Society*

*4.23 **Above, top, right** George William Bagby, copy of ca. 1860-65 photograph, Virginia Historical Society*

*4.24 **Above** Thomas Nelson Page, photograph by Frances Benjamin Johnston, albumen print, Virginia Historical Society*

all were quick to master the techniques of hyperbole and historical revisionism, in which their readers, both southern and northern, were apparently more than willing to indulge. With ingenious, but, from our perspective, at times muddled logic, they attempted to justify antebellum life, even going so far as to defend slavery, which most Americans by the 1870s considered to have been a deplorable institution. Exploiting the popular appeal of the aristocratic lifestyle, the techniques of what would come to be called the "local color" school of writing, and the literary convention of the ennobling of a fallen people,

4.25 *Left* A Magnificent Production of that Sterling Historical Drama Uncle Tom's Cabin or Life Among the Lowly, by Harriet Beecher Stowe, *ca. 1890s, broadside, 28 x 11 in., Virginia Historical Society*

4.26 *Below, center* "Plantation Songs and Melodies," from A Magnificent Production of that Sterling Historical Drama Uncle Tom's Cabin or Life Among the Lowly, by Harriet Beecher Stowe, *ca. 1890s, broadside, Virginia Historical Society*

4.27 *Below* "Legree Whipping Tom," from A Magnificent Production of that Sterling Historical Drama Uncle Tom's Cabin or Life Among the Lowly, by Harriet Beecher Stowe, *ca. 1890s, broadside, Virginia Historical Society*

these thinkers were successful enough that a number of authors followed their lead, thereby allowing their own readers to escape to what had been transformed into a sanitized southern past.

In the late 1850s, when he was not yet thirty years old, John Esten Cooke had already become nationally known for his many articles about southern life. Born in Winchester and raised in the Valley and in Richmond, he had turned to writing after studying law. He was a prolific author, now remembered for his Civil War titles and stories, as well as his histories of colonial Virginia. George Bagby, who spent most of his life in Lynchburg, was an editor of the *Southern Literary Messenger* and a highly popular public speaker. His *Old Virginia Gentleman*, a lecture that was eventually published as an essay, is a classic expression of the apologist's creed. Thomas Nelson Page played a critical role in the reimagining of the region's antebellum past because his accounts and stories about Old Virginia were widely read in both the United States and Europe. Born and raised in Hanover County, he was the son of a Confederate officer, a great-grandson of a governor (John Page), and was related to scores of Old Virginia families, including the Randolphs, Pendletons, Wickhams, Carters, Lees, and Nelsons.

The refutation of what many southerners deemed misinformation would underlie the postwar reinvention of Old Virginia. Page explains in the introduction to his classic apology, *Social Life in Old Virginia Before the War* (1897), that among his reasons for publishing the book was "the absolute ignorance of the outside world of the real life of the South in old times, and [his] desire to correct the picture for the benefit of the younger generation of Southerners themselves."[66] He complained that the wrong impression about the South had been put forward in Harriet Beecher Stowe's fantastically popular *Uncle Tom's Cabin* and in the "large crop of so-called Southern plays" that ridiculed the southerner. One of those postwar plays, *A Magnificent Production of that Sterling Historical Drama Uncle Tom's Cabin or Life Among the Lowly* (fig. 4.25) was advertised in a broadside that presents Stowe's novel as if it were fact instead of fiction: "DON'T FAIL TO TAKE THE CHILDREN AND GIVE THEM A LASTING LESSON IN AMERICAN HISTORY." This production would have offended Page in part because of two of the stereotypes that it perpetuated. The traditional image of simpleminded slaves dancing, playing the banjo, and singing happy songs furnished light comedy (fig. 4.26). The portrayal of a cruel slave driver with a whip in hand provided gripping tragedy (fig. 4.27). Each figure would have been anticipated by even the casual playgoer, as the production had been advertised as "Replete with Comedy and Pathos."

Neither the rollicking slaves nor the cruel slave owner would have been accepted as archetypal by the apologists, who attempted to present a more pleasing picture of the

4.28 *David Gilmour Blythe,* Old Virginia Home, *1864, oil on canvas, 20³/₄ x 28³/₄ in., Art Institute of Chicago*

lives of slaves and the interactions between the races. In *Social Life in Old Virginia*, Page set out to counter such sensationalism by telling a more complete story of Virginia life, which not surprisingly, was dominated by the viewpoint of the white southerner. He argued that slavery was but "one of the factors in that life." Yet, because that institution was thought of as the defining flaw in the society that he chose to celebrate, the apologist constructed nearly all of his arguments around its defense. Page even defined the subject of social life in Old Virginia not by the civility and entertainments of the gentry, but primarily in terms of the supposedly positive relationship between master and slave. If readers today tire of Page's strained logic, we must recognize that the legacy of slavery was profound in his day; it helped to form both national and international opinions about the region.

Page, Bagby, and Cooke often began their apologetic discourses with descriptions of a plantation, with particular attention paid to the house itself. They would next look at the people who made up the society, and then at the social activities in which those people engaged, which frequently included material related to black/white interactions. In the following pages we will follow this formulation, and, when appropriate, invoke their narratives. When we do so we look at their arguments critically, but with an understanding of the bias that inevitably clouded their remembrances as they struggled for cultural survival in the difficult climate of Reconstruction.

"God Bless My Old Virginia Home"

By the antebellum period, Tidewater Virginia had been so agriculturally depleted that for decades travelers to the region had described it as blighted, with unproductive fields and run-down buildings. Apologists for the old ways, however, chose to ignore that reality. Virginia's arcadian rural environment had inspired the region's then two-centuries-old flirtation with the pastoral. It was the land, above all else, that set Virginia apart from the urban North. The apologists reimagined antebellum life in the region as having unfolded in the idyllic setting of large, well-kept manor houses, whose inhabitants enjoyed the bounty of a healthy farm economy. These homes were either stately mansions or, in some cases, rambling structures with enough wings added to the core to accommodate large families and innumerable guests. The latter type of house, because it had expanded informally, seemed to offer a warmer environment than did the cold, symmetrical mansion that had become too much associated with a cruel slave system. A third type of building, the cottage, which was smaller and thereby even farther removed from the slave past, also intrigued Americans of this era and had its vogue as the exemplary "Old Virginia Home." The vocabulary presented by these structures would be used by both attackers and defenders of the South in the rhetorical battles that followed those of the military.

The idea of an old plantation house, if not always that precise term, was popularized before the war in fiction and song; lyrics such as Christie's "Carry Me Back to Old Virginia" (1847) and many of the works of Stephen Foster, the most popular songwriter of the day, including "Old Folks at Home" (1851) and "My Old Kentucky Home" (1853), used this motif. Even at this early date the prominent theme was often nostalgia for a home and a lifestyle that for unstated reasons had been abandoned.

This characterization would continue to be invoked during and after the war, and the apologists would make excellent use of the ideas of loss and recovery in their literature. However, in 1864 the Pittsburgh artist and satirist David Gilmour Blythe would employ the idea of the "Old Virginia Home" in an unusual painting that lampoons the domestic scene that it purports to picture (fig. 4.28). In this complex image, Blythe criticizes both the myth of southern, rural contentment and the Federal decision to end slavery and cast African Americans to whatever fate awaited them.

Blythe presents a newly liberated slave, who departs a dilapidated, burning classical dwelling that is labeled on its gateway "OLD VIRGINIA HOME." The ruined structure is meant to represent the demise of both the Confederacy and the old ways of the southern plantation. Pictured in the left background is a portion of the Union army that presumably set the slave free. The man's broken condition, however, and the apocalyptic vision in the sky suggest that emancipation will hardly solve the host of pressing problems that it had inevitably created. A raven, a bird representative of famine and carrion, points also to the perilous state of the freedman, who must now somehow survive in a land where death has become commonplace. In the right foreground the name of Henry A. Wise, a Confederate general and former governor of Virginia, is written on a broken barrel. Information about Wise and the fate of Rolleston, his Tidewater plantation, which in 1862 had been captured and used to house freedmen, must have come to Blythe's attention. The irony that the plantation of a prominent secessionist had served to house liberated African Americans was not missed by the artist. Blythe's bleak image also interestingly masks the surprising reality that Rolleston endured, would survive the war, and would ultimately be returned to the ownership of Wise. [67]

The architecture pictured by Blythe as the quintessential "Old Virginia Home" is as anomalous as his theme. With its classical portico and one-story height, the building is almost Jeffersonian; it is neither large nor small. At the time that Blythe conceived this peculiar vision, two types of Virginia architecture were already well known to the American public through their association with George Washington. These were the stately rural mansion and the picturesque cottage; the general had lived in the former and supposedly had been born in the latter. Both were anti-urban models, in which were offered settings where the virtues that were believed to accompany country life could be pursued.

Because of Washington's fame, no structure in America had been more frequently depicted in prints than Mount Vernon (fig. 4.29). By mid-century it was the best-known rural Virginia mansion; the giant piazza of this house was so renowned as to influence Greek Revival ar-

*4.29 **Above, top** C. B. Graham, lithographer, and J. Crutchett, publisher,* Mount Vernon, West Front, *1858, lithograph, 10 x 14³/₄ in., Virginia Historical Society*

*4.30 **Above, center** Currier and Ives,* The Birth-Place of Washington, *ca. 1860, lithograph, 10 x 12³/₈ in., Mount Vernon Ladies' Association, gift of Dr. and Mrs. Joseph E. Fields*

*4.31 **Above** Currier and Ives,* A Virginia Home in Olden Time, *1872, lithograph, 8¹/₂ x 12¹/₂ in., Virginia Historical Society*

chitecture throughout the antebellum South. Additional prints of the house were published when the estate was purchased and ultimately preserved by the Mount Vernon Ladies' Association. Washington's natal home at Pope's Creek in Westmoreland County, as it was imagined by Benson Lossing in *Mount Vernon and Its Associations* (1860), was a clapboarded Dutch cottage. Lossing's image was repeated in a Currier and Ives lithograph and marketed as *The Birth-Place of Washington* (fig. 4.30). Lossing's creation, it turned out, was pure fantasy. Archaeologists have since determined that Washington was born in a brick house that was something of a mansion for its time and place; however, Lossing's creation was of a type compatible with mid-century expectations.[68] Some ten years after Lossing's publication, the Currier and Ives print that mimicked Lossing inspired a similar lithograph by the same firm entitled *A Virginia Home in Olden Time* (fig. 4.31).

At mid-century, and for decades until the advent of the Colonial Revival, the picturesque cottage rather than the stately mansion captured the national imagination as the most appealing of the types of domestic architecture associated with Old Virginia. There were a number of reasons why this cottage myth emerged and persisted. In many popular songs, such as John T. Rutledge's "God Bless My Old Virginia Home" (1877), there are references similar to his narrator's nostalgic remembrance of the "dear old hallowed cottage"of his youth. There was the association with Washington's birth; later in the century Abraham Lincoln's early life in a log cabin would increase the pressure to see Washington as someone who had come from appropriately humble beginnings.[69] Third, in both Europe and America there was by mid-century a nostalgia for a simpler, rural way of life. Images of a less complicated time, which were recalled from childhood but had disappeared as progress brought change in the form of too rapid urbanization and industrialism, became attractive and called to mind a longed-for alternative. The cottage seemed a refuge of stability and simplicity, an uncomplicated environment that was conducive to the feelings of contentment that could at least be contemplated if not entirely recaptured. Fourth, as sectionalist tensions increased, America had begun to allow for the existence of a poor white population of the South. Fictional characters had emerged well before the war, finding expression in romances like John Pendleton Kennedy's *Horse-Shoe Robinson, A Tale of the Tory Ascendency* (1835) and Emily Clemens Pearson's *Cousin Frank's Household: or, Scenes in the Old Dominion* (1852), and by the 1850s there was a clearer sense that the South was not made up simply of great plantation houses and slave quarters. By the 1880s, with the increasing democratization of America, the smaller "Old Virginia Home" had greater resonance because a cottage could be built by

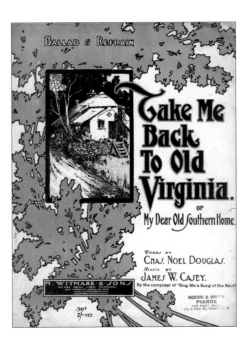

4.32 *Charles Noel Douglas and James W. Casey, "Take Me Back to Old Virginia, or, My Dear Old Southern Home," New York, 1903, sheet music, Virginia Historical Society*

anyone who owned land. Fifth, and perhaps most importantly, unlike the wealthy lord of the stately mansion house, the cottage owner was not a slaveholder. The cottage in this case served as an anti-myth, which, in a society steeped with abolitionist propaganda, made the perhaps surprising point that the lives of the majority of white Virginians had been at best untouched, at worst harmed, by slavery. When pictured, the inhabitants of such cottages, be they lower-class whites or blacks, were picturesque, in the same way as were the peasantry of Europe, survivors from an unpretentious time, meant to inspire in the viewer emotions that ranged from nostalgia to sentimentalism.

The myth of the cottage persisted for decades. In "Take Me Back to Old Virginia, or, My Dear Old Southern Home" (1903), Charles Noel Douglas "yearns" for "that dear boyhood's home, 'neath Southern skies" (fig.4.32). The cover to the sheet music illustrates a thatched-roof cottage, of a type that is more English than Virginian. About 1918, Gari Melchers painted an actual Virginia cottage that he had discovered in the landscape surrounding his adopted home near Fredericksburg (fig. 4.33). After having lived in the Detroit of his birth, and later in Düsseldorf, Paris, and other European cities, Melchers settled in Virginia late in his life. The idea of the Old Virginia cottage appealed to this acclaimed painter because similar elements of rusticity and nostalgia had appeared in his paintings of Dutch peasants that had won international acclaim. In the scene that he titled *In Old Virginia*, Melchers even followed the Dutch convention of including an appropriately picturesque cow. He looked back to a lifestyle that was leisurely and easy, and therefore an antidote to World War I and the other burgeoning ills of the modern world.

For more aristocratic Virginians, George Bagby would champion the rambling manor house, which seemed to this apologist to be a more intimate structure than the traditional mansion:

4.33 *Gari Melchers*, In Old Virginia, *ca. 1918, oil on canvas, 32 x 40 in., Belmont, Gari Melchers Gallery*

As a rule . . . it was neither planned nor built—it grew; and that was its great charm. . . . In the course of time, as children came along, as the family connexions increased, and as the desire, the necessity in fact, of keeping a free hotel grew upon him, the old gentleman kept adding a wing here and tacking a shed room there until the original building became mixed up and, as it were, lost in the crowd of additions.[70]

A house that was an organic, living thing could emphasize the close kinship of the family within.

Thomas Nelson Page begins *Social Life in Old Virginia* by describing the setting of his childhood, Oakland plantation (Hanover County, 1812, burned 1898), which the author celebrated as an "old Virginia home" that was a "plain 'weatherboard' house," one story and a half above a half-basement ground floor, "not a handsome place," and having "as many wings as Ezekiel."[71] As was true with the vogue of the cottage, Bagby would promote an architecture that "was neither planned nor built" and Page would celebrate a "plain" house with multiple wings because the mansion had fallen out of favor. If the classically inspired estate house had the burden of being the domain of the domineering trader in human flesh, a smaller house that had grown haphazardly by accretion did not. The nostalgia for a time gone by could survive, without invoking stereotypical master/slave relations.

There was at least a modicum of validity to this preference. A number of the buildings in antebellum Virginia were in fact rambling structures with wings, which had either been added by successive generations of owners, who seemed determined to make a statement in this way about lineage and longevity, or were built that way from the start because small units are simply easier for a carpenter to design and construct than are large ones. Rolleston (fig. 4.34), the home of General Wise, was such an edifice, an assemblage of at least three architecturally differentiated and separate structures. There can be no doubt as to the size of the house, but there is little unifying vision.

In the end, however, the apologists could not completely forget the stately mansions of early Virginia. In an article published in *Appletons' Journal* in 1872, John Esten Cooke describes Oaktree Hall, a house that he had known personally, as "a large brick mansion," for which he would only "employ adjectives of magnitude." "Every thing about the hall [house]," he argues, "was large and open, like the hearts of its inmates."[72] In 1877 George Bagby wrote that "the habitation of the old Virginia gentleman—house is too short a word to express it— . . . was sometimes stately, like the great, square house of 'Rosewell'" (fig. 4.35). As the principal Page family seat during the colonial era, Rosewell was a massive structure that in its size and lavish detailing outdid even the nearby governor's residence in Williamsburg that was always called a "Palace." Although Bagby had cited probably the grandest domestic building ever erected in all of colonial America, he chose not to discuss either the great classical

4.34 *Left* Rolleston, *Princess Anne County, ca. 1700; burned by 1900, photograph, Virginia Historical Society*

4.35 *Below, left* Rosewell, *Gloucester County, ca. 1721-41; burned 1916, photograph courtesy of The Valentine Museum*

4.36 *Below* Belmont, *late eighteenth century and later, Fredericksburg, photograph courtesy of Belmont, The Gari Melchers Estate and Memorial Gallery, Mary Washington College*

tradition that gave rise to such seats nor the large-scale slave operations that had been necessary to keep homes like Rosewell going. Size, not necessarily substance, was what was crucial in such descriptions.

Despite the cottage pictured in Gari Melchers's *In Old Virginia* (fig. 4.33 above), a work which was purposefully entitled to evoke nostalgia for a pre-urban, rural simplicity, the more traditional image of Old Virginia was as a landscape of mansion houses built in the classical tradition. This, in fact, was what had attracted Melchers to the region; a major influence in his choice of Virginia and the Fredericksburg area as his new home was the availability of Belmont (fig. 4.36), which the artist purchased in 1916. Admittedly, its double porch with columns was probably a nineteenth-century addition to an eighteenth-century structure, but otherwise the building reads as the typical southern mansion that was planned and built as a whole. By the mid-teens, when Melchers relocated to the

region, the national vogue for the colonial era had served to revive interest in the Virginia mansions. At that point the image of a large Virginia plantation house, with its associations of a lifestyle funded by immense wealth, had regained appeal. The grand tradition of Virginia architecture, which had influenced the nascent Colonial Revival movement a generation before, was being rediscovered and re-appreciated in its home state.

The cottage and the rambling house had offered alternative visions of Old Virginia domiciles that sidestepped the traditional image of the region as a land of slave masters, who were as cold and remote as their stony mansions, in order to downplay the legacy of slavery, which after Appomattox had increasingly become a liability for the image of Virginia. But the arch-apologists could not endorse the cottage myth—George Bagby's description of antebellum society in the Old Dominion was that it "had no equal since Greece," and so its patricians could not be shown to live in unsophisticated dwellings. The apologists felt the need to devise other methods whereby the liabilities caused by slavery could be deflected or turned on their accusers.[73]

The myth of the Old Virginia cottage inevitably had to fail, in part because there was nothing specifically Virginian about it and, more importantly, because such simple homes lacked a strong philosophical basis. This characteristic was missing as well in the attempts to picture the traditional Old Virginia residence as an unplanned assemblage of parts. In the final analysis, both conceptions fell short of the mansions that they were intended to replace. They were buildings, not architecture. The standards of virtue and gentility that had formed the bedrock of the imaginative Old Virginia society were lost in such unambitious models. The ideals of the Enlightenment had inspired not only fine architecture, but also fine living and great systems of government, whereas the cottage owner with a pipe in his hand might well be contented, but his dreams were not so lofty, and the rambling plantation house, which followed no plan, could not serve as a model for a well-ordered life. These imprecise buildings, because of their lack of direction and sophistication, stood as evidence that the philosophy that a century before had served as a guide for both the architecture and the society at large had been lost.

The mansions, by contrast, were clear, well-devised expressions of the gentility, of the striving for virtue, and of the humanism that were meant to accompany the pastoral life. The classical tradition had admittedly become associated with slavery, but eventually enough positive cultural values were remembered to outweigh the negatives. The great houses were themselves great ideas, and they carried great ideas within them. Once the mania for the picturesque Old Virginia cottage had subsided, the classical tradition of architecture in the Old Dominion would reassert itself and would have a profound effect on the reimagined relationship between the present and the colonial past that would gain momentum in the early decades of the twentieth century.

"Was This Actually So?": Still Longing for the Old Plantation

Halfway through *The Old Virginia Gentleman* (1877), his seminal essay that was exemplary of the apologists' defense of the old order, George Bagby pauses to wonder whether his reminiscences of antebellum society in the Old Dominion are accurate: "In the solitude of my room," he wrote, "I sometimes ask myself aloud, 'Was this actually so? Did I live in those days? Isn't it a dream? Did I ever know such women? Is there not some mirage, some rosy but false light thrown upon the picture as it appears in memory? It is very, very beautiful; but is it not of the fancy merely?'" He quickly answers his own query: "No! blessed be the Giver of every good and perfect gift, the picture is not imaginary. It is real."[74] Bagby's construction of this passage is revealing. He moves from a present reminiscence, back to the past, and then ends with his "picture" again in the present. "It is real"—the Old Virginia that he remembers still exists, if only in his mind and, he hopes, in the minds of his readers.

While commentators from Europe were reflecting the majority opinion in America that slavery had been the ruin of the South, Bagby crafted in response an alternative myth that many apologists would champion. He admits that his account of Old Virginia was not entirely true but was "a most exaggerated estimate of my State and its people." In his zeal to "awaken in our people a just pride in their Past," the author so confused myth and reality that the two had become intermingled, and would ultimately prove to be inseparable.[75]

Such articles as John Esten Cooke's "Old Virginia Manners" (1872) preceded *The Old Virginia Gentleman* and had reached a national audience, but it was Bagby who would produce the most emblematic work on the subject. Bagby wrote that he had intended to gather his ideas into a book entitled simply *Old Virginia,* but that he had failed to pull together "ample material" and feared that he best put down something "before I died." His essay purports to give the remembrances of an Old Virginia gentleman. The author's theme is that "beyond question there was in our Virginia country life a beauty, a simplicity, a purity, an uprightness, a cordial and lavish hospitality, a warmth and grace which shine in the lens of memory with a charm that passes all language at my command. It is gone with the social structure that gave it birth, and were I great, I would embalm it in the amber of such prose and verse as has not been written since John Milton laid down his pen."[76] His use of "embalm" suggests his concession of the demise of the old order. The embalming process preserves the form rather than the spirit of that which has departed.

A primary motivation of the apologists was to rectify supposed misconceptions about the principles of antebellum Virginians. The slaveholding society had gained the reputation both in the North and abroad as having been anything but virtuous. The long struggle by the Union army to end slavery had hammered into the northern consciousness the belief that the southern will to perpetuate a wicked system of human bondage had been the sole cause of the war, that those who engaged in such a practice were at best misguided, and that some of these rebels were actually evil. Through the creation of a geographically distinct mythology that would accent the positive qualities of its citizens, the apologists would attempt to reverse the South's negative legacy.

At the pinnacle of George Bagby's idealized picture of Old Virginia society were the virtuous plantation mistress and her husband the gentleman planter, who was imagined to be a serious individual who was ever preoccupied with thoughts about God, moral uprightness, honor, and responsibility. Admittedly, the planter had been pictured before the war in similar terms, but he was less grave in earlier manifestations. The apologists inserted into their fantasies about Old Virginia a heightened emphasis on morality so as to counter prevailing notions about the corrupt natures of many antebellum southerners.

Before the war, the plantation mistress was often described as a model of virtue. In some ways this adoration had been one means to placate the antebellum plantation wife, to keep her from rejecting her onerous, often rigorous, role of presiding over the domestic affairs of the household. As mentioned earlier, for many women the monitoring of the domestic slave population was a frustrating and thankless spiritual task, while the many chores involved in running a plantation house were physically exhausting. Although she was idealized simultaneously as a belle and an able administrator, such women, because they did not enter into the public sphere, often had their considerable efforts overlooked.

Old enough to have traveled the Virginia countryside during the 1850s and met many plantation mistresses, Bagby was positioned to convey credibility on the subject of their attributes and virtues. He and his fellow apologists resorted to making what now seem to be exaggerated claims about her virtue; indeed, they made the plantation mistress the focus of a vigorous post-war cult. She was saintlike, the inevitable inference being that slavery must not have been an evil if it was condoned and regulated at the household level by such paragons. One ploy of the new cult was therefore to denounce the northern critics who rejected the adoration of the mistress. On this subject Bagby assumed the posture of a religious revivalist:

> If ever I am tempted to call down the fire of divine wrath, it is upon the head of those (there have been such, incredible as it may seem,) who have wilfully and persistently misrepresented this best and purest of God's creatures as the luxurious, idle, cruel and tyrannical favorite of some Eastern hareem. The arch-fiend himself could not have originated a slander more gross, more infinitely and detestably foul.[77]

To counter any concern that Virginia women might not have relished the often difficult and distasteful duties that fell to them on the plantation, Bagby attempted to persuade his reader that the plantation wife in fact welcomed her role.[78] If she could be convincingly portrayed as actually enjoying hard work and savoring the development of intimate relationships with the host of people under her care, then the belief that given the chance she would have

4.37 *Maude Alice Cowles*, Tall lilies, white as angels' wings and stately as the maidens that walked among them, *frontispiece to Thomas Nelson Page*, Social Life in Old Virginia before the War, *1897, Virginia Historical Society*

rejected her position could be discarded as groundless:

> To feed, to clothe, to teach, to guide, to comfort, to nurse, to provide for and to watch over a great household and keep its complex machinery in noiseless order—these were the woman's rights which she asserted, and there was no one to dispute; this was her mission, and none ever dared to question it. Mother, mistress, instructor, counsellor, benefactress, friend, angel of the sick-room![79]

In her role as mother, "in the midst of her tall sons and blooming daughters," she had a "delicacy, tenderness, freshness, gentleness; [and] absolute purity of . . . life and thought, typified in the spotless neatness of her apparel and her every surrounding" that was "quite impossible to convey."[80]

> More grace, more elegance, more refinement, more guileless purity were never found the whole world over, in any age, not even that of the halcyon . . . . A complete, immaculate world of womanly virtue and home piety was theirs, the like of which, I boldly claim, was seldom approached, and never excelled, since the Almighty made man in his own image.[81]

Thomas Nelson Page believed that if he could establish that the southern woman's character was without flaw, then he would contribute to the image of Virginia a respectability that had been sadly lost. As the frontispiece of his *Social Life* he chose a picture of Virginia "maidens" amid "tall lilies, white as angels' wings" (fig. 4.37). This image is the work of Maude Cowles, a member of a well-known family of painting sisters from Farmington, Connecticut, who had strong Virginia connections. After the death of their mother, the Cowles sisters had been placed under the care of their mother's sister, "Miss Gwaltney," who traveled north from Virginia to assume that responsibility.[82] The plantation mistress is also the subject of Page's opening text, where she is described as the foundation of the society and remarkable in her attention to others:

> The mistress should be mentioned first, as she was the most important personage about the home, the presence which pervaded the mansion, the centre of all that life, the queen of that realm; the master willingly and proudly yielding her entire management of all household matters and simply carrying out her directions. . . .
>
> What she was, only her husband divined, and even he stood before her in dumb, half-amazed admiration, as he might before the inscrutable vision of a superior being. What she really was, was known only to God. Her life was one long act of devotion,—devotion to God, devotion to her husband, devotion to her children, devotion to her servants, to her friends, to the poor, to humanity.[83]

Page would have his readers understand that Virginia women were so caring as to look out for all of God's human creatures, and in particular that her "devotion to her servants" must have made slavery an institution that should have been admired rather than condemned.

The master apologist also manipulated his discussion of the girls of the plantation as a means to further associate the reputation of Old Virginia with virtue. In so doing Page left a period piece that tells as much about post-war Virginia values as about the antebellum society that it purportedly describes:

> [The girls of the plantation] were like the mother; made in her own image. They filled a peculiar place in the civilization; the key was set to them. They held by a universal consent the first place in the system, all social life revolving around them. So generally did the life shape itself about the young girl that it was almost as if a bit of the age of chivalry had been blown down the centuries and lodged in the old state. . . . In right of her blood (the beautiful Saxon, tempered by the influences of the genial Southern clime), she was exquisite, fine, beautiful; a creature of peach-blossom and snow; languid, delicate, saucy; now imperious, now melting, always bewitching. . . . She had not to learn to be a lady, because she was born one.[84]

At the other end of her life, the attractions of the southern woman were no less appealing. John Esten Cooke wrote of "the stately, mild, most charming old lady" who was his aunt as "one of the last links between the old age and the new." He added, "I seem to have touched hands, in clasping her thin, white fingers, with the age of Washington."[85] In the late nineteenth century Cooke's invocation of the memory of the foremost Founding Father served to bolster the image of the plantation wife as a figure of virtue. He would no doubt be surprised at the ambivalence that Washington inspires in many of our contemporaries.

The problem with reimagining the plantation mistress as a paragon carries us back to the issue of slavery. So virtuous a woman presumably could not have participated in a system based on human bondage, or, at the least, would have had trouble effectively directing the slaves who were her responsibility. The problems inherent for the mistress are personified by two of the women in Stowe's *Uncle Tom's Cabin*, which was criticized by apologists for its exaggerated depictions of southern life. Slavery could turn some women into monsters, like the harsh and thoughtless Marie St. Clare (the mother of the angelic Little Eva), who would instill fear in the slaves but in the process would keep the system in order. Or she could be benevolent, like Emily Shelby, who treated the slaves with Christian compassion but whose sympathy no doubt contributed to the financial problems at the Shelby plantation that led to the selling of Uncle Tom. Following emancipation, when Virginia women were freed from their responsibility for domestic slaves, the precarious position that many blacks found themselves in suggested that they might well have been better off before the war. The apologists played into this mythology, and went so far as to deny the existence of the problems that had no doubt caused serious moral dilemmas for many southern women.

Following the collapse of the old order, the wives of the planters were able to emerge from the shadow of the plantation and engage in various sorts of civic opportunities that provided a venue for the exhibition of patriotism. Pursuing a course plotted on the eve of the war by the Mount Vernon Ladies' Association and newly inspired by the nation's centenary, new historical and benevolent organizations were founded, such as the Association for the Preservation of Virginia Antiquities, the Daughters of the American Revolution, the National Society of the Colonial Dames of America, and the Confederate Memorial Literary Society. The preservationist impulses of many of these societies point to a sense that both Virginia's antiquities themselves, and what they tell us about the lives of previous generations, were in danger of being lost. These women, many of whom were from the old families, took it upon themselves to make sure that such items were conserved and protected.

4.38 *The Misses Cowles,* His thoughts dwelt upon serious things, *illustration in Thomas Nelson Page,* Social Life in Old Virginia before the War, *1897, Virginia Historical Society*

English commentator C. B. Berry had much to say about the postbellum Virginia gentleman:

> He wants energy. He may be high-spirited, hospitable, and honourable; but he is a drone. Assure him of his yearly income, give him a table at which to entertain his friends, and he is content. He is the good-hearted easy-going idler, seated in his cane chair with a cigar and a bottle of wine; but he is not the true energetic country gentleman, giving up his time to refining pursuits and the social welfare and elevation of his people. And this pernicious state of things in the South has beyond question been induced by slavery.[86]

This is the sort of sentiment with which the apologists would have to contend. In his 1872 article about "Old Virginia Manners," John Esten Cooke recalled one Old Virginia gentleman from before the war, his "much-loved Uncle Adam, who was a most excellent gentleman."[87] Page portrayed the southern man as epitomizing the most important of the chivalric ideals, piety, which in turn engendered a morality that guided his philosophy:

He believed in God, he believed in his wife, he believed in his blood. He was chivalrous, he was generous, he was usually incapable of fear or of meanness. To be a Virginia gentleman was the first duty; it embraced being a Christian and all the virtues.[88]

Although the problem of the distance that one had to travel to attend church services still applied as much as it did when William Fitzhugh complained in the seventeenth century, there can be little doubt that antebellum Virginians thought of themselves as devout Christians, and so the apologists were not exaggerating in pointing out their devotion.[89] Indeed, according to Page, one reason that the antebellum planter strove to be virtuous was that it fit his self image. The gentry of Old Virginia had risen in the national consciousness as the closest equivalent in America to a European-style aristocracy. Consequently, he wrote, the Virginia gentleman "believed in a democracy, but understood that the absence of a titled aristocracy had to be supplied by a class more virtuous than he believed any aristocracy to be."[90]

The apologists asserted that the planter's morality was manifested in his characteristically serious nature (fig. 4.38). He was the somber steward of the many responsibilities that he inherited. Bagby exaggerated the point: "In the depths of the Virginia character there was ever a stratum of grave thought and feeling that not seldom sank into sadness and even gloom."[91] Page imagined that the legacy of Virginia's Founding Fathers had much to do with this frame of mind:

> Responsibilities made him grave. . . . The greatness of the past, the time when Virginia had been the mighty power of the New World, loomed ever above him. . . . He saw the change that was steadily creeping on. . . . His thoughts dwelt upon serious things; he pondered causes and consequences. . . . He communed with the Creator and his first work, Nature.[92]

George Bagby had made the same connection in reference to the landscape: "Live wherever he might in Virginia, the breadth and grandeur of [the various] aspects of nature imparted their solemnity to him."[93] This notion was addended to the pastoral ideal; life in the country could make a gentleman virtuous, while concurrently allowing him the time to ponder more mundane yet no less grave subjects.

In *The Old Virginia Gentleman*, Bagby offers a bizarre list of the five types of the old-school gentleman. There was the figure of the squire as sketched by J. P. Kennedy in *Swallow Barn*. His Frank Meriwether is a tall, handsome, and genial gentleman who was philosophical about slavery, a bad arrangement that Virginians simply had inherited, but who saw no easy end in sight and recoiled at the instigations of outsiders in the matter. According to Bagby there was also the small, swarthy man; the fat,

4.39 *F. C. Yohn,* Katy dropped her head on his shoulder again, *illustration in F. Hopkinson Smith,* Colonel Carter's Christmas *(New York, 1903), Virginia Historical Society*

deeply pious gentleman with a soul of hospitality and kindness; the refined, scrupulously neat aristocrat, born and bred to that position; and the man with the gentleness and the humility of a devout Christian knight. Absent from the list is what we might call the "jovial" type, which was apparently well known from the post-war theater. "To me," Bagby wrote, "the strangest possible of mistakes is to reckon the broad-waisted, jovial, rollicking English squire as the true Virginia type."[94]

Thomas Nelson Page conceded that the Virginia gentleman could actually be cheerful when he chose to entertain:

> Yet, if he was generally grave, he was at times, among his intimates and guests, jovial, even gay. On festive occasions no one surpassed him in cheeriness. To a stranger he was always a host, to a lady always a courtier. When his house was full of guests, he was the life of the company.[95]

Figures in the oftentimes buoyant post-war literature, such as the protagonist in F. Hopkinson Smith's novel of 1891, *Colonel Carter of Cartersville,* tended more to be "the life of the company." The fictional Carter is grave only when concerned about his near-bankrupt estate. Created to appeal to a mass audience, the colonel was sufficiently

popular to reappear twelve years later in a sequel, *Colonel Carter's Christmas* (fig. 4.39).

The apologists gave their postbellum readers fictional plantation gentlemen who were often the personifications of the old virtues of piety, morality, and responsibility. A number of the actual members of the late-century Virginia gentry saw much in the past that was worth saving. Some joined such organizations as the Ku Klux Klan. Others rallied to restore the finances and rebuild the collections of the Virginia Historical Society, which had lost both its endowment (invested in Confederate bonds) and parts of its collection during the war, because that institution, by its constitution, preserved material evidence of the old values. Perhaps the most ambitious attempt to recapture antebellum life, however, was made by those like Major Augustus Drewry, then owner of Westover. As pictured by Richmond photographer Huestis Cook, Drewry looks as if he is assuming in real life the persona of the fictional Colonel Carter (fig. 4.40).

Persevering in the old beliefs, living in an appropriate setting, and dressing to suit the part is one way of making sure that the ideals of an earlier time survive. Such seemingly bizarre acts do allow those who are interested to understand better what life was like for their ancestors. Major Drewry's efforts thereby anticipated both the creation of what would be called Colonial Williamsburg, in which we find contemporary actors playing historical parts, and the attempts by later ruralists such as Paul Mellon to keep

4.40 *Huestis Cook,* Westover, with Major Drewry and Friends, *ca. 1890, photograph, Valentine Museum*

alive Virginia's pastoral ideal through a modern recreation of that agrarian life. In all of these instances the postwar Virginian was acting on the realization that while society would never be as it had been before Appomattox, the gentry would survive if it kept alive the old values.

Many of the wealthy plantation families had enjoyed a lavish social life on the model of European gentlefolk. In written remembrances, in illustrations, and in the way that Virginians of the postwar gentry strove to perpetuate traditional activities, the old rural society was remembered as having been a pinnacle of aristocratic social life in America. Contemporaries popularized the image of a lifestyle made up of balls, courtship and romance, camaraderie amongst the gentility, and adventure. In the decades after the war, regional bias was increasingly replaced by a national fascination with the wealth and leisurely lifestyle of Old Virginia. During the so-called Gilded Age, those who were beguiled by the excesses of Newport's wealthy elite found all the more intriguing the mystique of Old Virginia, the home of America's original aristocracy.

Extravagant entertaining on the great plantations was a tradition that had been established in the colonial era when isolated Virginians became so tired of their rural solitude that they regularly invited neighbors to extended dinners, sometimes of several days duration, and welcomed the company of travelers. There are many early examples of this tradition, such as the annual Christmas and New Years's festivities in Richmond County that progressed back and forth between Sabine Hall and Mount Airy, according to the late colonial era entries in the diary of Landon Carter, the master of the former estate.[96] Although the need to dispel boredom and loneliness underlies the Virginia tradition of hospitality, and slave labor allowed for such lavish entertaining, Thomas Nelson Page would find a different explanation for this apparent need for society, one that would better enhance the mystique of Old Virginia. He waxed instead about genetics, about "a recognized race characteristic . . . practised as a matter of course," one that was "universal," "spontaneous," and "one of the distinguishing features of the civilization."[97] It was in-bred in Virginians to seek out company, to entertain, which was not the case with their Puritan neighbors to the north who eschewed even traditional Christmas celebrations. Whether or not one agrees with Page's pseudo-scientific explanation, it is certain that large social gatherings were crucial to the enjoyment of rural life in early Virginia.

Much was made by commentators of the entertainments of the Christmas season. The holiday festivities were traditionally the grandest of the year, especially in those parts of the state where the old ways were most firmly entrenched. An image entitled "Christmas in Old

4.41 *Edwin Austin Abbey,* Christmas in Old Virginia, *1880, wood engraving, 12³/₄ x 20 in., signed* E. A. Abbey, London, Sept 1880, *from* The Graphic, *an English newspaper, 25 December 1880, Virginia Historical Society*

Virginia" (fig. 4.41) that appeared on 25 December 1880 in the English newspaper *The Graphic* demonstrates the international reputation that Virginians had achieved concerning their hospitality. Many elements of this scene are fantastic. Because the scale is that of an English country house, the architecture can only be described as having a grandeur far beyond anything actually erected in Old Virginia. The gentlemen and ladies, attended by cultured and contented slaves, are dressed in the finery of the early nineteenth century. They are shown to enjoy luxury and abundance, as did many of the landed aristocracy of late-Victorian England. The artist was an American in London, Edwin Austin Abbey of Philadelphia, who understood that Old Virginia was valued by his London audience as an offshoot of English civilization, one that had become all the more noteworthy because it had presumably vanished. Such scenes suggested that some aspects of the great rural tradition that had been passed across the Atlantic two centuries before had survived.

By explaining how this particular aristocratic tradition had been carried to Virginia and then retained, the apologists encouraged their readers to consider how other traits of the English gentry had in the same way become characteristic of the region. The Virginia Christmas mythology helped to affirm the belief that an American aristocracy had taken root on Virginia soil during the colonial period and had flourished.[98] The loss of the opulent agrarian lifestyle in postwar Virginia was disheartening, but the survival of its traditions, such as elaborate Christmas celebrations, suggested that such types of European usages could one day rekindle the dream of an idyllic, rural society.

Another component of antebellum social life that was recreated after the war was the sport of fox hunting, an activity that appealed to participants and observers because it carried associations with both colonial Virginia

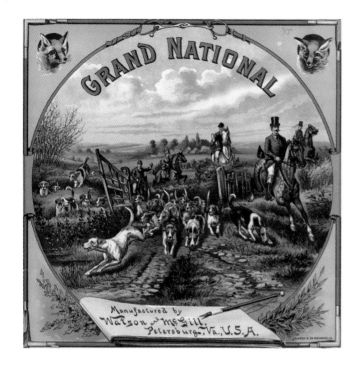

and aristocratic England. Hunting for entertainment rather than food was the exclusive domain of the wealthy, and the apologists may have sensed that a national audience would respond to remembrances of this defining pastime that had helped to set apart Virginians from the nouveau riche of the North. Thomas Nelson Page sketched a nostalgic scene of aristocratic life:

> The chief sport [in Old Virginia]. . . was fox-hunting. It was, in season, almost universal. Who that lived in that time does not remember the fox-hunts . . . . Many of [the foxes] had names. . . . There was one such that I remember: he was known as "Nat Turner," after the notorious leader of "Nat Turner's Rebellion," who remained in hiding for weeks after all his followers were taken. Great frolics these hunts were; for there were the prettiest girls in the world in the country houses around about. . . . Who does not recall the excitement at the house; the arrival in the yard, with horns blowing, hounds baying, horses prancing, and girls laughing.[99]

The sport's association with England was put to commercial advantage by Watson and McGill of Petersburg. In a postwar tobacco label, members of the Virginia gentry who are engaged in the spectacle of the hunt are shown to be remarkably similar to their counterparts abroad (fig. 4.42). In this way, as in the postbellum staging of jousting tournaments, the aristocrats of Virginia attempted to maintain their links to the culture that had served as the model for their ancestors.

A principal delight of antebellum social life was to vacation at the western spas, an activity that Page mentions in the context of summer travel. Long associated with Old Virginia, the mineral and thermal springs became increasingly popular after 1865 when the railroad

*4.42 **Above, top** Hoen & Company, Richmond,*Grand National (Tobacco)*, manufactured by Watson and McGill, Petersburg, ca. 1875?, lithograph (tobacco label), 10¼ x 10¼ in., Virginia Historical Society*

*4.43 **Above, center** Huestis Cook, Dining Room at White Sulphur, 1890s, photograph courtesy of The Valentine Museum*

*4.44 **Left** Cook studio, Richmond, Robert E. Lee at the Reconstruction Conference at White Sulphur, 1869, photograph courtesy of The Valentine Museum*

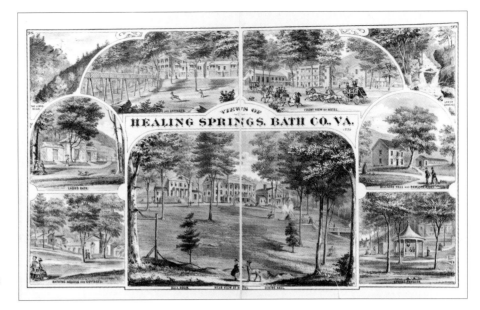

4.45 *F. W. Beers, publisher,* Views of Healing Springs, Bath Co., Va., *1876, lithograph, 15¼ x 25¾ in., in F. W. Beers,* Illustrated Atlas of the City of Richmond, Va., *Virginia Historical Society*

allowed them to be discovered by new audiences from the North and West.[100] In the postwar era, as the springs grew in size and in the lavishness of services provided, the mystique of Old Virginia, where such pleasures had long been enjoyed, was enhanced. At many of the springs it was easy to reimagine the grand lifestyle that had characterized the antebellum plantation, which many of the springs resembled in their architecture and landscape design. As suggested by a photograph taken by Huestis Cook in the 1890s of the dining room at White Sulphur (fig. 4.43), the springs could be marketed as offering the best of Old Virginia. One could enjoy there a leisurely visit supported by the labor of innumerable servants. Cook's image suggested that a traditional type of grandeur was available at the great spas of western Virginia that could no longer be found elsewhere.

Although it was then located in the new state of West Virginia, Thomas Nelson Page singled out White Sulphur as the best of the springs. It had inspired the publication of a number of songs and descriptive accounts, such as J. A. Rosenberger's "The Original Lover's Leap Galop or a Scene from the Greenbrier White Sulphur Springs."[101] The reference in the title is to those paths and open areas behind the rows of cottages that themselves became famous as "Lovers Leap," "Lovers Walk," "Lovers Rest," "Courtship Maze," "Hesitancy," "Rejection," and "Acceptance Way to Paradise." John Esten Cooke remarked about the new cosmopolitan nature of "the White," noting that in the postwar period the mayors of New York and New Orleans, former Confederate generals, and General Grant were all present there.[102] At White Sulphur Springs visitors from afar would be subtly encouraged to rethink their ideas about Old Virginia society.

The visit of Robert E. Lee to White Sulphur in 1868–69 brought the figure who best symbolized the old order to perhaps the grandest setting then associated with Old Virginia. The general traveled there with an eye to finding solutions for the problems being faced by reconstructed Virginians, but the presence of so prominent a

figure in so romantic a setting rekindled a nostalgia for the Old Virginia that had been lost. In a photograph of the key figures at the meeting (fig. 4.44), Lee is shown with the philanthropist George Peabody to his left. The general and other forward-thinking southerners successfully encouraged Peabody to contribute to educational institutions in the New South.

Travel to other celebrated resorts also increased during this period as the railroad network expanded farther into the western reaches of Virginia. One spa that enjoyed the new influx of visitors was Healing Springs in Bath County (fig. 4.45).[103] Located near the better-known Hot Springs, this complex was built in the late 1850s and ultimately functioned as a postwar resort. The main building was designed to resemble a Virginia plantation house; in fact it bore a remarkable similarity to Montpelier, James Madison's seat (page 179, fig. 4.82). The flanking buildings resembled Pavilion V on the lawn at the University of Virginia. Healing Springs may have been designed by one of Thomas Jefferson's workmen, Thomas Blackburn, who knew Montpelier from a sketch that he owned, who worked at the University, and who was then resident in nearby Staunton.[104] To look at this handsome complex, which was free of the run-down buildings that were so well known to visitors to the region, was to enjoy an idealized vision of the past. To visit must have seemed like a return to the remembered mansions and moonlight of Old Virginia. In its way, Healing Springs served as an apparition, a ghostly reminder of what plantation life must have been like.

Black Virginians were infrequently awarded dignity in late nineteenth-century images by white artists. One rare exception is a photograph taken in the 1890s by Huestis Cook of John Jasper (fig. 4.46), a Richmond minister who by his death in 1901 had built the congregation of Sixth Mount Zion Church to more than two thousand mem-

4.46 *Huestis Cook,* John Jasper, *1890s, photograph, Valentine Museum*

bers. Born in the Virginia Piedmont in 1812 to slave parents, Jasper was himself a field worker before he learned to read and write, and while still in bondage he managed to conduct a ministry in Petersburg. When freedom came, Jasper was able to found three churches; by the time of his appearance in the Cook photograph, he had developed into an imposing figure. Cook presents a man who had established a national reputation in his field and whose famous sermon, "The Sun Do Move," was well known throughout the state. While black viewers of this photograph no doubt took pride in Jasper's achievements, some contemporary whites may have been disturbed to recognize that liberated African Americans might move beyond the roles traditionally assigned to them in the field and the factory.

Most postwar images of black Virginians tended to follow one of two stereotypes. Although one was clearly more insulting than the other, both served to identify African Americans as different, and thereby to isolate them from the mainstream of American life. In the most popular of these stereotypes the subjects are ridiculed as comical figures from the world of minstrelsy. In the other they are shown to be picturesque characters in scenes of simple, often destitute, peasant life.

On the sheet music cover of an early edition of James Bland's popular song "Carry Me Back to Old Virginny" we see ridiculous black-face figures, musical clowns who derive from the stage of the minstrel shows, of whom Jim

Crow was the most famous (fig. 4.47). There, long before the war, white actors had made the black man into a comical type, a buffoon who would wildly sing and dance to entertain the white audience. In this particular case the selection of such imagery was not inappropriate for a plantation song that was written, at least in part, for performance in such a show. Images of banjo players and dancers, who would gesticulate wildly as if they were bewitched by the music, would become ubiquitous in postbellum America.

During the Civil War years the stereotype of the comical black figure was carried to northern troops by the young Winslow Homer (fig. 4.48). Sent to Virginia as an illustrator by the magazine *Harper's Weekly*, Homer additionally produced a series of six lithographs that he called *Campaign Sketches*. These depict camp life and were intended to answer the interest of northerners in the progress of the war. Four of the six scenes are humorous. Although after the war Homer would paint highly sympathetic images of African Americans, his rendering of *Our Jolly Cook* is a grotesque caricature. The Union soldiers who observe this dancing figure seem to expect their cook to perform for them as part of his duty. Peter Wood and Karen Dalton point out in *Winslow Homer's Images of Blacks* that the African American cook was a common image of the era: "Northern readers, long familiar with Negro cooks and servants, no doubt found reassurance in such portraits, which reinforced stereotypic associations of blacks with bountiful food, good-humored nurture, and nonthreatening service."[105]

The stereotyping of African Americans was perpetuated well into the twentieth century. One Virginia artist who on occasion depicted blacks in this manner was William Ludwell Sheppard, a Confederate veteran whose pair of drawings about the difficulties of hunting rabbits (fig. 4.49) is degrading on a number of levels. Whereas the white gentry participated in the aristocratic, equestrian sport of fox hunting, black hunters were often portrayed as sportsmen of a lesser nature. The idea that African Americans were obsessed in the pursuit of small game dates back at least half a century, when the story of the slave Ben and his midnight escapades after possums was developed as comic relief in *Swallow Barn* (1832). (In actuality such blacks in the South were simply pursuing the only part of the animal kingdom left to them by the ruling whites.) In the scenario imagined by Sheppard, even the down-home intelligence that is awarded to blacks in contemporary stories by Charles Chesnutt or the Uncle Remus tales is denied.

Sheppard was an appropriate choice to illustrate several scenes of black Virginians for Edward King's *The Great South*, in which this northern author also betrays a strong racial bias. On a train from Gordonsville to Lynchburg, King wondered if the African American as he

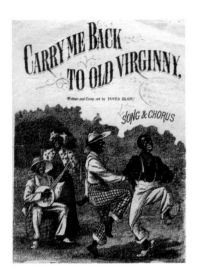

4.47 *Above, top, left James Bland, "Carry Me Back to Old Virginny," published by A. Cox and Company, after 1878, Virginia Historical Society*

4.48 *Above, top, right Winslow Homer,* Our Jolly Cook, *from Campaign Sketches, 1863, 14 x 11 in., L. Prang & Co., Boston, lithograph, Virginia Historical Society, gift of Paul Mellon*

4.49 *Above, left and right William Ludwell Sheppard,* Rabbit Caught *and* Rabbit Lost, *n. d. (late 19ᵗʰ century), wash drawings, each 17¹/₂ x 16 in., Virginia Historical Society, Lora Robins Collection of Virginia Art*

knew him from the comical stereotype would survive freedom:

> In the car where the colored people were seated there were a good many discouraging signs. Was it possible to mould these slouching and ragged fellows, who talked so rudely, whose gestures were so uncouth, and on whose features had been stamped the seal of ignorance, into . . . useful and trustworthy citizens . . . ? And if not, what would be the future condition of the lately liberated slave? Was he prospering, and hastening forward to the consummation of the independent manhood promised him?[106]

While in reality there was some social progress as the nineteenth century drew to a close, the continuing popularity of degrading images of blacks informs us of the expectations of white readers and audiences of the period.

The second predominant stereotype of the postwar era identified the African American as picturesque. As we have seen, before the war such American artists as Eastman Johnson who had lived in Europe were familiar with paintings there that celebrated a contented Old World peasantry. They understood that sentimental images of black Americans might in the same way evoke thoughts of a rural innocence that by the middle of the century had been lost on both sides of the Atlantic. The African American, whether he was a slave or emancipated, seemed to fit well with standard notions of the artistic and literary picturesque. He worked in a rural setting, he resided in a dilapidated cabin that could be perceived as a rustic cottage, he wore tattered clothing, he took delight in the simple power of music, he spoke in a strange, often humorous dialect, and he retained peculiar customs from his African past. Although most of the artists who invoked this stereotype followed the European vogue of presenting nostalgic scenes, a number of painters made subtle comments about the condition, and at times the humanity of their black sitters.

Lucian Whiting Powell, a Virginia artist from a respectable Upperville family, had studied in Philadelphia and Europe before he returned home to divide his time between northern Virginia and Washington, D.C.[107] While abroad, Powell had become familiar with the European interest in picturesque peasant types. In *The Old Log Cabin* (fig. 4.50) Powell included the expected musical ele-

4.50 *Lucien Whiting Powell,* The Old Log Cabin, *ca. 1865-70, oil on canvas, 30 x 25 in., Morris Museum of Art*

4.51 *A. B. Frost,* A Negro Funeral in Virginia, *1880, pen and ink, 11¹/₂ x 16¹/₂ in., drawn for* Harper's Weekly, *Virginia Historical Society, Lora Robins Collection of Virginia Art*

ments, but placed his figures in a cabin that could hardly be more run-down. Although the mistress of this homestead is hard at work, the two male figures have chosen instead to enjoy music, in poses that were well known from minstrelsy. These figures are not meant to be particularly comical, however, and they do not overtly degrade the African Americans. On the surface they establish a mood that to modern eyes seems more fanciful than real, more like that of a European fairy tale than an actual setting. But this painting, which was clearly intended for white viewers, also suggests that the black American belonged in a rural setting, where he was entirely comfortable living in poverty. In the aftermath of emancipation he would in theory continue to provide the manpower that would sustain Virginia's agricultural economy, but without his labor being forced, there would be little impetus for him to pick up the tools that are scattered about the foreground of Powell's scene.

The seemingly peculiar customs and mannerisms that rural African Americans retained both from Africa and from their slave past served to distance them from the modern world and thereby made them all the more picturesque. A. B. Frost was drawn to this subject in his rendering of *A Negro Funeral in Virginia* (fig. 4.51), which was published in *Harper's Weekly* in 1880. Although the scene recalls a pre-urban and pre-industrial past, it also inevitably brings to mind the subjects of slavery and racism in America. Such pictures made evident the survival of a distinct black culture; Frost is respectful of the event being depicted and of the emotions of his characters, but it seems as if these people inhabit a world that is considerably different from that of the readers of *Harper's Weekly.* Its white audience would appreciate the poignancy of such a scene, safe in the knowledge that they would probably never encounter such people in their daily lives.

Richard Norris Brooke of Warrenton followed his neighbor Lucien Powell to Paris, where he too learned the French tradition of painting the rural landscape and its peasantry. Although he settled in the nation's capital, it was in Virginia where Brooke could best implement what he had learned abroad. *A Pastoral Visit* (fig. 4.52), however, is not set in a rustic landscape; instead it records an actual interior in Warrenton. In this large canvas, the artist's first major undertaking upon his return, Brooke suggests that the old ways of America's black peasantry were worthy of nostalgic reconsideration because of their simplicity. In the end, however, the painting wound up with a different emphasis.

When Brooke offered *A Pastoral Visit* to the Corcoran Gallery of Art, he stated what we might expect to hear from a painter newly returned from the Barbizon countryside: Brooke would "elevate [Negro life] to that plane of sober and truthful treatment which, in French Art, has dignified the Peasant subjects of Jules Breton." But the artist admitted that he was also intrigued by "that peculiar humor which is characteristic of the [Negro] race," which he addresses in this painting by an interchange between the zealous pastor "Old George Washington" and his less-than-pious, musically inclined listener. If Brooke achieved his goal of "recognizing in proper measure the humorous features of my subject," he perhaps tried to do too many things in one canvas, because he was not as successful as Breton was in recalling the "dignity" of his "peasants." Indeed, the French artist's nostalgic longing for a pre-industrial past is given little expression here. In a comment written in a private journal, a Corcoran board member made no connection between this scene and a vanishing past; he only complained that he "dislike[d]" displays of "coarse homeliness" and that "there is *too much nigger* in [this painting]" [italics in the original]. The latter state-

4.52 *Richard Norris Brooke*, A Pastoral Visit, *1881, oil on canvas, 47³/₄ x 65³/₄ in., Corcoran Gallery of Art*

4.53 *Winslow Homer*, Blossom Time in Virginia, *ca. 1875, 14 x 20 in., The Detroit Institute of the Arts, bequest of Robert H. Tannahill*

ment dramatically underscores the national inclination at the time to keep the races separate, and suggests that Brooke's painting perhaps contributed more to that end than it did to attaining any of his more noble goals.[108]

In a optimistically labeled watercolor, *Blossom Time in Virginia* (fig. 4.53), Winslow Homer provides what by the mid-1870s was a typical scene of a black man working in a field. Homer, however, successfully goes beyond the stereotype. Knowing the artist's penchant for finding evidence of the self-sufficiency of the newly liberated population, many commentators have read his uplifting image of a confident, young black farmer as a statement that, contrary to the dire predictions of the slaveholder, the freedman was in fact capable of survival, and even success, on his own. An able provider, this young plowman demonstrates that his race never should have been enslaved, and therefore

that the northern war effort had been justified.

In *Blossom Time in Virginia* and a series of related postwar paintings of African Americans, Homer remembers the past as he examines the present and looks to the future. He takes great interest in the faces of his subjects, so that he can project their humanity as well as their concern about their newly changed destiny. Homer tends to conceive a perspective that places the head of each figure above the horizon line, so as to convey a spiritual as well as a physical elevation above the gravity of rural labor. The farmer here works alone, it seems on his own property, and so the fruits of his labors are his own. The flowering tree suggests the return of life, and a new beginning.

It is the spiritual nature of Homer's black ruralists that sets them apart from the Old World peasants. Homer scholars long ago traced the influence of such French art-

4.54 *Frank Blackwell Mayer,* Independence (Squire Jack Porter), *1858, oil on paper-board, 12 x 15⅞ in., Smithsonian's American Art Museum, bequest of Harriet Land Johnston*

ists as François Millet and Jules Breton, whose work he would have seen when he visited France in 1867–68. Wood and Dalton conclude that "in his use of these sources Homer identifies American blacks as the equivalent of the peasant class in Europe." They go on to cite the contemporary artist/critic Eugene Benson, who had encouraged Homer to travel to France and who wrote in *Appletons' Journal* in 1872 that "the peasant of France" is "a careless and unambitious being, much like the negro of the southern plantations. . . . He can hardly be said to think. He neither reads nor writes; the horizon of his field is the only one known to him . . . he seems a primitive man." Due, however, to "the great march of improvement and emancipation" in America, Benson adds, the analogy with the French peasant will break down. Benson had pointed the direction that Homer would follow. By depicting black American farm workers who are not bowed by the physical drudgery of excessive labor, and do not have "the patient dumb look" that Benson ascribed to Old World peasants who saw no future for themselves, Homer broke new ground. He managed to undo not only the stereotype of the picturesque African American, but also the analogy of that figure with the European peasant. These African Americans, Homer reminds us, are not slaves. They are free Americans, who presumably have much to look forward to.[109] Such optimistic portrayals, which suggest that these free black men are little different than their white counterparts, maintain however a clear distance from the white patrons of the arts who would have been interested in Homer's paintings. To wealthy white collectors, scenes of blacks working in the fields would have been expected, even after emancipation.

Before the war, white Virginians of almost any class could aspire to achieve the pastoral ideal. In 1858 Frank Blackwell Mayer conceived a painting entitled *Independence (Squire Jack Porter)* (fig. 4.54) that celebrates one manifestation of a southern white man's attainment of that model. Relaxing with pipe in hand on his porch, Jack Porter is a

"squire" because he owns his homestead and enjoys the freedom to relish life and to think philosophically. He is independent, self-sufficient, and dignified, a fine example of what could be attained by men from the middle-class in democratic America.

Although it would have been impossible before Appomattox, after the war a black man could be pictured similarly, as John Adams Elder illustrated in the painting that he called *Contentment* (fig. 4.55). This Virginia artist had also studied abroad; in 1850–55 he had traveled with Emanuel Leutze to Düsseldorf and had met Eastman Johnson there. On his return, predictably, Elder painted the African American in the guise of the peasant. However, he altered the stereotype that made the black man a picturesque reminder of the past in order to convey a more positive message. He was indeed picturesque, but he lived happily in rural Virginia. This property owner, who is generally well-dressed despite the tear in his trousers, is shown to be as contented as any white squire. He takes pride in his material achievements, and, perhaps because he is old enough to have been a slave, he is philosophical. Elder acknowledges his humanity and points to the potentially new status of the black Virginian. Given the pervasiveness during this period of negative opinions about African Americans, in this image Elder makes a significantly uplifting statement.[110] While it would be for Homer to look to the future, such figures as Elder's farmer point to a past to be remembered without any longing or nostalgia, and the wonderful possibilities of the present.

It might be imagined that a European artist who was familiar with the romantic vogue for peasantry would for that reason be drawn to communities of black Virginians when he journeyed during the postwar era to the Pied-

4.55 *John Adams Elder,* Contentment, *ca. 1880s, oil on canvas, 19½ x 23½ in., Virginia Historical Society*

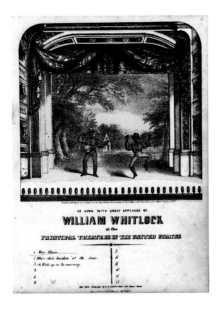

4.56 *Above, left C. G. Christman, publisher (New York), "Mary Blane," as composed and sung by Wm. Whitlock, 1846, sheet music, Virginia Historical Society*

4.57 *Above, right Frank Buchser,* The Song of Mary Blane, *1870, oil on canvas, 40³/₄ x 60³/₅ in., Kunstmuseum Solothurn*

mont and the Valley. But the Swiss painter Frank Buchser was apparently attracted to the African Americans of Virginia primarily because of his widespread travels through northern Africa, where he had encountered blacks who were appreciated by Europeans for their beauty and their mystique as exotic people who were independent of Old World conventions. It was therefore predictable that Buchser, like Homer, would reject stereotypical imagery and instead project the humanity of his sitters. He had come to America to paint Abraham Lincoln, but following the assassination of the president he had opted to paint Robert E. Lee instead. On his way to Lexington he produced a series of images of African Americans that are extraordinary for what is best described not as simply a lack of prejudice, but instead as an enthusiastic appreciation for the distinct qualities that make black people what they are.

The antebellum song "Mary Blane" had served minstrelsy as a vehicle to ridicule African Americans for decades (fig. 4.56). Perhaps for that very reason, Buchser seized upon this well-known subject to restore to the characters some measure of rightful dignity. In his painting entitled *The Song of Mary Blane* (fig. 4.57), we look not at ridiculous figures in blackface, but instead at what appear to be actual black individuals who bask in the bright Virginia sunlight, comfortable in a setting that has made them as healthy and vital as the tall corn that stands to the rear. To Buchser these people are physically attractive, intelligent, and energetic. If they are picturesque, it is due to their rural residency and inherent grace, not because their dwellings are dilapidated or their clothing

tattered. Most of the figures presented are in fact dressed in finery. A banjo and a watermelon are pictured, but these items are seen as fine belongings rather than as stereotypical elements belonging to simpleminded, poverty-stricken people.

Buchser's group listens as a member renders "The Song of Mary Blane" with pathos instead of comedy. When restored to its serious theme, the song tells about the fate of a young slave woman who loved a black singer until she was abducted by an evil white man. Only years later did the singer rediscover Mary Blane, by then dishonored and ill treated on the slave market. American slavery is remembered by Buchser as tragic, but the institution had not broken the spirit of these remarkable people. In making so positive a statement, Buchser was more explicit than his American contemporaries in his depiction of the humanity and potential of African Americans. Such inspired paintings, however, reached the eyes of far fewer viewers than did the insipid prints that appeared concurrently on the covers of popular sheet music and tobacco products.

The prevailing stereotypes of the African American were of little use to the apologists. They looked instead to portray antebellum slaves as contented rather than comical or picturesque. Taking a bold stand in order to defend effectively a troubled and much-criticized past, they dared to imagine that southern society had been idyllic during the antebellum years *because* of slavery. It was a system, they suggested, in which everyone knew and accepted his role. The white man headed the social order and directed the business of the plantation. The black man was pleased to be subservient and was well-treated for his labors. Virginians, they claimed, had been justified to hold slaves because the institution was benevolent and enriched the society at large. The best course for the new freedman, they inferred, was to accept his still grossly inferior social position and to continue providing the labor necessary to maintain the postwar economy.

The apologists suggested that when a slave was controlled and nurtured, he was not at all clown-like. Rather, through his acceptance of his role, he could develop into an emotionally and physically sound human being. In *Social Life in Old Virginia* Page describes a slave wedding as "a gay occasion" performed either in the great house by the master or in one of the quarters by a black preacher. The bride's trousseau would be arranged by her mistress and "the family was on hand . . . to recognize by their presence the solemnity of the tie."[111] Under slavery, Page tells us, Negroes behaved with morality. His illustrator, Genevieve Cowles, pictured the most refined wedding party imaginable, the antithesis of the comical, gross, or animalistic images then current (fig. 4.58).[112]

The sentimental image of the quaint black figure who lives in a dilapidated cabin and happily labors in the fields better fit their vision than depictions of rollicking dancers. It was important to the apologists to maintain that agrarian contentment was the condition of blacks before emancipation. Page describes a scene of laborers that is virtually the same as seen in *The Scarecrow*, a painting by the Virginia artist A. C. Redwood (fig. 4.59). In this image we see anonymous figures who use primitive hoes and plows in an age that knew mechanized farm machinery, and who toil in rows just as they had under slavery. In the simplicity and timelessness of their daily routine these black figures are picturesque, but there is little that is life-affirming here, especially when we consider the dead crow that is serving as the "scarecrow" of the title. While

such actual contrivances may have protected the produce of the fields from living birds, the dead crow might well have reminded white viewers of the Jim Crow laws that would keep many of the liberated African Americans in their menial position as field workers.[113]

In Page's verbal description, however, there is more of a feeling of contentment in the air:

> Far off, in the fields, . . . gangs of hands in lines performed their work in the corn or tobacco fields, loud shouts and peals of laughter, mellowed by the distance, floating up from time to time, telling that the heart was light and the toil not too heavy.[114]

Maude Cowles illustrated the scene for Page using anonymous figures seen from the rear, which is the same perspective that was chosen by Redwood (fig. 4.60). Her effort, however, is meant to emphasize the lightness of the load carried by the laborers.

What set the apologists apart from the majority of commentators, who emphasized the peasant-like aspects of southern black life, is that they had less to say about field hands than they did about house servants. The latter were described as refined, intelligent, and loving, characteristics that grew out of their years of intimate contact with the white family. The goal in such narratives was to see these African Americans as members of the household rather than as slaves.

The stories and accounts by Thomas Nelson Page enjoyed widespread popular acclaim. The master apologist imagined a fantastical past distinguished by the happiness, mutual love, and respect enjoyed by both master and servant. One of his most powerful pro-slavery creations was *Marse Chan*, which was first published in the *Century Magazine* in 1883–84 and then in repeated

4.58 *Genevieve Cowles,* A Negro Wedding, *illustration in Thomas Nelson Page,* Social Life in Old Virginia before the War, *1897, Virginia Historical Society*

4.59 *Above* Allen Christian Redwood, The Scarecrow, *ca. 1890s?,*
oil on canvas, 7 x 12 in., Virginia Historical Society, Lora Robins Col-
lection of Virginia Art

4.60 **Right** *Maude Cowles,* The Test of the Men's Prowess, *illustra-*
tion in Thomas Nelson Page, Social Life in Old Virginia before the
War, *1897, Virginia Historical Society*

4.61 **Below, right** *W. T. Smedley (?),* Now, Sam, from dis time you
belong to yo' young Marse Channin', *frontispiece to Thomas*
Nelson Page, Marse Chan: A Tale of Old Virginia, *in* In Ole Virginia *(1887), Virginia Historical Society*

reissuings. This emotional tale intertwines the loyalty of a
single slave with the epic fall of a great culture. Page tells
of the devotion between Sam and his master in a story of
pathos that is carried through the duration of Channing's
life, from his birth, when a slave is assigned to care for
him (fig. 4.61), through the upheaval of the Civil War
that brings the master's premature death. The old society
emerges as having been a grand achievement of American civilization, the loss of which is to be mourned by the
reader as fervently as the demise of Channing—a name
long associated with New England—and the resultant de-
spondency of the faithful Sam.

In *Social Life in Old Virginia before the War* (1897) Page
focused on the frequent interaction between the plantation's master and mistress and their house servants. Slavery, he argues, gave Old Virginia its distinct character,
and he went on to add that it was this peculiar institution
that had elevated its society to greatness. In a hypothesis
that seems outrageous to the modern ear, Page argued
that slavery actually inspired virtue in both races: "the social life formed of these elements combined was one of
singular sweetness and freedom from vice."[115]

4.62 *Left Genevieve Cowles, She was never anything but tender with the others, illustration in Thomas Nelson Page, Social Life in Old Virginia before the War (New York, 1897), Virginia Historical Society*

4.63 *Below William Ludwell Sheppard,* Master and Servant (Man Praying for a Sick Negro)*, ca. 1870, watercolor and ink on paper, 12⅝ x 9⅝ in., Valentine Museum*

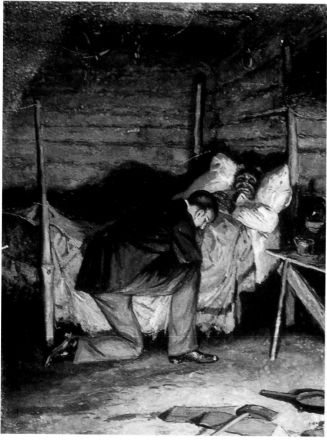

for a Sick Negro) (fig. 4.63). The attachment between the young white man and the old slave, like that of George for Uncle Tom, had become a common sentimental motif. Sheppard's watercolor of 1870 reminded its viewers of the affection in which some servants had been held.

In another remarkable passage that reads like a description of an angelic presence, Page credits the plantation mistress for her tireless care of the slaves in her charge:

> Who knew of the visits she paid to the cabins of her sick and suffering servants! often, at the dead of night, "slipping down" the last thing to see that her directions were carried out; with her own hands administering medicines or food; ever by her cheeriness inspiring new hope, by her strength giving courage, by her presence awaking faith; telling in her soft voice to dying ears the story of the suffering Saviour; with her hope soothing the troubled spirit, and lighting with her own faith the path down into the valley of the dark shadow. What poor person was there, however inaccessible the cabin, that was sick or destitute and knew not her charity![116]

When necessary, the mistress would put her own health in jeopardy to see to the needs of her "sick and suffering servants." Where are we to find such expressions of loyalty and devotion in the postwar world?

Ranking below only the personal body servants "in importance and rank" Page claimed, were the butler and the carriage driver: "these . . . were the aristocrats of the family, who trained the children in good manners and other exercises."[117] As another means to suggest that this system was in some ways advantageous for those enslaved, Page imagined that these domestics actually wielded power over the whites whom they served. He also stressed that they took genuine interest in how the lives of their masters unfolded, and that they felt, when appropriate, pride, joy, and sorrow. The master and mistress, of course, looked at their servants with benevolent feelings every bit as intense.

John Esten Cooke and George Bagby had made similar arguments a quarter century earlier. In his article "Old Virginia Manners," Cooke suggested of blacks that "There never was a more contented, happy, domineering, consequential, well-to-do class of people in the world." Bagby waxed poetically on the subject when remembering the "Old Virginia Gentleman":

> His castle was his country home
> Hard by the river James,
> Full two hundred servants dwelt around—
> He called them by their names;
> And life to them no hardship was,
> 'Twas all things else I ween;
> They were the happiest peasantry

voted to the fantasy of blissful racial relations on the old Virginia plantation. "The old mammies and family servants about the house," Page writes, were, after the master and mistress, the "other characters without mention of which no picture of the social life of the South would be complete." He argues that a lasting bond between the races was established during the infancy and childhood of the white master, when a mammy (fig. 4.62) and then a child slave (like the Sam of *Marse Chan)* cared for him. In turn, the master and mistress guarded the welfare of their slaves from cradle to grave, as suggested by William Ludwell Sheppard in his *Master and Servant (Man Praying*

This world has ever seen,
Despite the Abolition chevaliers
All of the Northern clime![118]

His rebuff of the abolitionists whose interference had led to the Civil War and the destruction of the life that had been enjoyed by both master and slave is not surprising. Bagby's invocation of the "peasantry" harkens back to the visual artists who were using European thematic models in their attempts to illustrate the lives of blacks, as well as the antebellum, pro-slavery theorists who argued that slaves in the American South were better off than the European poor or the often poverty-stricken workmen, women, and children who suffered in the factories of the North.

The three arch-apologists and their followers were doomed from the start to fail in their revisionary endeavors. Partly, this had to do with timing: a national audience—and particularly the generation of northerners who had lost fathers, sons, and brothers in the recent conflict—was not yet ready to hear about the great, lost civilization of the South. Too much had been sacrificed to end slavery. Americans of the postbellum period would not suddenly conclude that it had been a righteous system after all. John Esten Cooke would continue to write until his death in 1883, becoming best known for his historical works that looked backward beyond the nineteenth century to the colonial era. George Bagby also died in 1883, but his writings were kept alive in reprints; Thomas Nelson Page would publish an edition of Bagby's selected writings in 1910. As for Page himself, he would remain alive well into the twentieth century and so be able to witness the renewed interest in the lost civilization of the colonial South that began after its turn. He is remembered today as much as a "local colorist" as an "apologist," and he made successful forays into the fields of biography, social studies, and poetry, while continuing to write fiction until he was appointed ambassador to Italy, where he served from 1913 until 1919.

The arguments that had been made by pro-slavery theorists before the war concerning the fact that all of the great classical civilizations, and indeed, God's own "Chosen People" the Israelites, had held slaves were heard with some interest by thinkers throughout the still relatively young nation, which by the 1830s and 1840s seemed to be on the road toward the creation of a continental, if not a hemispheric, empire of its own. Such discussions would then continue with warnings against northern instigation in the ultimate continuance or demise of that institution. By war's end, however, slavery too had come to an end, and the country was too busy healing and dealing with the western Indians to rekindle its empire-building fires. Although staunch adherents to the Lost Cause were extant throughout the South, they were only one of the several audiences that the apologists felt needed to hear heart-warming tales about Old Virginia. Cooke, Bagby, and Page were faced with the unenviable task of trying to convince a war-torn nation that more had been lost than was gained in the conflict. Success was not in the offing. By early in the next century there would again be interest in the Old South, but this turn would not be influenced by the apologists' nostalgic, often overly sentimental narratives of antebellum life. Rather, the gaze would be back to the eighteenth century, before the heydays of northern abolitionists and southern defenders.

"Happy and Free from All Sorrow": The Aftermath of Emancipation

As the apologists were creating personae for antebellum African Americans that they hoped would have an effect on their status in the postbellum world, black writers and artists were also beginning to look at the nation's history to try to make sense of their own legacy of slavery and of the experiences of those who had been freed, and thereby to try to construct a place for themselves in American society. Eventually, as the generation born after emancipation grew to maturity, blacks began to document their view of past events, which was necessarily quite different from those of southern white chroniclers. Many struggled to come to terms with the idea that generations of their families had been enslaved, and some were saddened by the inequities left by Reconstruction and its backlash. Freedom had been accomplished; thoughts now turned to equality. However, it is perhaps surprising today to learn that Booker T. Washington (fig. 4.64), the

4.64 Booker T. Washington, *photograph, Virginia Historical Society*

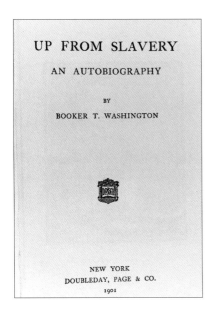

UP FROM SLAVERY

AN AUTOBIOGRAPHY

BY

BOOKER T. WASHINGTON

NEW YORK
DOUBLEDAY, PAGE & CO.
1901

4.65 *Booker T. Washington,* Up From Slavery, An Autobiography *(New York, 1901), Virginia Historical Society*

figure who was most influential in the last quarter of the nineteenth century in interpreting black history and in plotting a course for black progress, initially held a viewpoint not far removed from that of a number of his white contemporaries.

Emancipation had advanced the position of blacks so immediately and drastically that many of those who experienced the ending of slavery were ill prepared, at least initially, to consider further change. It was difficult to look much beyond the question of his or her immediate survival. Most slaves had little or no education, and other than those who had worked in the great houses or had learned a trade, their job skills were limited to the sorts of field work that they had carried out on the plantation.

Many black writers came to refer to the failure of Reconstruction as "the Revolution of 1876" because soon thereafter the black man's vote was suppressed along with his other civil and political rights. It was in this constrictive climate that Booker T. Washington, a shrewd observer of national and regional opinion, determined that blacks would best hold on to their newly won ground by conceding, temporarily, their ideas about real equality and by working cooperatively with the ruling white majority. This, it should be remembered, was also the period when James Bland, the black man who had composed "Carry Me Back to Old Virginny," felt compelled to cater to nostalgic white patrons, who were the audience for the minstrel shows and the purchasers of sheet music, because they longed to imagine that former slaves remembered their antebellum servitude fondly.

While some blacks may have wished again to be "happy and free from all sorrow" as the song suggests, what in fact was most often remembered with nostalgia were the often loving, at times tenuous, family relations. As Elizabeth Keckley put it in *Behind the Scenes, or Thirty Years a Slave and Four Years in the White House* (1868): "Dear old Virginia! A birthplace is always dear, no matter under what circumstances you were born, since it revives in memory the golden hours of childhood . . . and the warm kiss of a mother."[119]

"I was born a slave on a plantation in Franklin County, Virginia," wrote Booker T. Washington at the start of his autobiography, which became an international best seller. He added with the ingratiating humor that helps to explain his immense popularity, "I am not quite sure of the exact place or exact date of my birth, but at any rate I suspect I must have been born somewhere and at some time" (fig. 4.65). The year is believed to have been 1856, and the plantation that of a James Burroughs, which was in the Valley near Big Lick (later Roanoke). After the Civil War the Washington family moved to West Virginia, but Booker soon returned east to Hampton Institute and Industrial School, first as a student and then to serve on the staff. From that experience came the opportunity to head the normal school at Tuskegee, Alabama, in 1881, which Washington quickly developed into a national center of black education.

In a now-famous speech delivered in 1895 that became known as "the Atlanta Compromise," Booker T. Washington stated his philosophy of cooperation with the existing white hierarchy. "In all things purely social we can be as separate as the five fingers," he reasoned, "and yet one as the hand in all things essential to mutual progress."[120] Having concluded, correctly, that southern whites had effectively barred political and civil rights from the grasp of the freedman and were unwilling to share control of society, Washington opted to accept near total segregation as a fact of postwar life and simply move forward in those few areas where progress was possible, industrial education and employment in the trades. As to the past, Washington reasoned in *Up From Slavery* that nothing would be gained by bitterness and that slavery, which was perhaps even part of a divine plan for the black race, had actually advanced the welfare of the African American, an argument that ironically had also been made by the apologists. "I pity from the bottom of my heart any nation or body of people that is so unfortunate as to get entangled in the net of slavery," Washington wrote, but the past was no reason to "cherish any spirit of bitterness against the Southern white people." While acknowledging "the cruelty and moral wrong of slavery," Washington judged "the ten million Negroes inhabiting this country"—those who had been slaves or were descended from slaves—as being "in a stronger and more hopeful condition, materially, intellectually, morally, and religiously, than is true of an equal number of black people in any other portion of the globe." As slaves they had been introduced to Christianity, which gave Washington both "faith in the future of my race in this country" and a Biblical perspective on slavery as "the wilderness through which and out of which, a good Providence has already led us."[121] Washington's biographer Louis Harlan says that this American had become a "white man's black man," but "considering his background it is hard to see how he could have been anything else."[122]

By the end of the century, however, as a new and increasingly sophisticated generation of African Americans matured, the conciliatory approach of Booker T. Washington began to be supplanted. Such thinkers as W. E. B. Du Bois and the poet Paul Lawrence Dunbar had seen the difficulties in trying to be "happy and free from all sorrow" in the repressive postwar society. They would rewrite history in their own terms, exploring the black experience in a nation that was blind to the contributions of a population that had helped to shape its very identity, and attempt to forge a new road for their contemporaries.

The movement to abandon Booker T. Washington's course for a more aggressive path was led by William Edward Burghardt Du Bois (fig. 4.66), a New Englander who became a professor of sociology at Atlanta University and later was active in the National Association for the Advancement of Colored People. Du Bois initially supported Washington's conciliatory stance but soon became impatient for progress. "The slave went free," he complained, "stood a brief moment in the sun; then moved again toward slavery."[123] In *The Souls of Black Folk* (fig. 4.67) Du Bois marveled at the ascendancy of Washington as "the most striking thing in the history of the American Negro since 1876," attributing it to "a sense of doubt and hesitation [that] overtook the freedmen's sons."[124] He acknowledged Washington as the "greatest leader" of the black man, "the most distinguished Southerner since Jefferson Davis," which to modern eyes seems a striking comparison, "the one recognized spokesman of his ten million fellows," and a man with remarkable powers of diplomacy: "it is no ordinary tribute to this man's tact and power that, steering as he must between so many diverse interests and opinions, he so largely retains the respect of all."[125] But Du Bois objected that the "old attitude of adjustment and submission" was no longer timely; the "self-respect" of the African American had been lost. After ten years of implementation, Washington's "tender of the palm branch" had returned only disappointments: "The question then comes, Is it possible, and probable, that nine [sic] millions of men can make effective progress in economic lines if they are deprived of political rights, made a servile caste, and allowed only the most meagre chance for developing their exceptional men? If history and reason give any distinct answer to these questions," Du Bois concludes, "it is an emphatic *No*."[126] The rising generation of black leaders, whose opposition to Washington amounted "at times to bitterness," would not "sit silently by while the inevitable seeds are sown for a harvest of disaster to our children, black and white."[127] In a recent edition of *The Souls of Black Folk* (first published in 1903) editors David W. Blight

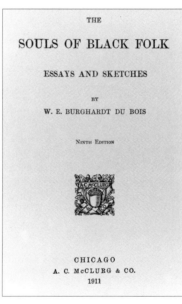

THE

SOULS OF BLACK FOLK

ESSAYS AND SKETCHES

BY

W. E. BURGHARDT DU BOIS

NINTH EDITION

CHICAGO
A. C. McCLURG & CO.
1911

4.66 Above William Edward Burghardt Du Bois, *photograph, Virginia Historical Society*

4.67 Left W. E. B. *Du Bois*, The Souls of Black Folk, *Essays and Sketches (Chicago, 1911), Virginia Historical Society*

and Robert Gooding-Williams describe this collection of essays as "an electrifying manifesto" that "mobiliz[ed] a people for bitter, prolonged struggle to win a place in history."[128]

Du Bois pointedly remarked that one task any black leader faced was "arguing with Mr. Thomas Nelson Page."[129] He wasted little time in directly refuting the apologist, however, choosing instead to provide his own remembrances of the past. By recounting history from a black man's perspective, by recording the joys of freedom and the pain of Reconstruction, and by pointing to the tragedies and contributions of a people who were rejected solely on racial grounds, the author provided his readers a clear alternative to Page and to the white supremacist thinkers of this era.

Du Bois opens *The Souls of Black Folk* with a question: "How does it feel to be a problem?" He answers that the "strange experience" of the African American is a history of the "strife" caused by racial injustice. He looks for a way "to be both a Negro and an American."[130] Blight and Godding-Williams eloquently describe the pathos in *Souls* as "a prayerful wail from the shipwreck of black freedom, as it lists on the shoals of segregation." As they suggest, the book is highly readable because of the author's remarkable talent for transposing history into lyrical expression that is at times powerful in its visionary quality. For instance, to characterize metaphorically the racial tension that persisted under Reconstruction, Du Bois imagined two specters that survived from the past, the slaveholder and the slave. For the black man these figures lingered visibly in the postwar present:

> Two figures ever stand to typify that day to coming ages—the one, a gray-haired gentleman, whose fathers had quit themselves like men, whose sons lay in nameless graves; who bowed to the evil of slavery because its abolition threatened untold ill to all; who stood at last in the evening of life, a blighted, ruined form, with hate in his eyes; —and the other, a form hovering dark and mother-like, her awful face black with the mists of centuries, had aforetime quailed at that white master's command, and bent in love over the cradles of his sons and daughter, and closed in death the sunken eyes of his wife,—aye, too, at his behest had laid herself low to his lust, and borne a tawny man-child to the world, only to see her dark boy's limbs scattered to the winds by midnight marauders riding after "cursed Niggers." These were the saddest sights of that woeful day; and no man clasped the hands of these two passing figures of the present-past; but, hating, they went to their long home, and, hating, their children's children live to-day.[131]

In the references to the intimacy of master and slave from cradle to grave we recognize in Du Bois's text subtle rebuttals of Page's too bold claims in *Social Life in Old Virginia Before the War*. (A year later, partly in response to Du Bois, Page would publish *The Negro: The Southerner's Problem* [New York, 1904].)

Du Bois was positive about the contributions of African Americans. He described how their gifts of "story and song . . . sweat and brawn . . . and spirit" had contributed to the identity of America.[132] The songs, however, haunted Du Bois as "the rhythmic cry of the slave," the "soul of the black slave [speaking] to men." He gives an entire chapter to these melodies that stand "not simply as the sole American music, but as the most beautiful expression of human experience born this side the seas."[133] This music is "the singular spiritual heritage of the nation and the greatest gift of the Negro people," he writes. Yet it had been "caricatured on the 'minstrel' stage" and, as Frederick Douglass had cautioned fifty-eight years before in his *Narrative*, had been "persistently mistaken and misunderstood" by whites as describing a joyful mood. Du Bois

reminds us that these songs had in fact originated with those who "walked in darkness"; it was the darkness of slavery, not the darkness of blackfaced minstrel figures, that created them. On that grim note the author starts "The Sorrow Songs."

The opposing philosophies put forth by Washington and Du Bois established an ideological conflict that would reemerge as a crucial set of parameters during what would later become known as the civil rights movement. In their own day, each of these views found expression in the writings of a young black poet and novelist. Before his premature death in 1906 at age thirty-four, Paul Lawrence Dunbar catered to the white man's interest in branding the African American as appealingly picturesque, and therefore so different as to be no threat to white society, while at the same time he served as a vibrant and clear voice for the rights of black people.

Born in Dayton, Ohio, and resident there all his life, Paul Lawrence Dunbar rose to fame in the 1890s when he published poems and short stories that were popular with white audiences for their stereotypical subject matter and their use of Negro dialects, both of which were associated with the prewar plantation days. He told nostalgic tales in poems like "Hunting Song" and "Dat Ol' Mare O' Mine" that addressed themes that were perceived as typifying Negro life in the South. He remembered the hunt humorously, with mock drama:

> Down th'oo de valleys an' ovah de hills,
> Into de woods whah de 'simmon-tree grows,
> Wakin' an' skeerin' de po' whippo'wills,
> Huntin' fu' coon an' fu' 'possum we goes.

Dunbar conceived an image of the broken-down horse, who was the coworker and companion of the pre-mechanized farmer, that is similar to the docile creature in Lucien Powell's painting *The Old Log Cabin* (page 157, fig. 4.50):

> Yes, huh coat ah long an' shaggy, an' she ain't
>   no shakes to see;
> Dat's a ring-bone, yes, you right, suh, an' she
>   got a on'ry knee,
> But dey ain't no use in talkin', she de only
>   hoss fu' me.

Although the language in such verse would have been seen as quaint by white readers, these compositions were not meant to be degrading to blacks. The danger of such an interpretation was lessened when Dunbar's poems were published with scores of illustrations—as many as one per every half-dozen lines of verse—by the Hampton Institute Camera Club (fig. 4.68). One of Dunbar's best poems in this genre is "The Deserted Plantation," which plays effectively with the same nostalgic sentiments as did "Carry Me

4.68 *Hampton Institute Camera Club,* The Deserted Plantation, *illustration for the poem of that name in Paul Lawrence Dunbar,* Poems of Cabin and Field, Illustrated with Photographs by the Hampton Institute Camera Club *(New York, 1899), Virginia Historical Society*

Back to Old Virginny" and Page's *Marse Chan,* the latter of which provided a similar recollection of the fall of the plantation lifestyle.

- - - - - - - - -

An' de big house stan's all quiet lak an' solemn,
Not a blessed soul in pa'lor, po'ch, er lawn;
Not a guest, ner not a ca'iage lef' to haul 'em,
Fu' de ones dat tu'ned de latchstring out air gone.

- - - - - - - - -

Whah's de da'kies, dem dat used to be a-dancin'
Ev'ry night befo' de ol' cabin do'?
Whah's de chillun, dem dat used to be a-prancin'
Er a-rollin' in de san' er on de slo'?

Gone! Not one o' dem is lef' to tell de story;
Dey have lef' de deah ole place to fall away.
Could n't one o' dem dat seed it in its glory
Stay to watch it in de hour of decay?

Dey have lef' de ol' plantation to de swallers,
But it hol's in me a lover till de las';
Fu' I fin' hyeah in de memory dat follers
All dat loved me an' dat I loved in de pas'.[134]

If Dunbar at times followed the same conservative current that guided Booker T. Washington, he concurrently championed the new course as well, every bit as strongly as did Du Bois. Both had rediscovered Frederick Douglass, who at his death in 1895 had again become an archetypal symbol of the black man's struggle for freedom. Du Bois remembered that the former slave refused to compromise: "Douglass, in his old age, still bravely stood for the ideals of his early manhood,—ultimate assimilation *through* self-assertion, and on no other terms."[135] In Dunbar's elegiac poem "Frederick Douglass," "Ethiopia . . . Laments the passing of her noblest born":

She weeps for him a mother's burning tears—
She loved him with a mother's deepest love.
He was her champion thro' direful years,
And held her weal all other ends above.
When Bondage held her bleeding in the dust,
He raised her up and whispered, "Hope and Trust."

- - - - - - - - -

And he was no soft-tongued apologist;
He spoke straightforward, fearlessly uncowed;
The sunlight of his truth dispelled the mist,
And set in bold relief each dark hued cloud;
To sin and crime he gave their proper hue,
And hurled at evil what was evil's due.

- - - - - - - - -

Oh, Douglass, thou hast passed beyond the shore,
But still thy voice is ringing o'er the gale!
Thou'st taught thy race how high her hopes may
    soar,
And bade her seek the heights, nor faint, nor fail.
She will not fail, she heeds thy stirring cry,
She knows they guardian spirit will be nigh,
And, rising from beneath the chast'ning rod,
She stretches out her bleeding hands to God![136]

In his "Ode to Ethiopia" Dunbar sets out to restore to his people the self-respect that Du Bois said had been lost by Washington's too-conciliatory stand. The poet encourages his black readers to "be proud" to have survived slavery, and to now reach for new glories:

No other race, or white or black,
When bound as thou wert, to the rack,
So seldom stooped to grieving;
No other race, when free again,
Forgot the past and proved them men
So noble in forgiving.[137]

The "nobility" gained by "forgiving" may sound Washingtonesque, but Dunbar was often concerned with moving on, with looking to the future, from a troubled past and, at times, a troubling present. In the clearly titled "To the South On Its New Slavery," Dunbar surprisingly laments his own day as being even worse than the slave era, which at least "held in some joys to alternate with pain." Now the freedman "toils hopeless on from joyless morn till night":

For him no more the cabin's quiet rest,
The homely joys that gave to labor zest;
No more for him the merry banjo's sound,
Nor trip of lightsome dances footing round.

For him no more the lamp shall glow at eve,
Nor chubby children pluck him by the sleeve;
No more for him the master's eyes be bright, —
He has nor freedom's nor a slave's delight.[138]

The poet concludes that what has brought this about is that the South has forgotten its high principles, which we can infer had been established long before by the Founding Fathers of the nation.

> Oh, Mother South, hast thou forgot thy ways,
> Forgot the glory of thine ancient days,
> Forgot the honor that once made thee great,
> And stooped to this unhallowed estate?[139]

If southerners can find a way to reclaim their honor—not based on the hubris of the slavemaster but on the humanism of those great men, many of whom were Virginians and who, whether they meant it or not, declared that "all men were created equal"—then the black race will have a chance to rise from this new species of servitude.

The "merry banjo's sound" was the subject of an extended poem by Dunbar entitled "A Banjo Song," in which he appears to perpetuate a stereotype that had been in use since the early days of minstrelsy. The banjo, a derivative of African instruments, was long associated with the slave era and, despite its "merry sound," with sorrow:

> Oh, de music o' de banjo,
> Quick an' deb'lish, solemn, slow,
> Is de greates' joy an' solace
> Dat a weary slave kin know!
> So jes' let me hyeah it ringin',
> Dough de chune be po' an' rough,
> It's a pleasure; an' de pleasures
> O' dis life is few enough.

4.69 Henry Ossawa Tanner, The Banjo Lesson, *1893, oil on canvas, 48 x 35 in., Hampton University Museum*

What is important in this poem is that the banjo can serve as a remedy for the trials and tribulations of life. It is kept on "de wall" and so is available when the tired worker returns home to provide one of the few pleasures of his life.

In this same decade of the 1890s, the black painter Henry Ossawa Tanner also engaged the stereotype of the black banjo player. Reacting to the two popular images of African Americans—the comical minstrel figure who plays the banjo and the picturesque peasant who lives in a dilapidated cabin—Tanner transformed the banjo into an instrument that ennobles rather than degrades, and points to the importance of home and familial love. In his masterpiece, *The Banjo Lesson* (fig. 4.69), the artist presents an elderly black man who with tenderness and patience teaches a child to play an instrument that he apparently had mastered long ago. In this way Tanner annihilates a second long-held stereotype, which for decades had been used by the proponents of slavery—that to break apart African American slave families was acceptable because the members of different generations of blacks feel little love for one another. In Tanner's painting the opposite is shown to be true. A grandparent who

clearly is old enough to have once been a slave shares love with a grandson who reciprocates that feeling. Tanner furthermore sets the scene in a respectable farmhouse, not a run-down, if picturesque, cabin. The white viewer is allowed to observe this revealing scene as almost a voyeur, in the same way that the young white woman in Eastman Johnson's *Negro Life in the South* (page 13, fig. 1) is permitted to investigate a way of life that is little known to her. Only here we are not simply entertained by the picturesque nature of the scene; we are instead carried beyond stereotypes to an enlightened understanding of African American life and values.[140]

Thinkers such as Washington, Du Bois, Dunbar, and Tanner struggled to understand and articulate the past and to launch black Americans into the new century with pride and confidence. Part of the problem that they faced was that the United States—the South in general, and Virginia in particular—were going through dynamic changes during this period. Although their reasons for doing so often differed, many commentators of the day, white and black, saw the need to look back, while simultaneously attempting to move society forward. In the next generation, Carter Woodson, a Virginian from Buckingham County and the "father of Negro history," would face the same enigma. In Virginia progress would mean to some a welcomed birth of new industries and their inherent possibilities for a better future; to others, however, each step toward modernity was a step away from what they believed had made their society great.

New Virginia and the Reinvention of the Landscape

While many writers in postwar Virginia turned their attentions toward a rekindling of the manners and mores of antebellum society, more forward-thinking leaders, the most visible of whom was William Mahone, the former Confederate general, railroad tycoon, and leader of the Readjuster movement, recognized the region's potential for growth and development. What was called the Progressive Movement spurred the creation of a more industrialized economy, which led to a more urbanized population. Edward King, writing in *The Great South* (1875), enthusiastically promoted the development of Virginia's resources, industries, and cities, finding "excellent chances for growth" seemingly in every place that he visited. Investors from the North and Europe looked to build new towns and to develop existing burghs into metropolises. The presence of new railroad lines across most of western Virginia, when linked with those in the east, made this development seem all the more feasible. A New Virginia began to emerge; the state was still predominantly agricultural but achieved a greatly expanded industrial base during this period. The hope was that the region would not only recover from defeat but would prosper and ultimately regain her national stature, now as part of a New South.

In Virginia, however, even charting the future could inspire nostalgia for the past. Progressives were looking for economic recovery, but they were not interested in societal change; their pocketbooks were necessarily in New Virginia but their values were in the old society. It was in their effort to maintain the social status quo that they too turned to Virginia's past. In *Preserving the Old Dominion, Historic Preservation and Virginia Traditionalism*, historian James Lindgren elaborates: "Progressives, as well as historic preservationists yearned for a more orderly and cohesive community that would foster economic progress. Politics would be reformed, social controls applied, and society purified in order that men be protected from their own weaknesses. . . . In the Old Dominion traditionalism and progressivism virtually became one."[141] It was this philosophy that in the early twentieth century would guide the Virginia-born president Woodrow Wilson to re-segregate the federal government.

Before the war, progress was a force that had threat-ened the old agrarian traditions, thereby prompting a countervailing mythology about the pastoral plantation lifestyle. After the war, when progressives supported traditionalists in preserving the old social order, progress again served to induce sentimental longings for an imagined Old Virginia. Writing about the beginnings of what he calls the "matrix of antimodernism," Jackson Lears argues that those at the turn of the twentieth century who were interested in finding another direction sought exemplars across the historical spectrum: "Whether they focused on premodern character or on more recent models, all these disparate pilgrims sought 'authentic' alternatives to the apparent unreality of modern existence."[142] In Virginia the look first was to antebellum society, which seemed to offer an escape from progress and its attendant discontents. Ultimately, however, the clock would be turned back farther, to the truly "premodern" world of the eighteenth century, in part because the region's memorable colonial history appealed to both national politicians and northern investors, and so by association could aid in the advancement of the political and economic goals of New Virginia, and because renewed attention to the pastoral society from which had emerged the greatest Virginians of the past might encourage a new generation of sons who could assume leadership positions. At the least, a turn to this moment was a subtle attempt by Virginians to maintain a social structure with which they were accustomed.

Just as progress and modernization in the Old Dominion had not unexpectedly evoked a nostalgia for earlier times, so did many contemporary representations of the landscape. In response to the urbanism of the Progressive Movement, Virginians looked anew at their seemingly disintegrating rural environment. The possibility of preserving some areas from the march of modernity, and thereby keeping open the porthole to the pastoral lifestyle of their ancestors, became more crucial as the twentieth century proceeded.

The new industrialization and urbanization were predictably played out first in the established cities of Richmond and Norfolk. In the Valley efforts to transform the Old Dominion into New Virginia had initially met with success, but the Panic of 1893 brought failure to many of the progressive schemes there. In Richmond the burned district that was destroyed in the Civil War was quickly rebuilt, and new businesses were boldly promoted, as is shown in a large advertisement for the Richmond Stove Works that appeared in a centennial-year atlas (fig. 4.70). So garish a commercial structure recalls the northern industrial complexes of the antebellum era that had long made the pastoral society of Virginia seem appealing. While manufacturing had not been an anomaly in Richmond before the war, the postwar turn toward northern-style industry was no doubt shocking to Richmond's re-

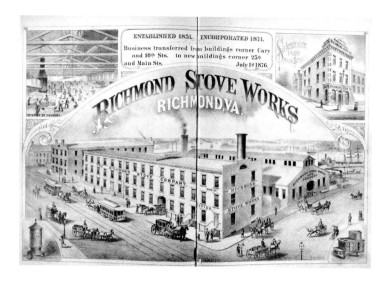

maining traditionalists. In fact, Edward King stated that the continuing growth of the capital brings sadness to the old school, because Richmond had become a symbol of the decay of the society that produced the old plantation type.[143]

In 1892, the anniversary year of Columbus's voyage to America, the state's premier port was chosen to be the site for an international naval review to be held the following year in conjunction with the Chicago World's Fair. Norfolk's urbanization had been meteoric in the years following the war. Its growth, and the concurrent idea that a New Virginia had emerged, were both boldly projected in a large lithograph entitled *Panorama of Norfolk* that was published by a local real estate company on the occasion of the naval review (fig. 4.71). King had seen unlimited potential for this seaport, which in the twentieth century would be realized when Norfolk would house the largest naval base in the world: "The importance of Norfolk as a port of the future is certainly indisputable," he wrote, adding, "A thorough system of internal improvements in Virginia, giving lines leading from the tidewater in that State to the North-west, would enable Nor-

folk almost to usurp the commercial preeminence of New York."[144] Although King's comment was perhaps somewhat overly ambitious, after the war, as a consequence of the commercial traffic passing through its port, the city grew in its size and industrial base.[145]

King's "internal improvement" that would link Norfolk to the West was the railroad, which in fact did dramatically spur the growth of both that city and, at the opposite end of the southwest line, a new urban center for the gathering of coal, minerals, and lumber that would be shipped through Norfolk to innumerable points beyond. This was the former village of Big Lick, which the progressives built into the city of Roanoke. King had much to say about the minerals and other natural resources that could be exported from the Valley, and investors soon took an interest. Southwestern Virginia, which in the antebellum era had been almost wholly rural, suddenly became the most industrialized portion of the state. Mines, mills, and a railway system were constructed. In 1885 Roanoke was described as the antithesis of Old Virginia:

> The city of Roanoke blazes up ahead like an illumination; red-mouthed furnace chimneys light like giant torches above the plain; the roar of machinery, the whistle of engines, the ceaseless hum of labor and of life in the very heart of a quiet, mountain locked valley! We roll into the finest depot in the state, and are escorted to a hotel that would do credit to the proudest city. We tourists go to bed dumb-founded![146]

A new era of prosperity, and even affluence, had come to the Valley, leaving spellbound those who had the old society of rural Virginia in mind.

Prior to the Panic of 1893, efforts had been made in the Valley to enlarge towns and establish industries. "We

4.70 *Above F. W. Beers, publisher,* Richmond Stove Works, *1876, lithograph, 15³/₄ x 24¹/₂ in., published in F. W. Beers,* Illustrated Atlas of the City of Richmond, Va., *Virginia Historical Society*

4.71 *Right American Publishing Company (Milwaukee),* Panorama of Norfolk, Va. and Surroundings, 1892, *Compliments of Myers & Company, Real Estate, 1892, lithograph, 19¹/₂ x 40 in., Virginia Historical Society*

4.72 Michael Miley, Lexington, ca. 1885 (post-1883, the completion date of the Robert E. Lee Episcopal Church, visible at the right), 10⅝ x 18¾ in., carbon print, Virginia Historical Society

all know the stories of wondrous development of towns in the New South," wrote Emory Allen in 1891, "The tide seems to be turning in the direction of old Virginia now. . . . Vast manufacturing plants, representing a capital of many hundred thousand dollars, are to found where but a short time previously there was a wilderness."[147] Allen's generic use of "old Virginia," which here clearly means the state as a whole rather than a particular Virginia society of the past, looks ahead to the loss of specificity that will diminish the usefulness of the term in the twentieth century.

The town of Lexington, which had received national attention in 1866 when Robert E. Lee settled there to head Washington College, was the focus of a series of development schemes that attempted, unsuccessfully, to urbanize and industrialize not only that community but the surrounding towns of Glasgow, Buena Vista, and Goshen.[148] Remarkably ambitious plans were under way for the transformation of Lexington about the time that photographer Michael Miley recorded and thereby preserved an image of the community's bucolic nature (fig. 4.72). He presents a typical western Virginia market town, akin to the ones painted by Edward Beyer in the 1850s (page 108, fig. 3.55). In October 1890, however, it appeared that the scene pictured by Miley might change. At that time the *Rockbridge County News* announced "Lexington's great awakening": "The old town has aroused from her lethargy, she has caught the spirit of the times."[149] With six passenger trains arriving daily, Lexington seemed destined to become a railroad center like Roanoke, its neighbor fifty miles to the south. Local citizens and outside investors all envisioned a modern-day migration of settlers to the expanded community. The Union Steel Company of Louisville prepared to relocate there. A headline in the *Lexington Gazette* announced the sale in two hours of "$100,000 Of Stock," enough to fund the purchase of 1,275 acres to the west of town. There the Lexington Development Company planned to lay out streets and lots, engineer a water supply,

and erect two grand hotels in order to build "the most beautiful and profitable city in the South to live in." One hotel was actually constructed: the Castle Hill (also called the deHart) remained unopened, however, when the *Rockbridge County News* announced the Panic of 1893: "It's a bust! The boom's busted." The Lexington Development Company soon folded. Today the foundations of the Union Steel Company's projected plant lie buried beneath tennis courts at Washington and Lee University. The Castle Hill Hotel soon burned. Lexington's planned expansion was over.

The progress that seemed inevitable in the Lexington of the 1880s had not been welcomed by all. Miley, perhaps fearful that the railroad would bring change, recorded what seems to be an already nostalgic view of the rural town. His image rejects the idea of New Virginia for a memory of what would soon be lost. Thus, progress in the western reaches of the state also spurred an interest in an imaginative Old Virginia.

While Progressives of New Virginia sought to maintain the social status quo, they also envisioned the recovery of the national stature that Virginia had enjoyed in the colonial era. To help in this pursuit, they would take what opportunities presented themselves to remind the nation of the eighteenth-century past, when Virginians had assumed leadership roles in affairs of state. To do so they would have to part ways, at least to a degree, with those traditionalists who by fondly remembering the Confederacy had self-imposed a type of isolation on the commonwealth. The Confederate past would ultimately have to be jettisoned altogether because it was detested in the postwar North, where the deaths of thousands of Union soldiers were vividly remembered.

Supporting the view held by many northerners was an entry published in the *Encyclopaedia Britannica* of 1878 (fig. 4.73), which Thomas Nelson Page remembered as having characterized the South as "an ignorant, illiterate,

AMERICAN

the poetry of the pioneer is unconscious. The attractive culture of the South has been limited in extent and degree. The hothouse fruit of wealth and leisure, it has never struck its roots deeply into native soil. Since the Revolution days, when Virginia was the nurse of statesmen, the few thinkers of America born south of Mason and Dixon's line—outnumbered by those belonging to the single State of Massachusetts—have commonly migrated to New York or Boston in search of a university training. In the world of letters at least, the Southern States have shone by reflected light; nor is it too much to say, that mainly by their connection with the North the Carolinas have been saved from sinking to the level of Mexico or the Antilles. Whether we look to India or Louisiana, it would seem that the tropical sun takes the poetic fire out of Anglo-Saxon veins, and the indolence which is the concomitant of despotism has the same benumbing effect. Like the Spartan marshalling his helots, the planter lounging among his slaves was made dead to Art by a paralysing sense of his own superiority. All the best transatlantic literature is inspired by the spirit of over-confidence—often of over-confidence—in labour. It has only flourished freely in a free soil; and for almost all its vitality and aspirations, its comparatively scant performance and large promise, we must turn to New England. Its defects and merits are those of the national character as developed in the Northern States, and we must seek for an explanation of its peculiarities in the physical and moral circumstances which surround them.

When we remember that the Romans lived under the sky of Italy, that the character of the modern Swiss is

4.73 Above, left The Encyclopaedia Britannica, *Ninth Edition (New York, 1878), volume A, "American Literature," The Homer Babbidge Library, University of Connecticut, Storrs*

4.74 Above, right T. K. Oglesby, The Britannica Answered and the South Vindicated *(Montgomery, Alabama, 1891), Virginia Historical Society*

cruel, semi-barbarous section of the American people, sunk in brutality and vice . . . a race of slavedrivers who contributed nothing to the advancement of mankind and who started a bloody war to protect their slave property."[150] In actuality, the *Britannica* entry, which addressed the subject of "American Literature," faulted the admittedly "attractive" culture of the South as a "hothouse fruit of wealth and leisure [that] has never struck its roots deeply into native soil" and thus "has been limited in extent and degree." The blame was attributed to climate and slavery: "it would seem that the tropical sun takes the poetic fire out of Anglo-Saxon veins, and the indolence which is the concomitant of despotism has the same benumbing effect. . . . the planter lounging among his slaves was made dead to Art by a paralysing sense of his own superiority."[151] One of the responses to this affront by the presumed source of all reliable knowledge came from Thaddeus K. Oglesby, who penned *The Britannica Answered and the South Vindicated* (fig. 4.74), wherein the many intellectual contributions of southerners over several centuries are enumerated. Oglesby sought to "lay before the public . . . a summary of historical facts, showing that to the South, far more than to any other section, is this Union indebted for the genius, wisdom, enterprise, patriotism and valor that have given it so proud an eminence among the nations of the earth."[152] This passionate response indicates that even twenty-six years after Appomattox Virginians were still sensitive to what they saw as a continuation of what seemed to be rehashed abolitionist rhetoric. It would not be until the celebrations of the next two decades that the state and the nation as whole would be better able to look beyond the Confederate past.

Indeed, it had become apparent that Virginia's advances into the national arena would be compromised if they were always preceded by the figurative parading of Confederate flags. Virginia's colonial heritage, by contrast, held national appeal. Even this author for the *Britannica* admitted that "Virginia was the nurse of statesmen" during "the Revolution days." Beginning in 1876, when the centennial of independence sparked nationwide interest in what would become the Colonial Revival, Progressives began to redirect attention to this less controversial history as they "worked to influence the nation." As James Lindgren explains, they "preserved a past that proved that the Old Dominion had founded the nation, established representative government, instituted racial order through slavery, and stood for civility and grace."[153] If this looking backwards at times seemed incongruous, in 1907 Progressives could skirt that problem when they were presented with the opportunity to look to both the past and the future at the same time, to utilize symbols of modernity to recognize the first episode of the nation's history. This occasion was the tercentennial of the founding of Jamestown. A ceremony held in modern Norfolk celebrated both Virginia's and America's proud past, as well as the future of the civilized world. The Norfolk event was advertised on a number of posters (fig. 4.75). If this imagery looks primarily forward, some of the events at the fair honored the past, particularly the exploits of John Smith and Pocahontas. The tercentennial was the ultimate triumph of the progressive's agenda to tie the modern world to the earlier periods in Virginia's history.

The postwar landscape also facilitated the mythologization of Old Virginia. Alfred Wordsworth Thompson, who regretted the progress that was transforming cities like Norfolk, longed for an escape into the countryside (fig. 4.76). Like so many American artists of the period, Thompson

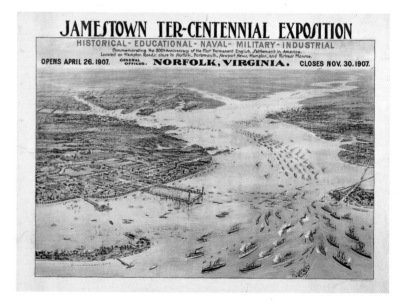

4.75 A. Hoen & Co., Richmond, Jamestown Ter-Centennial Exposition, Historical - Educational - Naval - Military - Industrial, Commemorating the 300th Anniversary of the First Permanent English Settlement in America . . . Norfolk, Virginia. . . . 1907, *1907, poster, 26¹/₂ x 36⁵/₈ in., Virginia Historical Society*

4.76 *Alfred Wordsworth Thompson,* Road Out of Norfolk, *1888, oil on canvas, 18 x 30 in., Chrysler Museum of Art*

had studied in Paris in the 1860s where he had seen the peasants in Barbizon paintings. He recognized their American equivalents in the Tidewater landscape when he pictured a "road out of" the newly industrialized Norfolk. Rural life still survived in the Tidewater; people still tilled the ground in order to survive. Admittedly, they lived in near poverty, but to many theorists, if not to the farmers themselves, the old lifestyle was nonetheless preferable to the new urbanization. The miseries brought on by progress are suggested by Thompson's inclusion of factories and their ever-present smoke in the distance of his painting, but the viewer does not get a sense that the thoroughfare upon which the travelers are escaping is a road to prosperity. Indeed, these people, even though they are moving, seem trapped in this evolving world, in which they are barred from participation in the new ways and so are left with the old, which assures their continued destitution. As Thompson shows us, the actual roads out of Norfolk in the postwar period led to a flat, bleak landscape of exhausted fields that promised little for the future of Virginia. If that landscape was to inspire its residents it would have to be reinvented and viewed through the eye of memory, either as what it had recently been, the setting for a great antebellum culture or, even better, as the landscape that bred the nation's Founding Fathers.

The plantation setting was remembered in detail by the apologists as a key component of antebellum society. Thomas Nelson Page and George Bagby described the gardens and fields that gave the old way of life its idyllic

quality and that helped set Virginia apart from the North. To George Inness the region's landscape was stamped with the history of a lost era. Indeed, so pervasive was the decades-old mythology about antebellum Virginia that this northern painter had formulated a conception about its landscape even before he visited the state. The mystique of Old Virginia lured America's leading landscapist of the 1880s to a place where he knew that he would find human history. In an interview six years earlier Inness had stated his preference for a "civilized landscape" that was imbued "with every act of man" such as the scenery that he had discovered on an extended tour of Italy.[154] In Goochland County, just west of Richmond, particularly in those settings where slaves had lived and endured, Inness looked in the landscape for what he called "the sentiment of humanity." Thus in *A Virginia Sunset* (fig. 4.77) two slave figures and a distant cabin seem almost to be apparitions on an expanse that is cold and flat yet has an entrancing beauty to it. Inness presents a still setting that is imbued with a mood of disappearance and loss. Any vibrancy that once engendered the life here has vanished, and there is a nostalgia for a time that has past, even though Inness's postbellum viewers would have been aware of all of the iniquitous associations of that life.

In these same years George Bagby associated similar sentiments with the land. He complained about the absence of human activity on the postwar Virginia landscape. The quiet, he said, was overwhelming to those who remembered the bustle and constant motion of workers

4.77 *Above* George Inness, A Virginia Sunset, *1889, 30 x 45 in., oil on canvas, Mead Art Museum, Amherst College*

4.78 *Left* Broadside: *"Get a farm in eastern Virginia while land is cheap, and can be had on easy terms: The undersigned has for sale a vast number of farms in King and Queen County, Virginia," Philadelphia, n. d. (postwar), 15⅛ x 9⁷/₁₆ in., Virginia Historical Society*

and playful children on the antebellum plantation. His melancholy description corroborates the imagery of Inness. The comparative quiet of the rural landscape no doubt served as a stimulus for remembering the old order for many inhabitants of the late-century Virginia countryside.

This stillness was corroborated in additional ways. For instance, a broadside of the period (fig. 4.78) records one reason that a number of the old Tidewater plantations were quiet—they had been broken up and were being sold off in the years following the war. Here, we see that

farms in eastern Virginia were being offered to potential northern buyers (in Philadelphia) on "cheap" and "easy" terms. From such evidence we can understand how to some writers the Virginia of the antebellum era must truly have seemed to be vanishing. Thomas Nelson Page wrote that rural Virginians initially withstood the effects of the war: "The old life survived for a period in a sort of afterglow; the people thought they could reconstruct the shattered fragments and live it over." But this was not for long: "The old life at the South passed away in the flame of war and in the yet more fiery ordeal of Reconstruction"; the "devastation," he wrote, was "complete." With outsiders being lured to the state, some of whom wanted to re-create what they imagined to be the idyllic lifestyle of Old Virginia, Page quipped that "Virginia, instead of being, as the cant phrase went, 'a good country to come from,' has become a good country to come to."[155]

While structures, cities, and civilizations might pass away, nature is constant. It is always there, ever renewing itself and offering a new beginning. As the century neared its end, the landscape of the Tidewater provided for its tenants and visitors what appeared to be the setting for a new beginning, which was sorely needed following the carnage of war and the political and ideological chaos that had followed. As the yearning by Progressives for national acceptance had brought about the rediscovery of a Virginia history that would meet with national approval, so the landscape itself also provided a path that led to a rediscovery of the region's glorious past, and even its pre-settlement purity.

In those areas where the land was abandoned after the war, it seemed to some observers that it became again the rugged environment that the first colonists had settled. Recognizing the potency of nature for physical renewal, Richard Norris Brooke looked to the land for spiritual renewal in an era that had experienced political upheaval and too rapid social and economic change. In his untitled landscape that has come to be called *Virginia Scene* (fig. 4.79), Brooke imitated the Barbizon artists in searching the landscape for traditional values that were difficult to come by in the modern age. Unlike the contemporary image of George Inness, Brooke creates a landscape where powerful forces have nearly obliterated man's efforts to level and fence a field. As in the final painting of Thomas Cole's antebellum series, *The Course of Empire*, the land is pictured as returning to its primeval innocence. Nature is shown to exist in a prelapsarian state; it carries the viewer far from the recent past of Civil War violence to a soon-to-be Edenic world, in which man will be able to begin again. This painting makes the point that man's attempts to assert dominance over the natural world will, according to Brooke, end as all such attempts have ended in the past, with the re-establishment of nature. It is only recently that the more dire effects of our

attempts at such control have taken on their often disastrous permanence.

The renewed attention to the past that was inspired by remnants that remained on the Virginia landscape became increasingly important in the early years of the twentieth century. In *Early Spring Landscape* (fig. 4.80), Gari Melchers presents a view in Falmouth, which is near Fredericksburg. Melchers produced a canvas that is crowded with elements of new and old. This is an "early spring landscape." It is fresh with a sense of new life; there are trees in bloom and newly cleaned laundry dries in the warm sunlight. The two buildings that consume large sections of the canvas, however, are both old, but recall differing eras from the past. In the foreground is a newer building of the cottage type, which is clearly inhabited, if not in the best of repair. It is of an age to have survived the nearby fighting and has made itself available for the renewal of human life. The more commanding of the two buildings looms above, in the distance.[156] This house is solemn and stately in its Georgian regularity and mass. It is almost menacing as it looks down upon the human habitations below, and as such becomes the inevitable focus of the viewer's attention. Nature appears almost to have parted its curtain of foliage to reveal this monument of eighteenth-century history. Melchers reminds his contemporaries to reconsider Virginia's preeminent past,

4.79 *Richard Norris Brooke,* Virginia Scene, *ca. 1900, oil on canvas, 20 x 30 in., Virginia Historical Society, Lora Robins Collection of Virginia Art*

4.80 *Above Gari Melchers*, Early Spring Landscape, *ca. 1918, oil on canvas, 17³/₄ x 21¹/₂ in., Belmont, The Gari Melchers Estate and Memorial Gallery, Mary Washington College, Fredericksburg, Virginia*

4.81 *Right Jean Leon Gerome Ferris*, Under My Own Vine and Fig Tree, 1798, *ca. 1910, oil on canvas, 29 x 20 in., Virginia Historical Society, Lora Robins Collection of Virginia Art*

which has ever been present in the landscape but is only in his day coming back into focus.

When in the early twentieth century Jean Leon Gerome Ferris set out to paint the life of George Washington, he visited the general's estate and studied the decorative objects and memorabilia preserved there. Most importantly, however, he paid careful attention to, and was moved by, the impressive building that had been Washington's home. In his depiction of Washington with Nelly Custis, the president's step-granddaughter, which is appropriately titled *Under My Own Vine and Fig Tree*, the scene is composed to give a dramatic presence to the architecture of Mount Vernon (fig. 4.81). This imposing classical structure stands as evidence of the vision and accomplishment of one of the nation's Founding Fathers, and of the ideas that were current in his day, which he

tried to include when redesigning his house. By the time of Ferris's visit, the building had long been in the hands of the Mount Vernon Ladies' Association, which had taken up the task of restoring what was arguably America's most important residence. As pictured by this artist, Mount Vernon is shown to embody solidity and permanence in a world of changing natural and political seasons.

The classical architecture of Virginia had, of course, always been present in the landscape, but many of the great houses had fallen on hard times through neglect, either because of the financial setbacks of their owners before the war, the ravages of the war itself, or their undeniable association with slavery after it. Their rural settings, like that of former President James Madison's home, Montpelier, also served to place them beyond the attentions of the postwar urban progressivists, most of whom who were not yet ready to retire to such estates (fig. 4.82). It would not be until after the centennial of 1876, and, for all intents and purposes, until the early decades of the twentieth century, when Americans would again be ready to rediscover this earliest and greatest Virginia architecture and the motives of those who had participated in its development. After a half-dozen owners in the second half of the nineteenth century, Montpelier was acquired in 1901 by William duPont, of Delaware and England, whose architecturally correct but outlandish-in-scale additions to the house doubled its size (fig. 4.83). By this time, most Americans, including even the old apologist Thomas Nelson Page, had come to the understanding that Old Virginia was best redefined as Colonial Virginia.

4.82 Above John Gadsby Chapman, Montpelier *(Orange County)*, *1836, engraved by J. F. E. Prud'homme, 3¼ x 4¼ in., Virginia Historical Society*

4.83 Above, top Montpelier, *following the alterations by William duPont, photograph, Virginia Historical Society*

179

5.1 *Thur de Thulstrup,* A Meet in Old Virginia, *1901, photogravure,*
18 x 24¹/₂ in., Virginia Historical Society

V. The Triumph of the Colonial Past

n 1901, Thur de Thulstrup, an award-winning New York painter and illustrator, produced for an expanding market of colonial enthusiasts a print entitled *A Meet in Old Virginia* (fig. 5.1). The scene is of fox hunters readying themselves for the chase; the setting is Westover, the tidewater plantation of the William Byrds, and the costumes are colonial. Thulstrup illustrates the mid-eighteenth century, a time that many turn-of-the-twentieth-century Americans believed was the golden age of the region. The title of the print reminds us that the meaning of the term Old Virginia had remained adaptable since its inception three quarters of a century earlier. This image is an exemplary product of the Colonial Revival, a national movement that had been inspired by the centenary of 1876 and had gained momentum in the waning years of the nineteenth century.

The rekindled patriotism of 1876 had served to revive interest in the colonial past, particularly in those eras most closely associated with representative government and America's quest for liberty. Much of that history had unfolded in Virginia. Thus, the centenary provided Virginians with a fortuitous opportunity to refashion their history for a national audience. By reintroducing the heritage of colonial Virginia to Americans of the post Civil War era, Virginians could deflect attention away from the recent conflict, and perhaps bring a degree of closure to that catastrophic era and its painful aftermath. The image of prewar Virginia as a virtuous pastoral society had been severely damaged; the myth of an antebellum arcadia could now appeal only as nostalgia. Old Virginia, however, could be reinvented as the region's colonial past, and thereby reinfused with the spirit of those invigorating times. That was a past that had a future.

The Colonial Revival was a movement in architecture, the decorative arts, preservation, and painting to return to the design ideals that were popular in eighteenth-century America, and to picture, write about, and otherwise remember episodes and figures from that era. It started with a nationalistic flourish at the Philadelphia Exposition of 1876, and, concurrently, with an unthinkable tragedy, as word filtered back to the east coast of the destruction of the Seventh Cavalry and its charismatic leader, General George Armstrong Custer, at Little Big Horn. Both events inspired Americans to greater patrio-

tism, and to reconsider how the nation had risen and what it had endured to survive.[1] The movement evolved erratically, however, slowing in the 1880s before becoming widely popularized at the turn of the century. The revival also, not surprisingly, developed differently in different parts of the nation. The remembering of colonial history would be directed to different purposes in New England. Michael Kammen writes of the revival that "as a manifestation of American memory it managed to be simultaneously symptomatic yet highly idiosyncratic."[2]

To understand the development of the Colonial Revival is to look beyond the aesthetics of the colonial houses that were restored or the homes that were conceived anew in the old styles, and beyond the artistic merit of the history paintings that recalled and celebrated the colonial past. More importantly, the revived interest in early America took on a social significance as traditionalists from the North and South directed public attention to the values of eighteenth-century Americans. In retrospect, the attempts by these revivalists to mold contemporary society to the model of elitist, Anglo-Saxon, colonial America is not surprising. Postwar northern traditionalists feared for the survival of both the established order of society and the values that had originated with the Founding Fathers because millions of European immigrants had come to America's shores in the latter decades of the nineteenth century, and because burgeoning industrialization threatened massive social change in their region. On the positive side, interest in the colonial past served to benefit tourism in what had been the thirteen original colonies. However, unlike Virginians, who, it must be said, paid little attention to the colonial past of New England, northerners after the Civil War tended to spread wide the nets of colonial revivalism to include, and at times to focus particular attention on, the history of colonial Virginia. This was in part because they found there the best precedent for the aristocratic life style that many of them chose to pursue in the modern era, as well as because the personages from the Old Dominion were simply too important to leave out of any reminiscence of the nation's birth.

Many Virginians had a different agenda. Although the aristocracy there was just as fervent, if not more so, in wanting to ban from the higher ranks of society all intruders, including popular-class radicals and newly liberated African Americans, such exclusivity had long been the norm in the region, where since the 1830s the emergent idea of Old Virginia had served to block the ascent of immigrants and outsiders. Immediately after Appomattox, the cult of the Lost Cause had arisen to perpetuate the old social order that the Confederacy had been established to defend. To be sure, the Colonial Revival would help in the battle waged by Virginia traditionalists to maintain order within local societies and to retain control of regional political power. But it was also quickly understood that this movement could serve as well the grander purpose of reviving the national status of Virginia. The literature and visual arts of the Colonial Revival era that reimagine colonial Virginia come into our story as expressions of a contemporary culture that was trying to redefine itself on the fly, to simultaneously return to a version of the antebellum social status quo while encouraging the nation as a whole to look beyond the Civil War and the philosophical debates of abolitionists and pro-slavery theorists to a grand colonial period that was peopled by thinkers and leaders with whom all Americans could identify and in whom all could take pride. The term Old Virginia, when it was invoked, was most often used as a buoy that marked one's entry into an imaginative colonial world, rather than the still vividly remembered Civil War era.

Evidence of the shift in the meaning of the term Old Virginia is to be found as early as the 1870s. In June of 1876, in recognition of the coming anniversary of the "Declaration of Independence," John Esten Cooke published in *Harper's New Monthly Magazine* an article entitled "Virginia in the Revolution."[3] Prominently illustrating the opening page is a wood engraving that is captioned *"In Old Virginny"* (fig. 5.2). Pictured is the ubiquitous banjo-playing slave, who serves to identify the setting. However, while Americans had come to associate this figure with the carefree lifestyle of the region during the antebellum era, the plantation master and mistress who are shown visiting their musical slave are clothed in colonial costume. By juxtaposing the title of his article with the imagery and caption, Cooke deftly transformed the term Old Virginia to mean the colonial era. In 1901, when Thur de Thulstrup did much the same, it would no longer have been a surprise.

By 1907, the anniversary year of the founding of Jamestown, this shift was for the most part complete. At that time of great sentiment for the region's colonial past, James J. McDonald, a retired state senator, published *Life in Old Virginia* (by way of the appropriately named concern, The Old Virginia Publishing Company, Norfolk). The frontispiece of his book pictures Captain John Smith. Opposite is the Foreword, which begins with lines remembered imperfectly from the 1847 "Carry Me Back to Old Virginia" song:

When I am old and feeble,
And cannot work any more,
Then carry me back to Old Virginia
To Old Virginia's shore.

The author then connects this passage, which had actually been written about antebellum Virginia, to the colonial past:

The purpose of this book is to give a brief history of the efforts of the English to establish permanent settlements in Virginia, and to follow with interesting stories of the life and customs of the people inhabiting particularly that part of Old Virginia, known as the 'Tidewater' section where American civilization began its first struggles for existence amid forests of a new world whose only occupants then were wild beasts and savage men.[4]

To James McDonald, Old Virginia is colonial Virginia. As evidence, we note that only twenty pages in his book of more than three hundred are given to "The Commonwealth of Virginia, 1776–1860"; only eight explain "Secession and Civil War."

This is not to say that all commentators after 1907 uniformly redefined Old Virginia as the colonial past. Some invoked Old Virginia with intentional vagueness to

5.2 *Unidentified artist,* In Ole Virginny, *wood engraving, 4½ x 4½ in., in John Esten Cooke,* "Virginia in the Revolution," Harper's New Monthly Magazine, *June 1876, Virginia Historical Society*

call to mind a heritage that was not to be precisely delimited. When the term was redefined to mean largely the colonial era, however, the idea of Old Virginia gained national primacy. Those in the North who prior to the Civil War had been mesmerized by the culture of plantation society could again admire the region. They could revere cavaliers like John Smith, who had founded the nation at Jamestown, and patriots like George Washington and Patrick Henry, who had wrestled independence from England. The new national interest in the colonial past thereby contributed notably to the ending of Virginia's isolation following the most recent war of rebellion.

While Mount Vernon had remained in the public consciousness throughout the nineteenth century, to the point where the warring parties had agreed that Washington's estate would be spared any military engagements, it seemed almost as if Jamestown and Williamsburg had been held in reserve by Virginians for this last campaign to regain national status. Both sites had been left virtually untouched when cities were being built elsewhere. Admittedly, Jamestown had been remembered throughout the nineteenth century whenever stories about Pocahontas and Captain John Smith had been told, but, other than the sectional debates about the veracity of Smith's accounts that began in the 1850s, the first colony had remained out of the mainstream of American thought until the tercentenary of its founding. At that time Theodore Roosevelt traveled to Jamestown, thereby lending his prestige to its importance as a national founding narrative as significant as, if not as well known as, the Pilgrims and Plymouth Rock. So fully had the Old Dominion been accepted as a member in good standing of the union that by 1913 a Virginia-born president, Woodrow Wilson, could be elected. So complete was the victory by the 1920s that W. A. R. Goodwin, the rector at Bruton Parish Church in Williamsburg, could approach John D. Rockefeller, Jr., one of the wealthiest of all northerners, to fund what would be the restoration of an entire town. Rockefeller accepted Goodwin's argument that Williamsburg should become a national, not simply a regional shrine, where the lives of the colonial patriots who had pointed the nation on the course toward independence could be reenacted. Moving far beyond the old arguments of sectionalists, Rockefeller accepted the minister's forward-looking premise that a restored colonial town would both educate visitors and inspire them to revive the values that drove such patriots. Caught up in the national enthusiasm for this period in our history, Rockefeller would make the Williamsburg project the culmination of the Colonial Revivalist belief that the material culture of colonial America could encourage the nation to return to the enlightened principles of its forefathers. Although in recent years the historians at Colonial Williamsburg have taken a critical

look at the problems that were inherent in life in that early Virginia city, in general terms Williamsburg has come to symbolize the colonial Virginia that patriotic Americans revere. Although the term Old Virginia was rarely used at Colonial Williamsburg, to this day many envision the restored town when they hear it.

The idea of a reborn Old Virginia would be carried as well to the countryside by new generations of gentry. As had the aristocrats of two-hundred years before, wealthy Americans of the mid-twentieth century sought out rural estates far from the centers of commerce and industry, where a genteel, virtuous life could be pursued in a conducive setting. Like the rebuilders of Williamsburg who strove to recover not only the old buildings but also the environment that had inspired the Virginian Founding Fathers to greatness, these modern lords of the manor took inspiration from the knowledge that their colonial predecessors had moved on the same stage for many of the same reasons. The pastoral lifestyle, with its intertwining of great wealth, humanism, historical consciousness, and the pursuit of virtue, was a worthy goal, either as an occasional escape from urban life or as a welcomed retirement from it. In their reimagining of plantation life—now styled one's "country place" or "farm"—these new ruralists would establish a pattern for gentry living that exists to this day.

The Colonial Revival and the Old Dominion

The process of rethinking the region's early past appealed to the patriotism of those who came to recognize that in order "to understand the history of the country it is . . . necessary to study the Virginia and New England of the seventeenth and eighteenth centuries."[5] This statement is by John Esten Cooke, one of the Virginia apologists, whose arguments were more easily crafted and thereby more credible when they concerned colonial history. In studying that mytho-historic past, Americans from both sections found reassuring roots. In stories about patriots, in colonial-style architecture, and even in household furnishings, they discovered symbols that could give expression to their aspirations for the present and their dreams for the future. Vincent Scully has characterized the Americans of the 1870s as "a self-conscious generation, tormented, as the men of the mid-century had seldom been, by a sense of history, of memory, and of cultural loss."[6] James Lindgren, writing in *Preserving the Old Dominion*, explains that at the time of the centenary most of America's elite wanted particularly to uphold old habits, including a respect for hierarchy, work, and law.[7] Reverence for the colonial past—remembered as a stable time when values were sound and the right people were in control of society, and therefore when immigrants and black people had no power—helped Anglo-Americans toward that objective. In Virginia, revivalists shared with proponents of the Lost Cause the common goal of maintaining the societal status quo.

Beyond its intellectual underpinnings, the movement had popular appeal. The Colonial Revival was seized upon by the masses at the turn of the century in part because the early history of America, and particularly of Virginia, was made up of dramatic episodes.[8] Writing in *The Birth of the Nation, Jamestown, 1607*, Mrs. Roger A. Pryor explained that "the story of a world emerging from the darkness in which it had been hidden for countless ages will always thrill the imagination."[9] Mary Newton Stanard, a prolific author, wrote in 1907 of her "pilgrimages into that charmed region, Virginia's past."[10] And R. T. Barton argued in his *Reports . . . of Decisions of The General Court of Virginia, 1728–1741* (1909) that the colonial was "by far the most interesting period of our American life."[11] Although there were remnants of the colonial period all along the eastern seaboard, Americans often looked to colonial Virginia when they attended to seventeenth-century history. Whether aspiring to revive the political and social principles of the Founding Fathers or attempting to perpetuate their forefathers's refined tastes for Georgian architecture, many of the better examples of which were produced in the Old Dominion, the life that had been created in that colony seemed emblematic of the ideals that had inspired the Colonial Revival in the first place. Also, because the Gilded Age was characterized by a nostalgia for an inegalitarian and undemocratic society, Virginia, which had been more elitist than any of the other colonies, became a favorite subject for artists, architects, and writers. By 1908 Thomas Nelson Page would be able to make the claim to a national audience that Virginia was "the first colony in America in influence, as she was in time, and more than any other contributed to the making of this nation."[12]

The society and architecture of colonial Virginia intrigued many northern revivalists. Authors like Sydney George Fisher, writing in *Men, Women and Manners in Colonial Times* (Philadelphia, 1902), lauded the region's early gentry for its love of "amusements of all kinds" and the "continual visiting between plantations." This gave Virginians "great social facility," a quality that had become difficult to find in the modern world.[13] The architectural appeal of the region is evident in such studies as *Virginia Beautiful*, published about 1930 by the celebrated Wallace Nutting, a prominent spokesman for the Colonial Revival, whom Michael Kammen argues personified the movement as much as any single person.[14] Nutting was one of many New Englanders who recognized that Virginia's early material history was much more adaptable to the modern world than was the Puritan legacy. He chose to write about this region because Virginia's past provided many examples of architecture and decorative furnishings that fit his vision; Nutting ranked the Georgian mansions of Virginia as unmatched elsewhere in the nation. It can be argued that northern revivalists like Fisher and Nutting could be unabashedly enthusiastic about the first colony precisely because they were not residents of the state. They were far removed from the Confederate legacy that lingered in postwar Virginia and at times diverted attention there to the more immediate past.

John Esten Cooke did as much as any single writer to boost the revival movement within the Old Dominion. Cooke, who had been an ardent secessionist and had served in the Confederate army throughout the war, was also a prolific author whose work spanned the second half of the nineteenth century. Early in his career, before the old regime had collapsed, Cooke had looked to the colonial past of his home state with an eye "to do for the Old Dominion what . . . Hawthorne [has done] for the Puritan life of New England."[15] In the 1850s Cooke therefore wrote primarily about cavaliers and the settlement of the Tidewater. The experience of the Civil War inspired him to produce histories and novels dealing with that traumatic period in Virginia's recent past, but it would not be long before Cooke again turned his attention to the earlier period. An 1867 article for *Hours at Home* identified John Smith as "The Last of the Knights,"[16] an interesting appellation considering the contemporary interest in such Confederate "knights" as Jackson and Stuart. His *Stories of the Old Dominion* (1879) told many "interesting incidents" about the early history of Virginia, and his *Virginia: A History of the People* (1883) devoted 472 pages to the colonial period and only twenty-eight to the era of "Modern Virginia."

In writing about the colonial age, Cooke celebrated the same pinnacles of Virginia's early history that had begun to attract interest in the 1830s: the Jamestown era of settlement and adventure, when civilization was established in America, and the later period of patriots and revolution, when a nation was founded. He focused on the two most revered of the Virginia Founding Fathers, Patrick Henry and George Washington, who towered far above the rest because of the personal risks that they had taken to inspire and secure American independence. Cooke imagined the society of the late colonial period to be a golden age, when planters amassed fortunes that enabled them to live like English lords and to pursue the idyllic pastoral life. This was the society that would appeal to wealthy revivalists nationwide who looked for colonial precedent for their own lifestyle of abundance.

Following the Civil War Cooke had "patiently studied the dusty archives" of such institutions as the Virginia Historical Society in order to "ascertain the truth" about the region's early history. He complained that no one had ever done so before, and that this subject had been so much neglected that no satisfactory account existed.[17] Al-

5.3 *Huestis Cook,* Jamestown, *ca. 1890s, gelatin silver print, 11 x 19¾ in., stamped on rear Cook studios, Virginia Historical Society*

though a number of histories of the early colony existed, such as those by Robert Beverley and William Stith, by 1876, other than in exciting tales about Pocahontas and Captain John Smith or Nathaniel Bacon, the history of Virginia in the seventeenth century was little known. Inspired by the centenary, Alexander Brown of Nelson County had begun working on his *Genesis of the United States*, which was finally published in 1890. Brown considered it his "patriotic duty" to compile "a full and fair account of our very beginning."[18] Had the Jamestown colony failed, Brown pointed out, the United States might never have come into existence.[19] Mary Tucker Magill, in writing her *History of Virginia, For the Use of Schools* (1876), judged the Civil War and its aftermath "too new to be described with that spirit of calmness and impartiality which should ever characterize the historian."[20] Accordingly she devoted nearly half of her text to the century of settlement. Philip Alexander Bruce wrote his *Economic History of Virginia in the Seventeenth Century* (1896) because he found that he could not "obtain a thorough understanding" of the economy of the periods that followed before he addressed the colony's early years. Later, Bruce argued that the history of the seventeenth century was even relevant to an understanding of the present. In his five-volume study *Virginia, Rebirth of the Old Dominion* (1929), the author identified as the two great constructive periods in the history of Virginia the interval between 1607 and 1700, and that between 1876 and 1927.[21] By the height of the Colonial Revival it was understood that the seventeenth-century history of the region held more than local significance. Royall Bascom Smithey pointed out that the Virginia colony was "the cradle of the English race in America," an assertion that would be repeated time and again by the revivalists.[22] The

settlers of Virginia established the "foundation of a new Nation," wrote Thomas Nelson Page, who argued that Virginia's early history belongs "not to the present Virginia alone. It is the heritage of every State carved from the mighty empire once embraced within her borders."[23]

Jamestown was always the most famous seventeenth-century site in Virginia. Admittedly the area had been abandoned, and few other than writers and artists, and the public on rare anniversary years, visited it until the end of the nineteenth century. Page said dramatically that it had "lain desert and untrodden by any feet save those of the wild beast and yet wilder savage."[24] Some antebellum writers, however, had boasted of the Jamestown achievement, particularly in the 1830s, and their insistence on its primacy had struck a chord in the expanding nation.

In the years following the Civil War, artists and writers in Virginia looked to the triumph of Jamestown as a means to forget the defeat of the Confederacy. The Richmond photographer Huestis Cook recorded the site, producing sedate, almost reverent imagery that is respectful of the antiquity of Jamestown and of the significance of its history (fig. 5.3). John Esten Cooke used William Ludwell Sheppard's sketch of *Captain John Smith Making Toys for Pocahontas* as both the cover illustration and the frontispiece to his *Stories of the Old Dominion* in which he asserts that Pocahontas was "only a child but [she] acted nobly" and thereby "deserves our love and respect."[25] Cooke's *My Lady Pokahontas: A True Relation of Virginia. Writ by Anas Todkill, Puritan and Pilgrim [pseud.], with Notes by John Esten Cooke* (1885), is perhaps the best-known novel about the princess. Some three decades earlier the reputation of Pocahontas had been slandered and the importance of the Jamestown settlement downplayed by the Massachusetts historian Charles Deane when he attempted to discredit John Smith's narratives. In his "true" account Cooke answered Deane and Henry Adams by defending the historicity of the great events of her life, although he goes on to create various imaginative subplots, including her previously unknown and certainly fictional crossing of paths with Shakespeare at a performance of *The Tempest*, where the playwright admits that many of the experiences of Miranda are based on those of the American princess.

Interest in Captain John Smith spread well beyond Virginia during this period. In 1881 the Massachusetts writer Charles Dudley Warner published *Captain John Smith . . . A Study of His Life and Writings*. Soon thereafter Smith's narratives from the early 1600s were reissued in the United States and England in an edition by Edward Arber that would remain the standard text of Smith's writings well into the twentieth century.[26] In still another answer to the New England historians who had doubted Smith, Katharine Pearson Woods of Baltimore set out in the *True Story of Captain John Smith* (1901) "to still once and for all those disturbing voices that have of late years been busy in aspersing his memory."[27]

The anniversary year of Columbus's voyage directed interest toward America's early past in general and toward Jamestown in particular. On that occasion William Wirt Henry credited the legislative assembly of 1619 as providing the underpinning of the government that Americans in 1892 were so "devoted to."[28] The convening of that first meeting of the House of Burgesses, added W. R. Garrett, was "among the decisive events of history."[29] In the year before the landing of the Pilgrims at Plymouth Rock and the creation of the "Mayflower Compact", the colony that would one day grow into the United States of America already had a form of representative government of which it could be proud.

Indeed, of vital importance to the status of Jamestown was the early date of the settlement. Thomas Nelson Page relished the opportunity to state that "from her northeastern territory of 'North Virginia,' charted by and cleared of invaders by her Governors, came New England."[30] Captain John Smith coined the term "New England" and the Pilgrim voyagers to Massachusetts used his maps to plot their journey. Page added that "the Anglo-Saxon civilization was established in this country before the *Mayflower*, under the encouragement and charter of the Virginia Company, brought her body of devoted Pilgrims to the shores of North Virginia."[31] He argued that as "the Birthplace of the American People: the first rude cradle in which was swaddled the tiny infant that in time has sprung up to be among the leaders of nations," Jamestown was "the key to the continent, and led to the supremacy of the Saxon Race, with its laws, its religion and its civilization in North America."[32] He also remem-

bered Sir Francis Bacon's statement that "in Kingdoms the first Foundation or Plantation is of more Dignitie and Merit than all that followeth."[33] Lyon Tyler added that Jamestown saw "the first trial by jury, the first English church, the first English marriage, the first birth of an English child in Virginia, and the first legislative assembly in America."[34] Another writer who was particularly generous toward the Jamestown settlers was Will T. Hale, who stretched the truth a bit in his *True Stories of Jamestown and Its Environs*. Hale wrote that "the earliest Protestant church, trial by jury, thanksgiving services, literary effort, and free school followed hard upon the day" when Jamestown was settled.[35] All this was to counter the impression that, as Page put it, "until just now . . . nearly everything that has counted for much in the history of this country, either sprang from or took its color from New England."[36]

A more widespread rediscovery of Jamestown was brought about through the efforts of several of the women's organizations that were established in the wake of the nation's centenary to aid in the unearthing of America's colonial past. The Association for the Preservation of Virginia Antiquities began its mission in 1889 with the belief that "every detail of the life of [the colony at Jamestown] is of concern to all true Americans," and that "scattered throughout Virginia are numerous ruins of these Colonial days" that should be restored and preserved.[37] It was joined in the following year by the Daughters of the American Revolution and the National Society of the Colonial Dames of America. The latter were national in membership; the APVA would be emulated nationwide. It was incorporated "for the purpose of acquiring, holding and preserving real and personal property relating to the history of Virginia, and particularly to restore and preserve the ancient historic buildings, tombs, monuments and grave-yards."[38] The APVA sought to enshrine those structures and sites as symbols of Virginia's history of greatness, and to popularize them through ceremonies and publications.

The association's first acquisition was the Powder Magazine in Williamsburg; in 1893 it acquired its most important property, a portion of Jamestown Island.[39] As explained by James Lindgren, it was Jamestown that best served the APVA in its effort to wage two concurrent wars on behalf of the established order. One was local, against the popular-class Virginians whom they sought to disfranchise. The second war was national, against those Yankee historians who had argued that the North had founded the nation and thereby should have greater political weight in defining its future direction.[40]

National appreciation for Jamestown escalated at the turn of the century as the tercentenary of 1907 approached. In 1902 the American Scenic and Historic Preservation Society, whose officers included such prominent New Yorkers as J. Pierpont Morgan and Samuel P. Avery, was "moved by the approach of this significant anniversary and the threatened obliteration of the [Jamestown] site." The Society petitioned Congress to purchase Jamestown Island, because "respect for our national traditions" and "justifiable pride in the annals of our race" demand that the site be "preserved forever as the birth-place of Anglo-Saxon America."[41] Also in 1902, a Jamestown Exposition Company was incorporated to plan appropriate ceremonies for 1907. Former president Grover Cleveland endorsed this idea, stating that the events, which would be staged at neighboring Norfolk, would stir in Americans "their best patriotism."[42] As the tercentenary grew nearer, the efforts of national politicians were aligned with those of Virginia Progressives, Colonial Revivalists, and the APVA. Northern disbelief in the romantic history of Jamestown, in which the first settlement had been established by honorable Englishmen and saved from annihilation by a virtuous Indian princess, crumbled under the pressure of the forces that were leveraged at Norfolk. The seniority of Jamestown over Plymouth Rock was almost universally, if begrudgingly, accepted, if only for the duration of the festivities.

The advent of the celebration and the actual anniversary of the founding of the Anglo-American nation inspired the publication of a plethora of books and essays that linked ideas about patriotism and representative government to Jamestown and Old Virginia. Thomas J. Wertenbaker would write in 1914 that during this period "a flood of light has been thrown upon Virginia colonial history," which included the unearthing of many letters, reports, and other sorts of colonial manuscripts.[43] Some of these efforts were serious historical studies, such as Lyon Tyler's *The Cradle of the Republic: Jamestown and James River* (Richmond, 1900), Thomas J. Wertenbaker's *Patrician and Plebeian in Virginia* (Charlottesville, 1910), and his *Virginia Under the Stuarts* (Princeton and London, 1914). Others were reissuings of primary texts, such as *The Colonial Virginia Register, A List of Governors, Councillors and Other Higher Officials* (Albany, N.Y., 1902), Susan A. Kingsbury's *Records of the Virginia Company of London* (Washington, D.C., 1905), and Tyler's *Narratives of Early Virginia, 1606–25* (New York, 1907).[44] The majority of the tercentennial books, however, were romantic histories written for the general reader. These confirmed for the masses the significant contributions that had been made by the sons and daughters of Old Virginia. Jamestown was presented as less a Virginia site than a national one. As a consequence, the reputation of the state was elevated to a status it had not enjoyed in nearly a hundred years.

Standing at the Jamestown site, Page proclaimed that the overwhelming pride felt at such a "sacred spot" must not be "sectional or personal-selfgratulation" but "must be National and Racial," because "had this Colony not had

being, it is possible that this republic might never have been, and . . . the blessing of human liberty, might never have been." To heighten the drama, Page recorded an almost mystical experience:

> I stood on the deck of a boat anchored on the bosom of the river and gazed on this Island as it lay under the moonlight. . . .
> Jamestown took on for me that night a new significance. It became the emblem of that earnest, devoted and patriotic zeal which inspires the heart of every true Freeman. In that mysterious haze all parochial lines and insular confines disappeared, and it became the real Cradle of the American People wherever they may be. . . .
> When I speak of Virginia it is not so much the present Virginia that I bear in mind as that 'Old Virginia,' whose eastern shores extended from her Floridian confines on the south to the forty-fifth degree of north latitude on the north, and whose border to the westward reached to 'the furthest sea.' . . .
> This occasion belongs to all America. This spot belongs to the continent. The heart of it is Old Virginia.[45]

In his *Three Hundreth Anniversary Address,* Page had articulated as forcibly as was possible the relationship between the first colony and the great nation, and his hope that all Americans would one day share in this type of patriotic zeal.

By the end of 1907, it seemed that a new, more elevated status had been firmly established for the first permanent settlement. Will T. Hale wrote in his *True Stories* that "Jamestown's memories deserve our reverence forever and a day." J. Warren Keifer added that the legislative exercise of power, initiated at Jamestown, "will not end while progressive civilization lasts."[46] The success of the tercentennial in popularizing the story of Jamestown for a national audience is suggested by the new interest in this subject and in early Virginia history in general. In 1915 the Ohio Society of the Colonial Dames of America began the printing of "Lectures on the Colonial Period for Use in the Public Schools." The first publication, which addressed the history of the Old Dominion, asked the question, "What caused Virginia to produce such great men and to become a leader in the struggle for national freedom?" The answer carried the reader "back to the history of England, for early Virginia was but a child of the 'Mother Country.'"[47] The close tie to England that had always been felt by colonial Virginians was reasserted in such writings, as was the sense that emulation, rather than separation, had been the foundation of the colony's early years.

Congratulatory endorsements had come in 1907 from such quarters as the United Kingdom, offered by King Edward VII, and the White House, offered by President Theodore Roosevelt. In fact, the "Rough Rider" was

5.4 *Jean Leon Gerome Ferris,* The Abduction of Pocahontas, 1612, *ca. 1910, oil on canvas, 24 x 35 in., Virginia Historical Society, Lora Robins Collection of Virginia Art*

at the time compared to Jamestown's first significant leader who was also dynamic, aggressive, and unconventional. The dedication of one of the tercentennial volumes, entitled *Jamestown Tributes,* is to that "VIVID figure standing out in as bold relief against the background of American life to-day as did that of Captain John Smith in the affairs of the infant nation at Jamestown."[48] Traditionalists in the Bay State were forced to concede that the history of early Virginia was at least as important as their own. In offering an entry for his state in *Jamestown Tributes,* Senator Henry Cabot Lodge of Massachusetts allowed that "Plymouth Rock marks one of the corners of the great republic of the United States as Jamestown marks the other."[49]

Among the northern artists who painted Virginia subjects at this time was Jean Leon Gerome Ferris. Not surprisingly, he was attracted to the story of Pocahontas. However, he sidestepped the well-known episode of the rescue of John Smith, selecting instead the obscure story of the kidnaping of the princess by Samuel Argall, who saw his captive as ransom to be used in negotiations with her father, the "emperor" Powhatan (fig. 5.4). In his notes about the painting, Ferris called Argall a "freebooter," meaning a plunderer or pirate.[50] In his image we see the beautiful Pocahontas pleading her case to the British,

but she would in the end be carried to Jamestown, converted to Christianity, married to John Rolfe, and taken to England, a trip from which she would never return. Ferris shows us what would be the last moment of her life as a Native American and her first as a political pawn.

When Page discussed the "heroic deeds" and "sublime fortitude and endeavor" that characterized the history of early Virginia,[51] he was referring to an era of romance and adventure in which a large part of the drama was stirred by encounters between the English and the resident Indians. Not all were favorable to the invaders. In 1622, the Native American population rose up and attacked the Old World settlers who constituted a foreign presence on what had once been exclusively their land. One of the many settings for what had often been described as a "massacre" was Falling Creek, which is situated on the James River east of the future location of Richmond. This area had been virtually forgotten since the early seventeenth century.

The Falling Creek site and its history were rediscovered by John Douglas Woodward, a Virginia-born artist who was raised in Kentucky and studied in New York City during the Civil War. After Appomattox, Woodward divided his time between that art center and Richmond. He also traveled widely and produced illustrations for such

5.5 *John Douglas Woodward,* Falling Creek, Virginia, *n. d. (ca. 1880s), sketch, 17½ x 15 in., Virginia Historical Society, Lora Robins Collection of Virginia Art*

publications as *Hearth and Home* and Appleton's *Picturesque America* and *Picturesque Europe*. In Virginia Woodward found a number of subjects of interest, including the unremembered Fallen Creek battleground (fig. 5.5). His sketch of this scene was possibly prepared as one of a number of illustrations of Old Virginia.[52]

To suggest the antiquity of the setting and nature's inevitable encroachment on human constructions, Woodward pictures an ancient building in an overgrown setting. A magnolia helps to identify the region as southern. The scene is visible through a round opening that is meant to suggest a portal into time, back to an event that had long ago vanished from the popular imagination. In turning to the land to reimagine the events that had unfolded on it, Woodward followed the same path taken by George Inness in the 1880s. In this case, however, the artist provides precise written information about historical occurences that were tied to this specific site. An inscription on the sketch identifies Falling Creek as both a setting for the 1622 uprising and, interestingly, as the location of the first iron furnace established on American soil. The Indian victory at this site would not assure their domination of it for long.

John Esten Cooke recounted the story of the massacre in his *Virginia, A History of the People* (1883) and men-

tioned the Falling Creek settlement by name:

> The Indians savagely attacked them when they least expected it, and no more spared the women and children than the men. Of twenty-four persons at Falling Creek, near Richmond, only a boy and girl escaped. . . .
> From the Falls to the bay, many of the plantations were entirely destroyed.[53]

However, writing in his later *Stories of the Old Dominion,* Cooke argued that the massacre "did not discourage people. More settlers came to make their homes in the country."[54] In his centenary *Address* Page maintained that the massacre "only served to excite both the Company and the colony to renewed efforts," adding that "this blow must have destroyed" Virginia had not the colony "been established on a firm foundation" at Jamestown.[55] The massacre, then, should in the end be seen as a measure of the strength, rather than the weakness, of the first English settlement. To Woodward, it was an opportunity both to rekindle the memory of a forgotten scene from Virginia's past and to make a point about the transience of human habitations which recede amidst the cyclical growth and renewal of nature.

The other great moment of the seventeenth century deemed worthy of reminiscence was Bacon's Rebellion, which was an attempt led by the young Nathaniel Bacon to protect the citizens of the frontier from hostile Indians after their request for aid had been turned down by Governor Sir William Berkeley. For decades revivalists had found the adventures of Bacon and Berkeley irresistible. In her *Story of Bacon's Rebellion* (1907), Mary Newton Stanard ranked this subject as, next to the early days at Jamestown, "the most portentous, the most dramatic, the most picturesque event of [the colony's] seventeenth century history."[56] John Esten Cooke, among others, interpreted this episode of 1666 as the first American revolution against British tyranny and a harbinger of the events of 1776:

> Just one hundred years before the American Revolution, a rebellion or revolution took place in Virginia, which resembled it in the most striking manner. The Virginians . . . made war on the English governor just as the Americans afterward made war on the King of England. They were led, too, by a man whose character was very much like Washington's.

Cooke posited that Bacon's underlying motivation was "a vast mass of real oppression and a whole world of misery and suppressed rage."[57] Page was more specific, arguing that both rebellions were provoked by the same cause, "the inalienable right of British subjects to have self-government. Both of them were based on the original Charters under which Virginia was planted."[58]

One later telling that is representative of the interest

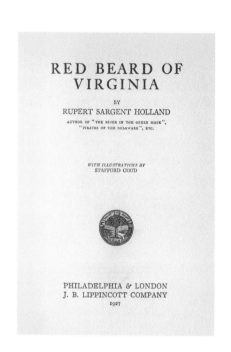

RED BEARD OF
VIRGINIA

BY
RUPERT SARGENT HOLLAND

AUTHOR OF "THE RIDER IN THE GREEN MASK",
"PIRATES OF THE DELAWARE", ETC.

WITH ILLUSTRATIONS BY
STAFFORD GOOD

PHILADELPHIA & LONDON
J. B. LIPPINCOTT COMPANY
1927

5.6 *Above* *Rupert S. Holland,* Red Beard
of Virginia *(Philadelphia, 1927), Virginia
Historical Society*

5.7 *Right* *Stafford Good,* Shining Shafts
Engaged and Disengaged in Lightning-
like Play, *1927, oil on board, 22 x 18 in.,
Virginia Historical Society, Lora Robins
Collection of Virginia Art*

in Bacon and his times is *Red Beard of Virginia* (fig. 5.6) by the prolific author of historical adventure tales, Rupert S. Holland.[59] This romance actually begins at mid-century in the countryside of England on a "warm and sweet-scented" December day, and then moves to the Virginia of the era of the uprising. Red Beard is the gentleman Nicholas Ross of Norfolk, who in the opening pages "burie[s] [his rapier] in [the] breast" of the evil Sir Basil Inchbald, who would have forced Lady Anne Brent of Devonshire to marry him. The scene where "Nicholas lunged and metal shivered on metal as the rapiers crossed," which appears as the dramatic cover and frontis-piece of the novel, was painted by Bernard Stafford Good, an Englishman who had studied at the Art Institute of Chicago and with George Bellows and N. C. Wyeth (fig. 5.7).[60] This image gives the reader a sense of the type of action to come. Ross and Lady Anne soon meet again on

her plantation, Burford, on the James River in Virginia, this following his being kidnapped to Puerto Rico and her fleeing from Inchbald, unaware of his death. Brother to an intimate of King Charles I, Ross allies himself first with Berkeley, the royal governor, but ultimately sides with Bacon, the rebel, whom Lady Anne supports and who "was a true, upright man, no matter what slanderers may say."[61] Following the death of Bacon and the retire-ment of Berkeley, Ross and Lady Anne wed and set up house at Burford, determined to "make it the fairest es-tate in Virginia, . . . the fairest in the New World!"

The imaginatively created Red Beards of seventeenth-century Virginia were allowed to play across a stage befit-ting their romantic lifestyle. Because excavations at Jamestown at the turn of the twentieth century had re-vealed that brick houses had once been erected there, these were envisioned as the norm throughout the colony

5.8 Frances Benjamin Johnston, Adam Thoroughgood House, *1935, gelatin silver print, 19¹/₂ x 15³/₄ in., Virginia Historical Society*

during its first century, and so it was this architecture that was often contrived for newer novels. It mattered little, and in fact was little known until the 1980s, that most Virginians of the seventeenth century actually lived in somewhat primitive conditions, in wooden, post-hole houses that would have been as unappealing to the eyes of Colonial Revivalists as were the wooden houses of Puritan New England. Old Virginia was made more attractive when its landscape was believed to have been stocked instead with houses like that of Adam Thoroughgood (fig.5.8).

The Thoroughgood house was built circa 1680 to the east of Jamestown. (It is located in what is now the expanded city of Virginia Beach.) This house is one of only a few standing brick structures in Virginia that actually date to the seventeenth century. It was a mansion for its time and place. When Frances Benjamin Johnston photographed the house in the 1930s, she took care to conceive an image that suggests how the form and materials of the building were then being valued for their aesthetic merits. Of such craftsmanship Wallace Nutting wrote:

> We take occasion here to mention the truly wonderful quality of the mason's work in the dwellings of Virginia. Some of this work nearly three hundred years old seems as perfect today as when it was

erected. . . . Why these masons were possessed of such an almost uncanny skill apparent in nearly all the Virginia work surpasses one's comprehension. The inevitable conclusion is forced upon us, that, both in architecture and in furniture the time of Queen Anne far surpassed anything that has followed it.[62]

Hand craftsmanship was readily appreciated in the early twentieth century because the Arts and Crafts Movement had rekindled an admiration for honest workmanship and uncontrived design. Thus, the craftsmen on the early plantations were esteemed by the revivalists. Nutting suggested that its hand craftsmanship alone made Old Virginia a culture to value, and therefore to revive: "Manufacturing was carried on to a considerable degree by trained servants on the plantation. Spinning, weaving, the making of all the servants' garments, shoe making, common harness making, wagon work, blacksmithing, malting and flour grinding was done in every great establishment."[63] In this case the author chose to overlook a fact that he would assert later in *Virginia Beautiful*: from the start and throughout the colonial period the best goods were imported to Virginia. During the mid-eighteenth century the great landowners and their scions would travel to England; later they would besiege their agents to find and deliver decorative items that matched the current styles and tastes in the mother country.

In John Esten Cooke's *Virginia, A History of the People* (1883), the author divides the colonial era into two periods, the Plantation, which ends in 1619 when a representative legislature was established, and the Colonial, which extends to the Revolution and saw "the gradual formation of a stable and vigorous society." During the latter era Virginia became one of the crucial players on the hemispheric stage.[64] John Fiske's *Old Virginia and Her Neighbors* tells the story of the colony from the age of Sir Walter Ralegh until 1753, "when the youthful George Washington sets forth," the French and Indian War is initiated, and "a new era" arrives. After 1753 Fiske "can no longer follow the career of Virginia" because the colony ceases then to be "the main stream of causation" in American history; instead, it is absorbed "into a mightier stream."[65] Both Cooke and Fiske recognized the importance of emphasizing the early period in Virginia's history in order to be able to elucidate successfully the colony's importance in the events that would follow. To Cooke, "The Golden Age of Virginia," was the entire eighteenth century, when the colony reached "the most peculiar and striking stage of its development":

> An immense change had taken place in society since the Plantation time. What was rude had become luxurious. The log-houses of the early settlers had given place to fine manor-houses. . . .
> What is certain is that life was easy and happy in

these "good old times" . . . . The planter in his manor-house, surrounded by his family and retainers, was a feudal patriarch, mildly ruling everybody; drank wholesome wine, sherry or canary, of his own importation; entertained everyone; held great festivities at Christmas, with huge log-fires in the great fire-places, around which the family clan gathered; and everybody, high and low, seemed to be happy. . . . The portraits of the time show us faces without those lines which carve furrows in the faces of the men of to-day. There was no solicitude for the morrow. The plantation produced everything and was a little community sufficient for itself.[66]

Cooke was certain to point out, however, the importance of "importation" even in a "little community sufficient for itself": "Such luxuries as were desired, books, wines, silk and laces, were brought from London to the planter's wharf in exchange for tobacco; and he was content to pay well for all, if he could thereby escape living in towns."[67] These links to Great Britain would be important elements in tales of early Virginia, which did not suffer through as tempestuous a relationship with the Mother Country as did her New England neighbors. He also uses "plantation" in two ways: as an adjective it speaks of the earliest period of the colony's existence, while as a noun it calls to mind what by this time was the stereotypical image of a southern estate. The linking of the two suggests that the qualities that had made the founding successful were still present in the eighteenth-century descendants of the original planters, who would make a political break from England that would be of even greater importance than the geographical break made in the early seventeenth century.

Cooke believed that so "prosperous and brilliant" a society merited a rebirth in attention from a national audience. In the early 1870s, in anticipation of the centenary of independence, he published a series of articles that looked at the most tangible surviving evidence of that past, the architecture. His piece about "Old Blandford Church" appeared in *Appletons' Journal* in 1871. Built between 1734 and 1737, the church is situated beside what is now the Petersburg National Battlefield, a site that was made famous during the epic siege of that city in 1864–65 by Union forces under the command of Ulysses S. Grant. The campaign there was climactic; after the fall of Petersburg, Robert E. Lee retreated to Appomattox and surrendered. Hundreds of Confederate soldiers are buried in the large cemetery that forms the churchyard of Blandford.

Cooke was with Lee at Appomattox and was almost certainly present for at least part of the Petersburg campaign. He pictures the old church in ruins (fig.5.9), but surprisingly makes no reference to the events of the recent war. This article, with its telling illustration, was a conscious effort by Cooke to deflect attention away from the painful Confederate past and toward the colonial and early national eras. The author presents a history of the church that ends in the year 1802, when the site was abandoned after the town had extended westward. Cooke discusses a "sad pleasure" in viewing the ruins, which at Blandford compose a setting where "the past seemed to return with . . . distinctness." That past, however, is the era "when George II was king."[68] The author then points out that he knows "many" ruined churches in Virginia that inspire similar memories of colonial history. Such remembrances are worthy of revival, and the reunited nation should once again learn to value this heritage.

Currier and Ives soon after issued an undated lithograph that is also titled *Old Blandford Church* (fig. 5.10); it is a similar image of ruin. To Virginians, however, who had been humiliated in defeat and had seen many great old structures reduced to rubble, such a depiction could simultaneously inspire a reminiscence of their glorious colonial past. And if northern viewers purchased the print to remember the recent history associated with Petersburg, they would in a way still be participating in the Colonial Revival movement. The threat of disunion had made all the more precious the period of nation building, with its traditional values and noble aspirations, that had existed only a century earlier. A site like Blandford Church stood as a symbol of that lost era, and thereby helped to recall commonalities rather than conflict.

Three years after the Blandford article, Cooke focused national attention on a house from Old Virginia, George Mason's Gunston Hall, which is pictured and described as a "curious old mansion [that] is a venerable and most interesting relic of the past" (fig. 5.11).[69] This was but one example from the rich architectural heritage of colonial Virginia that would be rediscovered in the following decades. Expansive surveys of these buildings would be undertaken, including Edith Tunis Sale's *Manors of Virginia in Colonial Times* (Philadelphia, 1909, with 67 illustrations and 22 coats-of-arms) and her *Interiors of Virginia Houses of Colonial Times* (Richmond, 1927, with 371 illustrations), Robert A. Lancaster, Jr.'s *Historic Virginia Homes and Churches* (Philadelphia, 1915, 527 pages, with illustrations), and Wallace Nutting's *Virginia Beautiful* (Framingham, Massachuseetts, circa 1930, with 330 illustrations of landscape and dwellings). These books pictured and described scores of colonial structures, the most impressive of which went on to be featured as well in national surveys like the massive *Great Georgian Houses of America* (New York, 1933-37, two volumes with illustrations), which was compiled by the Architects' Emergency Committee. These architectural histories played an important role in the early twentieth century in establishing a new definition for Old Virginia.[70]

The nationwide enthusiasm for the state's Georgian architecture was perhaps best explained by Wallace Nut-

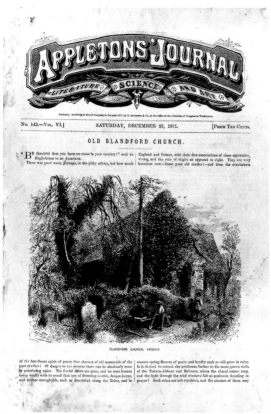

5.9 *Above,* Harry Fenn, Blandford Church, Virginia, *woodcut, from John Esten Cooke, "Old Blandford Church,"* Appletons' Journal, *23 December 1871, Virginia Historical Society*

5.10 *Above, top* Currier and Ives, Old Blandford Church, Petersburg, Virginia, *n. d., lithograph, 6¹/₂ x 9¹/₂ in., Virginia Historical Society*

ting. He asserted that "There are almost no places in the North of this character" because "it was the aim of the ambitious Virginian and of the South in general, to establish a handsome country place."[71] Virginians built "the finest houses in our country in the old time" because "they came to America to better their condition" and "they had the funds to pay for such homes."[72] This description differentiates the early planters of the Old Dominion from those who had landed in Plymouth and Massachusetts Bay, who during this period were thought to have emigrated primarily for religious freedom. Nutting continues, "Having then such a wealth of raw materials as the world had never known, all in the clay about, or in the forests pressing their very home lots, having a taste trained by English memories or education, it is not a marvel that the planters built many beautiful houses, but that they did not build more of them."[73]

Georgian design had been displaced in the nineteenth century by other styles, some of which, like the cottage and the rambling house, had even been recalled by the apologists as typically Virginian. But in the Old Dominion a legacy of quality had endured from the colonial era. Nutting credited the builders of the Tidewater with having established in the region a tradition of architectural excellence that was no small achievement:

I think we may attribute the great beauty and excellent taste of the Richmond dwellings of [the nineteenth century] to the examples, so numerous and

5.11 Gunston Hall, *woodcut from John Esten Cooke, "Historic Houses of America. Gunston Hall,"* Appletons' Journal, *4 April 1874, Virginia Historical Society*

so near at hand, of fine eighteenth century work. One has inevitably impressed upon him, that the Virginian carries on the gracious traditions of the past and is seeking to conserve the best of the eighteenth for the twentieth century. That is how civilization grows, by cumulative effect, for no one generation can plan or execute all the desirable achievements.[74]

One could "conserve the best" of eighteenth-century architecture in several ways: by picturing it; by remembering it in print as did Cooke and his contemporaries; by restoring the actual extant buildings; and by building anew in the Georgian style. One house that was actually conserved was one of the piles best known to the colonial revivalists, Westover, the Byrd family mansion below Richmond. Once again this house emerged as a symbol of Virginia. Nutting noted that "probably this place has been more seen and written about than any other in Virginia, aside of course from Mt. Vernon and Monticello."[75] He was thinking of accounts like that by Sale, who wrote in

1927, "There seems to be no question but that the finest example of existing Colonial architecture in Virginia is Westover."[76] To the revivalists this house came to epitomize the style and quality of Virginia Georgian design, a reputation that survives to this day.

A large photograph of Westover records the impressiveness of the complex after its Colonial Revival period restoration (fig. 5.12). At that time the originally detached dependencies were connected to the main building, thereby establishing the current design of the complex. The title of the photograph, *Westover in Virginia, The Seat of Mrs. Ramsay (Clarise Charlotte Sears Risley Harrold), 1878–1921,* is handwritten on the reverse. The image is three feet wide; so large a photograph would have been produced to hang in a hotel or train station to serve as a travel poster.

Following the death in 1814 of the widow of William Byrd III, the Westover plantation had been sold out of the family. It then passed through several hands: John Selden owned the house from 1829 until George McClellan's

"WESTOVER."   VIRGINIA.

ESTATE OF . . . . .
WM. MS C. RAMSEY.

M. J. DIMMOCK: ASSOCIATED:
G. R. TOLMAN: ARCHITECTS:

5.12 **Above** Westover in Virginia, The Seat of Mrs. Ramsay (Clarise Charlotte Sears Risley Harrold), 1878–1921, *after 1921, gelatin silver print, 24 x 36 in., Virginia Historical Society*

5.13 **Left** *Marion Johnson Dimmock and George R. Tolman, Westover, Virginia, ca. 1902, lithograph (replica of a presentation drawing), 4⁷⁄₈ x 8¹⁄₂ in., Virginia Historical Society*

Union army ravaged the site; Major Augustus Drewry presided there during the postwar years until his death in 1898, when it was purchased by Clarise Sears Ramsay, a collateral descendant of William Byrd II and also of the Sears family of colonial Massachusetts.[77] In 1902 Mrs. Ramsay commissioned the New York restoration architect William H. Mersereau to modernize the structure into an Edwardian country house. A presentation drawing (fig. 5.13) was made by M. J. Dimmock and G. R. Tolman, local architects who had contributed to the project. This drawing conveys more clearly than do photographs just how much the revivalists set out to transform the house.

When Mersereau designed the hyphens that lead to the kitchen and library wings he thoroughly reimagined the latter, which E. C. Henry had shown was burned during the Civil War (page 130, fig. 4.8). The new library was given a gambrel roof that is also different from the original gable-roofed dependency pictured in early sketches of the complex. To the core of the house Mersereau added new mantels, a new third-floor interior, and central heating. The restoration was largely completed by 1905.[78] Westover, which already had been admired as the epitome of American Georgian design, had been "improved"; Edith Sale voiced her approval by writing that with the wings "a manourial effect is attained."[79]

Rarely could the enthusiast for colonial architecture find a building to restore that was as grand as Westover. Most colonialists who wished to live in a spectacular period environment instead commissioned new buildings in the old style. They made country- and city-houses that were either replicas of, or included borrowings from, the more appealing of the early Virginia structures. Westover, predictably, was a popular model; copies were erected across the state. Some were as ambitious as the original. One of the finest of the new Westovers is Gallison Hall. Presentation drawings of the house (figs. 5.14, 5.15, and 5.16), which were made for the purpose of selling the architects' scheme to their prospective clients, record an enthusiasm for this design.

Gallison Hall is situated on forty-four acres at Farmington Country Club in Albemarle County, close to Charlottesville and Monticello. The country club takes its name from the original Farmington House, which has additions by Thomas Jefferson. Given the setting, it was inevitable that in the design of Gallison Hall a few concessions would be made to Jeffersonian architecture. Thus, the bricks are oversized as at Monticello, and an arcade recalls the ranges at the University of Virginia. But most of the other borrowings, which architects Stanhope Johnson and Raymond Brannan of Lynchburg took from multiple sources, are colonial. The debt to Westover, the overall form of which is copied, is the most obvious. The clustered chimney stacks are taken from Bacon's Castle (Surry County). On the interior the library borrows from the great room at Stratford Hall (Westmoreland County). The staircase in the entrance hall was modeled on the one at Gadsby's Tavern in Alexandria. The living room paneling takes features from Shirley (Charles City County), and the scheme of large arches in the drawing room was influenced by William Buckland's work at Gunston Hall (Fairfax County).[80] In the original structures the woodwork was elaborately detailed, and that flair was replicated in the copies. The revivalists defended such lavish treatment; Nutting wrote, "Why do men forget that Grinling Gibbons, the greatest English carver who ever lived, was turning out his wonderful work in the late seventeenth and early eighteenth centuries, at the very time when the planters were creating their dwellings?"[81]

The Johnson and Brannan presentation drawings imagine an interior richly furnished with handsome decorative objects. Nutting is persuasive in arguing that the best colonial Virginia homes were so finished: "To us, thinking of the great undeveloped country back from the shore fringe, it seems strange indeed to read the inventories of the old estates, rich in silver, drapery, furniture, carriages, and raiment, until the lists make us feel, what is the fact, that we are at the unlading of a ship from London, heavy with the latest and richest products of that world metropolis, ordered by successful planters, who desired their families to have such habitations and habiliments as might comport with the best society of the age."[82] The great country homes of England were without a doubt in the minds of those who would build their seats in the hinterlands of the colony.

Although the borrowings from the eighteenth century are many at Gallison Hall, the house is nonetheless a product of its own time. The interior design crafted by Johnson and Brannan is modern, in that the pale pastel colors that appealed to early twentieth-century eyes are used. Also, the rooms are oversized to match the revivalist's imagination, and furniture of mixed styles is arranged in conversation groups unimaginable two centuries earlier. These elements of modernity, though rooted in the Georgian past, are derived from such sources as the New York decorator and architect Ogden Codman, Jr., and soon-to-be novelist Edith Wharton's influential publication, *The Decoration of Houses* (1897). We are reminded that the Colonial Revival was in part fantasy, and that once again the idea of Old Virginia had been reimagined to match contemporary ideals. Richard Guy Wilson has written of the Gallison Hall interiors, "This design sighs with twentieth-century nostalgia for an imagined past, one of historical novels and celluloid images, a time that never existed, now made real with great conviction."[83]

Gallison Hall stands as evidence that Georgian architecture, when made grandiose, was relevant to the lifestyles of the wealthy landowners of twentieth-century Virginia. The name of the house derives from those of the owners, Mr. and Mrs. Julio Suarez-Galban. (The word "Galban" is combined with "Allison," the family name of the wife's mother.) Both parties brought wealth to their marriage; Julio's money was supplied by the sugar trade, which had also enhanced the fortunes of eighteenth-century planters. Although the couple lacked the Old Virginia ancestry that Clarise Ramsay had brought to Westover, such twentieth-century ruralists imagined themselves to be successors on the land and heirs to the pastoral ideal of Old Virginia.

The self image of the new ruralists evolved out of their perceptions of how their colonial predecessors had looked and lived. In his *Virginia Historical Portraiture*, Alexander Weddell offered a fairly realistic presentation of the leadership of the colony, in part because he was able to gather many life portraits. For the most part, however, the colonial figures who reemerged in the early twentieth century were the products of over-ambitious imaginations. They were often made to seem as important as were the Founding Fathers, as overly large in scale as were the public rooms at Gallison Hall. In twentieth-century oil portraits, in novels, and ultimately in films they were pictured romantically, more as the revivalists wanted them to have been than as they actually were.

5.14 **Above** *William Addison Staples, for Johnson & Brannan, Lynchburg (Stanhope S. Johnson and Raymond O. Brannan), Gallison Hall, Entrance Front,* 1930, *presentation drawing, colored pencil on tracing paper, 15 x 36 in., Jones Memorial Library, Lynchburg, Virginia*

5.15 **Left, center** *William A. Staples, Gallison Hall, Drawing Room,* 1930, *presentation drawing, colored pencil on tracing paper, 6³/₄ x 14¹/₂ in., Jones Memorial Library, Lynchburg, Virginia*

5.16 **Left** *William A. Staples,* Gallison Hall, Living Room, 1930, *presentation drawing, colored pencil on tracing paper, 5¹/₄ x 13³/₈ in., Jones Memorial Library, Lynchburg, Virginia*

Edith Sale effused about them in typical revivalist fashion when she reimagined the Golden Age at Westover and the lifestyle there. She remembered the time when William Byrd II (page 41, fig. 2.5) returned from London with his daughter Evelyn: "Kingdoms have been won and lost, but never will America know such picturesque grandeur, never will the pulse quicken as it did in dangerous Colonial days, but never will life be so gay and well worth living as when Evelyn Byrd was the Toast of two Worlds."[84]

In her first book, *Manors of Virginia*, Sale had pictured many of the coats of arms of the Virginia dynasties. No family was more important than the Carters, whose most celebrated member was Robert, the aggressive land agent for the Fairfax proprietary who amassed so great a fortune that he had earned the sobriquet "King" in his lifetime. Only the last years of Carter's life (d. 1732) fell during what had come to be thought of as the "Golden Age" of the Virginia aristocracy, but that mattered little. He was the "King," and the revivalists admired royalty. In the entry in Weddell's *Virginia Historical Portraiture*, Carter's prominence is succinctly rendered, with a mention only of "his immense possessions and overwhelming influence." Sale, however, considered him to be "one of the most picturesque and commanding figures of the country," adding that as "Speaker of the House of Burgesses, Treasurer, President of the Council, and acting Governor of Virginia, with his vast fortune, there was no office nor honor which he did not attain." She was also impressed that at his death Carter left "a princely fortune, consisting as it did of 300,000 acres of land, about £10,000 sterling, and 1,000 slaves."[85]

Sale accepted as authentic a large painting of Robert Carter (fig. 5.17) that reputedly was copied from a now-lost life portrait but was almost certainly a creation of the Colonial Revival. The subject, who is pictured imaginatively with a grand periwig and one hand beside a letter addressed to him in his capacity as president of the Council, resembles more the protagonists of revival novels, rather than the actual figure whose tombstone at the church that he built, Christ Church in Lancaster County, describes him as "neither a prodigal nor a parsimonious host." So much did this romantic image fit Sale's imaginative picture of Carter that she devoted a paragraph to a description of the painting:

> One portrait of King Carter as a young man represents a strikingly handsome figure in velvet coat and lace cravat, wearing the long, curling wig of the period. The luminous eyes seem to follow one everywhere. The firm mouth shows lines of pity next to curves of scorn, and the beautiful, tapering hand that rests easily on the hilt of his sword could only have been used for the most delicate of tasks.[86]

Multiple replicas of this image were produced for descen-

5.17 Attributed to Marietta Andrews, Robert "King" Carter, *ca. 1900, oil on canvas, 60 x 44 in., Virginia Historical Society*

dants and aficionados of the "King." Apparently everyone at the time accepted the image as accurate.[87] In the early 1960s Louise Anderson Patten of Winchester tracked down one of the replicas in a private collection in Baltimore, purchased it, and ultimately bequeathed to the Virginia Historical Society. This romanticized portrait illustrates one method by which Virginians brought to life their actual and figurative ancestors from the Golden Age.

In *A Meet in Old Virginia* (page 180, fig. 5.1), Thur de Thulstrup attempted to recreate visually the perception that the lives of the colony's aristocrats were filled with activities that would have been considered appropriate for gentry on either side of the Atlantic. He set his scene at Westover, the quintessential Virginia mansion, where William Byrd III, a horse enthusiast and spendthrift, would have enjoyed such spectacular rural entertainments. "These sports and amusements had a very wholesome influence," argued Sydney George Fisher in *Men, Women and Manners in Colonial Times* (1902).[88] The author reasoned that such "an education" was necessary training for the difficult task of running a plantation: "It was a large enterprise, somewhat resembling in the ability required our modern manufacturing industries."[89] Fisher imagined a festive outdoor society, "a gay, happy people; a race of sportsmen, cock-fighters and fox-hunters; bright, humorous, and sociable; in the saddle by day and feasting and dancing by night; and we go away with the impression that the hounds were always baying in Virginia, that the sun shone all day long, and all night the fiddlers scraped and the darkies sang." However, the propensity of colonial Virginians for such entertainments was more than just a taste that was derived from the pattern of country life in eighteenth-century England. Fisher argued that it was what early set these colonists apart from the original New England Puritans and their post-Revolutionary puritanical successors, whose philosophy about life seemed, in contrast, unworthy of revival in the twentieth century. The focus on entertainment "gave the people of all classes great social facility and an ease of manner and intercourse which still often astonishes travellers from the North." Fisher went on, "it is not uncommon to find a Virginian who has been born with a natural politeness and social instinct which the best people in other parts of America spend half a lifetime in acquiring."[90]

It mattered little to the artists and authors of Post-Reconstruction America that the lifestyle they celebrated had enormous social flaws. Thomas Nelson Page lauded the Virginians of the Golden Age for having "preserved far more" than did any of the other colonists "the traits of the English country life." He reasoned that the introduction of convicts and indentured servants "only served to widen the gap between them and the gentry, and to emphasize the distinctive aristocratic feature of Virginia society."[91] Fisher rejected the idea that colonial history should be dismissed as "a time of slavery"; more important, he argued, is our "re-discovering the debt we owe to the colonies." Besides, Fisher asserted, "the treatment of slaves in Virginia is generally admitted to have been mild and kindly."[92] This author even argued that slavery was a virtue because it gave the gentry "the habit of command and the desire for ascendancy."[93]

We are intended, and tempted, to accept such images as that by Thulstrup as universal, especially when we consider that it is well known that the young George Washington was a great horseman who would have enjoyed such a hunt. However, there is little to suggest that scenes of such grandeur were common at plantations throughout Old Virginia, even during its Golden Age. The explanation for such exaggerations seems to be that many of the colonial revivalists longed for socially acceptable immoderation in their own lives, and so they were determined to find it in the colonial past. They responded positively to, and therefore patronized, works of art and literature that supported such notions.

The renewed enthusiasm for the accomplishments of the Virginia Founding Fathers that emerged at the centenary of 1876 would be nurtured for decades by spokespersons for the Colonial Revival. In 1896 Dabney Herndon Maury wrote *A Young People's History of Virginia and Virginians* to foster in the rising generation an appreciation for

"the prominent part" that their forefathers bore "in the establishment of civil and religious liberty on this continent, and in the upbuilding of the great American Republic."[94] J. Warren Keifer added in an address delivered at the Jamestown exposition in 1907 that "no such constellation of men, fitted for the work of great statesmen and soldiers, was ever known as existed in Virginia in 1776."[95] Thomas Nelson Page praised those great statesmen for "leading [all of the other colonies] in their action of breaking the ties which bound them to the Old Country," and he pointedly credited Old Virginia with supplying "the Chief who led the Revolutionary Armies to final Victory."[96]

As they were concurrently intrigued by the founders of Jamestown and the national Founding Fathers, the revivalists linked the two by tracing the evolution of the latter giants of colonial history to the earliest settlement. The seventeenth-century settlers, claimed William Wirt Henry, were "a people superior to any existing in the world." Their experience as slaveholders, he added in terms that seem ironic to the modern reader, only made them "most proud and jealous of their freedom," and the form of government allowed by the early charters "was potent in the development of Virginia character" that guided the Revolution.[97] Following the Civil War it seemed that more than anything else it was character that was invoked as the quality that set Virginia's Founding Fathers apart from their contemporaries, enabled them to lead, and made them worthy of modern adulation. Page said that in Old Virginia a "new Civilization" had been brought forth "where Character and Courtesy went hand in hand; where the goal ever set before the eyes was Honor, and the distinguishing marks of the life were Simplicity and Sincerity."[98] For that reason, he continued, it was "no mere accident that George Washington, Patrick Henry, Thomas Jefferson, . . . and other leaders of the Revolutionary movement came from the shores of the rivers which pour into the Chesapeake"; they were "the product of the life established on those shores."[99] The northerner Sydney George Fisher had reached the same conclusion in 1902 in his *Men, Women & Manners in Colonial Times*. He decided that to have produced the men upon whom so much depended at the moment of the Revolution, colonial Virginia "must have been a remarkable community."[100]

The revivalists saw taxation as the principal issue that had stirred Virginia's Founding Fathers to greatness. The colonies had long prospered, wrote Cooke, and if England "had treated them justly, they might have remained a part of the British Empire."[101] Such sentiments reminded Americans of the closeness of Virginia to the crown, which had made that colony's turn toward rebellion so important in the unfolding events of the 1770s. In violation of a law passed in 1624 by the Virginia Assembly that reserved the right of taxation exclusively for itself, George III, in part to pay for the recent French and Indian War in which the armies of Great Britain had protected the colonies from their enemies of the frontier, had decided in the 1760s to tax the colonists directly. That ancient law, according to Page, was "the very ground on which one hundred and fifty years later the American Revolution was based."[102]

Cooke credited the Virginians of the Revolutionary era with "originat[ing] the principle that the right of the citizen is paramount to the will of the king."[103] Keifer ranked the Virginia Bill of Rights (1776), which embodied doctrines of personal liberty that were later woven into both the Declaration of Independence and the Constitution, as being "as immutable as the ten commandments given to the world by God, through Moses amid the thunder of Sinai."[104] And William Wirt Henry praised the "broad and national views" of the Virginians and their "efficient services in forming and securing our federal Union."[105] Those services, he implied, excused Virginians for attempting in 1861 to reassert their rights and dissolve the union; the earlier achievements were ample reason to revere once more the heroes of the independence movement.

As had been true throughout the antebellum era, the two figures from revolutionary Virginia who were most admired by the revivalists were George Washington and Patrick Henry. Washington was indisputably the greatest martial figure of the eighteenth century, while Henry was thought to have been the preeminent statesman. Washington's reputation had survived the Civil War intact, and although he had to share the spotlight with Lincoln in the latter days of the nineteenth century, there was still no doubt as to his greatness as both a military and political leader.

Patrick Henry was "the greatest orator that . . . ever lived in America," wrote Cooke; his "immense genius for oratory . . . was to shape the history of the North American continent."[106] To answer the bias that many Gilded Age revivalists held against persons of less than aristocratic status, Cooke claimed that Henry was not of "low origin," which was at best an arguable point, nor was he a man of "ignorance."[107] As we have seen, this country lawyer had won the adulation of his contemporaries in arguing the so-called case of the Parson's Cause, which addressed the king's right to determine the salary of minsters. The people cheered, wrote Cooke, when Henry made his "demand that the authority of the Burgesses of Virginia should take precedence [over] the authority of the King of England." Henry's stand against the Stamp Act was also significant as a concise expression of the Virginia claim that "from the earliest times the House of Burgesses had regulated the affairs" of the colony.[108]

Henry's finest moment, however, was when he spoke

5.18 *Edwin Austin Abbey,* "Give Me Liberty, or Give Me Death," *wood engraving in John Esten Cooke,* "Virginia in the Revolution," Harper's New Monthly Magazine, *June 1876; republished in Cooke,* Stories of the Old Dominion, *1879, Virginia Historical Society*

for liberty. Edwin Austin Abbey illustrated the episode for Cooke's readers (fig. 5.18). The occasion was the spring of 1775, when British soldiers and ships were poised in Boston to quell a revolt, and Virginia's leaders had gathered to determine the course that their colony would follow. Cooke recounted the story; his source was William Wirt, who in 1817 had attempted to piece together the famous speech for inclusion in his biography of Henry:

> When Patrick Henry moved that steps should be taken 'for embodying, arming, and disciplining the militia,' many of the members opposed the resolution. The result was one of the grandest of all the displays of Henry's oratory: 'If we wish to be free we must fight!' he exclaimed passionately. 'It is too late to retire from the contest. There is no retreat but in submission and slavery. The war is inevitable, and let it come! The next gale that sweeps from the north will bring to our ears the clash of resounding arms! I know not what course others may take, but as for me, give me liberty or give me death!'

Abbey imagined the speaker as poised like a fencer when delivering the most famous of his pleas. Cooke wrote that Henry uttered the words about liberty "with both arms raised and eyes on fire with excitement." He added that "a thrill ran through the whole assembly" and that "no

5.19 Above J. C. Bridgewood,
St. John's Church, Rich-
mond, *after 1879, oil on can-*
vas, 16 x 20 in., Valentine
Museum

5.20 Left Portion of a
wooden beam from St.
John's Church, *1700s, gift in*
1882 to the Virginia Historical
Society

further opposition was made." Cooke also made an additional assertion, out of a concern "to establish the truth
of history": the writer corrected the false "impression"
given by Henry's biographer "that a body of laggards
were again inspired by one man." The members of the
Richmond convention, Cooke insisted, were "already . . .
ready to resist."[109] While his declaration that the antithesis
of liberty is "submission and slavery" can be seen as problematic to the modern reader because Henry was himself
a slaveholder, his stirring remarks were not undermined
for this comparison during the Colonial Revival era. In
our day it is the final sentence, and especially the final
clause, that is remembered. The rest of the speech, like
the rest of "Light-Horse Harry" Lee's eulogy for Washington, has for the most part passed into the hands of historians.

The political leaders of the colony had assembled in
Richmond in 1775 to avoid interference by the royal gov-
ernor, Lord Dunmore, who was resident in Williamsburg.
They gathered in the largest building in town, and by the
nature and consequence of their deliberations they made
St. John's Church famous. "It is a plain old building,"
wrote Cooke, who then proceeded to tie St. John's to
Virginia's early history, "not far from Bloody Run, where
Bacon defeated the Indians, and in sight of Powhatan,
where the old Indian emperor was visited by Captain
Smith."[110] St. John's Church became a shrine to the colonial revivalists; it was remembered in paint, in the way
that architectural monuments had long been pictured on
canvas in Europe (fig. 5.19). In at least three nearly identical paintings of St. John's, J. C. Bridgewood shows the
building after its bell tower had been added to the north
front, which occurred around 1830. Interestingly, when
such alterations were made to the original fabric of the
church, architectural relics became available. One, an
eighteenth century wooden beam (fig. 5.20), was given to
the Virginia Historical Society in 1882 as a Colonial Revival memento of the power and patriotism of Patrick
Henry.

Cooke followed the innumerable admirers of George
Washington, including the future president Woodrow
Wilson, when he described the general as "one of those
men who rises above all the rest, and is looked upon as
one of the greatest human beings who have lived in this
world."[111] Little remained to be added to the already well-
known incidents in the life of the general and president.
Thus, in his *Stories of the Old Dominion,* Cooke offered
chapters only on "The Young Surveyor," "Washington in

the Wilderness" (an account of his French and Indian War adventures), and "The Surrender at Yorktown" (which looks less at the general than at the campaign). In his centenary article entitled "Virginia in the Revolution," Cooke uncovered an obscure story for those who longed to learn anything new about the father of their country. This was an account of the arrival at Boston early in the war of Morgan's Virginia riflemen: "Washington dismounted, came to meet the battalion, and going down the line with both arms extended, shook hands with the riflemen one by one, tears rolling down his cheeks as he did so."[112]

Because of the lack of documentary information about it, the greatest liberties taken with Washington's life often had to do with his childhood. At the start of the nineteenth century, Parson Mason Locke Weems had invented a number of incidents involving the young Washington, including those about his chopping down the cherry tree and the boy's manly strength that enabled him to hurl a silver dollar across a Tidewater river. Weems even reported a story that Washington "formed his schoolmates into companies, who paraded, marched, and fought mimic battles."[113] Such stories helped to apotheosize the newly deceased general, and to suggest that in childhood behavior we can see the greatness of the man to be. Following in the tradition established by Weems, writers and artists in the postbellum era continued to concoct tales about the boy who would be general. Frank Schoonover painted for Lucy Madison's biography of Washington as "retold for children" (1925) a scene that was invented by an author who reasoned that "to illustrate [Washington's] resourcefulness and boyhood inclinations, some little license [can be] taken with history."[114] Schoonover pictures the young Washington leading his classmates in a mock battle (fig. 5.21). The author provides her readers with the background of the war with Spain in which George's older brother served. Excited by news of Lawrence Washington's campaign, George leads an "English" contingent of his classmates to capture the enemy fort at Cartagena. (The actual garrison was in South America). To symbolize the victory, young George removes the "Spanish" flag. This "born soldier," Madison writes, had diverted his opponents's attention with a shower of apples.[115] Such stories, as well as the serious considerations of Washington's life, cast a reflected glory on the Old Virginia society that had produced him.

George Washington had settled the outcome of the war for independence at a spot remarkably close to what many Virginians of the postbellum period would claim to be the movement's place of origin. Cooke emphasized that "the Revolution ended at Yorktown, nor far from Williamsburg, where, in 1765, Patrick Henry sounded the first note of resistance to England."[116] The author went on to recount the important role played by the general in

this climactic campaign. Yorktown was important during the Colonial Revival not only because of the great historical significance of the victory, but also because the centenary of the battle, the year 1881, served as a second catalyst for the movement. Historically, Yorktown was seen as the turning point in the struggle for independence. Cooke noted: "In the first days of autumn (1781), few persons in England or America suspected that the Revolution, with its shifting scenes and varying fortunes, was approaching its end." Then, because of this battle and the unthinkable surrender of the British army under Lord Cornwallis, "suddenly the whole prospect changed."[117]

In 1881 a number of writers turned to this popular subject. A sketch of *The British Drummer Bearing a Parley for the Suspension of Hostilities* at Yorktown filled the cover of the October 22 issue of *Frank Leslie's Illustrated Newspaper* (fig. 5.22), and *Leslie's* and *Harper's Weekly* both covered the three-day Yorktown Centennial Celebration. Although the festivities were held in impermanent buildings, more public figures of note made appearances there than were present even at the great centennial event held at Philadelphia in 1876. The Yorktown celebration was funded by Congress, as was a towering Victory Monument, designed

5.21 *Frank Schoonover,* "Now Boys, a Rush Forward and in We Go," Shouted George, *1924, oil on canvas, 36 x 30 in., painted to illustrate Lucy Foster Madison,* Washington *(New York, 1925), Virginia Historical Society, Lora Robins Collection of Virginia Art*

5.22 *Above Hyde (?),* Centennial of Cornwallis's Surrender at Yorktown – The British Drummer Bearing a Parley for the Suspension of Hostilities, *1881, wood engraving published in* Frank Leslie's Illustrated Newspaper, *22 October 1881, VHS*

5.23 *Left Richard Morris Hunt,* Yorktown Monument, *ca. 1884, watercolor, 37⅝ x 23¾ in., American Institute of Architects Foundation, Washington, D.C.*

by architects Richard Morris Hunt and Henry van Brunt and the sculptor John Quincy Adams Ward, which was completed in 1884 (fig. 5.23). In 1907, the tourism inspired by the Jamestown tercentenary would bring an additional round of increased visitation to Yorktown. Guidebooks, such J. Blair Spencer's *An Illustrated Historical Sketch of Jamestown, Williamsburg, and Yorktown* (1907), were produced for the many national and international visitors to these sites.

Predictably, the campaign at Yorktown was a subject of great interest to Colonial Revival artists. Stanley Arthurs, a Wilmington, Delaware painter and illustrator,

imagined an affecting moment during Washington's return to his home state in 1781 (fig. 5.24). The reason that this crucial engagement took place in Virginia at all had much to do with the movements of his allies. The French admiral, the comte de Grasse, in command of a fleet of 29 warships supported by 3,000 troops, had been ordered to the American coast. He chose to steer clear of fortified New York City and to operate instead in the Chesapeake Bay. Washington moved quickly to make the most of the French presence in the South. He hastened to Virginia, while urging Lafayette "to prevent if possible the retreat of Cornwallis toward Carolina."[118] In route, Washington

5.24 *Stanley Arthurs,* George Washington at Mount Vernon, on His Way South to Yorktown in 1781, *ca. 1925, oil on canvas, 41 x 42 in., Virginia Historical Society, Lora Robins Collection of Virginia Art*

stopped for two days at Mount Vernon, which he had not seen in more than six years. He then set out for York-town—in his words, "almost all impatience and anxiety." Arthurs depicted the moment when the general again turned away from his beloved home, this time to partici-pate in a roll of the dice that would probably end the war, one way or the other.[119]

Sensing the popularity of Colonial Revival imagery, the New York painter James Walker briefly abandoned his usual Civil War subject matter to create two small canvases that depict the opposing commanders at the decisive battle of Yorktown (figs. 5.25 and 5.26). Walker provides

handsome images of the two leaders, the revered Wash-ington and the formidable Cornwallis, accepting the gal-lantry of both. These canvases pointed to the moment of victory and to the familial relations between the mother country and the colony most like her.

Another revivalist who celebrated the achievements of Washington was Jean Leon Gerome Ferris, the Phila-delphia artist who over three-and-a-half decades begin-ning in the 1890s painted more than a dozen canvases that brought to life the biography of the general, particu-larly the private existence that unfolded after the war. In *The Victory Ball, 1781* (fig. 5.27) we see the still uniformed

5.25 *Above, left James Walker*, George Washington, *ca. 1876, oil on canvas, 11⅝ x 9½ in., Virginia Historical Society, Lora Robins Collection of Virginia Art*

5.26 *Above, right James Walker*, Lord Cornwallis, *ca. 1876, oil on canvas, 11⅝ x 9½ in., Virginia Historical Society, Lora Robins Collection of Virginia Art*

5.27 *Left Jean Leon Gerome Ferris*, The Victory Ball, 1781, *ca. 1929, oil on canvas, 24 x 35 in., Virginia Historical Society, Lora Robins Collection of Virginia Art*

Washington enjoying a dance after his greatest triumph. Although there was no such gathering immediately after the campaign—Washington accompanied the widow of his step-son Jacky, who had died at Yorktown from "camp fever," to Mount Vernon—the sense that Ferris creates is one of jubilation, as it would have been experienced by the officers and gentry of the period. His inclusion of Washington's mother Mary, "dressed in the very plain but becoming garb of the Virginia lady of the old time," both points to Washington's devotion to his mother and links him to that earlier period, and thereby to the Virginians who had created the community from which he and his great contemporaries emerged.[120] In 1932, the bicentenary of Washington's birth, adulation peaked for both the general and the Old Virginia society that had produced him. By then the latter was familiar to Americans as it had been reimagined in the reconstructed town of Williamsburg.

The Creation of Colonial Williamsburg

As its culmination, and, as it would turn out, its swan song, the Colonial Revival brought about the recovery of an entire town. For decades the colonial past had been remembered in histories and novels, new portraits had brought to life figures from the pre-national past, and individual eighteenth-century houses had been restored and filled with colonial antiques. In the 1920s a more ambitious project was undertaken, one that was possible only in the wake of the revived national interest in Virginia's Founding Fathers. Would it be possible to bring an entire city back to life as it had been before the Revolutionary War? Detractors of the scheme to return Williamsburg to its colonial appearance predicted failure. The *Baltimore Sun* anticipated at best "a flivver imitation of departed glory." The president of the College of William and Mary actually feared that proponents of this idea would be run out of town.[121] Instead, the founders of what would come to be called Colonial Williamsburg would in the end be revered, and their accomplishment would continue to be an internationally renowned phenomenon to the present day.

The goal of the restorers of the second capital was to transform the present into the past, to reinvent the town as the setting where American ideas about liberty had been formulated and debated. It was believed that visitors to so unique an environment would rediscover the values of the Founders, which would be worth consideration in post-World War I America. To turn back the clock, however, was no easy task. Early buildings had to be restored, later ones removed, and lost ones rebuilt. Structures that were so poorly documented as to be problematic, along with those that were simply unappealing, could be omitted from what would become a purified urban environment. Park-like greens were constructed and settled with houses that reflected the simple style of Georgian architecture. These buildings had become fashionable again, for the first time in more than a century, and innumerable colonial-style houses and even modern stores and office buildings would soon be erected across America after Williamsburg types. If unwanted buildings could be omitted from the Colonial Williamsburg stage, so the more troublesome episodes of Virginia's history could be just as easily forgotten. Admittedly, many white Americans during the early twentieth century cared little about racial equality, but for those who did, the "new" second capital, with its colonial setting and attempt to revive colonial mores, was fraught with unsolvable problems. Because Williamsburg was a city, field hands and slave quarters would not have been greatly in evidence, but, while not so blatantly visible, slavery would have been present, and indeed an important aspect of life in the actual colonial city. Could, or should, this be represented? Would

attempts to render life with complete accuracy conjure up images of an institution that a long and bloody war had been fought to end?

The response to the restoration was overwhelmingly positive; almost overnight Colonial Williamsburg became something of a national shrine. Soon the restored town would be world famous, more renowned than the first Williamsburg had ever been. Visitors from north and south made pilgrimages to the site, thereby reaffirming the validity, if not the triumph, of Virginia's colonial past. The mystique of Old Virginia returned, and interest in that history reached a high water mark that had not been enjoyed for a hundred years.

Through most of the nineteenth century Williamsburg had been viewed as almost a ghost town. Following the removal of the seat of government to Richmond in 1780 and the winning of American independence, the second capital had rapidly declined. In 1793 Jedidiah Morse visited a "dull, forsaken and melancholy" setting. In *Letters from Virginia* (1816), George Tucker lamented that "this poor town has very little to recommend it to a stranger except the memory of its ancient importance, and this is but a sad sort of interest at best. . . . All is just as lifeless as the very Goddess of Dullness could wish. . . . It is but the shadow of itself, and even that seems passing away."[122] For a short while at the beginning of the 1830s, when the traditional agrarian society of Virginia was first seriously threatened by change, colonial Williamsburg was remembered in its glory, as emblematic of what was old and good. But that past was quickly forgotten. Eighty years later, John Sergeant Wise reported that the population of Williamsburg had diminished to even less than it had been in the colonial era, and that the boast of the town was that it had no wealth or trade.[123] Thomas Wilkinson was one of a number of artists in the late nineteenth and early twentieth centuries who painted melancholy views of the town that record its deserted appearance prior to restoration (fig. 5.28). It would have been difficult to imagine at that moment the sort of transformation that was in the offing.

The early years of the Colonial Revival had initiated some change, not in the nature of the town itself, which remained as decrepit as Wise and Wilkinson had described it, but in the way that colonial Williamsburg was remembered. If only on paper and canvas, writers and painters began the process of recapturing some of the town's ancient glory. In 1883 John Esten Cooke recounted the culture that had thrived there:

> During the winter large numbers of the planters went to live in Williamsburg, the vice-regal capital; and here were held grand assemblies at the Raleigh Tavern, or the old capitol, where the beaux and belles of the time in the finest silks and laces danced

5.28 *Thomas H. Wilkinson,* George Wythe House, *1903, watercolor, 12³/₄ x 17 in., Virginia Historical Society*

and feasted. . . . The youths passed on their fine horses going to prosecute their love affairs; and the poetical portion wrote love verses to their inamoratas, and published them in the 'Virginia Gazette.'[124]

Cooke imagines the town functioning as a gathering place for the wealthy planters and their progeny, a place of romance and fine living, in which the gentry could enjoy a respite from their often isolated lives on their country estates.

There was a problem for those artists who wished to recreate scenes comparable to the one that Cooke had imagined. Both Raleigh Tavern and the Capitol had long been lost to fire and so were unavailable as models. The town's spiritual center, however, Bruton Parish Church, had survived and was, to the thinking of Alfred Wordsworth Thompson, a plausible setting for presenting evidence of the cultural accomplishments of old Williamsburg (fig. 5.29). "Grand assemblies" were in fact held each Sunday at Bruton, both inside the church, where

members of the gentry entered last, paraded, and strategically seated themselves forward in the congregation, and outside, during the moments preceding and following the service, when the gentry arrived and departed on horseback or in coaches, wearing their "finest" clothing. Thompson recreated on canvas the outdoor spectacle at Bruton because he knew that such displays would find an appreciative audience among the Americans of the Colonial Revival era.

Thompson was a Maryland artist, a southerner at heart with a keen sympathy for Old Virginia. His painting of Bruton Parish Church gave expression to his regional pride. In the title of his canvas, the artist set the scene during the years 1771–75, when John Murray, earl of Dunmore, was royal governor. The lavish gentry lifestyle of Virginia's Golden Age appealed during Thompson's own era, the Gilded Age of the late nineteenth century. His painting depicts an era characterized by the kind of social stability and deference that revivalists in America longed to recover, an age devoid of modern workers' unions, strikes, socialism, and the migrations of many

5.29 *Alfred Wordsworth Thompson,* Old Bruton Church, Williamsburg, Virginia, in the Time of Lord Dunmore, *1893, oil on canvas, 18 x 27¹/₈ in., Metropolitan Museum of Art, gift of Mrs. A. Wordsworth Thompson, 1899, copyright 1983*

southern blacks to the urban centers of the North. Revivalists from all regions admired Thompson's image for the society of Old Virginia that it captures and celebrates.

Cooke and Thompson had recognized that the life that had once been led in the now sleeping capital would interest revivalists. A decade would pass after Thompson's painting had previewed, however, before the man who would make Williamsburg the shrine of the national Colonial Revival would arrive in town in 1903 to assume the rectorship at Bruton Parish. Rather than carry his parishoners into the twentieth century, William Archer Rutherford Goodwin, like Cooke and Thompson, chose to envision the colonial city as it had been peopled in its glory. He soon came to believe that "the ghosts of the past haunted the houses and . . . streets" of Williamsburg and that "these ancient personages had been too long silent."[125] What was different between the visions of Goodwin and Thompson was that the former was more attuned to the ghosts of the patriots than to those of the royal governors. By 1903 the mood of the nation had shifted in the direction of democratic ideas. The rector's biographer Dennis Montgomery writes that as Goodwin walked the unpaved streets of Williamsburg, it was the

ghosts of George Washington, Thomas Jefferson, and Patrick Henry with whom he communed, and that he felt the presence of those and other patriots "in the history of his parish, of his state, and of his nation." Goodwin himself wrote that he would often imagine "the music of the minuet . . . in the Raleigh Tavern as Jefferson returned to dance with his fair 'Belinda'" and "the eloquence of Patrick Henry in the House of Burgesses."[126] He was not uninterested in the history of Lord Dunmore and his circle at Bruton Parish; rather he simply saw greater virtue in the accomplishments of those figures who had ousted the royal governors.

Born on a farm in Virginia's Piedmont, in Nelson County, W. A. R. Goodwin had begun his ministry in Petersburg. He relocated to the Williamsburg parish on the condition that the interior of the church be returned to its colonial form, an idea that his predecessor at the church, the controversial William Thomas Roberts, had initiated.[127] Goodwin went quickly to work. A poster (fig. 5.30), which was displayed in the church about 1905, solicits financial contributions for the project and states that "Old Bruton is more than a Parish Church. It is a National Shrine." In 1907, the year of the Jamestown cel-

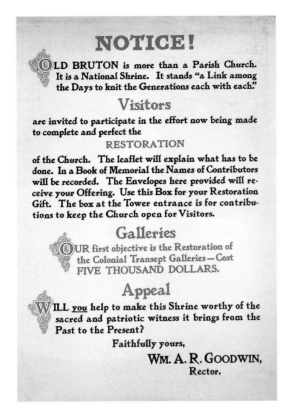

NOTICE!

OLD BRUTON is more than a Parish Church. It is a National Shrine. It stands "a Link among the Days to knit the Generations each with each."

Visitors

are invited to participate in the effort now being made to complete and perfect the

RESTORATION

of the Church. The leaflet will explain what has to be done. In a Book of Memorial the Names of Contributors will be recorded. The Envelopes here provided will receive your Offering. Use this Box for your Restoration Gift. The box at the Tower entrance is for contributions to keep the Church open for Visitors.

Galleries

OUR first objective is the Restoration of the Colonial Transept Galleries—Cost FIVE THOUSAND DOLLARS.

Appeal

WILL you help to make this Shrine worthy of the sacred and patriotic witness it brings from the Past to the Present?

Faithfully yours,

WM. A. R. GOODWIN,
Rector.

5.30 Old Bruton is . . . a National Shrine, *ca. 1905, poster, 28 x 21 in., Virginia Historical Society*

ebrations, Goodwin further associated this building with nationalism and American independence, commending the church "to the patriotic interest of the Nation" and crediting "the faith and devotion of the Nation Builders."[128] To Goodwin's thinking, Bruton Parish Church should serve to inspire not only religious sentiment but also patriotism. Montgomery believes that the rector "wanted his parishioners, indeed all Americans, to find inspiration not only in the faiths of their fathers but in the whole legacy of the people he called the nation-builders."[129]

Barely into the new century, the rector had established at Bruton Parish Church the nationalistic ideology that later would be used for the restoration of the entire town of Williamsburg. Goodwin, who would be the spirit and driving force behind both projects, stated that the recovery of Bruton "represented the beginning of the thought of the restoration" of the surrounding town.[130] A decade-and-a-half would pass, however, between the completion of the first restoration and the beginning of the second. During that time the rector served a pastorate in Rochester, New York. He returned to Williamsburg in 1923 to head the Department of Biblical Literature and Religious Education at William and Mary and to direct an endowment campaign at the college. In 1926 Goodwin began a second rectorate at Bruton Parish. As a developer he would be more successful with the town than with the college; even before he was resettled he had begun thinking about the possibilities for restoration on a grand scale.

The absence in nineteenth-century Williamsburg of "wealth and trade," the condition that was so apparent to John Sargeant Wise in 1897, had actually been strangely fortuitous, in that it allowed for the survival there of several dozen colonial structures; poverty had acted as a preservative. This is not to say, however, that many of those buildings were in even fair condition in 1923. Goodwin described a "canvas [that] was coming to be little more than a thin worn fabric of dreams." He concluded "that unless something was done there would soon be left in Williamsburg nothing but memories of what was no longer here, and regrets for the loss of the tokens and symbols of a glorious past."[131] The rector set out to restore those symbols of glory to the pristine condition that he had achieved at Bruton Parish Church.

Goodwin quickly transferred to the town as a whole the ideas that he had invoked for Bruton, reusing such terms as "nation builders," "shrine," and "patriotism" as he advocated the restoration of a city: "The Restoration [of Williamsburg] will be inspirational, in that it will recall to present and to future generations the faith and the sacrifice of the nation builders. Through this Restoration, a shrine will be created that will serve to stimulate patriotism."[132] According to his secretary, Goodwin even developed a spiritual analogy to describe his vision: he "often said that the city should be made a sacrament, an outward and visible sign of spiritual truth and beauty, through which the lives of visitors to the place would be inspired and enriched."[133] Outdistancing even those bold apologists for antebellum Virginia who had readily substituted emotion for analytical thinking, the rector had elevated the study of the town's colonial history to a religious experience. But Goodwin was not defending a regional past, as the apologists had done; he wrote that "Williamsburg Restored [will be] an inspiration, and . . . a witness to events that are memorable in the history of Virginia, of the nation, and of the world."[134] The past of colonial Virginia, which had nurtured and inspired those who would articulate and lead the struggle for liberty, could be called upon to inspire future generations.

Despite the many formidable obstacles in his path, Goodwin was confident that he would achieve his goal and that "America would respond with gratitude and appreciation when the significance of a restoration of the city was understood."[135] He was just as certain that he would find a patron for the project. In the 1920s such a Colonial Revival restoration would indeed prove to be fundable. Following the attention to early colonial Virginia at the Jamestown tercentenary and the resultant embrace of the state by the reunited nation, the southern location of Williamsburg was inconsequential. Thus, Goodwin could look for a patron where he was most likely to find one with sufficient wealth, in the North among the Gilded Age industrialists. He could reason with potential

5.31 W. A. R. Goodwin and John D. Rockefeller, Jr., behind the George Wythe House, *1928, photograph courtesy of The Colonial Williamsburg Foundation*

donors that Williamsburg could be transformed into a national shrine that would inspire all Americans, and could add that the opportunity at the early capital was unique:

> Williamsburg was the only city celebrated in connection with pre-Revolutionary and Revolutionary events that was capable of restoration. It would be impossible to acquire a territory one mile long and a quarter of a mile wide in Boston, with Faneuil Hall as its center; or in New York, with Wall Street and Trinity church as its center; or in Philadelphia with Independence Hall as its center. Whereas, here, in Williamsburg, equally famous, there remained at least seventy colonial buildings in a town surrounded by the untouched and unmarked countryside, presenting an opportunity to create a shrine that would bear witness to the faith and the devotion and the sacrifice of the nation builders.[136]

Goodwin was ultimately able to persuade the heir to the Standard Oil monopoly to fund the restoration. In 1924 in New York City, the rector introduced his ideas about the colonial capitol to John D. Rockefeller, Jr., who had spent part of the previous decade working in faraway Colorado dealing with the problems of management in the mining industry. But Rockefeller more recently had become involved with restorations in France, at Versailles, Fontainebleau, and Reims, where "beautiful and historic places and buildings [were] disintegrating," which caused the capitalist what he described as "very real distress."[137] This postwar period was a time of strong nationalistic spirit in America, and Rockefeller was more than willing to listen. Goodwin's biographer explains that the rector and the patron shared a perception, common to the era, that theirs was a country on the threshold of greatness but in doubt concerning the fundamentals of democratic

capitalism. They saw in their countrymen a need for reassurance and touchstones, and believed that Americans would respond emotionally to crucial moments in their own history.[138] They also recognized that the Colonial Revival had given Old Virginia a potency that it had lost during the previous century.

Rockefeller would later state in the April 1937 issue of *National Geographic* that the opportunity to restore an entire colonial town was "irresistible."[139] So apparently were Goodwin's powers of persuasion. Although at first the patron was simply intrigued with the idea of saving a town, he soon realized that their project would do more than just "preserve the beauty and charm of the old buildings and gardens." Under Goodwin's guidance he came to recognize that "an even greater value [is] the lesson that [the restored town] teaches of the patriotism, high purpose, and unselfish devotion of our forefathers to the common good."[140] Rockefeller had been won over to the nationalistic creed of the visionary rector, and even to his patriotic and idealistic vocabulary. Goodwin additionally talked about portals to history: "It has been said that the best way to look at history is through windows. There are windows here, and there were others, which might be restored, through which unparalleled vistas open into the nation's past."[141] He often cited a memorable epigram offered by the nineteenth-century British critic John Ruskin: "It is our duty to preserve what the past has had to say for itself, and to say for ourselves those things that shall be true for the future."[142] From this line of thinking, Rockefeller coined the phrase that became the motto of Colonial Williamsburg, "That the future may learn from the past."[143]

As they developed their shared dream, the rector and his patron, of similar age and temperament, developed admiration and respect for one another and a genuine friendship that lasted until Goodwin's death in 1939. The rector was always quick to credit Rockefeller, arguing, for example, that nothing "will prove more lasting, illuminating, and inspiring than what he has done, through the restoration of colonial Williamsburg, to wed truth and beauty here to be the interpreters of the past to the present and the future." Rockefeller would just as faithfully respond that "without Dr. Goodwin there would have been no restoration."[144]

In the beginning, no one knew precisely where the rector's vision would lead, or even how to proceed. A New York architect, J. Stewart Barney, who had assisted in the Bruton Parish renovation, advised Goodwin to deed to the College of William and Mary whatever buildings his patron would buy and renovate. These could be used as student and faculty housing, following a tradition that dated back to the age of Jefferson. This was the idea that the rector had initially carried to Rockefeller. It was discarded for the grander scheme of recovering the town

5.32 *William Graves Perry, Thomas Mott Shaw, and Andrew H. Hepburn (Perry, Shaw & Hepburn),* Sketch of the Restored House of Burgesses with Its Surroundings *and* Sketch of the Restored Court & Palace Greens with their Surroundings, *1927-28, colored pencil over photoprint, each 10³/₄ x 23³/₈ in., The Colonial Williamsburg Foundation*

and establishing the entire vicinity as an educational entity. Goodwin explained:

> Mr. Rockefeller did not in the beginning indicate his purpose of securing all, or of restoring the whole, colonial area of Williamsburg. He entered upon the work and proceeded with it gradually, buying certain pieces of property and finally committing himself to the restoration of the Main Building—or the Christopher Wren Building—at the college, . . . the rebuilding of the House of Burgesses, the restoration of the Duke of Gloucester Street, and the acquisition of Court Green and Palace Green.[145]

Those properties, when taken in total, constituted much of the colonial town.

As the first step of the restoration, Rockefeller agreed in 1926 to the hiring of an architect to provide preliminary drawings of what might be accomplished if the postcolonial structures were removed, the altered buildings

were renovated, and the lost ones were rebuilt. A Boston firm, Perry, Shaw & Hepburn, was engaged after several more experienced architects had declined so radical a commission. William Perry had recently donated his services at the George Wythe House, which through Goodwin's maneuvering the Colonial Dames of America had purchased so that it could serve as the rectory for Bruton Parish. Goodwin wrote that the recovery of that house "very strongly appealed to Mr. Rockefeller" when the patron first visited the town.[146]

Andrew Hepburn, however, would work most closely with the project. Among the early sketches that he provided for Goodwin and Rockefeller are several that follow a popular nineteenth-century type used for city views, the bird's-eye perspective (fig. 5.32). These sketches, which are not the first in the series, are perhaps most significant for what they do not depict, the modern landscape of Williamsburg. Here the town is shown purged of contemporary businesses to illustrate the goal of the restoration, the return of this prospect to its earlier appearance. The modern buildings were what Goodwin called "nightmares that disturbed [his] dream." There were "corrugated iron buildings on the Duke of Gloucester Street mixed in with highly colored filling stations" and "unsightly shacks and stores and cheap modern restaurants [that] were like blots on the painting of a master artist."[147]

In one of the views Hepburn projects the appearance of the second Capitol. The first structure had been lost to fire in 1747 and had been rebuilt with a double portico; in 1832 a second fire destroyed the rebuilt Capitol. As an inspirational symbol of the patriotism associated with Williamsburg, this seat of government was a key structure in Goodwin's perspective of the town. The rector remembered it as the site "where George Mason's bill of rights was adopted, where the resolution was passed instructing the Virginia delegates in the Continental Congress to offer there a resolution to declare the colonies free and independent states, [and] where Patrick Henry delivered his Brutus speech."[148] The second Capitol had been sketched prior to 1832, and archaeological evidence remained at the site, providing Perry, Shaw & Hepburn with a basis for the image that they conceived. In 1929, however, researchers discovered the so-called Bodleian Plate, a copperplate engraving housed at the Bodleian Library at Oxford University, which pictures the Capitol as it appeared initially, from 1701 until 1747. It was decided that this was the form in which it would reappear, despite the fact that it was the latter building that had housed the Virginia patriots. In this instance Colonial Williamsburg would get the best of both, the early and more accomplished design and the association of the site with American independence.

The second view by Hepburn presents a broad perspective of the purged town, with a reimagined squat, three-bay Governor's Palace pictured at the top center. The Bodleian plate would ultimately prove that Hepburn's conjecture about the Palace was far from the mark in describing what had once stood on the site. Architectural historian Richard Guy Wilson notes that "a liberal dose of imagination" underlies Hepburn's vision. Beyond issues concerning the building itself, his trees, along with the pristine houses and the well-kept yards and gardens, are not rooted in historical fact; instead they give what Wilson calls "a bucolic vision of a twentieth-century, upper-middle-class suburban town."[149] However, once Goodwin, Rockefeller, and their architects embraced the bold recovery plan that these views document, the triumph of Colonial Williamsburg was assured, and so, thereby, was Virginia's place as a bedrock of the United States.

Hepburn's sketches achieved the far-reaching effect that Goodwin desired. As the rector recounts, they persuaded Rockefeller to authorize the acquisition of the property that lies within the areas that they picture. The first building purchased was the Ludwell-Paradise house, which came on the market in December of 1926, making that year the accepted birth date of Colonial Williamsburg. To avoid an escalation of the real estate market, the identity of the actual purchaser of that property and of those that followed was kept secret until 1928, when public lands and buildings, such as the Palace green, the market square, and the courthouse, were eyed by Goodwin. At that point the project had to be opened to both public scrutiny and review by the city fathers. They quickly approved Rockefeller's patronage, however, and so the restoration continued.

Once the Palace green was acquired, plans were made to rebuild the lost edifice. Given the early date of the fire, 1781, the redesigned structure would have to be based upon scant historical evidence. Rockefeller, however, according to Goodwin, was "extremely" interested in "historic verity."[150] Thus the site was subject to archaeological scrutiny, Thomas Jefferson's notes about the building were studied, and teams of architects and historians were hired to conduct research in Williamsburg and the Tidewater and to scan records offices and libraries in England and France. It was in this way that the Bodleian Plate was discovered. Although that print gives only a single view of the building's main facade, Rockefeller convinced himself that the image carried his designers out of "the dark" and allowed them to move forward "with absolute certainty and conviction."[151]

One of young architects assigned to the Palace project, and apparently the draftsman of the elevation that is pictured here (fig. 5.33), was Thomas Tileston Waterman, who was born in New York City and apprenticed with architects in Boston before joining the Williamsburg team. Waterman is remembered today for his work on that project, and for several books that he later wrote about early Virginia architecture. He transformed Hepburn's less than inspired conception of how the building might have looked into the tall and elegant structure that was finally completed in 1930. The Palace immediately became the centerpiece of the Williamsburg restoration. Goodwin called it "a treasure," although he generally had less to say about this building than he did about the Capitol. This is probably because the Palace, if only by its very name, was associated with Virginia's royal governors. It was a sumptuous setting where a patriot like Patrick Henry might well have seemed out of place.

When blocks along the Duke of Gloucester Street were reimagined by Perry, Shaw & Hepburn, a remarkably tidy colonial village emerged (fig. 5.34). This improved environment is pictured in a drawing that Robert Dean prepared for Rockefeller's approval. A sense of

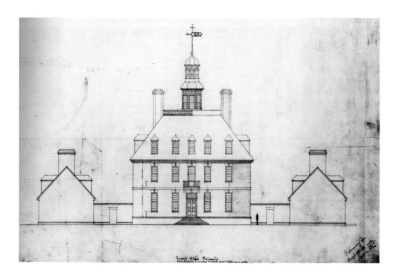

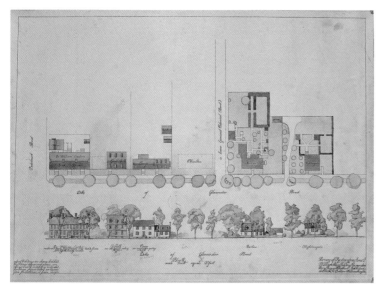

5.33 *Above, left Attributed to Thomas Tileston Waterman, for Perry, Shaw & Hepburn,* Front Elevation of the Governor's Palace, *1930, working drawing, 23¼ x 38½ in., graphite pencil on tracing paper, Library of Congress*

5.34 *Left Robert Dean for Perry, Shaw & Hepburn,* Duke of Gloucester Street, Block X, *plan and elevations, ca. 1931, watercolor and ink on paper, 27¼ x 37⅜ in., The Colonial Williamsburg Foundation*

5.35 *Above Perry, Shaw & Hepburn,* House Number 1, *for* House & Garden *(November 1937, "Williamsburg Issue"), Virginia Historical Society*

overall order is conveyed by the architect, due in no small part to the rhythmic placement of the many trees that would characterize the new Williamsburg.[152]

In looking at the smaller houses pictured by Dean, which are prominent throughout the town, Goodwin came to recognize their importance in establishing the tone of the landscape. "It is fortunate," the rector wrote, "that Williamsburg . . . will bring to mind, and perpetuate the simple architectural designs of that period in Virginia and American history before wealth had become obvious."[153] This, of course, was a sentiment that differed from the earlier stance of the colonialists who thought that wealth and the mansions that it could build, which had come back into favor during the Gilded Age, was a requisite for revivalism. Goodwin was attuned to more modern values, and was even somewhat prophetic in that the simple domestic architecture of Williamsburg was soon copied in twentieth-century neighborhoods across the United States, and the streets themselves became the pattern for suburban developments far removed from Virginia. As suggested by the design published by *House & Garden* magazine in 1937 (fig. 5.35), the press of the

1930s brought Williamsburg models to a receptive national audience.

The recovery of the Duke of Gloucester Street was completed in 1934, a momentous year in the history of the Williamsburg restoration. At that date President Franklin D. Roosevelt visited to dedicate this purged avenue and to celebrate the completion of an important phase of the restoration. Not only had a principal axis of the town been restored, but also the new Capitol and the Palace had both been completed. The president was no doubt impressed by the revivalist activities in Virginia. He certainly knew about the rebuilding of an early English mansion in Richmond that would become "Virginia House" because a year earlier he had called its owner Alexander Weddell back into diplomatic service. At Williamsburg, Roosevelt stated, "What a thrill it has been . . . to have the honor of formally opening the reconstructed Duke of Gloucester Street, which rightly can be called the most historic avenue in America; what a joy . . . to see 61 colonial buildings restored, 84 colonial buildings rebuilt; . . . to see how . . . the atmosphere of a whole glorious chapter in our history, has been recaptured."[154]

By 1941 an informational leaflet printed for tourists at Colonial Williamsburg touted further accomplishments, particularly in the area of removal: "591 modern Buildings have been demolished or removed from the colonial Area; 188 colonial Buildings have been reconstructed, most of them on original Foundations; 77 colonial Buildings have been restored."[155] Today the 173 acres of Colonial Williamsburg present some 200 historical buildings, 88 of which are original structures.

Given such impressive statistics, historians have ranked Colonial Williamsburg as the most extraordinary restoration project ever completed in America.[156] This is not to say, however, that any factual past can be easily traced to the particulars of the restored city. At Williamsburg, a historical period has been reimagined. From the manipulation of the landscape elements, to the selection and design of the buildings, to the presentation of the history itself, elements of fantasy have been prominent in the restoration of Williamsburg from the very start. In fact, architectural historian Richard Guy Wilson sees the restored town as inseparable from the twentieth-century tastes that molded it. "Although promoted and popularly viewed as an authentic recreation of Virginia's colonial capital on the eve of the Revolution in the eighteenth century," he writes, "in reality Colonial Williamsburg more accurately reflects the values held during its re-creation by the architects who restored it."[157] Thus there are city blocks in the new section of Williamsburg that are perhaps more similar to a twentieth-century suburban town than to colonial Virginia. Merchant's Square, the commercial run of modern stores, has little to do with the city's past. Its architect, William Perry, wrote of his creation, "It has been assumed that had the people of Williamsburg been faced with a similar problem in the eighteenth century, they might have solved it in this manner and with buildings similar in appearance to these."[158]

George Yetter explains that the founders of Colonial Williamsburg stretched their recaptured moment in time to extend a full century and a half:

> The architects defined the restoration as a "composite representation of the original forms of a number of buildings and areas known or believed to have existed in Williamsburg between the years 1699 and 1840." The overall ambience was not intended to express a particular date, but rather the feeling and appearance of a continuum of time reflecting the colonial experience, together with the classical tradition of the early republic which evolved from it.[159]

Thus, for example, the rebuilt Capitol of 1701–47 can stand in the restored town beside the Public Records Office that was originally constructed as a consequence of the fire of 1747. Nearby is another example of a landscape element that was never seen by visitors to the first Capitol. The James Semple House was not built until the time of the Revolution.

The difficult story of race relations in the second capital underscores the extent to which the image of early Virginia had to be reimagined there. Admittedly, slavery was less visible in a colonial town than on the large plantations, where slaves could outnumber their masters by the dozens. But census data from the late colonial period shows that fifty-two percent of the population of the capital was African American. This sizable slave presence was downplayed by the revivalists, who chose instead to create Colonial Williamsburg as a more idyllic and less problematic environment. The unpleasant aspects of slavery were brushed under the new, colonial-style carpets.

In the early years, restoration architects were happy to find little evidence in the town of slave quarters, or much in the archaeology or documentary evidence to suggest how the private hours of the slave population had been spent. Once the decision was made to people the setting with costumed actors, however, an African-American presence was a necessity. At the outset, those in service would become visible only if their appearance would not make white tourists uncomfortable. Blacks were largely presented in eighteenth-century livery, or as deferential and contented servants. In fact, the modern black population of the area was far from content. The behemoth that became Colonial Williamsburg disrupted the lives of many local African Americans. "The most tragic aspect of the whole enterprise," writes Michael Kammen, "is that it resulted in the destruction or relocation of homes and community institutions of blacks, and it strained relationships between blacks and whites."[160]

In the wake of the national civil rights movement, the administration at Colonial Williamsburg reconsidered the image that it was projecting of a colonial society that was somehow free of the evils inherent in slavery. Early Williamsburg was reimagined again with the goal of giving more accuracy to the African-American presence there. In 1982 an African-American Studies Department was established in the Colonial Williamsburg research division. A tour entitled "How the Other Half Lives" was offered to visitors, who after dinner might hear the sound of African folk songs. Critics, however, complained that the distressing aspects of human bondage still remained hidden in the restored town so as not to offend the tourists who might withdraw financial support. In response, in 1994, the foundation boldly staged the reenactment of a slave auction (fig. 5.36). Visitors were moved to tears, but the NAACP criticized the presentation as "crass entertainment." The program was dropped in 1995.[161] Try as it might, the administration at Colonial Williamsburg continues to struggle in its attempts to deal forcefully yet respectfully with the issue of slavery.

The failure of this reenactment proves that the entire truth about the city's history is still more than many Americans care to experience. Unable to right the wrong of eighteenth-century slavery, the administrators at Williamsburg have returned to the positive components of the town's legacy. Colin Campbell, the current president of the operation, argues today that "if we do not instruct our children and remind ourselves how [our] freedoms were won, then surely we will awake one day to find them lost—along with all the rest."[162] What Richard Guy Wilson has called "Virginia's great creation of the twentieth century" continues its popularity into the twenty-first.[163] And as long as Colonial Williamsburg continues to prosper, the image of a glorious Old Virginia may well remain invulnerable to the barbs of detractors.

At mid-century, before the efforts to provide a more realistic semblance of black life in the second capital had begun, a Virginia painter resident in New York City used the landscape of Tidewater Virginia to posit that the social history of the region was in fact too painful to inspire Colonial Williamsburg-type nostalgia. Because blacks in Virginia had been oppressed as slaves and given few opportunities as freedmen, and because in the 1940s such injustice continued unabated, the legacy of the region seemed more worthy of shame than celebration to Robert Gwathmey, an eighth-generation Virginian. He stated that on returning to the Old Dominion, to the Tidewater countryside just up the road from Colonial Williamsburg, "Suddenly, I saw with terrible clarity . . . how it was for the Negro in the South."[164] His paintings of oppressed black agricultural workers attacked the racial and social problems that had survived with the perpetuation of Old Virginia values. Gwathmey set a course for a growing awareness of racial injustice that would eventually challenge, and in some ways undermine, the appeal of the state's colonial and antebellum past.

In paintings like *Hoeing* (fig. 5.37) Gwathmey pointed to the often destitute lives of contemporary African Americans, which existed alongside the stereotypical views that had been perpetuated by *Gone With the Wind* and the novels and films about antebellum life that had followed in its wake. He takes Winslow Homer's image of the freedman as an agricultural worker and updates it to show that fifty years later there has been little change. Many blacks in Virginia still toiled in the fields as sharecroppers, who were lucky to eke out a living on the land.

5.36   *Left* African-American Costumed Actors at Colonial Williamsburg, *1994, photograph courtesy of The Colonial Williamsburg Foundation*

5.37   *Below Robert Gwathmey,* Hoeing, *1943, oil on canvas, 40 x 60¼ in., Carnegie Museum of Art*

They still labored with primitive hoes, as in the days of slavery.

Gwathmey updated the style and characterizations that had been popularized by Homer and his contemporaries. As he thought about the traditional ways that blacks had been portrayed, he was determined to avoid the pitfalls of the past: "When any people can depict any other people as picturesque, it degenerates into romantic mockery."[165] Gwathmey devised a flat style, influenced by that of Henri Matisse, whereby symbols could be made of strong and simple visual elements. In *Hoeing*, these include the church, which points to the black family's strong religious faith; the stark, single corn plant and single post that alert viewers to the failures of a society that still denied the contributions of the African American; the barbed wire, which speaks of the segregation and inhuman treatment of the black man; and the child carrying a baby, a motif that reminds us both that each parent was obliged to work if a black family was to survive in Virginia, and that future generations will face the same struggle.[166] This was the true aftermath of plantation life. And while there is hope in this scene, both in the fact that the family has managed to remain together and in the power and dignity of the young laborer, there is also pathos. Such efforts to portray the difficulties of the present, even when providing a glimmer of hope for a possibly better future, held up popular attempts to celebrate the society of the Old South—be they through re-enactments such as Colonial Williamsburg or the representations in the many historically based films of the mid-twentieth century—to a heightened degree of scrutiny.

The history that was reconstructed at Williamsburg originally consisted simply of rebuilding the old houses and replacing lost structures. It evolved to include the peopling of the town with actors and craftsmen, who ran the gamut from slaves, to common people, to the great men of the era. On a regular basis one could hear Patrick Henry deliver his "Brutus" speech that had so interested Rector Goodwin or see such luminaries as Washington, Mason, or the young Thomas Jefferson. The next logical step was to make use of the available technology to increase the educational and entertainment possibilities. Thus in 1956 Colonial Williamsburg engaged Paramount Pictures to produce a movie that recreated important events from the critical period between 1769 and 1776, when the leadership of Old Virginia did so much to shape a burgeoning nation. Little expense was spared. Experienced directors and professional actors were hired for the making of *The Story of a Patriot*, which in an updated version is to this day still screened for visitors to the restored capital. The short film tells the story of a fictional planter, John Fry, who supposedly met with leaders like Washington and Jefferson and witnessed the move toward independence.

5.38 *Paramount Pictures,* The Virginian, *1929 (reissued 1935), poster, Virginia Historical Society*

Two earlier, very successful, Hollywood films had actually directed attention away from the colonial period. *The Virginian*, the celluloid version of Owen Wister's best-selling novel (1902), appeared in 1929 and was reissued in 1935 (fig. 5.38). In it Gary Cooper starred as the often laconic Wyoming ranch-hand, who lives by his own, deeply entrenched moral code in the "Wild West" of the second half of the nineteenth century. Wister had warned his readers that he was writing of a time that no longer existed, and he set up his story so as to provide both an exciting tale of the frontier days and a mythic story of a lone hero, known only as "the Virginian," who had to use his in-bred abilities to conquer evil and win the heart of Molly Wood, a pretty schoolmarm from Vermont. In such films as *The Virginian* and the later *High Noon* (1952), many of the still existing parameters of the "Western" were successfully rendered, thanks in part to the ability of Cooper to straddle the roles of everyday man and mythic hero.

Victor Fleming, who directed *The Virginian*, had his greatest success later in the 1930s with another adaptation of a successful novel. Margaret Mitchell's *Gone With the Wind* had been an international best-seller and a Pulitzer Prize winner in 1936. Interest in the film was such that there were spirited debates about who should play Scarlett O'Hara, Ashley Wilkes, and Melanie Hamilton; there was little doubt that Clark Gable was the only choice for Rhett Butler. Producer David Selznick's epic about a Georgia family before, during, and after the Civil War was a sensation, and remains to this day one of the most popular films ever made. Its presentation of antebellum southern life sparked tremendous interest in that period and created images of the Old South that are still indelibly imprinted in the popular consciousness. One of the plot contrivances that Mitchell set before her

5.39 *Above, top Columbia Pictures,* The Howards of Virginia, *1940, poster, Virginia Historical Society*

5.40 *Above Paramount Pictures,* Virginia, *1941, poster, Virginia Historical Society*

readers without much elaboration is the fact that the Wilkes family was originally from Virginia. This, in part, provides an explanation for the attraction felt by Scarlett to the gentlemanly, intellectual, somewhat stiff Ashley, who to many viewers paled in comparison to the rakish Rhett.

Selznick and Fleming had demonstrated that cinema could fuel a latent nostalgia in modern America for stories about a glorious and aristocratic southern past, which by the 1930s could be wistfully remembered. They also proved that a film could have an almost unimaginable power to shape the popular understanding of history. The remarkable success of *Gone with the Wind* almost immediately inspired the production of three motion pictures about Old Virginia, which attempted to combine the state's mystique with lively tales from its history.

The first of the Virginia films to follow in the wake of *Gone With the Wind* was a Revolutionary War romance that starred the young, remarkably handsome Cary Grant and Martha Scott. In 1940 Columbia Pictures released *The Howards of Virginia*, a lavish black-and-white epic about an impoverished Virginia surveyor who by his all-American charm, and with a little help from his lifelong friend Thomas Jefferson, marries into an aristocratic family of the first colony and is swept into events of the Revolutionary War (fig. 5.39). It too was adapted from a best-selling novel, *The Tree of Liberty* (1940) by Elizabeth Page. If the author named her Virginia novel in such a way as to evoke national associations—of the Sons of Liberty of New England or the Liberty Bell of Philadelphia—Hollywood cared little for her idea.

A number of scenes in *The Howards of Virginia* were filmed at the newly restored Colonial Williamsburg (including interiors that were supposedly set in the Piedmont). Rockefeller's new town actually emerges as one of the stars of the show. *The Howards*, empowered by the charisma of its male lead, served to introduce Colonial Williamsburg to the nation, and no doubt inspired Williamsburg's administrators, a decade-and-a-half and two wars later, to commission *The Story of a Patriot*.

Two of the other Virginia-based films that were produced on the eve of World War II were blatant sequels to *Gone with the Wind*. The first and most transparent of these is *Virginia* (fig. 5.40), which was released by Paramount Pictures. As *Gone with the Wind* was set in rural Georgia, *Virginia* was set in the small (nonexistent) town of Fairville, Virginia. As *Gone with the Wind* presented lavish scenes filled with hooped skirts, columned architecture, green fields, and faithful black retainers, then *Virginia* would do the same. As *Gone with the Wind* starred an Englishwoman, Vivian Leigh as Scarlett O'Hara, then the British actress Madeleine Carroll would serve well in *Virginia* as the southern belle Charlotte Dunterry. As Scarlett was hot-tempered, then Charlotte would be a former

5.41 *Paramount Pictures,* Virginia, *1941, poster, Virginia Historical Society*

5.42 *Metro-Goldwyn-Mayer,* You're a beautiful bride . . . like your mother!, *from* The Vanishing Virginian, *1941, poster, Virginia Historical Society*

showgirl. As Scarlett was heir to Tara, then Charlotte would take control of her family plantation. As Scarlett faced financial insolvency, so would Charlotte. As Hattie McDaniel, an African American, had won the Academy Award for Best Supporting Actress for her work in *Gone with the Wind,* several black retainers would be written into the screenplay for *Virginia* (fig. 5.41). One of the black actors, Leigh Whipper, who portrays an elderly former slave who returns to Fairville to die, gave a memorable performance. Critic Hal Erickson writes of Whipper that "he doesn't sing 'Carry Me Back to Old Virginny,' but one can hear it anyway."[167] And, perhaps most importantly, as Scarlett pined for her beloved Ashley yet at the same time was attracted to Rhett Butler, Charlotte would enter into a loveless marriage with the wealthy norther-

ner Norman Williams, played by Sterling Hayden, while she longs for an impoverished local aristocrat, Stonewall Elliot, played by a young Fred MacMurray. Erickson adds that while Charlotte Dunterry wavers between Elliot and Williams, the audience settles in for a good long nap.

Metro-Goldwyn-Mayer's own sequel to *Gone with the Wind, The Vanishing Virginian* (fig. 5.42), was an adaptation of the popular autobiographical novel of the same name written in 1940 by Rebecca Yancey Williams. The story is set in the Piedmont, where Williams's father grew to maturity during the post-Civil-War era, and focuses on family life. When the daughter becomes involved in the suffragette movement, it becomes apparent that the ways of Old Virginia that Captain Bob Yancey knew are on the way out. Although Yancey, played by Frank Morgan, is a loveable figure, audiences and critics apparently found little else to praise in *The Vanishing Virginian.*

Such films failed in part because it was impossible to compete with the *Gone with the Wind* phenomenon. Much of the material seemed at best dated, at worst clearly derivative of the Gable/Leigh blockbuster, and so offered little new in terms of plot or context. What must also be considered, however, is that by the mid-twentieth century the history of Virginia was so tied to the colonial period that there would have been little interest in anything not directly related to the Founding Fathers. Such failures ultimately led to widespread rejection of the antebellum South by many filmmakers, which had an unanticipated result. The lack of consideration of this period has allowed for the survival of the plantation myth as it was told in the greatest and by far the most popular film on the subject, *Gone with the Wind.* The failure to engage slavery in a thoughtful manner until the production of such films as *Roots* in the 1970s served to freeze dry scenes of Tara and its environs in the popular consciousness. For better or worse, *Gone with the Wind* would be remembered by succeeding generations whenever the Old South was invoked.

The Recovery of the Pastoral Ideal

Nancy, Lady Astor of Mirador in Albemarle County, who would become the first woman to sit in the British House of Commons, once wrote, "To be a Virginian is a tremendous responsibility. So much is expected of us." The responsibility is tied to the region's great legacy of leadership and achievement. The expectation—the additional component that would emerge during the Colonial Revival—would involve the preservation of the pre-statehood past, the importance of which had receded in the turbulent years of the mid-nineteenth century.

One of the tenets of the ruralist movement of the eighteenth century had been the sense that one could re-enact in America, with its open, Edenic spaces, the quest for the pastoral ideal that had existed in the imaginations of Old World thinkers since the Classical Age. In nineteenth-century Virginia this quest had become linked to the great historical events that had taken place in the colony. One could not consider the ideals sought by the landed gentry of the mid-eighteenth century without eliding into the great purposes of the Revolutionary era which they inspired. This connection would be reaffirmed during the Colonial Revival, and would become inextricably linked by the time of the new agrarians of the early twentieth century, who understood that a crucial part of their design had to be a focus on the trials and accomplishments of those who had come to Virginia in previous generations. In this sense, the pastoral ideal survives to this day in the commonwealth, particularly in the hills

5.43 *Philip De Laszlo,* Alexander Wilbourne Weddell, *1937, oil on canvas, 35³/₄ x 25³/₄ in., Virginia Historical Society*

of the Piedmont and along the rivers of the Tidewater. And if this pursuit remains viable in the nation as a whole, it is due in part to the successes of such Virginians as Alexander Weddell and Paul Mellon, who in their respective eras personified what could be attained when men of means seek refuge on the land.

In recent decades archaeologists have proven that the importation of quality goods from England and other Old World countries was an important characteristic of life in colonial Virginia from the time of the earliest settlements. In the most extreme case imaginable of the importation of accouterments of culture, a prominent Virginian of the twentieth century chose to import not the small decorative objects that would have provided reminiscences of the Elizabethan and Jacobean lifestyle, but an actual English mansion. While other colonial revivalists restored old Virginia houses of the eighteenth century or built anew in the Georgian style, Alexander Wilbourne Weddell (fig. 5.43) did them one better by reconstructing an ancient English manor house that he had disassembled and shipped across the ocean. Starting with a Tudor building that had stood in the midlands of England for nearly three-and-a-half centuries, Weddell created one of the most extraordinary revival-style houses of the modern era (fig. 5.44).[168]

5.44 Virginia House, *1926-28, built west of Richmond in Henrico County (now Richmond), photograph in Alexander Weddell,* A Description of Virginia House in Henrico County, near Richmond, Virginia *(Richmond, 1947), Virginia Historical Society*

A highly visible player in the recovery of Virginia's seventeenth-century legacy and a social force in Richmond, Washington, D.C., and international circles, Weddell was ever conscious of what he called "the great glory of Virginia," a heritage to which he contributed significantly. Weddell's paternal grandfather had emigrated from Scotland in the nineteenth century, and his father, Alexander Watson Weddell, became rector of St. John's Church in Richmond, the site made famous by Patrick Henry. The father also served as private secretary to Confederate secretary of state Judah P. Benjamin, and two of the Reverend Weddell's brothers were killed in the Civil War fighting for the Confederate cause. Weddell's mother, Penelope Wright, was the daughter of Dr. David Minton Wright, a civilian physician in Norfolk who in 1863, following a fatal altercation with a Union officer, was executed by northern troops. Dr. Wright would become a Confederate martyr, to whom Abraham Lincoln had denied a pardon. Alexander Weddell, however, put aside his family's Confederate past when as a young man

he pursued a diplomatic career. He served in Africa, the Mediterranean, India, and Mexico between 1910 and 1928. The ambassador then retired to a life of civic interests, during which he helped Virginians to rediscover that portion of their past that he believed had greater significance than did the Confederate legacy.

Initially Weddell had intended simply to build a new mansion in the English Tudor style, which would harken back to the Elizabethan age when the first voyages to Virginia were undertaken. The Jacobean variation of this earlier pattern had been introduced into seventeenth-century Virginia. By building in that manner, Weddell could celebrate the antiquity of a colony so old that it had been named for the virgin queen. Fortuitously, however, Weddell discovered in 1925 a sixteenth-century mansion, Warwick Priory, that was undergoing demolition. The building appealed to Weddell and to his new wife, Virginia, a midwestern heiress with Virginia family roots, because of its association with Queen Elizabeth and John Evelyn, both of whom had visited there. The Weddells soon purchased Warwick and began the process of transporting the house to America.

Weddell immediately hired a New York architect to modify the priory's late medieval design. Henry Grant Morse added distinctive Flemish gables that are reminiscent of those that had originally existed at Warwick, and he also made extensive changes to the floor plan, including the addition of west and east wings. The west wing, which includes Weddell's library, is a replica of the central portion of Sulgrave Manor, the English ancestral home of George Washington's family, to which Weddell was distantly related through his mother's side of the family. The east wing is a replica of the tower of Wormleighton, an estate of the Spencer-Churchill family who are also related to the Washingtons. With these architectural links to the clan that would produce the Father of His Country, Weddell managed to celebrate both Virginia's late colonial and early national history, as well as the earlier era that had produced the original building.[169]

Weddell called his new estate Virginia House. He valued its grounds (fig. 5.45) as part of the huge land grant that had been awarded to William Byrd I, which was ultimately a gift from Charles II. In that way, the English history of the nine acres that surrounded him could be carried nearly as far backward in time as the era when Warwick Priory was first built. Innumerable country retreats were developed along the east coast of the United States during the period when Virginia House was constructed; this phenomenon has been labeled the American Country Place movement.[170] Weddell's selection of a site outside urban Richmond, where he had spent his

childhood, was a conscious maneuver intended to link his new lifestyle with the rural traditions of Old Virginia. He also expressed his interest in the classical pastoral ideal when he traced this type of life to its ancient Rome roots. In his book *Description of Virginia House in Henrico County, near Richmond, Virginia*, Weddell cites a letter of Pliny the Younger, who lauds "the charm of [his own] villa [outside Rome], the advantages of its situation, and the extensive prospect." The ambassador would have agreed with Pliny's conclusion: "Surely you are unreasonably attached to the pleasures of the town if you have no hankering after [so agreeable a retreat]."[171]

With characteristic charm, Weddell explained that the name Virginia House honored his wife, Virginia. But his coincident purpose was to celebrate the Old Virginia of the colonial era, particularly the colony's sixteenth-century bond to England, which no other region in America could duplicate. In 1947 Weddell stated that the reason he built Virginia House was to glorify the state: "ad majorem Virginiae gloriam." For that reason he had conveyed the estate in 1929 to the Virginia Historical Society, reserving a life interest for himself and his wife.[172] Perhaps fearing that a visitor to Virginia House might miss the point, one year earlier he had commissioned Fred Dana Marsh to paint for the overmantel of his library, which housed an impressive collection of books about early Virginia, a huge, eight-foot-long enlargement of John Farrer's small map of 1651, which pictures Sir Frances Drake and credits him for taking possession of Virginia in 1577 "in the name of Q. Eliza." (fig. 5.46; see page 30, fig. 1.18). Farrer had charted the domain of

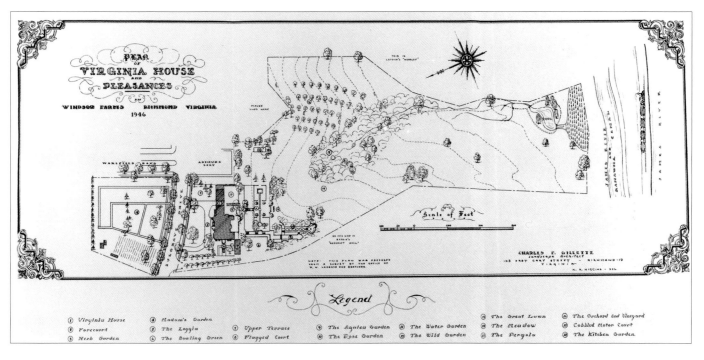

5.45 Plan of the grounds of Virginia House, *in Alexander Weddell,* A Description of Virginia House in Henrico County, near Richmond, Virginia *(Richmond, 1947)*

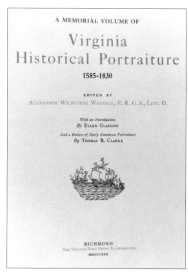

5.46 *Above, top, left John Farrer,* A Mapp of Virginia Discouered to Ye Falls, *London, 1651, as painted by Fred Dana Marsh for Alexander Weddell's Virginia House*

5.47 *Above, top, right Alexander Wilbourne Weddell,* A Memorial Volume of Virginia Historical Portraiture, 1585-1830 *(Richmond, 1930), Virginia Historical Society*

5.48 *Above Unidentified artist,* Sir Francis Drake, *19th century?, 20½ x 18½ in., Virginia Historical Society, bequest of Alexander Wilbourne Weddell*

what he labeled "Ould Virginia" as encompassing nearly the entire New World, stretching from Florida to New England and westward to "the Sea of China and the Indies." Weddell was proud of that heritage; he would picture the overmantel prominently in a massive volume that he published and titled *A Memorial Volume of Virginia Historical Portraiture, 1585–1830* (fig. 5.47).

In 1930 Weddell organized and presented at Virginia House the largest exhibition ever held of early Virginia portraiture, a group of some two hundred oil portraits of Englishmen and Virginians that he had assembled from collections near and far. This was a monumental undertaking that few museums even today would attempt. The accompanying catalogue, the size and weight of a lectern Bible and bound in gold-stamped full morocco, is itself a work of art, an appropriate home for so important a collection. The time span for the material included, 1585–1830, expands the idea of Old Virginia from the earliest date ever considered for the term until well into the nineteenth century. Weddell gathered portraits of most of the important figures associated with early Virginia. First on his list, of course, was the virgin queen herself, who in the entry written by Mary Newton Stanard, entitled *Elizabeth, by the Grace of God, Queene of England, Fraunce, and Ireland, and of Virginia,* is introduced as the "slender, erect, bejewelled woman who made English America possible."[173] During this period Weddell purchased for his own collection a portrait of undetermined date of Sir Francis Drake (fig. 5.48), the explorer who is pictured on the Farrer map. He commissioned replicas of such figures as John Murray, the fourth Earl of Dunmore, Virginia's

5.49 *Charles X. Harris, after Sir Joshua Reynolds,* John Murray, fourth Earl of Dunmore, *1929, oil on canvas, 94 x 58 in., Virginia Historical Society, bequest of Alexander Wilbourne Weddell*

last royal governor (fig. 5.49). The latter was copied when the original by Sir Joshua Reynolds traveled to Virginia House from Scotland.

The visitor to Weddell's portrait exhibition was intended to be awed by the solemnity of this gathering of Virginia's founders and friends, and to acknowledge the great heritage personified by the scores of images that lined the paneled walls of Virginia House. The architecture of the exhibition space no doubt left an equally lasting impression. Although it is no longer in a rural setting—Virginia House is now surrounded by a residential neighborhood—the magnificent mansion and its contents still evoke thoughts of the Elizabethan age while also serving as exemplary of the American Country Place movement. The preservation of Alexander Weddell's great achievement remains a crucial responsibility of the Society.

The racehorse Shark was so successful on eighteenth-century English courses that his portrait was taken twice by the great animal painter George Stubbs, once in 1775 and again in 1794 (fig. 5.50). This image of Shark with his trainer was repeated in watercolor by the artist's son and was even engraved, the bill for which was reputedly paid by the Prince of Wales. If the several portraits of Shark point to his importance in the history of racing in England, he is also relevant to the sport in America; he was exported to the new nation to serve as a sire. In the 1830s a number of the leading racehorses in the Old Dominion were descended from this champion. The biography of Shark and other such sires illustrates another example of the transmission to Virginia of Old World diversions. The breeding and racing of horses had long been an important component of English country life. The beautiful portrait of Shark by so fine an artist as Stubbs depicts the pastoral nature of that culture, and thereby serves to encourage the perpetuation of the rural lifestyle.

Not surprisingly, this painting appealed to the Virginia philanthropist Paul Mellon, who purchased it in the late twentieth century and in 1999 bequeathed it to the Virginia Museum of Fine Arts. Mellon, who years before had selected the northern Piedmont of Virginia as the place where he could best recreate the rural way of life that Stubbs celebrates, was by then the world's premier collector of English sporting art. As a privileged heir, he had set for himself the lofty goal of contributing to the continuation of what he saw as important aspects of both English agrarian culture and its American descendant. Not only would he live like the rural gentry of old; he would also salvage representations of the pastoral lifestyle of Georgian England, which he greatly admired, to save those images for posterity. Mellon stands apart as the most significant of the modern Virginia ruralists who transmitted the region's ancient pastoral culture into the modern world.[174]

The new agrarians, however, gave the old ideal a new twist. Following the rekindled national interest in Virginia's past that had been ignited by the Jamestown tercentennial and stoked by the restoration of Williamsburg, these new gentry attempted to keep the fires burning, not as much through renovation as by pointing out that viable elements of the great colonial history of the region were still visible, indeed were part of the landscape itself, and so were available for contemplation if one took the time and energy to seek them out. The inspirational quality of a setting is perhaps easier sensed than put into words, but in 1930 Wallace Nutting tried to explain. Thinking of the colonial past, he wrote, "[An old] home in Virginia seems to cry out to its children: 'I have done all I could for you, all any country could do for you. Now, grow up!' And the best products are every inch men."[175] An understanding of the relationship between these old structures and the land was crucial to the achievement of

5.50 *George Stubbs,* Shark with his Trainer Price, *ca. 1794, oil on canvas, 40⅛ x 50⅛ in., Virginia Museum of Fine Arts, Richmond, bequest of Paul Mellon*

a type of exultation that had been long forgotten. As the Reverend Goodwin had founded Colonial Williamsburg on the notion that inspiration could be derived from a such a setting, and Alexander Weddell had built Virginia House and amassed his extraordinary collection in the hope that viewers would be so moved as to reconnect to their wondrous heritage, so Mellon and his generation would see the importance of the landscape to the rebirth of enthusiasm for Virginia's past. Such new ruralists were still interested in history; they would simply see its relationship to the present in a new way. In 1958 Mellon began to purchase manuscripts and rare books related to early Virginia. Soon he was the greatest private collector ever of Virginiana, which filled the library of his rural retreat. These objects helped Mellon to appreciate the historical heritage that was tied to the landscape that surrounded him in northern Virginia.

The story of Paul Mellon (fig. 5.51) has served to enhance the mystique of Old Virginia. His biography is so remarkable as to seem more fantasy than fact. On the jacket of his memoir, *Reflections in a Silver Spoon* (1992), Mellon is said to have experienced "one of the most enjoying, compelling, fascinating, and valuable lives of this American century."[176] It was "valuable" in part because of his great philanthropy to such public institutions as the National Gallery of Art, the Yale Center for British Art, the Virginia Museum of Fine Arts, and the Virginia Historical Society. If as a young man this wealthy heir had worried "about what [he was] going to do with the rest of [his life]," Mellon had answered that question by the 1950s. He would work to perpetuate the values that he considered representative of the best of western culture. Two often related ways that this could be accomplished were through collecting and philanthropy.[177]

5.51 *Bernard Hailstone,* Paul Mellon, *1970, oil on canvas, 41⅛ x 34¼ in., Virginia Historical Society*

Mellon cites at the start of his memoir a passage written by John Adams to his wife Abigail in 1780:

> I must study politics and war, that my sons may have liberty to study mathematics and philosophy. My sons ought to study mathematics and philosophy, geography, natural history and naval architecture, navigation, commerce, and agriculture, in order to give their children a right to study painting, poetry, music, architecture, statuary, tapestry, and porcelain.[178]

Mellon's grandfather was an Irish immigrant who would become the founder of the dynasty. His father, Andrew Mellon, the banker and later secretary of the Treasury, had made himself one of the four wealthiest men in America (along with Henry Ford, John D. Rockefeller, Jr., and Andrew's brother Richard). Paul Mellon was the grandchild who, in Adams's scenario, was able to "study" the arts. His inheritance not only "gave him the right" to immerse himself in culture; perhaps more importantly it provided the means for him to do so.[179]

Pittsburgh, where Paul Mellon was born and raised, was never to his liking. Nor were banking or business in general. He tells his readers so in surprisingly blunt terms. The "belching flames of the steel mills and coke ovens" of the city could seem like "a prelude to hell." The

young Mellon felt "repugnance at the thought of spending [his] life [like his father] as a banker." As a director of the family coal business, Mellon attended meetings where he "never knew what was going on and . . . didn't really care." The son rejected the lifestyle of his father. His "heart was always longing for the fields and woods of [his] farm in Virginia," a property that he had purchased in 1935.[180]

Nora, Mellon's mother, was English. During time spent in England he had learned to love the rural tradition of "racing, chasing, and hunting," as well as the history of the Georgian era:

> From childhood and from Cambridge days [as a graduate student] I acquired a fondness for the English landscape and for the ever-changing English light. . . . I became interested in English history, in particular the period from the start of Robert Walpole's ministry to the accession of Queen Victoria, roughly from 1720 to 1840.[181]

Nora Mellon, who had divorced Andrew in 1912, owned an estate in northern Virginia near Upperville named Rokeby Farm. This property is not far from Washington, D.C., where Nora's daughter Ailsa Mellon Bruce was at that time resident. Paul would purchase Rokeby Farm in 1935, and its four hundred acres, which he would eventually expand to 4,500. In this setting he rediscovered the pleasures of English country life. Mellon soon came to value Virginia as both one of the few places in America "where there is . . . any real country, in the English sense, left," and as the "country that I love." Virginia became his adopted home; he moved there permanently in 1937.[182]

Following those colonials who knew the pastoral lifestyle firsthand from their connections with and visits to England, Mellon soon began to spend "a lot of time" in the Virginia countryside. The 1930s was the bicentennial decade of George Washington's birth and 1937 was the first year that John D. Rockefeller, Jr.'s restored Williamsburg attracted significant visitation.[183] Resident in a region that two centuries earlier had been a part of the Fairfax proprietary, and where the first president, a foxhunter, had once reigned, Paul Mellon became a revivalist, who built at Rokeby an appropriate colonial mansion. He engaged New York architect William Adams Delano to design a replica of the Hammond-Harwood house, an imposing Georgian structure that was erected in Annapolis in 1773–74 by William Buckland, an English-born craftsman who George Mason had brought to Virginia to build Gunston Hall. Mellon called his replica the Brick House (fig. 5.52). It was not completed, however, until after the start of World War II. For the next four years the owner would be absent, serving in the United States Army first in the cavalry and then in the Office of Strategic Services (OSS). The Brick House is handsome,

5.52 *William Adams Delano,* The Brick House, *completed 1941, Rokeby Farm, near Upperville, photograph by Heinz Kluetmeier, courtesy of* Sports Illustrated

but Mellon came to think that it "never was a convenient house to run and had the added drawback of noisiness." Following the death of Mary, Mellon's first wife, and his marriage in 1948 to Rachel "Bunny" Lloyd, the Brick House seemed to him a "souvenir of another existence." Mellon quickly built a new residence a quarter of a mile away that "represented my new life with Bunny." Oak Spring is a rambling stone house of a less formal style, more akin to Lord Fairfax's Greenway Court than to the more classical Georgian manor houses of the colonial era. The Brick House would eventually become a museum to house Mellon's English paintings and his library of Virginiana.[184]

Comfortable at Oak Spring, Paul Mellon at mid-century reestablished his life on the land. Once again the scene at Rokeby became bucolic:

> The paddocks and fields near the house are . . . reserved for horses in order that we may have the pleasure of seeing them from the house or when we go for a walk. I don't think there is anyone who enjoys racing more than I do, or the sight of mares and foals grazing in green fields. . . . The sights and sounds of the countryside, as well as the color and action and excitement of the racecourse, are what turn me on.[185]

In the Virginia countryside, the lives of Mellon and his wife and children came to resemble those of the Georgian gentry who are pictured in the English paintings that a decade later he would begin to collect (see page 24, fig. 1.7).

By the early 1950s Paul Mellon was purchasing art, if only because "father's paintings were always around me in my childhood." He first collected French canvases, because "Bunny had always been interested in French history and in French nineteenth-century painting, partly inspired by her lifetime love of gardens and landscape gardening."[186] It was in 1957 that his thoughts were redirected to the colonial history of his adopted state. At that time, to celebrate the three-hundred-and-fiftieth anniversary of the founding of Jamestown, John Fleming, a New York dealer, put together a remarkable collection of early Virginia rare books and manuscripts that he advertised in a catalogue entitled *Virginia's Role in America's History.* Mindful of the significant personages and events that were linked to the landscape that surrounded him, Mellon bought the entire collection. In 1961 Fleming followed with a second grouping of materials that he published as *Virginia and Her Illustrious Sons*; Mellon bought *en bloc* again. He would continue to purchase Virginiana in future years, although on a lesser scale, because in

1959 the collector's interests had been refocused a final time, toward the field of British sporting art. From this point forward Paul Mellon would contribute to the survival of the pastoral ideal in Virginia not only by his own example at Rokeby, but also as a guardian of many tangible representations of that lifestyle.[187]

Mellon recounts in his memoir his pursuit of English sporting paintings. "Apart from buying a beautiful Stubbs of the racehorse Pumpkin and some colorplate sporting books before the war," he writes, "I didn't start collecting British art until I was well into middle age. There had always been something else to do."[188] Part of the impetus for this shift came from the exhibition *Sport and the Horse* that director Leslie Cheek presented at the Virginia Museum of Fine Arts in 1960. Cheek persuaded Mellon, a trustee of the museum since 1938, to serve as chairman of the British and American exhibition committees, which included English nobles and had the patronage of both the president of the United States and the queen of England. Mellon explained, "Leslie believed in going to the top."[189] Basil Taylor of the Royal College of Art in London wrote the catalogue for the exhibition and became Mellon's adviser concerning the acquisition of British art. The purchases followed quickly and *en masse*, partly because the market was so underpriced as to allow for collecting on a large scale. But more than that, the artists of these British paintings were, to Mellon's eye, "committing to canvas their wonder at the splendors of nature and at the beauty of light." Their efforts therefore mirrored the appreciation of nature that he enjoyed first hand at Rokeby Farm. Such pictures, it seemed, warranted preservation. Most of his acquisitions are housed today at the Yale Center for British Art and the Virginia Museum. They constitute what Mellon described in 1960 at the opening of the Virginia show as an "English tree" that had been "transplanted to Virginia soil" and that might "grow new branches, brighter leaves, as times goes on." As a purveyor of taste he added:

> I hope the high qualities of English Art will more and more be enjoyed throughout the Western World and that the pleasure inherent in it, and its beneficent influence, will gradually become better and better known.[190]

For the remaining years of his life, Mellon's "tree" of English culture would continue to flourish in his adopted home state.

The books about Virginia and the English sporting art all fit into Paul Mellon's understanding of what a genteel life should be. Through these volumes and pictures Mellon the collector could imaginatively return to the origins of the American and British pastoral. His effort was to gather records and representations of that life and to save them for posterity. Mustering such objects on an estate in the Virginia countryside fit into his larger scheme of preserving that lifestyle in a setting where it had long existed. Placing them in public museums was a way for their "beneficent influence" to bear fruit. When the authors of the current study set out to find the ways in which Old Virginia had been reimagined, the Rokeby books and paintings helped us to understand the development of early Virginia culture, its evolution over the centuries, and its potential for revivification in the modern world.

A devoted sportsman who for years participated in Virginia's annual "100 Mile Trail Ride," which carries its participants far across the western reaches of the state, Paul Mellon continuously looked for ways to preserve the pastoral setting of rural Virginia. Such feelings came to the surface during his first trips to the region. Mellon early on questioned his father's lack of interest in land preservation: "Why does he think it is foolish for me to own 400 more acres in Virginia?" Over the years Mellon became increasingly active in what he believed would be an essential effort "if we care at all about the sort of world our children and grandchildren will inherit." In 1973 he proudly donated to the Commonwealth of Virginia 1,100 acres of land near his home, which became Sky Meadows State Park. In his memoir Mellon asserted that "the preservation of land in large estates has effectively, so far, prevented the countryside from being ruined through development in spite of its proximity to Washington." He added,

> I have placed most of Rokeby in a permanent land conservation program administered by the Virginia Outdoors Foundation. . . . The dedication of my land to open-space use assures that only compatible uses will be permitted in our beautiful countryside. . . . Many of my closest neighbors [have done] likewise so that our part of Fauquier County will always be protected.[191]

In 1993, however, the plans of these preservationists were disrupted when the entertainment giant Walt Disney Company set out to place an American history theme park at Haymarket, in nearby Prince William County. Popular history, akin to that thoughtfully reimagined by the scholars at Colonial Williamsburg, would in such a venue more obviously replace the real thing. Further, the inspirational value of the landscape itself, and its relationship to the foundational events of Virginia's past would be sacrificed to amusement. Mellon and many of his neighbors rose to the challenge to defeat this new and unexpected threat to the pastoral environment that was being conserved for the gratification of all Americans. So powerful was the opposition that Disney was forced to scuttle the proposal. The success of the new ruralists in

5.53 *Kenneth Garrett,* Oak Hill, Loudoun County, the home of James Monroe, *photographed for Piedmont Environmental Council,* Hallowed Ground, *ca. 1996*

this matter was evidence of their will to preserve what is left of the countryside, as well as their will to perpetuate the traditions of Anglo-American country life.

The victors at Haymarket published a picture book to celebrate the defeat of Disney. *Hallowed Ground* (1996) presents a plethora of stunning photographs that suggest the extraordinary beauty of the Old Virginia Piedmont. The ground is "hallowed," to use the well-known term from the "Gettysburg Address," not only because of the Civil War activity that unfolded there. One must also consider the activities of Virginia's Founding Fathers. Pictured on the cover is James Monroe's Oak Hill in Loudoun County (fig. 5.53), nestled in the shadows like the many eighteenth- and early nineteenth-century buildings that still exist in the Virginia landscape. The hope is that such houses, and such vistas, will continue to be preserved as greater numbers of modern ruralists turn their attentions toward the land and the way of life that it nurtures.

Conclusion

In 1971, the year following Douglas Wilder's protest concerning the lyrics of "Carry Me Back to Old Virginia," Virginius Dabney published an important history of the region. In *Virginia: The New Dominion* Dabney explains that he sought "to describe the events and personalities, both good and bad, that make up the long and exciting Virginia story," and that while "some Virginians are nostalgic at this hour for the *Old* Dominion, and all of us must cherish and revere its virtues," we must today "salute the *New* Dominion, with its challenge and its promise."[1] As a consequence of the industrialization and urbanization of Virginia during the World War II era, and in the wake of the landmark social changes initiated by the Civil Rights movement, the state by 1971 had entered a new age. The time had come to make a conscious break with the past. Dabney asked his readers to move with him beyond the parameters that had long defined Old Virginia. In order to do so, however, one had to renew one's acquaintance with those parameters, which led to the perhaps surprising discovery that there were precepts from the earlier eras that could be still valued in the modern world.

In the present study we have attempted to follow Dabney's lead, to ask our readers to see the totality of Virginia's history, both the high aspirations of the colonial aristocrats that led to the triumph of independence, as well as the troubling history of race relations in the colony and commonwealth that was their concurrent legacy. The hope was that by demystifying Virginia's mytho-historic past we would come to better understand the strong feelings, whether of revulsion or nostalgia, that are often the result of reconsiderations of the state's long history. Today, although the term Old Virginia, no matter how one defines it, is a relic of the past, the idea of Old Virginia continues to survive and alternately to be construed as the basis for the state's either positive or problematic heritage. Old Dominion, on the other hand, has survived as a more morally neutral appellation, and so its antonym was available for Dabney when he wanted first to attend to the past, and then to posit a new beginning for the region. The more precise terms for particular historical periods, such as "colonial," "early national," and "antebellum," would not have been appropriate to this purpose because none describe Virginia's past in its entirety.

Many of the qualities present in the early days of the Old Dominion that Dabney would have his readers recall were tied to the ideal of rural virtue. Worthy attributes such as honor, integrity, gentility, and the ability to lead were born under the "vines and fig trees" of plantation-era Virginia. If we can resist rejecting what was commendable in the state's history because it is conceptually bound to an abomination, then we become free to better comprehend the geographic, climactic, and economic factors that led to the development of Virginia's early society. We thereby are better able to recognize that the visions of many of the patriots at the forefront of the move toward independence and the thinkers who conceived of our enlightened form of government were products of the pastoral landscapes of what would come to be called Old Virginia, as well as of the institution that provided plantation owners with the leisure time necessary to pursue the ideals of the Enlightenment. The Piedmont philosophers were driven not only by a political dream but also by a social vision to perpetuate their agrarian society, so that future, admittedly white, Americans could live in an arcadian environment, which they saw as the antithesis of the corrupt urban settings of eighteenth-century Europe and the growing cities of the northern colonies. As we have depicted the idealism that gave birth to the notion of Old Virginia, and the history that has served at times to support, at times to undermine, that creation, we have argued that the pursuit of rural gentility, with its attendant humanistic concerns, was a crucial factor in the molding of Virginia society.

Early Virginia should not be judged solely on its failings, nor should it be remembered only to insure that its heinous social system never re-emerges. If the comments of Professor Charles Andrews of Yale University to the membership of the Virginia Historical Society in 1931 are correct—"No state can point with greater pride than can Virginia to the ideas and influences that have been woven into the very fabric of our national life and government"[2] —then we must continue to seek out such influences and, when appropriate, to commend the society from which they emerged. The preservation of artifacts, such as those at the Virginia Historical Society, and the conservation of the landscape, to which Paul Mellon and others have contributed, are important in that they remind us that there are aspects of Virginia's past that should be celebrated.

To the public-spirited gentlemen who resolved in 1831 to establish the historical society, the scholar and author George Tucker delivered this charge: "the object of the proposed Society was to collect and preserve material for the Civil and physical history of Virginia." He reminded his audience that "The time would come when our Revolution would be looked at as the most important event [not only] in fixing the destinies of the hundreds of millions who would inhabit the Continent, but also in the influencing of all mankind."[3] The consequences of the Revolution, which could not have occurred without the contributions of the great Virginians of the period, will have repercussions of long duration. To Tucker, any study of that past, even if only the analysis of a rural ideal, will allow us to gain a greater understanding of the present and to effect the events of the future.

The renowned architectural historian Vincent Scully has said that one duty of good doctoral dissertations—and we might add a worthy purpose for any historical study—should be to "bring back great areas of human experience that have been jettisoned. Everything in the past is always waiting, waiting to detonate."[4] There are few areas of American history that have been "jettisoned" as effectively as the day-to-day lives of colonial and antebellum southerners, and if historical moments or events when reconsidered have the potential to be combustible, few topics have the inherent flammability of the Old South in general, or Old Virginia in particular. The recent responses to "Carry Me Back to Old Virginia," to the attempt to re-enact a slave auction at Colonial Williamsburg, and to the recent unfurling of a banner of Robert E. Lee, point to the powerful feelings that still smolder under the surface in many Americans, black and white, who find it difficult to escape the significations tied to any text or image that relates to the antebellum past. Such sentiments are certainly understandable, yet they oversimplify what was a complex culture and deny the existence of any potentially redeeming qualities. Our intention was to follow in the direction set by Virginius Dabney; our hope is that future studies will effectively bring the more worthy aspects of Virginia's history to the attention of the public.

In 2007 the nation will concurrently celebrate the 400th anniversary of the founding of Jamestown and the 200th anniversary of the birth of Robert E. Lee. During the former events, as we commemorate the great figures of the early colony, the highest praise will rightfully be bestowed on a self-promoting, self-congratulatory braggart, who according to his own accounts charmed, manipulated, or killed a number of the Native Americans whom he encountered, and fell out on numerous occasions with the lawful commanders of the expedition. Nevertheless, we now recognize that without the leadership skills, natural abilities, and common sense of Captain John Smith, there would have been no Jamestown founding to celebrate. As to the latter observance, we will commend one of the greatest Virginians, a man who was recognized in his day by friend and foe as a person of honor

and decency, and who maintained an allegiance to a code of behavior that hardly seems possible to modern sensibilities. Yet while Smith's reputation continues to be on the rise, Lee's in recent decades has plummeted. The captain is seen to have been endowed with intelligence, sagacity, charisma, a fighting spirit, and bravery in the face of the enemy, all qualities with which Americans like to identify. The general has taken upon his memory the worst of the Old South, and has been sacrificed in the crucible of its lamented antebellum history as a symbol of the evil that is identified with the cause for which he fought. Smith's rebellious nature seems to look ahead to those patriots who would found a nation; he therefore inspires our admiration. Lee's patriotism for his region, for all of its faults of which he was well aware, seems to look ahead to those who attempted one hundred years later to hold the line against civil rights for all Americans; he therefore inspires in many of us feelings of detestation if not of loathing. The attention that will be paid to the details of their lives in 2007 will no doubt encourage a reassessment of both figures. As scholars have learned more about the always controversial Smith, he has garnered increasing, if at times, grudging respect. It remains to be seen if Lee's reputation will be enhanced or further depreciated by such a reconsideration. The outcome of that attention may tell us much about how we in the early twenty-first century relate our past to our present, and ultimately to our future.

Notes

Abbreviation

VMHB   *Virginia Magazine of History and Biography*

Introduction

1. Emily J. Salmon and Edward D. C. Campbell, Jr., eds., *The Hornbook of Virginia History: A Ready-Reference Guide to the Old Dominion's People, Places, and Past* (Richmond, Va., 1994), 88; John Esten Cooke, "Why Virginia Was Called the 'Old Dominion'" in *Stories of the Old Dominion, From the Settlement to the End of the Revolution* (New York, 1879), 56-64.

2. In George Tucker, *Letters from Virginia, Translated from the French* (Baltimore, 1816), the new gentry in Richmond made up of foreigners is contrasted with "many of the true old Virginia breed" who are "frank, generous, and hospitable" (p. 200). In Tucker's, *Valley of the Shenandoah, or the Memoirs of the Graysons* (New York, 1824) characters lament that only a few of the "old families" are left (I:84); a slave grandmother recalls the grandeur of the colonial era (I:83); and Williamsburg is remembered wistfully ("those days are gone, never more to return!"; II:48-51). In Nathaniel Beverly Tucker, *George Balcombe* (New York, 1836), architecture is described as "old" and past its prime ("a fine old house there, somewhat decayed"), 46.

3. Leo Marx, *The Machine in the Garden: Technology and the Pastoral Ideal in America* (Oxford and New York, 1979 [1964]), 3.

4. Lewis P. Simpson, *The Dispossessed Garden: Pastoral and History in Southern Literature* (Baton Rouge, La., 1983 [1975]), 23.

5. Richard L. Bushman, *The Refinement of America: Persons, Houses, Cities* (New York, 1992), xii.

6. Raymond H. Pulley, "The Old Virginia Mystique and the Progressive Impulse," in *Old Virginia Restored: An Interpretation of the Progressive Influence, 1870-1930* (Charlottesville, Va., 1967) 1-23.

7. Jessie J. Poesch, "Growth and "Development of the Old South: 1830-1900," in Ella-Prince Knox, et al., *Painting in the South: 1564-1980* (Richmond, Va., 1983), 85; Michael David Zellman, *300 Years of American Art* (Secaucus, N.J., 1987), 1:209.

8. Knox et al., *Painting in the South*, 85.

9. Such temporal ambiguity is also evident in Johnson's *Washington's Kitchen at Mount Vernon* (c. 1857, Mount Vernon Ladies' Association), in that is unclear to the viewer whether the scene depicts Washington's time or the present.

10. Stephen Foster, "My Old Kentucky Home" (1853).

11. William Edwin Hemphill, "Endearing Imperfections: James A. Bland and the Virginia State Song," *Virginia Cavalcade* 1 (Spring, 1952), 36-43.

12. The creation of a generic "Old South" glossed over regional differences. The types of lives being led, for instance, in antebellum New Orleans, Charleston, Richmond, and in the new settlements in Alabama and the deep South were in many cases quite different.

13. Hemphill, "Endearing Imperfections," 36-43.

14. *Richmond Times-Dispatch*, 28 Jan. 1994; *Richmond Free Press*, 10 March 1994, 12 March 1994.

15. Geoffrey C. Ward, Ric Burns, and Ken Burns, *The Civil War* (New York, 1990), 228.

16. Robert S. Tilton, *Pocahontas, The Evolution of An American Narrative* (Cambridge and New York, 1994), esp.145-175.

17. Herbert Ravenel Sass, "They Don't Tell the Truth About the South!" *Saturday Evening Post* 226 (9 Jan. 1954): 25, 67-68; Bernard DeVoto, "That Southern Inferiority Complex" *Saturday Evening Post* 226 (16 Jan. 1954): 27, 112-114; Ann Uhry Abrams discusses these alternative founding myths in detail in *The Pilgrims and Pocahontas: Rival Myths of American Origin* (Boulder, Colo., 1999), esp. 221-59.

Chapter I

1. Alan Wallach, "Thomas Cole: Landscape and the Course of American Empire," in William H. Truettner and Alan Wallach, eds., *Thomas Cole: Landscape Into History* (Washington, D.C., 1994), 90-91.

2. Joseph Addison, *The Spectator*, 28 June 1712, 417.

3. Leo Marx, *The Machine in the Garden: Technology and the Pastoral Ideal in America* (Oxford and New York, 1979 [1964]), 19, 23.

4. C. Day Lewis, trans., *The Georgics of Virgil* (Oxford and New York, 1947), ix.

5. John Dixon Hunt and Peter Willis, eds. *The Genius of Place: The English Landscape Garden, 1620-1820* (Cambridge, Mass., 1988 [1975]), 11.

6. Plutarch, quoted in Ehrenfried Kluckert, *European Garden Design: From Classical Antiquity to the Present Day*, ed. Rolf Toman (Cologne, 2000), 17.

7. See J. H. Westcott, *Selected Letters of Pliny* (Norman, Okla., 1965 [1898]), xxi-xxii.

8. Richard D. Brown, "William Byrd II and the Challenge of Rusticity Among the Tidewater Gentry," in *Knowledge Is Power: The Diffusion of Information in Early America, 1700-1865* (New York, 1989), 47; Cato, *De Agri Cultura* in *Marcus Porcius Cato on Agriculture: Marcus Terentius Varro on Agriculture*, trans. William Davis Hooper, rev. Harrison Boyd Ash (Cambridge, Mass., 1936), 3.

9. Kluckert, *European Garden Design*, 176-79. We wish to thank Kenneth Gouwens of the History Department at the University of Connecticut for his guidance on the subject of *Villegiatura*.

10. Olive Cook, *The English Country House: An Art and a Way of Life* (London, 1974), 160.

11. Kluckert, *European Garden Design*, 176.

12. We wish to thank Jack Manning of the English Department at the University of Connecticut for his advice concerning the literary pastoral in the English Renaissance.

13. Howard Mumford Jones, *A Strange New World* (New York, 1964), 238.

14. Marx, *Machine in the Garden*, 39.

15. Hunt and Willis, *Genius of Place*, 12-13.

16. Hunt and Willis, *Genius of Place*, 82.

17. Westcott, *Pliny*, xxii.

18. Cook, *English Country House*, 159.

19. Quoted in Rudy J. Favretti, *Gardens and Landscapes of Virginia* (Little Compton, R.I., 1993), 9.

20. Cook, *English Country House*, 160.

21. Oliver Goldsmith, *The Deserted Village* in *Collected Works of Oliver Goldsmith* (Oxford, 1966), 4:302 (lines 395-398).

22. Goldsmith, *The Deserted Village*, 4:303 (lines 402-406).

23. Richard Payne Knight, fr. *An Analytical Inquiry into the Principles of Taste* (1805), in Hunt and Willis, *Genius of Place*, 350.

24. Lewis, *The Georgics of Virgil*, 43.

25. Cato, *De Agri Cultura*, 3.

26. James C. Kelly and William M. S. Rasmussen, *The Virginia Landscape, A Cultural History* (Charlottesville, Va., 2000), 26.

27. Marx, *Machine in the Garden*, 40 ff.

28. *Genesis* 3:17.

29. Arthur Barlowe (1584), quoted in Marx, *Machine in the Garden*, 37.

30. C. Allan Brown, "Eighteenth-Century Virginia Plantation Gardens: Translating an Ancient Idyll," in Therese O'Malley and Marc Treib, *Regional Garden Design in the United States* (Washington, D.C., 1995), 135.

31. Sydney Ahlstrom, *A Religious History of the American People* (New Haven, 1972), 184.

32. Karen Ordahl Kupperman, *Settling with the Indians: The Meeting of English and Indian Cultures in America, 1580-1640* (Totowa, N.J., 1980), 27.

33. Kupperman, *Settling with the Indians*, 27. See also Perry Miller's well-known essay, "Religion and Society in the Early Literature of Virginia," reprinted in his *Errand Into the Wilderness* (New York, 1956), 99-140.

34. Brown, "Virginia Plantation Gardens," 126.

35. William M. S. Rasmussen and Robert S. Tilton, *George Washington: The Man Behind the Myths* (Charlottesville, Va., and London, 1999), 241-43.

36. Brown, "Virginia Plantation Gardens," 126.

37. See Philip L. Barbour, ed., *The Complete Works of Captain John Smith (1580-1631)* (Chapel Hill, N.C., 1986), 2: 98-99.

38. Emily J. Salmon and Edward D. C. Campbell, Jr., eds., *The Hornbook of Virginia History: A Ready-Reference Guide to the Old Dominion's People, Places, and Past* (Richmond, Va., 1994), 88.

39. Thomas Ludwell to Lord Arlington, 18 July 1666, in W. Noel Sainsbury, ed., *Calendar of State Papers, Colonial Series, America and West Indies, 1661-1668* (London, 1880), 399-401.

40. Jack P. Greene, *Defining Virginia: Studies in the Formation of Identity, 1584-1775* (Richmond, Va., 1996), 31.

41. Edward Waterhouse, *A Declaration of the State of the Colony and Affaires in Virginia* (London, 1622), 12-13; John Oldmixon, *The British Empire in America* (London, 1708), I: 319- 20.

42. Virginia Company Council, *A True Declaration* (1610), cited in Greene, *Defining Virginia*, 13.

43. Greene, *Defining Virginia*, 40.

44. Oldmixon, *British Empire*, 319-20; Robert Beverley, *The History and Present State of Virginia* (London, 1705), 297.

45. King James I, *The Order [banishing rogues to the New Found Lands]* (London, 1603).

46. William Crashaw, *A Sermon Preached in London before the right honorable the Lord Lavvarre, Lord Gouernour and Captaine Generall of Virginia . . .* (London, 1610), cited in Robert F. Strohm et al., *Treasures Revealed from the Paul Mellon Library of Americana* (Charlottesville, Va., 2001), 14.

47. John Donne, *A Sermon Preached to the Honourable Company of the Virginia Plantation. 13 November 1622* (London, 1622), in George R. Potter and Evelyn M. Simpson, eds., *The Sermons of John Donne* (Berkeley, Cal, 1959), 4:272.

48. Peter Linebaugh and Marcus Rediker, *The Many-Headed Hydra: Sailors, Slaves, Commoners, and the Hidden History of the Revolutionary Atlantic* (Boston, 2000), 59.

49. Beverley, *History*; cited in Strohm et al., *Treasures Revealed*, 4.

50. William Bullock, *Virginia Impartially Examined, and Left to Publick View* (London, 1649), 37; cited in Greene, *Defining Virginia*, 37.

51. Henry Hartwell, James Blair, and Edward Chilton, *The Present State of Virginia, and the College* (London, 1697), 3; cited in Greene, *Defining Virginia*, 37-40.

52. Brown, *Knowledge Is Power*, 42.

53. Letters of 18 May 1685 to William Fitzhugh (a nephew in England), 30 Jan. 1686/7 to London friend Nicholas Hayward, 18 May 1685 to cousin William Fitzhugh, and 22 April 1686 to brother Henry Fitzhugh; account of the French traveler Durand, who visited Virginia from September 1686 to March 1687; in Richard Beale Davis, ed., *William Fitzhugh and His Chesapeake World, 1676-1701* (Chapel Hill, N.C., 1963), 169, 201-08, 169-71, 18.

54. Letters of 1 June 1688 and 2 June 1681 to John Cooper and Nicholas Hayward, in Davis, ed., *Fitzhugh*, 244-46, 91.

55. Davis, ed., *Fitzhugh*, 203.

56. Helen Hill Miller, *Colonel Parke of Virginia, "The Greatest Hector in Town"* (Chapel Hill, N.C, 1989), 144-45.

57. Miller, *Parke*, 179-204.

Chapter II

1. Paul Williams, *Vain Prodigal Life*, cited in Jack P. Greene, *Defining Virginia: Studies in the Formation of Identity, 1584-1775* (Richmond, Va., 1996), 34.

2. John Oldmixon, *The British Empire in America* (London, 1708), I: 288-89, cited in Greene, *Defining Virginia*, 61; Greene, *Defining Virginia*, 62; Robert Beverley, *The History and Present State of Virginia* (London, 1705), 287-88, 58, cited in Greene, *Defining Virginia*, 60-61.

3. Wayne Craven, *Colonial American Portraiture: The Economic, Religious, Social, Cultural, Philosophical, Scientific, and Aesthetic Foundations* (Cambridge and New York, 1986).

4. Guthrie Sayen, "'A Compleat Gentleman': The Making of George Washington, 1732-1775" (Ph.D. diss., Univ. of Connecticut, 1998), 3.

5. Richard L. Bushman, *The Refinement of America: Person, Houses, Cities* (New York, 1992), 30.

6. See Francis Makemie, *A Plain and Friendly Perswasive to the Inhabitants of Virginia and Maryland, for Promoting Towns and Cohabitation* (London, 1705) in Robert F. Strohm et al., *Treasures Revealed from the Paul Mellon Library of Americana* (Charlottesville, Va., 2001), 160.

7. G. A. Stiverson and P. H. Butler III, eds., "Virginia in 1732: The Travel Journal of William Hugh Grove," *VMHB* 85 (1977): 18-44; cited in C. Allan Brown, "Eighteenth-Century Virginia Plantation Gardens: Translating an Ancient Idyll," in Therese O'Malley and Marc Treib, *Regional Garden Design in the United States* (Washington, D.C., 1995), 139.

8. Greene, *Defining Virginia*, 64.

9. Richard D. Brown, *Knowledge Is Power: The Diffusion of Information in Early America, 1700-1865* (New York, 1989), 63.

10. Greene, *Defining Virginia*, 73.

11. Hugh Jones, *The Present State of Virginia Giving A particular and short Account of the Indians, English and Negroe Inhabitants of that Colony* (London, 1724), vi, ii; cited in Strohm, *Treasures Revealed*, 204.

12. Jones, *Present State*, 43.

13. Jones, *Present State*, 47.

14. Jones, *Present State*, 48.

15. Jones, *Present State*, 96.

16. Sydney Ahlstrom, *A Religious History of the American People* (New Haven, 1972), 191-92.

17. Virginius Dabney, *Virginia: The New Dominion* (New York, 1971), 97.

18. Samuel S. Hill, Jr., *The South and the North in American Religion* (Athens, Ga., 1980), 4-5; Lewis P. Simpson, *The Dispossessed Garden: Pastoral and History in Southern Literature* (Baton Rouge, La., 1983 [1975]), 15; Brown, *Knowledge Is Power*, 56.

19. For example, the entry in Byrd's diary for 25 April 1719 records that he "spoke to the Duke of Argyll who was very kind to me"; cited in Louis B. Wright and Marion Tinling, eds., *The London Diary (1717-1721) and Other Writings* (New York, 1958).

20. Wright and Tinling, eds., *The London Diary*.

21. Thomas Glover, "Account of Virginia," *Philosophical Transactions*, XI, no. 126 (June, 1676), 623, 635; cited in Greene, *Defining Virginia*, 30.

22. Kenneth A. Lockridge, *The Diary, and Life, of William Byrd II of Virginia, 1674-1744* (Chapel Hill, N.C. and London, 1987), 11.

23. Quoted in Lockbridge, *Byrd*, 27-30.

24. In the small social world of early eighteenth-century London, Byrd had the opportunity to meet two beautiful sisters from the aristocratic Roman Catholic Blount family, Teresa and Martha. Both were friends of Alexander Pope, who was also a Roman Catholic; he had made their acquaintance about 1707. Pope's relationship with Martha is best known and was so intense that contemporaries suspected that the pair might secretly have been married; one family tradition suggests that this portrait depicts Martha Blount. It was, however, the rich curls of Teresa that are said to have inspired *The Rape of the Lock*. We find no mention of either of the Blounts in Byrd's London diary, but this volume covers only four of the years between 1714 and 1726. How well Byrd might have known either of the Blount sisters or Alexander Pope is entirely a matter of speculation, for in the portrait gallery at Westover, beside the portraits of his friends and family, Byrd hung as well likenesses of figures that he only admired from a distance. See Curtis Price and William Rasmussen, "Musical Images in a Portrait of Teresa Blount," *Early Music* (Feb. 1996), 64-76.

25. Quoted in Lockbridge, *Byrd*, 27-30.

26. Byrd to Orrery, 5 July 1726, in Marion Tinling, ed., *The Correspondence of the Three William Byrds of Westover, Virginia, 1684-1776* (Charlottesville, Va., 1977), I: 354-56.

27. Byrd to Orrery, 2 Feb. 1726-27, in Tinling, ed., *Correspondence of the William Byrds*, I: 356-59.

28. Byrd to Orrery, 5 July 1726, in Tinling, ed., *Correspondence of the William Byrds*, I: 354-56.

29. Byrd to Orrery, 20 July 1732, in Tinling, ed., *Correspondence of the William Byrds*, II, 447-48.

30. This survey is titled "A Plan of Westover Including the Land of Mr. Minge and the church Land"; it is bound in the title book of lands owned by William Byrd II. The Minge land came to Byrd in 1701 but the church land was not released to him until 1731 ("William Byrd Title Book," *VMHB* 47 [1939]: 304). In 1735, when Byrd considered selling Westover, he wrote to Peter Beckford (6 Dec.) that he had "got a person to make a draught of [his seat of Westover]": "Many particulars are left out, which could not conveniently be crowded into so small a plan, but the gardens & chief of the buildings are comprehended" (Tinling, ed., *Correspondence of the William Byrds*, II: 464). It is possible that fig. 2.6 is a copy of or is in someway related to that plan.

31. Brown, *Knowledge Is Power*, 55; Simpson, *The Dispossessed Garden*, 23-24.

32. Maria Byrd married Landon Carter in 1742 at age fifteen and produced a daughter before her premature death in 1745.

33. Jack P. Greene, ed., *The Diary of Colonel Landon Carter of Sabine Hall, 1752-1778* (Charlottesville, Va., 1965), 4-5.

34. Greene, *Landon Carter*, 59.

35. Greene, *Landon Carter*, 9.

36. Greene, *Landon Carter*, 10.

37. Greene, *Landon Carter*, 20-21.

38. James Gibbs, *A Book of Architecture* (London, 1728), plate 58.

39. Gibbs, *Architecture*, Introduction, i.

40. Bushman, *The Refinement of America*, 113-14; Brown, *Knowledge Is Power*, 49-51.

41. Greene, *Defining Virginia*, 76-83.

42. William M. S. Rasmussen and Robert S. Tilton, *George Washington: The Man Behind the Myths* (Charlottesville, Va., and London, 1999), esp. chapters 1-4.

43. See Bertram Wyatt-Brown, *Southern Honor: Ethics and Behavior in the Old South* (New York, 1982).

44. "An American," *Virginia Gazette* (Purdie & Dixon), 21 Nov. 1771; cited in Greene, *Defining Virginia*, 83.

45. [Arthur Lee], *An Essay in Vindication of the Continental Colonies of America* (London, 1764), iii, 20-23, 30; cited in Greene, *Defining Virginia*, 86.

46. Richard W. Stephenson and Marianne M. McKee, eds., *Virginia in Maps, Four Centuries of Settlement, Growth, and Development* (Richmond, Va., 2000), 83.

47. See *The Case of the Separate Traders to Africa with Remarks on the African Company's Memorial* (London, 1709) in Strohm, *Treasures Revealed*, 164.

48. Slavery would not be abolished in the British Empire until 1833.

49. "Brutus" to Printer, *Virginia Gazette* (Rind), 1 June 1769; cited in Greene, *Defining Virginia*, 100.

50. Franklin's marginalia in Israel Mauduit, *A Short View . . .* (London, 1769), in Leonard W. Labaree et al., eds., *The Papers of Benjamin Franklin* (New Haven, Conn., 1959–), XVI: 296-97; cited in Greene, *Defining Virginia*, 99.

51. Greene, *Defining Virginia*, 99.

52. Jones, *Present State*, 75-76, 130; Samuel Jenner, *Newly Discovered Eden*, 9; Peter to Moses Fontaine, 30 March 1757, in Ann Maury, ed., *Memoirs of a Huguenot Family* (New York, 1907), 352; all cited in Greene, *Defining Virginia*, 94-95.

53. Jones, *Present State*, 75; Lee, *Essay*, v, 11-13, 15; cited in Greene, *Defining Virginia*, 96.

54. "Associator Humanus," *Virginia Gazette* (Purdie & Dixon), 11 July 1771; Richard K. MacMaster, ed., "Arthur Lee's 'Address on Slavery': An Aspect of Virginia's Struggle to End the Slave Trade, 1765-1774," *VMHB* 70 (1972): 153-57; [Lee], *Essay*, 39-43; Amelia Mott Gummere, ed., *The Journal of John Woolman* (New York, 1922), 167; Peter to Moses Fontaine, 30 March 1757, in Maury, ed., *Huguenot Family*, 352; all cited in Greene, *Defining Virginia*, 97-98.

55. See Virginia House of Burgesses, *Petition to King George III* (1772) in Strohm, *Treasures Revealed*, 168.

56. See Pauline Maier, *American Scripture: Making the Declaration of Independence* (New York, 1997), 239.

57. Virginia Legislature to the Crown, 18 May 1769, in William J. Van Schreeven, comp., and Robert L. Scribner, ed., *Revolutionary Virginia: The Road to Independence*, 7 vols. (Charlottesville, Va., 1973-83), I: 75; cited in Greene, *Defining Virginia*, 100.

58. Rasmussen and Tilton, *George Washington*, 114-27, 174-78.

59. In at least two of Sir Joshua Reynolds's portraits of the 1760s a black manservant is similarly portrayed. These are "Frederick, Count of Schaumburg-Lippe," c. 1764-67, and "John Manners, Marquess of Granby," 1766; See John Caldwell and Oswaldo Rodriguez Roque, *American Paintings in the Metropolitan Museum of Art* (New York, 1994), I: 201.

60. It is suggested by Caldwell and Roque that the background is possibly meant to show West Point, a fort that was never actually attacked.

61. Rasmussen and Tilton, *George Washington*, 128.

62. Washington to John Augustine Washington, 6 - 19 Nov. 1776, in Dorothy Twohig, ed., *The Papers of George Washington, Revolutionary War Series*, 7 vols. (Charlottesville, Va., 1985–), VII: 102-6.

63. Rasmussen and Tilton, *George Washington*, 128-29.

64. Rasmussen and Tilton, *George Washington*, 155.

65. Rasmussen and Tilton, *George Washington*, 202-3.

66. *Virginia Gazette*, 14 Sept. 1769.

67. Thomas Jefferson, *Notes on the State of Virginia*, ed. Thomas Perkins Abernethy (New York, 1964), Query XVIII, 155.

68. Jefferson, *Notes*, ed. Abernethy, Query XVIII, 155-56.

69. Robert A. Rutland, ed., *The Papers of George Mason, 1725-1792*, 3 vols. (Chapel Hill, N.C., 1970), I: 147-60; Helen Hill, "George Mason," *Dictionary of American Biography*, ed. Dumas Malone (New York, 1933), XII: 361-64.

70. Joseph J. Ellis, *Founding Brothers: The Revolutionary Gen*

eration (New York, 2000), 96.

71. Cynthia A. Kierner, "'The Dark and Dense Cloud Perpetually Lowering Over Us': Gender and the Decline of the Gentry in Postrevolutionary Virginia." *Journal of the Early Republic* 20 (Summer, 2000), 185-86.

72. Charles J. Farmer, "Persistence of Country Trade: The Failure of Towns to Develop in Southside Virginia During the Eighteenth Century." *Journal of Historical Geography* 14 (Oct. 1988): 331-41.

73. Rasmussen and Tilton, *George Washington*, 105-9.

74. Kierner, "Decline of the Gentry," 187.

75. William Byrd III to Ralph Wormeley V, 4 Oct. 1775, Virginia Historical Society.

76. Louis Morton, *Robert Carter of Nomini Hall* (Williamsburg, Va., 1945), 35.

77. Rasmussen and Tilton, *George Washington*, 28.

78. See David Hackett Fischer and James C. Kelly, *Away, I'm Bound Away: Virginia and the Westward Movement* (Richmond, Va., 1993).

79. Alexander Cluny, *The American Traveller: or, Observations on the Present State, Culture and Commerce of the British Colonies in America* (London, 1769), 86.

80. Edward C. Carter II, John C. Van Horne, and Charles E. Brownell, eds., *Latrobe's View of America, 1795-1820, Selections from the Watercolors and Sketches* (New Haven, Conn. and London, 1985), 130.

81. Isaac Weld, Jr., *Travels Through the States of North America, and the Provinces of Upper and Lower Canada, During the Years 1795, 1796, and 1797* (London, 1799), 109; cited in Carter, Van Horne, and Brownell, eds., *Latrobe's View of America*, 130.

82. Brown, *Knowledge Is Power*, 58.

83. Close examination of the actual painting reveals that the painted flag has the stars and stripes of the American flag, but much of it is rendered in the same mustard color as the nearby buildings. The stripes alternate white and yellow (not red), and the stars are brick (like the flagpole) on a yellow field (not blue). The artist apparently simplified his task by limiting his palette.

Chapter III

1. Milbert copied the 1808 aquatint by William Roberts. See James C. Kelly and William M. S. Rasmussen, *The Virginia Landscape, A Cultural History* (Charlottesville, Va., 2000), 11-13.

2. Sutton, "Nostalgia, Pessimism, and Malaise, The Doomed Aristocrat in Late-Jefferson Virginia," *VMHB* 76 (1968): 42.

3. William Davis produced the finished drawing of the Bishop Madison map and Frederick Bossler, an immigrant from Switzerland, engraved Davis's drawing.

4. Mason Locke Weems, *The Life of Washington*, ed. Marcus Cunliffe (Cambridge, Mass., 1962), 4-5.

5. William Wirt, *Sketches of the Life and Character of Patrick Henry* (Philadelphia, 1817), I: 261; cited in Sutton, "Nostalgia, Pessimism, and Malaise," 45.

6. Dumas Malone, "John Randolph," *Dictionary of American Biography*, ed. Dumas Malone (New York, 1935), XV: 366-67.

7. Henry Adams, *History of the United States of America* (New York, 1890), I: 157.

8. *Proceedings and Debates of the Virginia State Convention of 1829-30* (Richmond, 1830), 320.

9. *Convention of 1829-30*, 404-5; cited in David Hackett Fischer and James C. Kelly, *Away, I'm Bound Away, Virginia and the Westward Movement* (Richmond, Va., 1993), 198.

10. *Convention of 1829-30*, 313-15; cited in Fischer and Kelly, *Bound Away*, 198.

11. *Convention of 1829-30*, 321.

12. Hugh A. Garland, *The Life of John Randolph of Roanoke*, 2 vols. (New York and Philadelphia, 1850), II:15; cited in Fischer and Kelly, *Bound Away*, 84.

13. Fischer and Kelly, *Bound Away*, 66, 83-87.

14. Quoted in Fischer and Kelly, *Bound Away*, 84.

15. 16 Oct. 1827 to John Randolph, University of Virginia, cited in Sutton, "Nostalgia, Pessimism, and Malaise," 42.

16. Quoted in Fischer and Kelly, *Bound Away*, 87.

17. Fischer and Kelly, *Bound Away*, 86-87.

18. John Taylor, *Tyranny Unmasked*, ed. F. Thornton Miller (Indianapolis, 1992), x. Agrarian republicanism was sometimes called "Country" republicanism.

19. George Tucker, *Valley of the Shenandoah or the Memoirs of the Graysons* (New York, 1824), II: 30, 32.

20. Bryan Clark Green, Calder Loth, and William M. S. Rasmussen, *Lost Virginia: Vanished Architecture of the Old Dominion* (Charlottesville, Va., 2001), 11.

21. Melvin I. Urofsky, *The Levy Family and Monticello, 1834-1923: Saving Thomas Jefferson's House* (Charlottesville, Va., 2001), 41-42.

22. Notice for the sale of Monticello, *Richmond Enquirer*, 22 July 1828; pictured in Urofsky, *Monticello*, 41.

23. Newspaper clipping from the Elkhorn, Wisconsin *Independent*, 14 June 1956, reprint of an 1856 account; library, Mount Vernon Ladies' Association.

24. Published in the Rochester *North Star*, 3 Aug. 1849; library, Mount Vernon Ladies' Association.

25. Joan E. Cashin, "Landscape and Memory in Antebellum Virginia," *VMHB* 102 (Oct. 1994): 491.

26. Cashin, "Landscape and Memory," 480-81, 498.

27. This landmark had become internationally famous after the publication in 1803 of the poem "The Lake of the Dismal Swamp" by the Irish bard Thomas Moore.

28. Kelly and Rasmussen, *Virginia Landscape*, 80-82.

29. [Nathaniel] Beverley Tucker, *The Partisan Leader, A Tale of the Future* (Washington, D.C., 1836), cited in Sutton, "Nostalgia, Pessimism, and Malaise," 45.

30. Tyler was seemingly destined to be a national leader. His father, a judge and governor of Virginia, had raised his son in the circle of Jefferson and Madison; the latter was the father's college friend. A talent for oratory had carried the young lawyer to Congress, to the governor's mansion, and to the Senate, before his inclusion on the ticket and succession to the presidency. By refusing to modify the Jeffersonian states' rights principles of the 1790s in an era changed by the growth of industry and the expansion of slavery, and almost despite his successes in foreign affairs (particularly in the annexation of Texas), Tyler did little to reverse Virginia's political decline on the national stage. Although another Virginian, General Zachary Taylor, would soon, briefly, occupy the White House, the Old Dominion would never again rise to the political heights that it had experienced during the colonial and early national eras.

31. Michael Chevalier, *Society, Manners and Politics in the United States: Being A Series of Letters on North America* (Boston, 1839), 327.

32. Brissot de Warville, J. P., *New Travels in the United States of America. Performed in 1788* (Boston, 1797), 159.

33. James Kirke Paulding, *Letters from the South, Written during an Excursion in the Summer of 1816* (New York, 1817), I: 97.

34. Virginius Dabney, *Virginia: The New Dominion* (New York, 1971), 241.

35. Dabney, *New Dominion*, 241.

36. Lieutenant Francis Hall, *Travels in Canada and the United States, in 1816 and 1817* (London, 1818), 357.

37. Frances Trollope, *Domestic Manners of the Americans* (New York, 1832), 247.

38. Brissot de Warville, *Travels*, 159.

39. Charles Dickens, *American Notes for General Circulation* (London, 1842), 158.

40. Dickens, *American Notes*, 160.

41. Dickens, *American Notes*, 160.

42. Tucker, *Valley of the Shenandoah*, II: 206-7.

43. Tucker, *Valley of the Shenandoah*, II: 194, 211.

44. Dickens, *American Notes*, 158.

45. Some scholars feel that the importance of this network has been exaggerated. Only a thousand of three million slaves in America at mid-century were in fact fugitives. See Dabney, *New Dominion*, 242.

46. Harriet Martineau, *Retrospect of Western Travel* (London, 1838), 105.

47. According to Virginius Dabney, in the period between independence and the end of the Civil War, only 56 masters, 11 mistresses, and 7 overseers in Virginia had been murdered by their slaves (*New Dominion*, 243).

48. Dabney, *New Dominion*, 224.

49. Martineau, *Western Travel*, 327.

50. Marquis de Chastellux, *Travels in North America in the Years 1780, 1781 and 1782*, 1963 reprint of 1786 ed., 439.

51. Martineau, *Western Travel*, 75-76.

52. George Tucker, *Letters from Virginia, Translated from the French* (Baltimore, 1816), 30-34.

53. Tucker, *Valley of the Shenandoah*, I: 61-63.

54. Tucker, *Valley of the Shenandoah*, I: 61.

55. Martineau, *Western Travel*, 75.

56. Dabney, *New Dominion*, 226-27.

57. James Fenimore Cooper, *Notions of the Americans: Picked Up by a Travelling Bachelor* (Philadelphia, 1838), 261.

58. Thomas R. Dew, *Review of the Debate in the Virginia Legislature, 1831–'32*, republished in *The Pro-Slavery Argument, as Maintained by the Most Distinguished Writers of the Southern States* (Philadelphia, 1853); cited in Dabney, *New Dominion*, 228.

59. William Gilmore Simms, *The Morals of Slavery*, republished in *The Pro-Slavery Argument*, 263, 271, 274.

60. Simms, *Slavery*, 266, 265.

61. Tucker, *Valley of the Shenandoah*, I: 63.

62. Frederick Douglass, *Narrative of the Life of Frederick Douglass, an American Slave* (Cambridge, Mass.), 1967 reprint of 1845 ed., 153.

63. Harriet Beecher Stowe, *Uncle Tom's Cabin; Or, Life Among the Lowly* (Boston and New York), 1889 reprint of 1852 ed., iv, 493-94.

64. Ibid.

65. Thomas Nelson Page, *Social Life in Old Virginia before the War* (New York, 1897), Introduction, 2.

66. Mary H. Eastman, *Aunt Phillis's Cabin* (Philadelphia, 1852), 11, 22.

67. Eastman, *Aunt Phillis's Cabin*, 271, 280.

68. John Pendleton Kennedy, *Swallow Barn, or A Sojourn in the Old Dominion* (New York), 1962 reprint of 1853 ed., 71, 35.

69. Kennedy, *Swallow Barn*, xvi.

70. Kennedy, *Swallow Barn*, xxii-xxiii.

71. So radical a view was not exclusively the purview of the old school Virginia planter. In these same years, as we saw in Chapter I, the New York artist Thomas Cole expressed the fear of many Americans that when a civilization rejects the pastoral lifestyle for urban decadence—whether by choice or through the inevitable evolution of society—the collapse of that culture is imminent. Cole would have his viewers remember that history is replete with examples of this lesson, which was worth remembering as the new nation began to exhibit its own empiric tendencies.

72. Richard N. Current, *Northernizing the South* (Athens, Ga., 1983), 42. Current quotes Charles G. Sellers, ed., *The Southerner as American* (Chapel Hill, N. C., 1960), viii.

73. Tucker, *Letters from Virginia*, 200.

74. Kennedy, *Swallow Barn*, 34.

75. Brissot de Warville, *New Travels*, 246.

76. Chevalier, *Society, Manners and Politics*, 326.

77. Green, Loth, and Rasmussen, *Lost Virginia*, 175.

78. Kennedy, *Swallow Barn*, 8-9.

79. Dabney, *New Dominion*, 281.

80. "Trip to Richmond—Old Virginia," *New York Express*, re-printed in the *Staunton [Virginia] Spectator and General Adviser*, 25 March 1841, 1; Dabney, *New Dominion*, 282.

81. Dabney, *New Dominion*, 283.

82. "Trip to Richmond—Old Virginia," *New York Express*, 1.

83. William M. S. Rasmussen and Robert S. Tilton, *George Washington: The Man Behind the Myths* (Charlottesville, Va., and London, 1999), 103.

84. Dabney, *New Dominion*, 215.

85. Dabney, *New Dominion*, 221.

86. Tucker, *Valley of the Shenandoah*, I: 47-49, 54-55.

87. In *Away, I'm Bound Away: Virginia and the Westward Movement*, David Hackett Fischer and James C. Kelly identify aspects of this way of life, including the architecture (the cabin of earth, stone, brush, or wood), the distinct English dialect (which survives today as "the speech of country and western singers, cinematic cowboys, and backcountry politicians"), the food ways (a spartan diet of food prepared by "pot boiling and hearth baking"), and the social structuring around the clan ("mutually supportive nuclear households sharing a common name"). They add that among the codes of the clan were the rules of retribution ("a system of *lex talionis*"), personal loyalty, and personal freedom ("a man's natural right to be let alone, with plenty of elbow room and as little government as possible") (54-55, 155-57).

88. Fischer and Kelly, *Bound Away*, 52-53, 153.

89. Fischer and Kelly, *Bound Away*, 54, 155.

90. Kennedy, *Swallow Barn*, 8-9.

91. Henry Wadsworth Longfellow, "The Village Blacksmith" (1841).

92. Charles H. Bohner, "*Swallow Barn*: John P. Kennedy's Chronicle of Virginia Society," *VMHB* 68 (1960): 320.

93. Chevalier, *Society, Manners and Politics*, 119, 385-86, 406, 414, 420.

94. Chevalier, *Society, Manners and Politics*, 115-16.

95. Chevalier, *Society, Manners and Politics*, 114.

96. Francis J. Grund, *Aristocracy in America. From the Sketch-Book of a German Nobleman* (London, 1839), 15, 16, 19, 24-27.

97. Dickens, *American Notes*, 271.

98. Chastellux, *Travels*, 434-35.

99. Trollope, *Domestic Manners*, 37.

100. Cooper, *Notions of the Americans*, 293.

101. Chastellux, *Travels*, 435; Luigi Castiglioni, *Viaggio (Travels in the United States of North America, 1785-87)* (Syracuse, N.Y.), 1983 reprint of 1790 ed., 194-95.

102. Hall, *Travels*, 392.

103. Brissot de Warville, *New Travels*, 155, 252.

104. Tucker, *Valley of the Shenandoah*, I: 70.

105. Lewis P. Simpson, *The Dispossessed Garden: Pastoral and History in Southern Literature* (Baton Rouge, La., 1983 [1975]), 43, 51.

106. Tucker, *The Partisan Leader*, 9, 391.

107. Kennedy, *Swallow Barn*, 34-35.

108. That void had been defined by William Fitzhugh in the seventeenth century, when he complained of the "want of spiritual help & comforts" in the rural parishes, due to the distances that were an inherent part of country living (Rasmussen and Tilton, *George Washington*, 3).

109. Bertram Wyatt-Brown, *Southern Honor: Ethics and Behavior in the Old South* (New York, 1982), xvii, vii, 61, 114. Wyatt-Brown also notes that beginning in the Jeffersonian era, as the number of southern whites who were evangelized by the revival movements increased, the code of honor declined, at least among the middling ranks and the poor.

110. On dueling in literature see Bradley Johnson, "A Succinct and Formal Violence: The Function of the Duel in Southern Literature, 1825-1950" (Ph.D. diss., Univ. of Connecticut, 2000.)

111. Kennedy, *Swallow Barn*, 34.

112. Kennedy, *Swallow Barn*, 452-55.

113. Kennedy, *Swallow Barn*, 457-58.

114. Simpson, *The Dispossessed Garden*, 43, 51.

115. Kennedy, *Swallow Barn*, xxiv.

116. Robert P. Hilldrup, *Upper Brandon* (Richmond, Va., 1987), 53.

117. Cecil D. Eby, Jr., "Porte Crayon in the Tidewater," *VMHB* 67 (1959): 438-49.

118. Hilldrup, *Upper Brandon*, 41-43, 63, 74.

119. Hilldrup, *Upper Brandon*, 54-57.

120. Joseph Hadfield, *An Englishman in America, 1785*, ed. Douglas S. Robertson (Toronto, 1933), 8.

121. Evelyn L. Pugh, "Women and Slavery, Julia Gardiner Tyler and the Duchess of Sutherland," *VMHB* 88 (1980): 186.

122. Virginia Cary, *Letters on Female Character* (Richmond, Va., 1838), 172-73.

123. Pugh, "Women and Slavery," 186-202.

124. Pugh, "Women and Slavery," 200.

125. For a discussion of courtesy books, see Wayne Craven, *Colonial American Portraiture: The Economic, Religious, Social, Cultural, Philosophical, Scientific, and Aesthetic Foundations* (Cambridge and New York, 1986).

126. Pugh, "Women and Slavery," 187.

127. Cary, *Female Character*, vi.

128. Maury Klein, *Days of Defiance, Sumter, Secession, and the Coming of the Civil War* (New York, 1999), 65.

129. Kennedy, *Swallow Barn*, 228-37, 362-68.

130. Brissot de Warville, *New Travels*, 246.

131. Alexander Mackay-Smith, *The Race-Horses of America, 1832-1872, Portraits and Other Paintings by Edward Troye* (Saratoga Springs, N.Y., 1981), 29.

132. Kennedy, *Swallow Barn*, 36, 437-45.

133. Douglas Southall Freeman, *R. E. Lee, A Biography* (New York and London, 1934-35), IV: 495.

134. A classic example is David Meade who in 1798 moved from the James River to Kentucky, where he established a Virginia-style plantation. "Chaumiere des Prairies" in Jasamine County was distinguished as much for its forty-acre gardens as for the entertainments supported by Meade's staff of household slaves. See *Bound Away*, 113, 117.

135. Chevalier, *Society, Manners and Politics*, 110.

136. Paulding, *Letters*, I: 92.

137. Cited in Kelly and Rasmussen, *Virginia Landscape*, 158.

138. Ibid.

139. Brissot de Warville, *New Travels*, 159.

140. Daniel W. Crofts, "Late Antebellum Virginia Reconsidered," *VMHB* 107 (1999): 260.

141. In a preliminary sketch now at Indiana University the scene seems even more desolate because the wagon and figures, which were clearly an afterthought, are absent from the empty road. Though nearly invisible here, a large slave population remained in the Tidewater; in 1832 some 476,000 African Americans were in bondage in the east, while there were only 53,000 slaves in the western counties. See Bishop Davenport, *A New Gazetteer, or Geographical Dictionary, of North America and the West Indies* (Baltimore, 1832), 91-93.

142. Crofts, "Late Antebellum Virginia," 254.

143. Of course, no such market towns had existed in colonial Virginia because Britain had then provided the market. However, they would be necessary if the old ways were to survive in the post-colonial period, especially in areas west of easy access to the Tidewater network of rivers that provided cheap transportation.

144. Kennedy, *Swallow Barn*, 34.

145. Castiglioni, *Travels*, 186, 190.

146. Paulding, *Letters*, II: 163-74.

147. W. Williams, *Appleton's Railroad and Steamboat Companion* (New York, 1849), 286.

148. T. Addison Richards, *Appleton's Illustrated Hand-Book of American Travel* (New York, 1857), 222.

149. Paulding, *Letters*, II: 189.

150. Richards, *Appleton's Illustrated Hand-Book*, 232; Williams, *Appleton's Railroad and Steamboat Companion*, 286.

151. Notes to *Album of Virginia*, cited in Kelly and Rasmussen, *Virginia Landscape*, 65.

152. Rasmussen and Tilton, *George Washington*, 261-62.

153. Weems, *Washington*, ed. Cunliffe, 1.

154. John Marshall, *The Life of George Washington* (Philadelphia, 1804-07), Preface, iii, iv, xi.

155. George Washington had no children of his own.

156. See *Eulogy for Patrick Henry*, by an unidentified hand, c. 1799, manuscript, Lee Family Papers, Virginia Historical Society.

157. William Wirt, *Sketches of the Life and Character of Patrick Henry* (New York), 1903 reprint of 1817 ed., 434.

158. Tucker, *Letters from Virginia*, 149-52.

159. Kennedy, *Swallow Barn*, 16-17.

160. William M. S. Rasmussen and Robert S. Tilton, *Pocahontas: Her Life and Legend* (Richmond, Va., 1994), 18-21.

161. William Makepeace Thackeray, *The Virginians; A Tale of the Last Century* (London, 1857-59), I: 2.

162. "Historical Society," *Richmond Whig*, 7 July 1846.

Chapter IV

1. Douglas Southall Freeman, "Robert Edward Lee," *Dictionary of American Biography*, ed. Dumas Malone (New York, 1933), XI: 128.

2. Freeman, "Robert Edward Lee," 121.

3. Douglas Southall Freeman, *R. E. Lee, A Biography* (New York and London, 1934-35), I: 371.

4. Freeman, *Lee*, I: 372.

5. Freeman, *Lee*, I: 372-73.

6. Freeman, *Lee*, I: 373.

7. Bertram Wyatt-Brown, *The Shaping of Southern Culture: Honor, Grace, and War, 1760s-1890s* (Chapel Hill, N.C., 2001), xvii.

8. Lee offered the same explanation regarding his decision to accept the Virginia command in letters of April 20. He wrote to his commander Winfield Scott, "Save in defence of my native State, I never desire again to draw my sword." He wrote to his sister Mrs. Marshall: "I have not been able to make up my mind to raise my hand against my relatives, my children, my home. I have therefore resigned my commission in the Army, and save in defence of my native state, with the sincere hope that my poor services may never be needed, I hope I may never be called on to draw my sword." He wrote to his brother Smith: "I am now a private citizen, and have no other ambition than to remain at home. Save in defence of my native state, I have no desire ever again to draw my sword" (Freeman, *Lee*, I: 441-44).

9. *Journal of the Virginia Convention of 1861*, 186-88; cited in Freeman, *Lee*, I: 466-67.

10. Freeman, "Robert Edward Lee," 121-22.

11. Freeman, *Lee*, I: 469.

12. Freeman, *Lee*, I: viii; George William Bagby, *The Old Virginia Gentleman* (Richmond, Va.?, 1877), 20.

13. Freeman, *Lee*, IV: 505; David J. Eicher, *Robert E. Lee, A Life Portrait* (Dallas, Tex., 1997), 15.

14. Thomas L. Connelly, *The Marble Man: Robert E. Lee and His Image in American Society* (New York, 1977), 3.

15. Freeman, *Lee*, I: viii.

16. Ibid.

17. John Esten Cooke, *Surry of Eagle's-Nest; or, The Memoirs of a Staff-Officer Serving in Virginia* (New York, 1866), 241.

18. Connelly, *Marble Man*, 3.

19. Freeman, "Robert Edward Lee," 128; Emory M. Thomas, *Robert E. Lee—A Biography* (New York, 1995), 20.

20. Freeman, *Lee*, IV: 494, 496, 498-500.

21. Freeman, *Lee*, IV: 503.

22. Freeman, *Lee*, IV: 504-5.

23. Freeman, *Lee*, IV: 494.

24. Connelly, *Marble Man*, xiv-xv.

25. Thomas, *Lee*, 14.

26. Thomas, *Lee*, 18-20. Franklin Delano Roosevelt was similarly described.

27. Geoffrey C. Ward, Ric Burns, and Ken Burns, *The Civil War* (New York, 1990), 284-85.

28. Craig Timberg, "Lee's Portrait Opens Wounds in Richmond," *Washington Post*, 4 June 1999, B-1; Timberg, "Richmond is Seeking Civil Solution," *Washington Post*, 17 June 1999, B-4.

29. *Richmond Times-Dispatch*, 14 June 1999.

30. "City Council Supports Mural of Lee on Floodwall," *Richmond Times-Dispatch*, 27 July 1999, A-3.

31. *Washington Post*, 17 June 1999, B-4.

32. Bagby, *Old Virginia Gentleman*, 20.

33. James Lindgren, *Preserving the Old Dominion, Historic Preservation and Virginia Traditionalism* (Charlottesville, Va. and London, 1993), 1-12.

34. Quoted in Michael P. Branch and Daniel J. Philippon, eds., *The Height of Our Mountains: Nature Writing from Virginia's Blue Ridge Mountains and Shenandoah Valley* (Baltimore and London, 1998), 189.

35. Henry Chester Parry to his parents, 29 Dec. 1864, Virginia Historical Society; cited in James C. Kelly and William M. S. Rasmussen, *The Virginia Landscape, A Cultural History* (Charlottesville, Va., 2000), 138.

36. A third White House, a Gothic Revival structure designed by Richmond architect Albert L. West and built after the Civil War, burned in 1880. See Bryan Clark Green, Calder Loth, and William M. S. Rasmussen, *Lost Virginia: Vanished Architecture of the Old Dominion* (Charlottesville, Va., 2001), 46.

37. Robert Knox Sneden, *Eye of the Storm: A Civil War Odyssey*, ed. Charles F. Bryan, Jr., and Nelson D. Lankford (New York, 2000), 65.

38. Sneden, *Eye of the Storm*, 109.

39. Sneden, *Eye of the Storm*, 104-6.

40. E. L. Henry to Edward V. Valentine, 21 Sept. 1870, Valentine Museum; cited in Kelly and Rasmussen, *Virginia Landscape*, 139.

41. See Green, Loth, and Rasmussen, *Lost Virginia*, where the architecture and history of the house are discussed.

42. Captain George A. Armes, *List of Knights to Participate in a Tournament*, to be held 5 Sept. 1865 at Fairfax Court House, Virginia, Virginia Historical Society, bequest of Paul Mellon.

43. "Address to the Knights, by Hon. Philip Oglestifer," broadside, Virginia Historical Society.

44. A. Lawrence Kocher and Howard Dearstyne, *Shadows in Silver: A Record of Virginia, 1850-1900, In Contemporary Photographs Taken by George and Huestis Cook, With Additions from the Cook Collection* (New York, 1954), 174.

45. "Notice of New Books," c. 1866, *American Memory, Library of Congress, The Nineteenth Century in Print*, @ memory.loc.gov, 11 April 2002.

46. Cooke, *Surry of Eagle's-Nest*, 1.

47. Cooke, *Surry of Eagle's-Nest*, 164-65.

48. Cooke, *Surry of Eagle's-Nest*, 203-4, 217, 222.

49. Cooke, *Surry of Eagle's-Nest*, 82-83.

50. Harry of Navarre was Henry IV, the first Bourbon king, who in the late sixteenth century brought an end to forty years of religious civil wars that had devastated France. Because he granted religious freedom to Huguenots, Henry was a sectional hero in a country that was predominantly Roman Catholic. Prince Rupert of Prague, also known as "Prince Rupert of the Rhine," was a nephew of Charles I and a Royalist general. If he failed to save his uncle's throne and life, he was nonetheless a brilliant cavalry leader during the English Civil War. By mentioning Harry of Navarre and Prince Rupert, Cooke imagined that the reputation of J. E. B. Stuart would rise to match that of other gallant figures in history who had supported a noble cause against formidable odds.

51. William M. S. Rasmussen, "Making the Confederate Murals, Studies by Charles Hoffbauer," *VMHB* 101 (1993): 433-56.

52. Douglas Southall Freeman, "James Ewell Brown Stuart," *Dictionary of American Biography*, ed. Dumas Malone (New York, 1936), XVIII: 172.

53. Thomas Cooper De Leon, *Belles, Beaux, and Brains of the Sixties* (New York, 1909), 284-92.

54. A Philadelphian, Charles P. Tholey, would cater further to the southern audience the next year when he produced a lithograph that depicts George Washington and friends hunting at Mount Vernon.

55. Cooke, *Surry of Eagle's-Nest*, 459.

56. Cooke, *Surry of Eagle's-Nest*, 483.

57. Thomas Campbell, "Lochiel's Warning," *Clan Cameron Archives* @ lochiel.net/archives/arch065.html, 16 April 2002.

58. Thomas Nelson Page, *Red Rock, A Chronicle of Reconstruction* (New York, 1899), viii.

59. Page, *Red Rock*, vii, 228, 232, 235.

60. Page, *Red Rock*, 237-38.

61. Page, *Red Rock*, 239.

62. Page, *Red Rock*, 352; see also 407.

63. [Alex Rivington,] *Reminiscences of America in 1869 by Two Englishmen* (London, 1870), 42.

64. C. B. Berry, *The Other Side, How It Struck Us* (London and New York, 1880), 92-93.

65. Edward King, *The Great South* (Baton Rouge, La.), 1972 reprint of 1874 ed., 638. For progressivism, see Raymond H. Pulley, *Old Virginia Restored: An Interpretation of the Progressive Influence, 1870-1930* (Charlottesville, Va., 1967).

66. Thomas Nelson Page, *Social Life in Old Virginia Before the War* (New York, 1897), Introduction, 1.

67. In 1862, when Union forces occupied the region, the house at Rolleston was used by the American Missionary Association as a school for blacks, then as a home for displaced former slaves liberated by the Union forces, and finally as a regional headquarters and school for the Freedmen's Bureau. Although Henry Wise eventually regained title to the property, he never returned to live there. The house burned sometime in the late nineteenth century. See Green, Loth, and Rasmussen, *Lost Virginia*, 5.

68. William M. S. Rasmussen and Robert S. Tilton, *George Washington: The Man Behind the Myths* (Charlottesville, Va., and London, 1999), 5-6.

69. Between the Virginia Dynasty and Lincoln had come a succession of "log cabin" presidents.

70. Bagby, *Old Virginia Gentleman*, 5-6.

71. Page, *Social Life*, 7-8.

72. John Esten Cooke, "Old Virginia Manners," *Appletons' Journal* (20 April 1872): 437.

73. Bagby, *Old Virginia Gentleman*, Preface.

74. Bagby, *Old Virginia Gentleman*, 10.

75. Bagby, *Old Virginia Gentleman*, Preface.

76. Ibid.

77. Bagby, *Old Virginia Gentleman*, 10.

78. This argument that Virginia women did not relish their duties had been suggested by prewar abolitionists.

79. Bagby, *Old Virginia Gentleman*, 9-10.

80. Bagby, *Old Virginia Gentleman*, 10.

81. Bagby, *Old Virginia Gentleman*, 7-8.

82. The Misses Cowles—Maude Cowles and her sisters, Genevieve, Mildred, and Edith—who illustrated Page's book were Farmington, Connecticut artists who specialized in stained glass window design and murals. (Information courtesy of Ann J. Arcari, Farmington Library, Farmington, Connecticut.)

83. Page, *Social Life*, 34, 38.

84. Page, *Social Life*, 52-54.

85. Cooke, "Old Virginia Manners," 439.

86. Berry, *The Other Side*, 93.

87. Cooke, "Old Virginia Manners," 439.

88. Page, *Social Life*, 45.

89. Page, however, mentions "the old church" only in the context of Christmas festivities, when "Young men rode thirty and forty miles to 'help' dress the church" (*Social Life*, 86).

90. Page, *Social Life*, 45.

91. Bagby, *Old Virginia Gentleman*, 13.

92. Page, *Social Life*, 45-47.

93. Bagby, *Old Virginia Gentleman*, 14.

94. Bagby, *Old Virginia Gentleman*, 13.

95. Page, *Social Life*, 50-51.

96. Jack P. Greene, ed., *The Diary of Colonel Landon Carter of Sabine Hall, 1752-1778* (Charlottesville, Va., 1965), 907 (30 Dec. 1774) and 533 (16 Jan. 1771).

97. Page, *Social Life*, 77.

98. See John Esten Cooke, "Christmas Time in Old Virginia," *Magazine of American History* (Dec. 1883): 443-59, and Page, *Social Life*, 81-82.

99. Page, *Social Life*, 71-74.

100. King, *Great South*, 566, 671.

101. For an account, see *A Treatise on the White Sulphur Springs and Its Waters* (Richmond, Va., 1887).

102. John Esten Cooke, "The White Sulphur Springs," *Harper's New Monthly Magazine* 57 (1878): 337, 350-52.

103. A broadside in the collection of the Virginia Historical Society entitled "Healing Spring, Bath County, Va.," not dated, announces the opening of "these celebrated springs."

104. Many of Blackburn's drawings are preserved at the Virginia Historical Society. The sketch of Montpelier is not in his hand but may have been made by another of Jefferson's workmen. This information was provided by Bryan Clark Green, who is studying the career of Blackburn. The lithograph that we picture was published in the centennial year, when interest in the Founding Fathers and their architecture was revived.

105. Peter Wood and Karen Dalton, *Winslow Homer's Images of Blacks, The Civil War and Reconstruction Years* (Austin, Tex., 1988), 36-37.

106. King, *Great South*, 554.

107. Upperville was the region where Paul Mellon would settle three quarters of a century after Powell. By that time the image of picturesque black peasantry had necessarily faded from the landscape.

108. Guy C. McElroy, *Facing History, The Black Image in American Art, 1710-1940* (San Francisco, 1990), 93; Ella-Prince Knox et al., *Painting in the South: 1564-1980* (Richmond, Va., 1983), 92-93.

109. Wood and Dalton, *Homer*, 95-97.

110. In a related work by Elder, *A Virginny Breakdown*, c. 1877 (Virginia Museum of Fine Arts), African Americans are shown to be content and even happy with their condition.

111. Page, *Social Life*, 102.

112. In the Virginia Historical Society collection see, for example, the sheet music illustrations for Maurice C. Steinberg, "At An Ole Virginia Wedding, March Characteristic" (T. B. Harris & Co., c. 1899), where the black figures are projected as moronic, even evil; and Howell C. Featherston, "I'm an Old Virginia Nigger: A Plantation Melody and Song" (Sanders & Stayman Co., c. 1903), a northern publication (Washington and Baltimore) that regresses to the worst of the antebellum stereotyping.

113. Page, *Social Life*, 102.

114. Page, *Social Life*, 28.

115. Page, *Social Life*, 64.

116. Page, *Social Life*, 41.

117. Page, *Social Life*, 60-63.

118. Bagby, *Old Virginia Gentleman*, 19.

119. Elizabeth Keckley, *Behind the Scenes. Or, Thirty Years a Slave, and Four Years in the White House* (New York, 1868), 165.

120. Cited in W. E. B. DuBois, *The Souls of Black Folk*, eds. David W. Blight and Robert Gooding-Williams (Boston and New York), 1997 reprint of 1903 ed., 63.

121. Booker T. Washington, *Up From Slavery, An Autobiography* (New York, 1901), 16-17.

122. Louis R. Harlan, *Booker T. Washington in Perspective: Essays of Louis R. Harlan*, ed. Raymond W. Smock (Jackson, Miss., 1988), 22.

123. W. E. B. Du Bois, *Black Reconstruction: An Essay toward a History of the Part which Black Folk Played in the Attempt to Reconstruct Democracy in America, 1860-1880* (New York, 1935), 30; cited in Wood and Dalton, *Homer*, 98.

124. Du Bois, *Souls*, 62.

125. Du Bois, *Souls*, 72, 63, 64.

126. Du Bois, *Souls*, 67-68.

127. Du Bois, *Souls*, 63-64, 70.

128. Du Bois, *Souls*, 3.

129. Du Bois, *Souls*, 71.

130. Du Bois, *Souls*, 37-39.

131. Du Bois, *Souls*, 54-55.

132. Du Bois, *Souls*, 12.

133. Du Bois, *Souls*, 185-86.

134. Paul Lawrence Dunbar, *Poems of Cabin and Field, Illustrated with Photographs by the Hampton Institute Camera Club* (New York, 1899), 35; *Candle-Lightin' Time, Illustrated with Photographs by the Hampton Institute Camera Club* (New York, 1901), 25.

135. Du Bois, *Souls*, 66-67.

136. Dunbar, "Frederick Douglass."

137. Dunbar, "Ode to Ethiopia."

138. Dunbar, "To the South On Its New Slavery."

139. Ibid.

140. Tanner is not from Virginia, nor were his sketches for *The Banjo Lesson* drawn there. However, the banjo appears in so many late nineteenth-century images that are firmly tied to Virginia that many Americans of the era simply associated it with the black population of that region.

141. Lindgren, *Old Dominion*, 21.

142. Jackson Lears, *No Place of Grace: Antimodernism and the Transformation of American Culture, 1880-1920.* (New York, 1981), 5.

143. King, *Great South*, 636.

144. King, *Great South*, 590-91.

145. Kelly and Rasmussen, *Virginia Landscape*, 123.

146. Ernest Ingersoll, *To the Shenandoah and Beyond* (New York, 1885), 61; cited in Kelly and Rasmussen, *Virginia Landscape*, 125.

147. Emory A. Allen, *A Jolly Trip* (Cincinnati, 1891), 86-87; cited in Kelly and Rasmussen, *Virginia Landscape*, 125.

148. For information about the Rockbridge Hotel in Glasgow and the Alleghany Hotel in Goshen, see Green, Loth, and Rasmussen, *Lost Virginia*, 186, 188.

149. Green, Loth, and Rasmussen, *Lost Virginia*, 191-92.

150. Lindgren, *Old Dominion*, 177.

151. *The Encyclopaedia Britannica*, Ninth Edition (New York, 1878), volume A, "American Literature," 719.

152. Thaddeus K. Oglesby, *The Britannica Answered and the South Vindicated* (Montgomery, Ala., 1891), 1.

153. Lindgren, *Old Dominion*, 9.

154. Kelly and Rasmussen, *Virginia Landscape*, 160-61.

155. Thomas Nelson Page, "The Old Dominion," *Harper's New Monthly Magazine* (Christmas 1893): 20, 24; Page, *Social Life*, Introduction.

156. The distant building is said to have once been a cotton warehouse; see Joseph G. Dreiss, *Gari Melchers: His Works in the Belmont Collection* (Charlottesville, Va., 1984), 150.

Chapter V

1. See Richard Slotkin, *The Fatal Environment: The Myth of the Frontier in the Age of Industrialization, 1880-1890* (New York, 1985).

2. Michael G. Kammen, *Mystic Chords of Memory, The Trans*

formation of Tradition in American Culture (New York, 1991), 146. See also Karal Ann Marling, *George Washington Slept Here: Colonial Revivals and American Culture, 1876-1986* (Cambridge, Mass., 1988).

3. John Esten Cooke, "Virginia and the Revolution," *Harper's New Monthly Magazine* 53 (June 1876): 1.

4. James J. McDonald, *Life in Old Virginia* (Norfolk, 1907), iii-iv.

5. John Esten Cooke, *Virginia, A History of the People* (Boston, 1883), iv.

6. Cited in Kammen, *Mystic Chords of Memory*, 146.

7. James Lindgren, *Preserving the Old Dominion, Historic Preservation and Virginia Traditionalism* (Charlottesville, Va. and London, 1993), 5.

8. The Colonial Revival did not earn widespread popularity until the last decade of the nineteenth century and the first of the twentieth. See Kammen, *Mystic Chords of Memory*, 147- 53.

9. Mrs. Roger A. Pryor, *The Birth of the Nation, Jamestown, 1607* (New York and London, 1907), 2.

10. Mary Newton Stanard, *The Story of Bacon's Rebellion* (New York and Washington, D.C., 1907), dedication.

11. R. T. Barton, *Reports . . . of Decisions of The General Court of Virginia, 1728–1741* (New York and London, 1909), iv.

12. Thomas Nelson Page, *The Old Dominion, Her Making and Her Manners* (New York, 1908), 63.

13. Sydney George Fisher, *Men, Women and Manners in Colonial Times* (Philadelphia, 1902), I: 71.

14. Kammen, *Mystic Chords of Memory*, 152.

15. Marshall William Fishwick, *Virginia: A New Look at the Old Dominion* (New York, 1959), 157. Cooke turned out dozens of novels before and after the war; the Virginia Historical Society library holds some 130 books (including duplicates). A Cooke biographer has written that "His popularity has suffered somewhat from the unwinnowed abundance of his writings" (John O. Beaty, "John Esten Cooke," *Dictionary of American Biography*, eds. Allen Johnson and Dumas Malone [New York, 1930], IV: 385-86).

16. John Esten Cooke, "The Last of the Knights," *Hours at Home* (Jan. 1867): 210-17.

17. Cooke, *Virginia*, iv-v.

18. Alexander Brown, *Genesis of the United States* (New York, 1890), xv.

19. Brown, *United States*, v.

20. Mary Tucker Magill, *History of Virginia, For the Use of Schools* (Baltimore, 1876), 257. Not until 1890 did a new edition of Magill add a hundred pages to tell the story of Virginia through the 1880s.

21. Philip Alexander Bruce, *Economic History of Virginia in the Seventeenth Century* (New York, 1896), 1.

22. Royall Bascom Smithey, *History of Virginia* (New York, 1898), 7.

23. Page, *Old Dominion*, vii, viii.

24. Thomas Nelson Page, *Address at the Three Hundredth Anniversary of the Settlement of Jamestown* (Richmond, Va., 1907), 3.

25. John Esten Cooke, *Stories of the Old Dominion, From the Settlement to the End of the Revolution* (New York, 1879), 46.

26. See *Captain John Smith*, ed. by Edward Arber (Birmingham, England, 1884); Captain John Smith, *A History of the Settlement of Virginia* (New York, 1890); Captain John Smith's *True Relation* (New York, 1896).

27. Katharine Pearson Woods, *True Story of Captain John Smith* (New York, 1901), vii.

28. William Wirt Henry, *The First Legislative Assembly in America* (Washington, D.C., 1894), 301.

29. William Robertson Garrett, *The Father of Representative Government in America* (Nashville, Tenn., 1896?), 29.

30. Page, *Three Hundredth Anniversary of Jamestown*, 28.

31. Page, *Old Dominion*, 61.

32. Page, *Old Dominion*, 58-61.

33. Page, *Old Dominion*, 58. Page cribbed phrases like "cradle of the nation," comments about Anglo-Saxon superiority, and arguments about the Spanish threat and the limited opportunity to settle America from APVA spokespeople and from writers like Royall Bascom Smithey and Lyon Tyler. Tyler had also used the Sir Francis Bacon statement.

34. Lyon Gardiner Tyler, *The Cradle of the Republic: Jamestown and James River* (Richmond, Va., 1900), 21.

35. Will T. Hale, *True Stories of Jamestown and Its Environs* (Nashville, Tenn. and Dallas, Tex., 1907), 9.

36. Page, *Old Dominion*, 362.

37. *Year Book of the Association for the Preservation of Virginia Antiquities, for 1896 and 1897* (Richmond, Va., 1898), Introduction.

38. "A Bill Incorporating the Association for the Preservation of Virginia Antiquities," 1891/92.

39. Jamestown Island is today preserved and administered by both the APVA and the National Park Service.

40. Lindgren, *Old Dominion*, 91-152.

41. Edward Hagaman Hall, *Jamestown, A Sketch of the History and Present Condition* (New York, 1902), 6.

42. Julia Wyatt Bullard, *Jamestown Tributes and Toasts* (Lynchburg, Va., 1907), 13.

43. Thomas Jefferson Wertenbaker, *Virginia Under the Stuarts, 1607-1688* (Princeton, N.J., 1914), vii.

44. A few publications of this type had appeared in the late nineteenth century, such as Philip Alexander Bruce's *Economic History of Virginia in the Seventeenth Century* (New York, 1896). An early primary text is the modest *Colonial Records of Virginia* (Richmond, 1874).

45. Page, *Three Hundredth Anniversary of Jamestown*, 26-28.

46. Hale, *True Stories*, 10; J. Warren Keifer, "Address Delivered at the Jamestown Exposition, Virginia, July 30, 1907, The House of Burgesses, and The Development of Legislative Bodies in America" (1907), 1.

47. Mary Schuyler Phillips, *"Colonial Virginia," Lectures on the Colonial Period for Use in the Public Schools* (Cincinnati, Ohio, 1915), 5.

48. Bullard, *Jamestown Tributes*, 3.

49. Bullard, *Jamestown Tributes*, 50.

50. William M. S. Rasmussen and Robert S. Tilton, *Pocahontas: Her Life and Legend* (Richmond, Va., 1994), 23. Argall was the same adventurer whom Thomas Nelson Page the sectionalist had lauded for "rooting out" the French colonies "planted" in Maine and thereby clearing the way for the Pilgrim's later settlement of New England.

51. Page, *Old Dominion*, vii.

52. Woodward worked in a similar vein in New England, depicting old mills and forges. His goal was to stir nostalgia for the nation's earliest history. See Sue Rainey, "John Douglas Woodward, Shaping the Landscape Image, 1865-1910," *American Art Review* IX (April 1997): 104-13.

53. Cooke, *Virginia*, 127-28.

54. Cooke, *Stories of the Old Dominion*, 65.

55. Page, *Three Hundredth Anniversary of Jamestown*, 21.

56. Mary Newton Stanard, *The Story of Bacon's Rebellion* (New York and Washington, D.C., 1907), 9.

57. Cooke, *Stories of the Old Dominion*, 65; Cooke, *Virginia*, 230.

58. Page, *Three Hundredth Anniversary of Jamestown*, 24.

59. Holland was a Harvard-educated Philadelphia attorney who turned to the writing of novels at age twenty-eight; he published fifty-five of them by the time he retired at age sixty-five. These were often adventure stories that celebrated the excitement associated with the settlement and maturing of colonial America. Included in Holland's oeuvre are such titles are *Knights of the Golden Spur* (1912), *William Penn* (1915), *Blackbeard's Island* (1916), *Historic Events of Colonial Days* (1916), *Lafayette, We Come* (1918), *The Splendid Buccaneer* (1928), and

Steadfast at Valley Forge (1939).

60. Good worked out of Wilmington, Delaware and illustrated as well a second Holland novel, *The Splendid Buccaneer*, along with articles for *Scribner's* and *McCall's* magazines.

61. Rupert S. Holland, *Red Beard of Virginia* (Philadelphia, 1927), 283.

62. Wallace Nutting, *Virginia Beautiful* (Garden City, N.Y., 1930), 233.

63. Nutting, *Virginia Beautiful*, 122.

64. Cooke, *Virginia*, vi.

65. John Fiske, *Old Virginia and Her Neighbors* (Boston and New York, 1897), v-vi.

66. Cooke, *Virginia*, 365, 370-71.

67. Cooke, *Virginia*, 371.

68. John Esten Cooke, "Old Blandford Church," *Appleton's Journal* VI (23 Dec. 1871): 702.

69. Cooke, "Historic Houses of America. Gunston Hall," *Appleton's Journal* 11 (4 April 1874): 417-20. See also Cooke, "Christ Church, Alexandria," *Appleton's Journal* 12 (15 Aug. 1874): 193-96.

70. Other early publications of note are Lewis A. Coffin, Jr. and Arthur C. Holden, *Brick Architecture of the Colonial Period in Maryland and Virginia* (New York, 1919), and Thomas T. Waterman and John A. Barrows, *Domestic Colonial Architecture of Tidewater Virginia* (New York, 1932).

71. Nutting, *Virginia Beautiful*, 184.

72. Nutting, *Virginia Beautiful*, 173-74.

73. Nutting, *Virginia Beautiful*, 177-78.

74. Nutting, *Virginia Beautiful*, 125.

75. Nutting, *Virginia Beautiful*, 145.

76. Edith Tunis Sale, *Interiors of Virginia Houses of Colonial Times* (Richmond, Va., 1927), 449.

77. Edith Tunis Sale, *Manors of Virginia in Colonial Times* (Philadelphia, 1909), 147.

78. Mark R. Wenger, "Westover: William Byrd's Mansion Reconsidered" (M.A. thesis, University of Virginia, 1981), 11-12.

79. Sale, *Interiors*, 461.

80. Richard Guy Wilson in Charles E. Brownell, Calder Loth, William M. S. Rasmussen, and Richard Guy Wilson, *The Making of Virginia Architecture* (Richmond, Va., 1992), 378.

81. Nutting, *Virginia Beautiful*, 178.

82. Nutting, *Virginia Beautiful*, 174.

83. Brownell, Loth, Rasmussen, and Wilson, *Making Virginia Architecture*, 378.

84. Sale, *Interiors*, 461.

85. Alexander Wilbourne Weddell, *A Memorial Volume of Virginia Historical Portraiture, 1585-1830* (Richmond, Va., 1930), 166; Sale, *Manors*, 19-22.

86. Sale, *Manors*, 22.

87. One canvas is pictured in Marietta Andrews, *Memoirs of a Poor Relation* (New York, 1927), opposite p. 164, with the caption, "Robert Carter of Corotoman, Portrait by Mrs. Andrews after Sir Godfrey Kneller in the Possession of Mrs. Randolph Harrison McKim of Washington." A second, slightly different canvas is pictured in Thomas Allen Glenn, *Some Colonial Mansions* (Philadelphia, 1899), I: 226. A third canvas, also slightly different, is pictured in Louise P. du Bellet, *Some Prominent Virginia Families* (Lynchburg, 1907), II: 198.

88. Fisher, *Colonial Times*, I: 76.

89. Fisher, *Colonial Times*, I: 84.

90. Fisher, *Colonial Times*, I: 16, 71.

91. Page, *Old Dominion*, 134, 137.

92. Fisher, *Colonial Times*, I: 7-8, 37.

93. Fisher, *Colonial Times*, I: 15, 70.

94. Dabney Herndon Maury, *A Young People's History of Virginia and Virginians* (Richmond, 1896), 5.

95. Keifer, "Address Delivered at Jamestown," 16.

96. Page, *Three Hundredth Anniversary of Jamestown*, 25.

97. William Wirt Henry, *The Causes Which Produced the Virginia of the Revolutionary Period* (Washington, D.C., 1892), 18, 21, 22.

98. Page, *Old Dominion*, viii.

99. Page, *Three Hundredth Anniversary of Jamestown*, 25.

100. Fisher, *Colonial Times*, I: 15.

101. Cooke, *Stories of the Old Dominion*, 159.

102. Page, *Old Dominion*, 141.

103. Cooke, *Stories of the Old Dominion*, 159.

104. Keifer, "Address Delivered at Jamestown," 13.

105. Henry, *Causes Which Produced . . . Virginia*, 24.

106. Cooke, *Stories of the Old Dominion*, 162; Cooke, *Virginia*, 381.

107. Cooke, *Virginia*, 379.

108. Cooke, *Virginia*, 382-83.

109. Cooke, *Virginia*, 427-29; Cooke, *Stories of the Old Dominion*, 175-76.

110. Cooke, *Stories of the Old Dominion*, 174.

111. Cooke, *Stories of the Old Dominion*, 94.

112. Cooke, "Virginia and the Revolution," 14.

113. See Mason Locke Weems, *The Life of Washington*, ed. Marcus Cunliffe (Cambridge, Mass., 1962); William M. S. Rasmussen and Robert S. Tilton, *George Washington: The Man Behind the Myths* (Charlottesville, Va., and London, 1999), 16.

114. Rasmussen and Tilton, *George Washington*, 16.

115. Ibid.

116. Cooke, *Stories of the Old Dominion*, 319.

117. Cooke, *Virginia*, 462.

118. Rasmussen and Tilton, *George Washington*, 141.

119. Rasmussen and Tilton, *George Washington*, 141, 143.

120. Rasmussen and Tilton, *George Washington*, 149-50.

121. Dennis Montgomery, *A Link Among the Days: The Life and Times of the Reverend Doctor W. A. R. Goodwin, the Father of Colonial Williamsburg* (Richmond, Va., 1998), vii.

122. George Humphrey Yetter, *Williamsburg Before and After: The Rebirth of Virginia's Colonial Capital* (Williamsburg, Va., 1988), 33; George Tucker, *Letters from Virginia, Translated from the French* (Baltimore, 1816), 120.

123. John Sergeant Wise, *Diomed, The Life, Travels, and Observations of a Dog* (Boston, London, and New York, 1897), 307, 311; cited in James C. Kelly and William M. S. Rasmussen, *The Virginia Landscape, A Cultural History* (Charlottesville, Va., 2000), 94.

124. Cooke, *Virginia*, 372.

125. Montgomery, *Goodwin*, xvii.

126. Ibid.

127. Montgomery, *Goodwin*, xii.

128. Bullard, *Jamestown Tributes*, 87.

129. Montgomery, *Goodwin*, xii.

130. Montgomery, *Goodwin*, xvi.

131. Montgomery, *Goodwin*, xviii.

132. "The Far-Visioned Generosity of Mr. Rockefeller," *Colonial Williamsburg* (Winter 2000-2001): 19.

133. Yetter, *Williamsburg Before and After*, 49.

134. "Far-Visioned Generosity of Mr. Rockefeller," 14. Goodwin used the word "inspire" repeatedly.

135. Montgomery, *Goodwin*, xviii.

136. "Far-Visioned Generosity of Mr. Rockefeller," 14.

137. "Far-Visioned Generosity of Mr. Rockefeller," 19.

138. Montgomery, *Goodwin*, xvi.

139. Cited in "Far-Visioned Generosity of Mr. Rockefeller," 19.

140. Yetter, *Williamsburg Before and After*, 54-55.

141. Yetter, *Williamsburg Before and After*, 51.

142. Colin G. Campbell, "Seventy-Five Years of Preserving a Past for the Future," *Colonial Williamsburg* (Winter 2000-2001): 5.

143. Ibid.

144. Yetter, *Williamsburg Before and After*, 55; Montgomery, *Goodwin*, ix.

145. "Far-Visioned Generosity of Mr. Rockefeller,"

17-18.

146. "Far-Visioned Generosity of Mr. Rockefeller,"
16-17.

147. Montgomery, *Goodwin*, xviii.

148. "Far-Visioned Generosity of Mr. Rockefeller," 19.

149. Wilson in Brownell, Loth, Rasmussen, and Wilson, *Making Virginia Architecture*, 362.

150. "Far-Visioned Generosity of Mr. Rockefeller," 19.

151. Yetter, *Williamsburg Before and After*, 66.

152. Wilson in Brownell, Loth, Rasmussen, and Wilson, *Making Virginia Architecture*, 368.

153. "Far-Visioned Generosity of Mr. Rockefeller," 19.

154. Yetter, *Williamsburg Before and After*, 69-71.

155. *Williamsburg Virginia Official Information Concerning the Restored Colonial Capital, . . . An Official Leaflet Issued by The Williamsburg Restoration* (Williamsburg, Va., 1941).

156. Kammen, *Mystic Chords of Memory*, 361.

157. Wilson in Brownell, Loth, Rasmussen, and Wilson, *Making Virginia Architecture*, 362.

158. Wilson in Brownell, Loth, Rasmussen, and Wilson, *Making Virginia Architecture*, 368.

159. Yetter, *Williamsburg Before and After*, 60.

160. Kammen, *Mystic Chords of Memory*, 368.

161. *Richmond Times-Dispatch*, 15 July 2001 (75th anniversary of the founding of Colonial Williamsburg).

162. Colin G. Campbell, "In Celebration of Tomorrow," *Colonial Williamsburg* (Spring 2001): 5.

163. Wilson in Brownell, Loth, Rasmussen, and Wilson, *Making Virginia Architecture*, 362.

164. Michael Kammen, *Robert Gwathmey, The Life and Art of a Passionate Observer* (Chapel Hill, N.C. and London, 1999), 20.

165. Ella-Prince Knox et al., *Painting in the South: 1564-1980* (Richmond, Va., 1983), 129.

166. Kammen, *Gwathmey*, 40-42.

167. Hal Erickson, *All Movie Guide*, cited in *Virginia, www. blockbuster. com*, March 2002.

168. Weddell's importation of an English building was imitated by his soon-to-be immediate neighbor at Virginia House, the Richmond attorney and philanthropist Thomas C. Williams, Jr., who erected Agecroft Hall in 1926-28 and employed the same architect and the same gardener used by Weddell, Henry Grant Morse and Charles F. Gillette. A half-timbered manor house erected near Manchester, England in the fifteenth century by John Langley, Agecroft stood neglected in 1925 when Williams purchased it.

169. Two decades later, in 1946, another New York colonialist, William Lawrence Bottomley, by then the premier Georgian Revival architect active in Virginia, added a small loggia to one side of the house.

170. See Gary M. Inman, "Virginia House: An American Country Place" (M.A. thesis, Virginia Commonwealth University, 1993).

171. Alexander Weddell, *A Description of Virginia House in Henrico County, near Richmond, Virginia* (Richmond, Va., 1947), x.

172. Ibid.

173. Weddell, *Virginia Historical Portraiture*, 19.

174. For information about the racehorse Shark we thank Malcolm Cormack, Paul Mellon Curator at the Virginia Museum of Fine Arts.

175. Nutting, *Virginia Beautiful*, 15.

176. Paul Mellon, with John Baskett, *Reflections in a Silver Spoon, A Memoir* (New York, 1992), jacket.

177. Mellon, *Silver Spoon*, 117.

178. Mellon, *Silver Spoon*, 17.

179. Ibid.

180. Mellon, *Silver Spoon*, 32 ("prelude to hell"), 147 ("banker"), 136 ("didn't really care"), and 22 ("longing for the fields").

181. Mellon, *Silver Spoon*, 265, 276.

182. Mellon, *Silver Spoon*, 151.

183. Annual visitation at Colonial Williamsburg jumped in 1937 to 151,036, from 95,497 in 1936 (Kammen, *Mystic Chords of Memory*, 367).

184. Mellon, *Silver Spoon*, 225-26.

185. Mellon, *Silver Spoon*, 259-60.

186. Mellon, *Silver Spoon*, 270.

187. Robert F. Strohm et al., *Treasures Revealed from the Paul Mellon Library of Americana* (Charlottesville, Va., 2001), ix-x.

188. Mellon, *Silver Spoon*, 276.

189. Mellon, *Silver Spoon*, 276-77.

190. Mellon, *Silver Spoon*, 323, 290-91.

191. Mellon, *Silver Spoon*, 151 ("foolish"), 376 ("care"), 259 ("development").

Conclusion

1. Virginius Dabney, *Virginia: The New Dominion* (Garden City, N.Y., 1971), xiii, xv.

2. C. M. Andrews, "Virginia's Place in Colonial History," *VMHB* 40 (1932): 214.

3. Virginius Cornick Hall, Jr., "The Virginia Historical Society, An Anniversary Narrative of Its First Century and a Half," *VMHB* 90 (1982): 4, 6.

4. Howard Mansfield, "Exporting New England Style," *Yankee Magazine* (June 2002): 66.

Index